The Airline Revolution

When starting new airlines in response to government deregulation, entrepreneurs in the US and Europe reduced some traditional service qualities (to reduce costs), concentrated on non-stop services between city pairs not already so connected, improved on-time performance, and offered low fares to win leisure travellers from the incumbents and to encourage more travel.

In recent developments, some of the new airlines have offered optional extras (at higher fares) to attract business travellers and entered major routes alongside the legacy carriers. Within both the US and Europe, deregulation removed most geographical barriers to expansion by short-haul airlines. Later, limited deregulation spread to other world regions, where many short-haul routes connect city pairs in different countries, and where governments have retained traditional two-country mechanisms restricting who may fly. To gain access to domestic routes in other countries, some new airlines are setting up affiliate companies in neighbouring countries, with each company legally controlled in the country of domicile. With air travel growing strongly, especially in Asia, a common result is intense, but potentially short-lived, competition on major routes. The recent developments give clear signposts to likely mid-term outcomes, and make this an opportune time to report on the new-airline scene.

The Airline Revolution will provide valuable economic analysis of this climate to students, airline professionals advancing to senior positions, public servants and others who provide advice to governments.

Gordon Mills is Honorary Professor of Economics at the University of Sydney. His academic experience has been leavened by consulting engagements in the UK and Australia, and by membership of some Australian Government committees.

The Airline Revolution

Economic analysis of airline
performance and public policy

Gordon Mills

Routledge
Taylor & Francis Group

LONDON AND NEW YORK

First published 2017
by Routledge
2 Park Square, Milton Park, Abingdon, Oxon OX14 4RN

and by Routledge
711 Third Avenue, New York, NY 10017

Routledge is an imprint of the Taylor & Francis Group, an informa business

British Library Cataloguing in Publication Data
A catalogue record for this book is available from the British Library

Library of Congress Cataloging in Publication Data
Names: Mills, Gordon (Honorary professor of economics), author.
Title: The airline revolution: economic analysis of airline performance
and public policy / Gordon Mills.
Description: Abingdon, Oxon; New York, NY: Routledge, 2016.
Identifiers: LCCN 2016005209 | ISBN 9781472432346 (hardback) |
ISBN 9781315612348 (ebook)
Subjects: LCSH: Airlines. | Airlines—Government policy.
Classification: LCC HE9780. M55 2016 | DDC 387.7/1—dc23
LC record available at https://lccn.loc.gov/2016005209

ISBN: 978-1-4724-3234-6 (hbk)
ISBN: 978-1-315-61234-8 (ebk)

Typeset in Times New Roman
by Keystroke, Station Road, Codsall, Wolverhampton

Printed and bound by CPI Group (UK) Ltd, Croydon, CR0 4YY

Contents

Tables

Preface

While the approach offered here is that of the economist, my account serves those with a professional or student interest in aviation, and little or no formal training in economics. The book serves also those who have some background in economics, and want to learn about the major economic issues arising in the management of airlines.

In Part I of the book, I give descriptive accounts of *new-airline* developments in the various world regions. The focus is on low-cost, *short-haul* airlines that operate jet aircraft able to fly non-stop for up to about five hours, and sometimes also fly turbo-prop aircraft on so-called regional routes, usually with flight sectors of no more than (say) 600 kilometres.

Parts II and III develop the generalisations about airline operation that are needed when analysing business conduct and when formulating government policy that is intended to serve the public interest.

By *first* reporting on some real-world settings, I hope to persuade the reader that the ensuing generalisations are both sensible and important. That sequence is followed also in much economic-policy research. An experienced economist often muses: Oh, that practice looks interesting! I wonder why they do that. What would they do if the business conditions were different? And so on. In turn, such ruminating may prompt thinking about the underlying fundamentals, which can lead ultimately to general models that give new insights.

While I try to use economics jargon sparingly, it would be foolish not to introduce the proper terms and frameworks for the basic concepts that appear in various chapters. Accordingly, when introducing a technical term, I aim to give a clear explanation. And in the index, each such term is shown *in italics*, with the page number identifying the place where the term is introduced and explained.

Like any introductory account, much in this book rests on the writings of other authors. Where a source document is substantial and may be of wide interest, I have used the Harvard method for referencing within the text (e.g. 'Bloggs, 2009'), and the full publication details are given under the name Bloggs in the References section at the end of the book. The other cited publications are usually short in length, and of interest only in regard to the matter discussed at the point of citation; in such cases, I give the reference details within parentheses, at that point in the text.

There may be readers who – like the author – are not familiar with the conventional representation of section numbers. In that convention, §12.3.2 (for example) refers to section 3.2 in Chapter 12. The digit(s) appearing before the first point report the chapter number, and always appear in the number that identifies the start of any particular section. In making a cross-reference, the chapter number appears even when the reference is to a section within the same chapter.

Gordon Mills
Sydney, 2 November 2015

Acknowledgements

The University of Sydney has accommodated my labours throughout the book's long gestation. To the early drafts, Corinne McKenzie brought outstanding typing skills and a considerable cultural knowledge of immediate practical value. At Ashgate (and eventually at Routledge), commissioning editor Guy Loft combined friendly advice with immense patience.

When Routledge put the manuscript into production, I found Hamish Ironside to be a conscientious and author-friendly copy-editor. And the crew at Keystroke were very attentive, and keen to follow the schedule for typesetting.

For a scholarly author, unusual sources of information have been several daily/ weekly newsletters and other reports published by various aviation companies and other organisations. Witness to the importance of those sources are the frequent appearances of their names and/or web addresses, among the in-text references to be found in many of the chapters. In order to help the reader to identify those sources, it is opportune to list them here (together with their web addresses):

- Centre for Aviation (also known as CAPA, acronym for its earlier name) – centreforaviation.com
- *Air Transport World* – atwonline.com
- *Airline Network News & Analysis*, more commonly known by its web address – anna.aero
- ch-aviation – ch.aviation.com

In addition, daily listings and summaries of aviation-related reports (appearing in United States newspapers) are published by Airlines for America (also known as A4A) – airlines.org and a4a@smartbrief.com.

G.M.

Introduction

In September 1938, the 70-year-old British Prime Minister, Neville Chamberlain, made his own *first-ever* flight, to meet Hitler in Germany, and so try to avert war in Europe. Chamberlain soon made two more flights, the last to Munich – where he sought to appease Hitler by making concessions regarding control over parts of Czechoslovakia. Upon his return to London, Chamberlain explained his position by saying he did not believe that the British would want to go to war 'because of a quarrel in a faraway country between people of whom we know nothing' (as quoted in Clarke, 1997, p. 188).

Nowadays, a flight from London to the Czech capital, Prague, takes less than two hours. Following the advent of low-cost airlines, a weekend there became a favoured short break for British travellers. While routes and frequencies vary from time to time, in October 2015, four low-fare airlines (EasyJet, Ryanair, Jet2 and WizzAir) between them offered, on average, a total of about nine flights daily, serving ten ports in England, while British Airways flew five flights daily from London Heathrow and CSA offered one flight daily at London Gatwick. No doubt, the many British visitors to Prague learn something of the people (as well as the lager).

Much of the increase in air travel since the 1930s, and the consequent changes in popular experience and social attitudes, is due to the entry of low-cost airlines. Their precursors in the UK and in some other European countries were the charter flights organised by travel firms that packaged international travel and hotel rooms. Those firms marketed the packages at prices that were lower – often, much lower – than just the airfares of the scheduled airlines. The UK legislation allowed such charter flights even though the prevailing government regulations precluded entry by new airlines offering *scheduled* services. And the legacy carriers were content to shelter behind those regulations, which allowed them to maintain their high fares.

It was only as governments removed the restrictions on the entry of scheduled air carriers that the legacy airlines decided they needed to reduce their fares, in order to compete with the new low-cost airlines. Generally, those responses came only after the new airlines had demonstrated that lower fares greatly increased the numbers of passengers on routes such as London–Prague.

In the years since Chamberlain's travels, there have been remarkable technical developments in civil aviation. In the late 1930s, air transport was still in its infancy. Although 25 years had elapsed since man's first powered flight, the piston engines of the day were still small and very limited in capacity. Consequently, aircraft too were small – and restricted in commercial range. However, the world war that Chamberlain was not able to prevent served to stimulate the development of jet and turbo-prop engines. After that war, airline companies reorganised and extended their services, to take advantage of the increases in speed, range and aircraft size enabled by the advances in engineering.

In the early years of aviation, governments had become involved in *technical* regulation. National operating procedures were established. And, by licensing pilots and aircraft engineers, governments sought to improve training and lift safety standards. To facilitate international flights, inter-governmental organisations were set up to standardise technical and administrative arrangements.

However, it was then all too easy for governments and established airlines to go on to introduce and support *economic* regulation. For several decades *after* World War II, such regulation served to hinder and often to preclude entry by new firms. This allowed the incumbent airlines a quiet life, with little or no pressure to compete.

For the early commercial passenger-carrying flights of the 1930s, the primitive technology inevitably made production costs high – and there were fares to match. Business travel apart, only an affluent few could afford to travel by air. As costs declined over the years, a non-competitive airline industry found it opportune to raise service quality – and to employ perhaps more people than strictly necessary, and certainly more than would have been needed for a more basic style of service.

Though fares did decline (in real terms), they did not fall as much as the costs of providing a basic service. Sometimes government regulators determined the fare levels. On international routes, there were agreements between the two participating airlines, one from each country; and a government-endorsed agreement might even specify pooling of the airlines' route revenues, together with rules on how the revenue was then to be shared between the two companies. The airlines then 'competed' only on peripheral matters such as the quality of in-flight meals, and other supplementary features that were included in the price of the ticket.

In such a regulated world, airports too enjoyed a cosy life. Most were owned by national or local government agencies. Usually each port was the only one in the area, and was able to rely on its spatial monopoly when deciding on the quality of the services it provided, and the level and structure of the charges that it levied. In setting those charges, big-city airports could tap in to the handsome revenue streams of airlines that faced little competition. Over the post-war decades, many such ports used these financial proceeds to increase the quality of their passenger terminals, without much thought on whether passengers really 'wanted' such luxury (that is, would have been prepared to pay additionally for it, if given a choice in the matter).

The absence of competitive pressures on airlines did more than merely fail to promote the greatest possible fare reductions. It resulted also in airline management having little if any stimulus to *innovate*. This applied particularly to the design of route networks. In European countries the monopolistic 'national' airline was based in the national capital, and most flights radiated from there. International passengers travelling from or to regional cities usually had to travel via one or both of the national capitals. Within the United States, the Federal government's regulation of the industry also commonly resulted in passengers having to change planes when travelling to or from even a medium-size city, let alone a small one. In both continents, airline networks were to change dramatically after deregulation.

The movement to abandon (most) economic regulation started in the US, and then took hold in Western Europe and in other developed economies such as Canada, Australia and New Zealand. There followed some remarkable changes in the organisation of civil aviation, and in the character and reduced price of airline services. Elsewhere in the world, though economic regulation generally remains in place, governments have become less restrictive in their attitudes; in most countries, there has been enough competition and other innovation to reduce fares – and to increase network connectivity, which also encourages more air travel.

It is the purpose of this book to report and analyse these developments in respect of *short-haul* airline services, regarded here as those having flight sectors of up to five hours' duration. The aircraft so used by almost all the new, 'low-cost' airlines are the Boeing 737 and Airbus A320 families, together with the larger models of the relatively new family of Embraer jets. On the whole, *long-haul* routes have remained the preserve of the older, established airlines – though a few recent entrants have begun to compete, to the extent permitted by the ongoing bilateral government regulation that applies to most international routes.

In the short-haul context, it is the new airlines that have pioneered many of the changes. Among the many recent innovations, only two have depended on new technology: widespread access to the computer internet has helped airlines to sell directly to individual travellers; and the internet together with the introduction of passenger-access computers in airport terminals permits self-check-in. While new airlines were sometimes ahead of the others in introducing these practices, some traditional airlines were also among the pioneers. And in this area, the innovations have spread rapidly throughout the industry.

In implementing other changes, however, the new companies have had a distinct advantage: being without the burden of old habits, the entrepreneurs have found it relatively easy to adopt new (often, simpler) operating procedures, and to establish economical arrangements for staffing. Together with (generally) superior management, these changes have brought higher standards of customer service, especially in punctuality.

In contrast, many of the old companies have found it difficult to adapt to new ways, thanks largely to work-force resistance and managerial inertia. As a result, some of those companies have reduced the scale of their operations, quite a number have merged and a few have gone out of business.

While much the same forces are at work in most countries of the world, some features of the airline revolution differ between countries. The United States of America was the first country to undertake the deregulation that has helped to promote the changes in industry structure and airline practice; the story of deregulation there is taken up in Chapter 1. The later, even more dramatic structural changes that took place within the European Union are the subject of Chapter 2, while the following four chapters look at the developments in the other world regions.

Chapter 7 presents a case study of domestic airline services in Australia. There, the traditional regulatory arrangements were extreme and transparent; and both before and after deregulation, the market has been served by only two major airlines (though the cast list has changed). Those features make the case a ready source of insights into the processes of competition.

The second part of the book looks at various features of the current world scene. Chapter 8 examines how the new airlines have adopted some modified – even, new – ways of operating an airline. It looks also at some of the consequences.

While the old airlines had developed flexible pricing of airline tickets, Chapter 9 records how the new companies have introduced even greater pricing flexibility. The aim has been to increase profitability by more forceful targeting of passenger categories that are separated according to customers' willingness to pay, and by coupling that with good management of available-seat inventories.

Competition between airlines is the subject of Chapter 10; there is special emphasis on how incumbent airlines can and do impede entry by new ones, and on how the route networks of the new airlines often differ from those of the incumbents.

Chapter 11 considers so-called 'regional services', most of which are flown on routes at the fringes of the main route-networks; the principal issues there are relationships between major airlines and smaller regional carriers, and the desire of some governments to subsidise air service to small and remote communities.

In Chapter 12, attention turns to airline relations with airports. Instead of the old idea that all airlines using a port should access (and pay for) passenger terminals of a uniform standard, low-cost airlines often want only basic terminal facilities. In recent years, some ports have built such terminals – for which low-cost airlines pay lower charges. Furthermore, in some countries, airports are no longer required (by local or national governments) to apply a uniform tariff for all users of a given terminal. In such a situation, a port may seek *higher* charges from airlines who can afford to pay more; and a large, low-cost airline may seek to pay *lower* charges. In such bargaining situations, the outcome depends on the relative strengths of the market power enjoyed by the airline and the port.

The final part of the book looks to the future. Chapter 13 considers the prospects for continuing airline competition and further airline entry. The last two chapters deal with issues arising in public policy. The continuing need for a limited but important government role in *regulating* both airport conduct and the provision of air navigation services is the subject of Chapter 14. The final chapter looks at public policy concerns arising from airline conduct in traditional areas such as airline collusion, predatory fare setting and financial protections for air passengers, and in the new field of environmental protection with regard to aero-engine emissions.

Part I

New airlines around the world

1   USA and Canada

1.1 Deregulation in the US: the early effects

1.1.1 Airline services before deregulation

For *inter-state* airline services, regulatory power rested with the US (Federal) government, which had long controlled both route entry and fare levels. During that era, the list of major airlines changed little; and the regulators shaped the route networks of each of the airlines in the 'club'. In the light of later experience, it is notable that the overall airline network included quite a number of (so-called) 'milk-runs': in order to provide service to small cities, a flight commencing at a major port might stop at intermediate ports (sometimes three or four of them) before reaching its destination at another major city. The regulated fare structure also favoured local travel: low fares there were cross-subsidised by the airline's profits from the mandated high fares on dense, longer routes that provided non-stop service between large cities.

For routes *within* a single state, however, the power to license and control lay with the government of the state. Although most states are too small in area to support much by way of intra-state services, Texas and California were and are major exceptions. As aviation developed after World War II, each of those states became home to an important (low-cost) airline that was later to grow and challenge the established national and regional carriers.

In the post-war years, California saw a number of airline start-ups, notably that of Pacific Southwest Airlines. When founded at San Diego in 1949, that company leased a single DC3 aircraft, and started a *weekly* service between San Diego and Oakland (just across the Bay from San Francisco), with an intermediate stop at Burbank (in northern Los Angeles). With very limited financial resources, the new airline needed to be a low-cost carrier.

Less predictable was its adoption of an informal style, intended to make the flight a 'fun' experience for passengers. The informality also supported good staff relations – of particular importance when many staff, including pilots, had to help with tasks other than their principal roles. (The informality was later adopted by some other new carriers, notably Southwest Airlines, a Texas intra-state airline which launched in the 1970s – on which, see §1.2.1 below.)

From 1949, Pacific Southwest grew larger, though with mixed financial results. It sold shares to the public and to employees in 1962, and began operating B727 jets in 1965. It and other Californian carriers attracted hostile reactions from some of the major inter-state airlines, which engaged in localised price-competition.

The 1980s saw the absorption of the surviving local carriers. In 1988, Pacific Southwest itself became part of US Air (later merged into US Airways, which in turn became a part of American Airlines; see www.psa-history.org and en.wikipedia.org/wiki/Pacific Southwest Airlines, both accessed 18 April 2009).

1.1.2 Deregulation and the entry of new carriers

In 1978 the US Congress passed the Airline Deregulation Act, and the long-standing structure of inter-state services was soon transformed. Many new airline companies were established; almost all of them adopted a low-cost, low-fare strategy. And almost all of them died at an early age – usually by bankruptcy. A most spectacular example involved People Express which grew at an astounding rate but then collapsed dramatically (see Borenstein, 1992 on events in the first decade or so after deregulation).

While the task of managing an established airline that serves (truly) *competitive* markets is a demanding task, steering and expanding a new airline company is even more difficult. The penalty for error is usually considerable: one significant mistake or mis-judgement can bankrupt a small company. (In contrast, the managers of a large, established airline can make the occasional medium-size error without imperilling the company.) Thus for many of the new airlines, inadequate managerial performance contributed to the company's demise.

Needless to say, the established airlines often helped. In particular, they engaged in targeted fare-discounting on routes entered by the new airlines (Kahn, 1991). For the large companies, such discounted tickets were but a small proportion of all the tickets they sold, and so their strategy was financially affordable. In contrast, the entrant airline that matched the discounts on all of its (few) routes could easily run out of cash, notwithstanding its lower cost level. Although much of the selective fare-discounting of the established majors might be regarded as 'predatory' (in simple terms, deliberately 'selling below cost', with malevolent intent), the few anti-trust/trade practices challenges from government have not been warmly received by the courts; see, in particular, US District Court of Kansas (2001).

The established, major airlines also sought additional strength from mergers. Even when a merger resulted in diminished competition on some non-stop city-pair routes, regulatory scrutiny was not always effective. Eventually the number of remaining majors became small enough to permit (tacit) cartelisation (on which see §15.2.4).

1.1.3 Changes in the structure of the incumbents' airline networks

A major consequence of deregulation was the re-shaping of airline networks. In general, the majors adopted a hub-and-spoke pattern, usually with at least one daily flight to each non-hub port. Though the airline might still offer direct flights between the very largest cities, many passengers travelling between non-hub ports were required to change planes at an airline hub, usually found at a major city. While such an indirect journey takes more time than would be needed for a direct flight, many such port pairs were thought to have insufficient traffic to support direct flights. Thus a hub-and-spoke network was said to allow the airline to serve more ports than would otherwise be (financially) possible.

Usually, each hub port was a hub for one airline only. An airline that served most regions of the country established perhaps four or five hubs. For some non-hub port pairs, the established airlines competed with each other by offering indirect travel via different hubs.

The hub-and-spoke pattern was also thought to defend an established airline from entry by new carriers. In particular it allows a large airline to offer a frequent service between non-hub ports that is generally beyond the reach of a small entrant. Furthermore, a hubbing airline's frequent flights *may* bestow market power in respect of journeys having the hub port as origin or destination (Hergott, 1997). In support of that view, it should be noted that the fares for such journeys can be higher than the fares on otherwise comparable routes where neither port is a hub (Lijesen and others, 2001). Furthermore, the hubbing airline generally (wins a disproportionate share of the passengers whose travel *originates* at its hub, especially in the case of routes having a large proportion of business travellers. Such passengers are swayed by the size of the airline's hub presence on all routes served from the hub (Borenstein, 1989).

In short, for the established major airlines, the hub-and-spoke network was seen as helping to convert size into market power and consequent profitability. In the 1980s, a common view was that such a network was essential for survival (Kaplan, 1986, p. 54). Kaplan goes on to say (p. 70) 'Hub-and-spoke networks will continue to dominate carrier route planning.' Of course, the subsequent growth of low-cost airlines has qualified that view.

1.1.4 Entry strategies of low-cost carriers

In the US (and, later, in other countries around the world), most of the new airlines favoured a different route structure, namely a *point-to-point network*, in which each flight provided non-stop service between a single city-pair, and most travellers reached their destination without change of plane. Furthermore, most of the new airlines did not encourage travellers to book connecting flights, and generally did not guarantee connections. A traveller who nevertheless did organise a connecting sequence usually had to collect any checked baggage at each intermediate port, and re-check it for the next sector. (Further discussion of hubbing and point-to-point networks appears in §§8.2.2–3.)

1.2 New airlines in the US

In 2014, there remained only six significant, *'new'* airlines – that is, airlines widely launched on interstate routes since the deregulation of the airline sector.

As seen in Table 1.1, Southwest Airlines is *by far* the largest of these, thanks largely to it being much older than the others. Indeed, it has become much the same size as each of the three large 'network' carriers (American, Delta and United) that remain after the many mergers among the legacy carriers. One further new carrier, America West (based in Phoenix), became successful enough to merge with a legacy carrier, US Airways. Still headquartered in Phoenix, the merged company retained the US Airways name, until its merger with American Airlines.

The remainder of the US industry comprises: two important airlines, Alaska and Hawaiian, each with a network initially focussed on the eponymous state, but now pursuing ambitions to grow by extending its geographical reach; and several so-called regional airlines, mainly operating small aircraft on thin and/or local routes, usually under contract to one or more of American, Delta and United. (Those regional airlines are considered later, in §11.1.4.)

The six 'new' airlines are profiled in the following six sections.

1.2.1 Southwest Airlines (including AirTran Airways)

Though incorporated in Texas in 1967, Southwest did not begin service until June 1971 – thanks to legal obstacles initiated by the incumbent airlines in the region. Its initial fleet of three, second-hand Boeing 737 aircraft served three Texas cities – Dallas, Houston, and San Antonio. Its headquarters was (and is) at Dallas, where it began service from the in-town Love Field at a time when the established airlines had agreed to move their flights away from Love to the new, green-field Dallas–Fort Worth regional airport.

In the early years, Southwest's growth rate was very modest. About a year after start-up it was so short of cash that it had to sell one of the four, second-hand aircraft in its fleet. It was 1976 before the fleet grew to six aircraft. In 1979 deregulation of inter-state services gave the company the opportunity to fly outside Texas, its first such route being to New Orleans. However, the so-called Wright Amendment (which was included in Federal legislation) severely limited the set of ports to which *any* airline was allowed to fly *directly* from Love Field (see §12.2.1). Despite that limitation, the company was then growing strongly; by 1981 it was operating 27 aircraft (the airline history: 'We weren't just airborne yesterday' – version of 1 August 2007, accessed at www.southwest.com).

Notwithstanding the increased opportunities for expansion, the company continued to pursue a conservative growth policy, carefully adding nearby links to its point-to-point network. Even in the year 2000, the network was focussed mainly on its origins in Texas and the nearby states. Since then, the company has branched out more boldly, to add (for example) more services in the north-east and also some trans-continental routes. (In 2011, it purchased another low-cost carrier, AirTran Airways, as discussed below.)

To some extent the company's network has begun to take on some hub-and-spoke characteristics, and the booking engine offers many connecting flights. Many of the Southwest routes radiate from base ports at Chicago Midway,

Table 1.1 Significant US 'new' carriers: operations in 2014[1]

	Southwest[2]	JetBlue	Frontier	Virgin America	Spirit	Allegiant
Rev. passengers (millions)	126.7	26.4	11.3	6.3	12.6	8.1
RPM[3] (billions)	100.5	30.5	9.8	9.8	12.6	7.7
Load factor (%)	82.6	84.7	89.8	82.4	86.8	89.3
Flights (000s)	1,162	245	85	57	92	53
Main cities[4]	Chicago	New York	Denver	San Francisco	Fort Lauderdale	Las Vegas
	Las Vegas	Boston	Trenton	Los Angeles	Dallas/Fort Worth	Sanford
	Baltimore	Orlando	DC	New York	Las Vegas	Phoenix
	Denver	Fort Lauderdale	Las Vegas	Las Vegas	Chicago	St Petersburg

Source: US Department of Transport, BTS (transtats.bts.gov/carriers) accessed on 21 May 2015

Notes

1 Scheduled services, flights departing US airports during the twelve months ending December 2014.
2 These data exclude the (remaining) operations of AirTran.
3 Revenue passenger miles, being the total miles flown by paying passengers.
4 The lists refer to cities rather than to individual airports in a city. For each airline, cities are ranked according to the number of passengers carried by the airline from the city.

Las Vegas, Baltimore–Washington (BWI), Phoenix and Denver. Even so, at the end of 2013, Southwest (by itself) flew non-stop between 524 city-pairs; and the average stage length was 693 miles. Furthermore, about 72 per cent of journeys made by Southwest passengers in 2013 were non-stop. At 31 December 2013, the combined fleets operated by Southwest and AirTran numbered 614 B737 and 66 B717 aircraft (2013 Annual Report, Form 10-K, pp. 1 and 2).

AirTran Airways was formed in 1997 by a merger of two companies – ValuJet and Conquest Sun – which had started in the early 1990s. When Eastern Air Lines went out of business, there was a 'void at ... Atlanta International Airport'. ValuJet Airlines 'was founded by airline industry veterans including an executive group from the former Southern Airways and pilots, mechanics and flight attendants from the defunct Eastern Air Lines.' ('AirTran Airways history', accessed at AirTran website, 3 October 2007). ValuJet launched in October 1993.

The other company, *Conquest Sun* (later renamed as AirTran), was also started by former Eastern Air Lines personnel. The company moved its base to Orlando, Florida, and soon had a fleet of 11 Boeing 737 aircraft serving 24 cities in the east and mid-west.

In November 1997, ValuJet acquired AirTran, and the combined company kept the name AirTran. That company then grew very substantially, with principal hubs at Atlanta (non-stop service to 54 cities in January 2009) and Orlando (31 cities). To reduce its dependence on Atlanta, it increased its presence in Baltimore and Milwaukee (2010 Form 10-K, p. 4).

At 31 January 2011, a majority of AirTran's aircraft were B717s (AirTran 2010 Form 10-K, p. 5), while Southwest had always operated B737s only. As the two airlines integrated, the B717s were displaced.

1.2.2 JetBlue Airways

Based at John F Kennedy Airport in New York, the company launched in 2000, deploying new A320 aircraft. Its initial focus on east-coast routes (notably from the north-east to Florida) suggest a wish to avoid flying routes already served by Southwest Airlines. Regarding its choice of JFK Airport, however, JetBlue said 'We believe that by building our operations in the nation's largest travel market, more market opportunities will become available to us than if we focused our operations elsewhere' (2006 Form 10-K, p. 2). In its 2008 Annual Report (Form 10-K, p. 4), it pointed out that at JFK, at the end of 2008, the number of domestic passengers it served was almost as large as the number served by all the other airlines combined.

However its focus on some high-yield routes came at a cost: 'We are committed to operating our scheduled flights whenever possible; however, this commitment to customer service, along with operating at three of the most congested and delay-prone domestic airports, contributed to a 72.9% on-time performance in 2006, which was lower than all but one major US airline' (JetBlue, Annual Report 2006, p. 1).

JetBlue's early, profitable success led to aggressive expansion both on the east coast and (later) on some trans-continental routes. In 2005 JetBlue added to its fleet a smaller jet type, the 100-seat Embraer 190; this enabled it to serve 'thinner' routes, and to fly fewer seats at quiet times on some of the major routes.

At about the same time, however, the company's profitability declined. In 2005 it reported a net loss of US$20 million. During 2006, it 'introduced initiatives to reduce fuel consumption through more fuel efficient operating practices, renewed [its] focus on low-cost carrier spending habits and implemented more efficient staffing in all aspects of [its] business' (2006 Annual Report, Form 10-K, p. 1). Despite slowing its expansion, the company continued to lose money, and the adverse circumstances of 2008 led to a US$76 million deficit (2008 Form 10-K, p. 44).

The company then focussed successfully on selective growth on routes likely to earn good profits. It soon enjoyed operating profits in each of the four quarters in its financial year, notwithstanding the major increases in its outlays on jet fuel – which reached almost 40 per cent of its operating expenses in 2011 (2011 Form 10-K, p. 10).

By 31 December 2013, JetBlue was flying to 82 cities in 25 continental states, Puerto Rico, US Virgin Islands and 15 countries in the Caribbean and Latin America. In 2013, some 87 per cent of aircraft capacity was devoted to three route groups (2013 Form 10-K, p. 8): service between the North East and Florida absorbed 31 per cent, transcontinental routes (28 per cent), and services to the Caribbean and Puerto Rico (28 per cent). And, besides its top position at JFK, JetBlue had become the largest operator of domestic flights at Logan Airport, Boston.

From the very outset, the airline enjoyed a reputation for innovative management. In 2003 it removed one row of seats from each of its A320s, reducing capacity from 162 seats (already a small number) to 156 ('JetBlue add more legroom across fleet', media release, 13 November 2003). Then, apparently in response to its 2006 financial difficulties, the company moved (further) *up*-market: beginning in February 2007, it removed a further seat row, leaving only 150 seats, with at least 36 inches between rows 1 to 11 and at least 34 inches between rows 12 to 25, giving 'the most legroom in coach of all US airlines' (2006 Form 10-K, p. 2).

There was a compatible fare initiative:

> In 2005, our load factor was 85.2% and our yield per passenger mile was 8.02 cents. During 2006, we made ... a strategic decision to price our product to achieve a higher yield, at the expense of load factor. By year end, our load factor was 81.6% and our yield per passenger mile climbed to 9.53 cents – nearly a 19% increase year-over-year.
>
> (2006 Annual Report, introduction)

At the end of 2011, JetBlue operated 120 A320s and 49 E190s. Later, however, it deferred orders for further E190s, converted an order for A320s to one for A321s (with 190 seats per aircraft), and ordered still more A321s (2013 Form

10-K, pp. 19–20). No doubt this turn towards larger aircraft (with lower fuel consumption per available seat mile) reflected the continuing high price for jet fuel.

In anticipation of Robin Hayes becoming JetBlue's CEO (in February 2015), there was press speculation that JetBlue might start charging for bags, and add more seats in some of its aircraft. Such changes were thought likely to lead to increased profits (Reuters, 'New CEO could send JetBlue shares flying', 28 September 2014). When accessed on 25 January 2015, the airline website (jetblue.com) reported 'Your first checked bag is free', subject to weight and size limits. A second bag attracted a fee of US$50, while for a third bag the fee was US$100; in both cases, limits applied on weight and size. (For a principled discussion of bag charges, see §9.4.)

1.2.3 Spirit Airlines

Founded (as Charter One) in Detroit in 1980, the airline's initial role was to fly passengers taking package holidays. Under its new name, it became a scheduled carrier, and moved its main base to Fort Lauderdale (Florida) and its headquarters to Miramar (Florida). Over the two-year period ending in September 2006, it switched its entire fleet to *new* Airbus A319 and A320 aircraft. While the leisure focus remained, it developed an emphasis on destinations in the Caribbean, Bahamas and Latin America. Unusually, almost all the passengers flying to ports outside the US travel via its Fort Lauderdale hub.

In 2006, Spirit was struggling to make profits. In July that year, it secured an important recapitalisation when Indigo Partners LLC obtained a majority stake in the company. (At that time, the managing partner of Indigo was William Franke, former CEO of America West Airlines.) In that year, Spirit also appointed a new CEO, Ben Baldanza, who had started his life-long airline career in the finance department of American Airlines (Associated Press interview with Baldanza, *Las Vegas Sun*, 14 July 2011).

Spirit then embarked on a drive to reduce its costs, and soon started calling itself an Ultra Low Cost Carrier (ULCC). It also began to levy separate charges for all checked baggage, on-board beverages and snacks, and Big Front Seats (front rows with 2 + 2 seats, rather than the standard 3 + 3, and 36-inch legroom instead of 31 inches). Indeed, Spirit claims it was the first airline in the US to unbundle its pricing.

Spirit also strictly enforced its penalty charges for passengers who cancelled or changed booked tickets, and firmly declined to accept financial responsibility for extra costs incurred by passengers when it cancelled a flight. According to reports (see particularly 'Don't come crying to this airline', *New York Times*, 28 March 2009), some passengers complained about this approach. Yet enforcement of some of those rules is standard practice for low-cost airlines in other world regions.

Following a tiny net income in 2007, Spirit earned US$33 million in 2008, and between US$72 million and US$83 million in each of the following three years.

In those years (from 2009 to 2011), it enjoyed operating income margins of (respectively) 15.9, 8.85 and 13.5 per cent (2011 Form 10-K, pp. 38 and 43).

These improved results did *not* depend on great growth in the size of the company. Indeed, the fleet size at the end of 2011 was the same as that at the end of 2007. However, the aircraft worked rather harder than before. Even though the average stage length *decreased* slightly, from 956 miles in 2007 to 921 miles in 2011, average aircraft daily utilisation increased from 11.5 hours to 12.7 hours, and the load factor went from 81.0 per cent to 85.6 per cent.

Improved profitability did come in part from an increase in 'passenger flight segments', from 7.0 million in 2007 to 8.5 million in 2011. (No doubt, the choice of that unit of measurement reflects the fact that passengers travelling between US and Caribbean ports generally undertake two separate flights for a one-way journey.)

Upon introducing separate ancillary charges, Spirit (unlike many airlines) *did* reduce its base fare, from US$98 per passenger flight segment in 2007, to US$77 in 2010, while the revenue from ancillary charges increased markedly, rising from US$11 to US$35. Total revenue per passenger flight segment increased only from US$109 to US$112. However that figure increased to US$126 in 2011 (2011 Form 10-K, p. 40), and reached US$135 in 2013.

On 1 June 2011, Spirit completed its initial public offering (IPO) of common stock. In conjunction with a recapitalisation, the outcomes included repayment or conversion of all debt instruments, and receipt of net proceeds of US$150 million. The ongoing business plan was to increase the size of the business, in order to reap economies of scale.

At the end of 2011, Spirit still had only 37 Airbus aircraft (mainly A319s with 145 seats each). Over the next two years the fleet grew markedly, to comprise 29 A319s, 23 A320s (178 seats) and 2 A321s (218 seats). Thereafter, there was continuing emphasis on larger aircraft, with delivery of 11 A320s in 2014 – giving a total fleet of 65 aircraft by the end of that year. The plans for the following years envisaged more A320s and A321s, partly offset by annual *reductions* in the number of A319s ('Spirit Airlines Fleet Plan, as of July 29, 2014', accessed at the airline website, 1 October 2014).

By early 2012, Spirit's network included some trunk routes between major ports. At the end of 2013, it flew 130 routes serving 56 airports in North America, Central America, South America and the Caribbean. The ports included Los Angeles, Denver, Minneapolis/St Paul, Chicago O'Hare, Dallas/Fort Worth, Boston, NY La Guardia, Tampa, Orlando and Fort Lauderdale (2013 Form 10-K, pp. 6–7).

While the number of ports then remained stable, the number of routes ('markets') rose to 151 by the end of 2014: 'we target underserved and/or overpriced markets'. In most markets, Spirit faces competition from one or more of the four largest US airlines. 'Our single largest overlap, at approximately 51% of our markets as of January 12, 2015, is with American Airlines' (2014 Form 10-K, pp. 6–7).

Following the 2011 IPO, Spirit's net income continued to increase – to US$108 million in 2012, then US$177 million in 2013, and US$225 million in 2014. The respective operating profit margins were 13.2 per cent, 17.1 per cent and 18.4 per cent. Of course, the increase in total profit was due largely to the increase in the number of passengers. Indeed, total RPM rose from 6 billion in 2009 to 14 billion in 2014 (2014 Form 10-K, pp. 33–5).

1.2.4 Frontier Airlines

'The original Frontier Airlines was Denver's hometown carrier for 40 years' ('Our history', accessed at www.frontierairlines.com on 3 December 2007). In 1986, however, it ceased to exist as an independent airline, and the name disappeared. Later, when Continental Air Lines was scaling back its Denver hub, a group of 'founders', including executives from the former Frontier Airlines, judged that Continental's plans would leave much unserved demand at Denver, and so would present an opportunity for an entrant.

In February 1994, the founders established a new low-fare airline under the old Frontier name, and by April they had raised about US$9 million as start-up capital. Frontier began service in July, using two ageing B737-200 aircraft flying from Denver to small local ports. As Continental withdrew from further Denver routes, Frontier began to focus on routes to ports in larger cities, such as Las Vegas, Phoenix and Chicago (Midway).

Frontier received its first Airbus (an A319) in 2001, and became an all-Airbus operation in 2005. By mid-2008, its fleet had grown to 11 A318s, 47 A319s, and two A320s. This gave a smaller average aircraft size than usual for major Airbus operators. On the other hand, in the year to 31 March 2008, Frontier enjoyed a (high) average utilisation of 12.1 block hours per aircraft.

From its Denver base, Frontier operated what was largely a hub-and-spoke network. On routes from Denver, 44 of its top 50 destinations had direct flights from Denver (Form 10-K, March 2007, p. 6). This made it particularly susceptible to competition at Denver, In March 2007, United had 55 per cent of the Denver passengers, and Frontier came second with 21 per cent. Furthermore, Southwest Airlines had returned to Denver in January 2006, and had reached a five per cent passenger share in March 2007. Frontier competed with one or the other on almost all its routes (Frontier Form 10-K, March 2007, p. 10).

From mid-2007, Frontier started incurring a series of monthly financial deficits, in part because of the rising jet-fuel prices that were soon to trouble all US airlines. Then, as reported by Frontier (2009 Form 10-K, p. 4), its principal bankcard processor sought to increase the processor's 'holdback' of funds paid by passengers for tickets, a move that threatened Frontier's liquidity. On 10 April 2008, Frontier filed for Chapter 11 protection under the US Bankruptcy Code.

In the outcome, Frontier was purchased out of bankruptcy in August 2009 by Republic Airways Holdings, which beat off a rival bid by Southwest Airlines. Republic's plans included: adding six seats to each of the A320 aircraft, developing profitable point-to-point routes in areas away from Denver and, of course, reducing costs! In short, Republic was moving Frontier towards becoming an Ultra Low-Cost Carrier (ULCC).

Despite that campaign, Frontier was still incurring financial deficits, and in November 2011, Republic announced it planned to seek a buyer (Doug Cameron, *Wall Street Journal*, 8 November 2011). *Eventually*, there was a rumour that Indigo Partners would bid (Steve Raabe, *Denver Post*, 9 April 2013). At Indigo, William Franke resigned from the Spirit Airlines board in August, and Indigo began to divest its shares in Spirit (Hugo Martin, *Los Angeles Times*, 1 October 2013.) Republic signed a conditional contract with Indigo in October, and the sale was finalised in December (Associated Press *Star Tribune* (Minneapolis), 3 December 2013).

Under the new owners, Frontier recruited some executives with ULCC experience at Allegiant, Ryanair and Spirit. And it introduced two fare classes: one in which *all* optional services required extra payment; and the other a fully refundable 'classic' fare.

There was renewed emphasis on seeking out promising route opportunities in places other than Denver. In August 2014, Frontier opened a base at Washington Dulles, and within a few weeks had launched more than ten routes from that port (reports in anna.aero, 27 August and 10 September, 2014). It also started new routes from Cleveland, where United finally closed its hub, and from Cincinnati where earlier Delta had reduced its services (CAPA, 'Frontier Airlines moves on Cincinnati and Cleveland', 14 September, 2014). On most of its new routes, it was in competition with other airlines – notably Allegiant at Cincinnati. Of course, when introducing so many new routes, it is almost inevitable that some do not work out as well as hoped.

1.2.5 Allegiant Air

Founded in 1997 and headquartered in Las Vegas, Allegiant has pursued a very distinctive strategy: it is a ULCC that is marketed to leisure travellers, initially those living in small cities. In February 2014, it served 86 markets, offering non-stop service to 13 US leisure destinations, including Las Vegas, Phoenix (Arizona), Orlando, Tampa/St Petersburg and Fort Lauderdale (Florida), Los Angeles and Honolulu (Allegiant, 2013 Form 10-K, p. 2).

In May 2014, the Allegiant fleet comprised 53 MD80 aircraft (average age about 24 years, with an average of 166 seats per aircraft), six B757s (223 seats), three A319s (156 seats) and seven A320s (177 seats). The company had recently acquired the B757s; only in 2013 had it begun to acquire used Airbus aircraft – with seven more A319s and two more A320s to be delivered in 2014 and 2015 (Allegiant, Annual Report 2013, introductory statement, and 2013 Form 10-K, p. 19; see also Allegiant Management Presentation, 'Introduction of used Airbus A319 to ALGT', July 2012).

Though operating some charter flights, Allegiant's main business is the provision of scheduled services, with weekly frequencies of four or fewer flights on most of its 225 routes. At 1 February 2014, it faced direct competition on only 23 of those routes (2013 Form 10-K, p. 6). It usually enjoys load factors of around 90 per cent.

In 2013, Allegiant's fleet averaged about 5.5 block hours per day per aircraft; this figure varied seasonally, ranging from 7.1 hours in March to 3.9 hours in September (2013 Form 10-K, p. 3). No doubt, the modest deployment reflects the age of the fleet. Older aircraft are less reliable and need more maintenance; but the consequent low market value results in low daily holding costs. This helps Allegiant when it varies its amount of flying during the travel seasons.

In 2013, Allegiant sold 92 per cent of its tickets through its own website – a very high proportion for an airline in the US. The average (one-way) total fare was US$137; this included almost US$46 in ancillary charges. Its handsome *net* operating income in 2013 amounted to almost 11 per cent of its operating revenues (2013 Form 10-K, p. 27).

Allegiant's approach to ancillary charges is both comprehensive and distinctive. The list of charged services includes seat selection, priority boarding, call centre booking, boarding-pass printing (at the airport), checked *and carry-on* bags, and bags checked at the departure gate.

For many of the charges, the dollar amounts depend on detailed classifications, which generally *reflect* differences in the incremental costs incurred by the airline – though the charges do not necessarily *equate* to those costs. A modest example concerns credit-card transactions: to 'cover merchant-processing costs, [there is] a surcharge of 3.2%, not to exceed $8 each way, per passenger ... There is no fee to use a personal, US-issued Visa or MasterCard *debit* card' (italics added) ('Optional Services & Fees', allegiantair.com, accessed 27 January 2015).

Now for the baggage fees! 'Bags are priced *by route*, per segment' (italics added). The website table lists fees for each individual route; for example, for up to four checked bags, a per-bag charge of US$20, US$22, US$25 or US$30 depending on the distance to be travelled; and corresponding per-bag charges for carry-on bags of US$15, US$16, US$18 and US$20. In addition there are weight and size limits and additional charges for overweight and oversize bags. (See §9.4 for some general discussion of the structure of bag charges.)

Allegiant's very high profit rate has encouraged the airline to grow rapidly. It carried 13 per cent more scheduled passengers in 2014 than in 2013 (BTS, carrier snapshot). In 2015, new routes included particular expansion of services to Florida, and first-ever flights serving Indianapolis, New Orleans, Omaha, Pittsburgh and Richmond ('Allegiant Air loves Florida; sets passenger record in March as Indianapolis, New Orleans and Pittsburgh are added to network', anna. aero, 22 April 2015).

The airline seems to be more inclined to seek passengers living in larger cities; it thereby competes more directly with the large network carriers.

1.2.6 Virgin America

During a lengthy planning period beginning in 2004, the new, privately-held company had to satisfy the US Department of Transportation that – despite the 'Virgin' appellation – its shareholder structure met the requirements that foreigners must hold no more than 25 per cent of the voting shares and no more than 49 per cent of the capital.

The company chose San Francisco International (SFO) as its base port, and opted to fly brand-new A320 and A319 aircraft. These aircraft had both First Class and Main cabins, with seat pitches of 55 and 32/33 inches, respectively. Later, the airline added Main Cabin Select, with a 38 inches seat pitch. In 2015, it remained a point-to-point carrier, with a fleet of 53 aircraft, having 145–149 seats (A320) and 119 seats (A319) (Virgin America, Annual Report 2014, Form 10-K, p. 3).

When Virgin America launched on 8 August 2007, it flew routes from San Francisco (SFO) and from Los Angeles (LAX) to New York (JFK), to Dulles International in Washington, and (in 2009) to Boston Logan. It also began to fly several west-coast routes, serving Seattle, San Diego and Las Vegas from SFO and/or LAX. In 2014, it obtained gates at Dallas Love Field, and started several new routes there.

On some of its routes, the airline is in direct competition with legacy carriers, notably United Airlines and Alaska Airlines. Thus its strategy differs from that adopted by many start-ups which commonly seek to find lesser routes with little or no competition. To help it compete, Virgin America sought to offer superior service, and this drew favourable customer response, with the airline winning a service award even in its first year.

As seen in Table 1.2, the carrier expanded vigorously, and soon enjoyed quite good load factors. Yet, Virgin America continued to incur large financial deficits; by the end of 2012, the (simple) cumulated net loss was about US$700 million.

In its early years, Virgin America faced rising fuel prices and sharp fare competition on some of its routes, and so found it difficult to increase its fares to an economic level. Indeed, some recent fare and capacity decisions of rival airlines have posed questions as to whether those decisions constituted fair competition (see CAPA, 'Virgin America faces familiar and fierce competition on potential routes from New York LaGuardia', 13 December 2013). CAPA notes Virgin began service (in April 2013) from Newark (New York) to San Francisco, thereby breaking United's monopoly on that city pair; United responded by adding capacity on that route, and by reducing its fares to undercut Virgin.

In 2013, Virgin America deliberately *reduced* its offered capacity (available seat miles) by about 2.2 per cent (compared with 2012), and reduced the number of new route launches; those changes secured a one point increase in the percentage load factor, while sold output (RPM) fell by about one per cent. Despite a decline in the average stage length, the average fare increased by about 4 per cent, and (for the first time) the airline earned a *positive* annual operating margin.

Furthermore, the airline 'completed a debt restructuring in May 2013, eliminating more than $300 million of debt and accrued interest and reducing interest rates on a majority of the remaining debt' (Virgin America press release, 26 March 2014). That financial restructuring helped the company to report for 2013 a small, positive annual *net income*, also a first.

Table 1.2 Virgin America: operating statistics and financial results, 2007–14

Calendar years:	2007[1]	2008	2009	2010	2011	2012	2013	2014[2]
Passengers (m)	0.38	2.54	3.64	3.83	5.01	6.21	6.17	6.35
RPM[3] (billions)	0.58	3.41	5.42	6.24	8.02	9.92	9.57	9.82
Load factors %	61.7	76.6	82.8	81.5	81.4	79.3	80.3	82.4
Op. revenue ($m)	52	378	548	725	1,037	1,333	1,425	1,490
Op. margin[4,5] %		(49.7)	(7.1)	(1.7)	(2.6)	(2.4)	6.5	6.2
Net income[5] ($m)	(98)	(210)	(81)	(67)	(100)	(145)	12	60

Source: US Bureau of Transportation Statistics, Carrier snapshots; the operating statistics are for flights departing from US airports

Notes
1 These data are for the period 8 August–31 December 2007.
2 The data for 2014 are those shown on the BTS website on 6 May 2015.
3 Revenue passenger miles, being the total miles flown by paying passengers.
4 This percentage margin measures operating revenue relative to operating expenses.
5 Parentheses denote negative amounts.

In a press release (28 July 2014), Virgin announced plans for an Initial Purchase Offer. Thus, while the private owners had contributed to the debt restructuring, they could now expect to benefit from a higher selling price for the shares. In the outcome, the November IPO netted some US$276 million, and the initial trading on 18 November closed at a favourable share price, valuing the company at about US$1.6 billion (CAPA, 'Virgin America's powerful market debut. Corporate travel will be a key part of its business model', 19 November 2014).

Following a second (and larger) positive net income in 2014, the company planned to resume fleet expansion in late 2015 and start a new growth phase in 2016.

1.2.7 Lessons from the experiences of Allegiant, Spirit and Virgin America

Most airline newcomers seek routes with little or no direct competition. For their part, Allegiant and Spirit both noted that the major legacy carriers – with their focus on hub-and-spoke networks – were little interested in the demand of leisure travellers (especially those living in smaller cities) for non-stop flights to tourist destinations. And both airlines have earned handsome profits from serving that demand, at fares much lower than those charged by the major legacy carriers.

Yet there are also major differences *between* Allegiant and Spirit. Until Allegiant began to introduce *used* A319s it had relied solely on *very* old aircraft having low capital cost but high operating costs. That strategy was little changed when it started flying the Airbus aircraft. Nevertheless, its profitability suggests that the approach is well suited to its market niche.

In contrast, Spirit switched to *new* aircraft with higher capital costs but lower operating costs and also greater reliability, resulting in higher service quality. No doubt, that reliability has helped Spirit's prospects when it started to compete with major legacy carriers on dense routes. Also noteworthy is the strategic skill deployed when experienced investors took a stake in Spirit: the airline returned to profitability *before* expanding to new routes.

While Allegiant and Spirit are outside the legacy-airline club, both have been in business for quite some time. In contrast, Virgin America is still a recent start-up. By choosing San Francisco as its base, it sought some differentiation from the legacy carriers. On the other hand, by entering major routes, it inevitably had to compete directly with those carriers. Its long period with financial deficits show how difficult it is for a newcomer to cope with such a situation. Its survival depended on having investors with sizeable financial resources and a willingness to take risks. They also remained *patient* while the company bought market share and so reduced its unit costs. The company's other major advantage is an ability to motivate the cabin crew and other employees, thereby securing a reputation for good service and reliability.

1.3 Route competition in US domestic markets

1.3.1 The numbers of 'air traffic hubs' and hub city-pairs

Reflecting the great size of the domestic (mainland) airline network, the US Bureau of Transportation Statistics identifies about 120 so-called air traffic hubs. As of June 2011, the BTS classified 35 of them as 'medium' (each having between 0.25 and 1 per cent of total enplaned (boarded) passengers in the US) and 24 as 'large' (more than 1 per cent). Each traffic hub corresponds to a metropolitan area. (A few such areas have more than one jet airport; for example, Washington, DC.)

Disregarding the minor hubs, the 59 large and medium hubs yield 1711 hub pairs. However, some of those pairs (especially on the east coast) are too close together to support airline service. At the end of 2013, Southwest Airlines (excluding the remaining AirTran flights), operated non-stop service between 'only' 524 port pairs (Southwest Airlines, 2013 Form 10–K, p. 2). Thus even the large Southwest had considerable scope for further expansion of its point-to-point network.

By 2014, when the United States domestic market was served by only four 'national' airlines, together with the seven (independent) smaller companies, the nature of the competition between airlines was influenced by the number of airlines on each of the city pairs that do have non-stop airline service. For two selected ports, the following sections give some insights into airline numbers on individual routes.

1.3.2 A first example: airline routes at Salt Lake City

In 1978, this airport built a second terminal – initially for Western Airlines, which went on to establish an operating hub at Salt Lake City (SLC) in 1982. Western was merged into Delta Airlines in 1987, and ever since then, Salt Lake City has been a major hub for Delta and its regional carriers ('History of the airport', www.slcairport.com, accessed 12 May 2009). The Bureau of Transportation Statistics classifies it as a large hub.

For the year to 30 June 2014, Delta and its regional affiliated carriers – mainly Skywest – boarded more than 73 per cent of the passengers departing SLC (BTS Airport Snapshot for SLC). The shares for Southwest, American and Frontier were (respectively) 11.7, 3.1 and 2.4 per cent, while the remainder was shared among other airlines (notably Alaska and JetBlue).

The adjacent BTS large hubs are at Denver and Las Vegas, at sector distances of 394 miles (634 km) and 370 miles (595 km), respectively. While Salt Lake City has numerous local services to small ports, there are also services to large and medium hubs throughout the US.

For September 2014, the airport website recorded 334 daily domestic jet departures to 82 non-stop destinations. There were 63 route monopolies: Chicago Midway was served only by Southwest, though flights to Chicago O'Hare are a close substitute; the other 62 routes are served only by Delta (together with its regional carriers). While many of those ports are at small cities, Delta (with its affiliates) monopolised the services to several major cities: Atlanta (8 flights daily),

Boston (2), Cincinnati (2), Detroit (4), Kansas City (3), Minneapolis (6), Orlando (2), Sacramento (4), St Louis (2), Tucson (3), and Washington (2, both to DCA).

Details for the 19 *contested* non-stop routes in September 2014 are presented in Table 1.3. Though Delta had competition on many of its most dense routes, it is only on six busy routes (to Chicago O'Hare, Denver, Houston, Las Vegas, Los Angeles and Phoenix) that Delta encountered more than one competitor. Note also the limited presence of each major carrier.

The post-merger American flew only to Charlotte, Dallas/Fort Worth, Philadelphia and Phoenix. In marked contrast to June 2012, United (itself) flew only to Houston. And Southwest reduced from nine such routes to six.

In contrast, Alaska began flying (twice daily) from Seattle to SLC in April 2013. Then, in June 2014, it launched seven further routes at SLC, including two

Table 1.3 Carriers serving contested[1] non-stop routes from Salt Lake City (SLC), June 2012 and September 2014

Routes between Salt Lake City and these ports		Carriers other than Delta and its regional affiliates[2]	
		June 2012	*September 2014*
Baltimore	BWI	Southwest	Southwest
Boise	BOI	–	Horizon
Charlotte	CLT	US Airways	American
Chicago O'Hare	ORD	American, Shuttle America, United	Shuttle America, Republic
Dallas/Ft Worth	DFW	American	American
Denver	DEN	American, Frontier, Southwest, United	Frontier, Shuttle America, Republic, Southwest,
Houston	IAH	United	Express Jet, United
Las Vegas	LAS	Southwest	Horizon, Southwest
Long Beach	LGB	JetBlue	JetBlue
Los Angeles	LAX	American, Southwest, United	Alaska, Southwest
New York	JFK	JetBlue	JetBlue
Oakland	OAK	Southwest	Southwest
Philadelphia	PHL	–	American
Phoenix	PHX	Southwest, US Airways	Southwest, American
Portland	PDX	Southwest	Alaska
Reno	RNO	Southwest	–
San Diego	SAN	–	Alaska
San Francisco	SFO	United	Alaska
San Jose	SJC	–	Alaska
Seattle/Tacoma	SEA	Southwest	Alaska

Sources: Based on Daily Domestic Jet Departures from SLC, June 2012 and September 2014, slcairport.com

Notes
1 An 'affiliated' regional carrier flies on behalf of one or more of the major airlines. A route that is served *only* by Delta and/or any of its affiliated regional carriers is deemed not to be a contested route. Each of the routes recorded in the table has two or more *independent* carriers.
2 Delta and/or its affiliates (mainly Skywest) served every one of the contested routes (16 routes in June 2012; 19 in September 2014).

short routes (to Boise and Las Vegas) flown by its in-house regional carrier, Horizon, deploying Q400 turbo-props. Alaska's initial frequencies were twice-daily to Portland, San Diego and Las Vegas, and once daily on the other four routes (Alaska Airlines, 2013 Form 10-K, pp. 29–30, and media release, 9 June 2014). It also added a third daily flight between Seattle and SLC.

On those routes, Alaska faced considerable competition from the incumbent airlines, principally Delta and its affiliates (anna.aero, 19 June 2014). It remained to be seen how Alaska would fare. (See also the commentary in §13.2.1.)

1.3.3 A second example: airline routes at Oklahoma City

While large hubs are usually well connected, medium hubs generally have non-stop flights to only a modest proportion of the entire set of (domestic) large and medium hubs. As a second example, Oklahoma City airport (OKC) had about 3.5 million (arriving and departing) passengers in the 12 months to the end of March 2012 (BTS, 'Airport fact sheet'), and was at rank 65 in the BTS list of airports (not hubs). In that year, Southwest carried 36 per cent of the passengers and American came second with 17 per cent. A regional carrier, Skywest was third with 10 per cent. Several smaller carriers shared the remaining 37 per cent.

For June 2012, OKC had non-stop service to 19 ports (Table 1.4). Of those routes, only two were served by competing airlines. Notwithstanding the rather modest number of non-stop routes, the listed ports include many of the

Table 1.4 Ports served non-stop from Oklahoma City (OKC), June 2012 and October 2014

Contested routes	Competing airlines June 2012	Competing airlines October 2014
Atlanta	–	Delta, Southwest
Chicago O'Hare	American, United	American, United
Denver	Frontier, Southwest, United	Frontier, Southwest, United
Los Angeles	–	American, United
Airlines	*Routes monopolised June 2012*	*Routes monopolised October 2014*
American	Dallas/Ft Worth	Charlotte, Dallas/Ft Worth
United	Houston Intercontinental, Los Angeles (LAX), New York (Newark), Washington (Dulles)	Houston Intercontinental, New York (Newark), San Francisco, Washington (Dulles)
Delta	Atlanta, Detroit, Memphis, Minneapolis, Salt Lake City	Detroit, Minneapolis, Salt Lake City
Southwest	Baltimore, Dallas (Love), Houston (Hobby), Kansas City, Las Vegas, Phoenix, St Louis	Baltimore, Chicago (Midway), Dallas (Love), Houston (Hobby), Las Vegas, Phoenix, St Louis
Allegiant		Orlando–Sanford (seasonal)

Source: Oklahoma City Airport (flyokc.com, accessed June 2012 and October 2014)

major-airline hubs; clearly many domestic journeys from or to OKC could be accomplished with at most one change of aircraft.

In October 2014, although the overall picture was not greatly changed, several changes by individual airlines are of interest. Two additional routes were contested: Southwest joined Delta in offering non-stops to Atlanta; and American joined United in flying non-stop to Los Angeles (LAX). And the list of monopoly routes had several changes: overall, Delta reduced its role marginally, and American increased its role modestly, as did United and Southwest.

1.4 Airline services in Canada

Although a large proportion of the Canadian population lives close to the border with the US, Canada's network of domestic airline routes is still somewhat separate from the domestic network in the US. Canada did not embark on deregulation of its domestic aviation market until ten years after the US deregulation. Both governments have maintained separate national ownership requirements for airlines serving domestic routes. Thus the much smaller Canadian market is served by a distinct and small set of Canadian carriers.

However, each government readily grants permission for an airline domiciled in the other country to operate transborder (international) services between the two countries. The major Canadian scheduled airlines do fly to some US ports. While several US legacy carriers serve some Canadian ports, the *new* US airlines have not enthused about flying to Canada.

1.4.1 Domestic aviation before 2001

Aside from the presence of local regional airlines, aviation in Canada was long the preserve of two major airlines, both with railway antecedents. In the late 1930s, the Canadian government established Trans-Canadian Airlines (as it was then called), making it a subsidiary of the government-owned Canadian National Railways. In 1965, the name was changed to Air Canada, and this eventually became an independent Crown corporation.

The other major airline was established in 1942 when (the privately owned) Canadian Pacific Railways bought several small airlines and formed Canadian Pacific Airlines, based in Vancouver. Financial difficulties in the 1980s induced that railway to sell the airline company to a (western) regional airline; the merged entity took the name Canadian Airlines.

The *Canada Transportation Act 1987* deregulated domestic airline services from 1 January 1988, and Air Canada was privatised soon after. Following the 1999 relaxation of government control of the structure of the aviation industry, Air Canada acquired Canadian Airlines in July 2000 and merged the two operations on 1 January 2001.

The only other significant *scheduled* jet airline is the much newer company, WestJet Airlines, which launched in 1996, and is considered below, in §1.4.3. Canada also has an independent turbo-prop operator, Porter Airlines, discussed in §1.4.4. (Some very small regional operators are considered in §11.1.6.)

1.4.2 Air Canada from 2001

Though a large airline by world standards, Air Canada has long had problems over cost levels. In April 2003 it filed for protection from its creditors. A funding package came with new owners, and the company emerged from protection on 30 September 2004 (Air Canada, Initial Annual Information Form, March 2007). Following that re-organisation, the airline continued to expand. At the end of 2007, Air Canada (together with an affiliate Jazz) served 57 Canadian ports. And Jazz also flew some transborder routes on behalf of Air Canada.

In response to the low-cost competition of WestJet, Air Canada embarked on some low-cost initiatives of its own. In 2001, it started Air Canada Tango, which operated A320 aircraft on low-fare services between major cities. And in 2002, it established Zip as a low-cost airline operating old B737-200 aircraft in western Canada, in direct competition with WestJet. Neither of those ventures was particularly successful; both were closed in 2004.

In 2012, Air Canada still suffered from high cost levels. However during that year it reached new agreements with unions and suppliers. And, again, the company sought advantage from a low-cost initiative. It announced plans for a launch in 2013 of a subsidiary, Air Canada Rouge, a low-cost leisure airline, which was to fly tourists to North American and other international destinations. Air Canada's existing tour operator business, Air Canada Vacations, would work with Rouge (Air Canada, Annual Report 2012, pp. 7–8).

When Rouge started in July 2013, it flew routes to Athens, Edinburgh and Venice, and to several Caribbean ports. Its initial fleet comprised two 2 B767–300 aircraft and two A319s; by the end of the year, it was operating a further six A319s.

When in service with Rouge, those aircraft had unit operating costs (cents per available seat mile, CASM) about 21 per cent lower for the A319s and 29 per cent lower for the B767s, than when they had been operated by the main-line carrier. This was said to be thanks (in part) to *rouge* having higher seat densities, lower wage rates, and 'more competitive work rules in labour agreements' (Air Canada, Annual Report 2013, p. 9).

The launch of Rouge may be interpreted as a response to the success already enjoyed on such tourist routes by the newcomer WestJet. Also serving the tourist markets was Air Transat, offering charter flights as part of an integrated group supplying package holidays (CAPA, 'Air Transat braces for more pressure from currency headwinds than the challenge from rouge', 2 July 2014).

Air Canada financial data for 2013 and 2014 are included in Table 1.5, below. For the airline taken as a whole, the drive for improved profitability remained a work in progress.

1.4.3 WestJet Airlines

WestJet launched in February 1996 – flying three ageing B737-200 aircraft between its Calgary base and four other western ports, Vancouver, Kelowna,

Table 1.5 Operating and financial statistics, Air Canada and WestJet, 2013 and 2014

	Air Canada[1]		WestJet[2]	
	2013	2014	2013	2014
Revenue passengers carried (millions)[3]	35.8	38.5	18.5	19.7
Revenue passenger miles (RPM) (billions)	56.8	61.6	19.6	20.8
Revenue passenger load factor (%)	82.8	83.4	81.7	81.4
Number of aircraft in fleet, end of year	352	364	113	122
Block hours per aircraft per day	10.0	9.9	12.0	11.8
Revenue (C$ billions)	12.38	13.27	3.66	3.98
Net income (C$ millions)	10	105	269	284

Sources: Air Canada, Annual Report 2013, p.2, Annual Report 2014, p. 4; WestJet, Annual Information Form 2013, p. 22, Annual Information Form 2014, p. 5

Notes
1 The Air Canada operating statistics include the performance of the third party carriers (including Jazz) that fly under capacity purchase agreements with Air Canada.
2 The data include the operations of WestJet's turbo-prop unit, Encore, which launched in June 2013.
3 Air Canada counts revenue passengers on a flight number basis (which is consistent with the IATA definition). WestJet reports passenger segments flown: any passenger flying (say) two flight segments in the course of one journey is counted once for each segment. Because WestJet is largely a point-to-point airline, the measure might differ little if WestJet had used the same convention as Air Canada.

Edmonton and Winnipeg. It then had some quiet years before getting into its stride. In 1999 it added a few more ports, notably Prince George and (going further east) Thunder Bay. That year also saw its Initial Public Offering of shares. In 2000, it started an eastern network with Hamilton (Ontario) as hub, and services to Ottawa and to Moncton (New Brunswick); yet it was 2002 before it started services to the big smoke, Toronto ('Company history', accessed at westjet.com).

In 2004, WestJet began service to US ports on the west coast and in Florida. The following year saw the start of seasonal routes to Honolulu and Maui. The first international route beyond the US was to Nassau (in 2006), soon followed by further services to the Caribbean and some to Mexico.

Because Canadians like to holiday in warm climates during their winter, such leisure traffic helps to reduce the seasonal fluctuations in aircraft utilisation. By 2013, trans-border and international flights accounted for 45 per cent of WestJet's total available seat miles (Annual Information Form 2013, p. 8).

The key fleet decision that supported such growth came in 2001, when WestJet took delivery of its first Boeing next-generation aircraft, a 737-700. It retired its last 737-200 in 2005, and by December 2008 it had 76 Boeing NG aircraft, predominantly 737-700s. After several years of further growth, the fleet at 31 December 2014 comprised 13 B737-600 aircraft, 64 B737-700s, 30 B737-800s (now with 174 seats, being eight more seats than before), and 15 Q400 turboprops (78 seats) (Annual Information Form 2014, pp. 16–17).

The growing fleet carried more passengers each year, except for a small downturn in 2009. The total reached almost 20 million passengers in 2014 (Table 1.5).

Compared with the new US carriers (which fly in a much larger domestic market), WestJet's passenger total then came in-between JetBlue at 26 million and Frontier at 11 million passengers (cf. Table 1.1 above). In recent years, WestJet's load factor has been around 80 per cent. Since 2005, the company has been profitable in every year, including 2009 (Annual Report 2008, p. 4; Annual Report 2011, p. 23; Annual Information Form 2014, p. 5).

In 2012, WestJet confirmed its intention to start a regional subsidiary, flying Q400 turbo-props (made in Toronto by Bombardier). This new carrier was duly named WestJet Encore, and launched on 24 June 2013. With WestJet gradually switching to larger B737 models, Encore's role was to serve new local (regional) routes, and to increase frequencies on some of its existing minor routes. Based in Calgary, it started by serving five other ports in western Canada (Annual Information Form 2013, pp. 22–3, and a news release of 24 June 2013). A year later, Encore launched routes in eastern Canada, and carried its millionth passenger (WestJet news releases, 27 June and 10 July 2014).

As seen in Table 1.5, its profits in 2013 and 2014 were far ahead of those of the (larger) Air Canada. Even so, WestJet decided to try to get its main-line cost levels down to those attained by low-cost airlines in the US. In January 2013, it started a three-year campaign to reduce its annual operating costs by C$100 million, and reported some early success (Annual Information Form 2013, p. 23).

Like Southwest Airlines, WestJet emphasises that good staff relations are crucial in securing the high performance standards that (in turn) underpin the growth of the airline. For many years, WestJet has been honoured for its relations with its staff. To staff members, WestJet pays a share of its profits – in 2013, the total payment amounted to C$51.6 million (Annual Report 2013, p. 28).

1.4.4 Porter Airlines and Toronto City Airport

In the late 1930s, the Toronto city government recognised the new-fangled transport mode, and built two airports: a main one on Toronto Island, immediately adjacent to the CBD; and a secondary port on a green-field site at Malton, about 16 km to the west of downtown Toronto. The events of World War II and the subsequent development of jet aircraft of increasing size soon made the latter the primary port, now called Toronto Pearson International Airport.

Meanwhile, the Toronto City Airport (as it is now called) continued to serve commercial aviation, under the Toronto Port Authority (torontoport.com). By 1961, it had a 1200m runway, sufficient for use by many types of turbo-prop aircraft; a few small companies flew scheduled services. In 2001, the sole survivor, Air Ontario, became an affiliate of Air Canada, and continued a limited service.

In February 2006, a new company, Porter Airlines, announced 10 firm orders and 10 options for new Q400 turbo-prop aircraft (manufactured by Bombardier, in Toronto). From its base at Toronto City Airport, Porter planned to serve business travellers on flights to Canadian and US destinations within 500 nautical miles of Toronto (Porter Airlines news releases, 1 and 2 February, flyporter.com).

Porter belonged to a privately held company, since renamed Porter Aviation Holdings, which also controlled the East terminal at Toronto City. That group announced (news release, 16 February 2006), it would renovate that terminal, which then would be used by Porter Airlines. During the construction period, existing scheduled airline operations from the terminal would be suspended.

That edict was aimed at (Air Canada's) Jazz, which said (news release, 15 February, flyjazz.ca) that because of its eviction from the terminal, it was suspending its Ottawa service (five round-trip flights each weekday). Soon after, Porter Airlines stated (news release, 27 February) that the Ontario Superior Court of Justice had ruled against Jazz's request for an injunction regarding the termination of its month-to-month lease at Toronto City Airport.

Using two new Q400 aircraft (70 seats at 34-inch pitch), Porter started *its* Ottawa service on 23 October, offering 10 round-trips each weekday and two daily at weekends; the flight duration was about 60 minutes (Porter news release, 2 October).

In the next several years, Porter took delivery of further Q400 aircraft, and started more routes. In particular, the US Department of Transportation granted licences allowing Porter to start services to New York (Newark) in March 2008 and to Chicago (Midway) in November. By mid-2012, Porter had added Boston (Logan) and Washington (Dulles), and seasonal flights to Myrtle Beach, SC and Burlington, VT.

In 2011, Porter flew 1.3 billion available seat miles (ASM), and had a passenger load factor of 61.7 per cent – a modest figure that was appropriate (however) for a service for business travellers. For someone working in downtown Toronto, the City Airport was conveniently located; and the jet flight from Pearson to Ottawa took slightly longer than Porter's Q400 flight! Furthermore, Porter offered so many daily flights on its big-city routes that the even greater frequency of the Air Canada service from Pearson brought little advantage.

Of course, Porter is not a low-fare airline: a small-scale study of fares (anna. aero, 7 September 2007) for commuter day-return trips to Toronto from Montreal showed that WestJet was much the cheapest, with Porter generally slightly more expensive than Air Canada.

Air Canada eventually began rival services from Toronto City, also using Q400 aircraft, which were operated for Air Canada by a regional airline. A service to Montreal began on 1 May 2012, with 15 flights each weekday. In Air Canada's October 2014 timetable, Montreal remained the only route from Toronto City; however, a few of those flights went on from Montreal to Moncton.

During 2009, the Porter fleet increased from eight to eighteen Q400 aircraft, and the passenger numbers grew commensurately. On 21 May 2010, Porter issued a preliminary prospectus for an Initial Purchase Offer. Yet, in a news release on 1 June 2010, the company said it was deferring the IPO because of unfavourable conditions in equity markets.

Instead, the company's attention turned to diversification: Porter announced plans to seek permission from Toronto City Council (and other authorities) to operate *jet* aircraft at Toronto City Airport, and to lengthen the runway by about 300 metres to support the use of the CS100 jet – then being developed (in Toronto) by Bombardier – for which Porter would be the launch customer.

In an undated statement posted on its website, Porter notes the unanimous, April 2014, vote of the Toronto City Council to negotiate with Porter on terms and conditions that might allow deployment of the jet aircraft. Porter then hoped that jet operation could start in 2016.

The airport is slot-restricted on environmental grounds, and the use of jet aircraft may increase the noise disturbance. Conflicts between airport use and other neighbourhood land uses have been studied by a city agency, Toronto Waterfront (toronto.ca/waterfront; see in particular an explanatory 'Update' by John Livey, 9 September 2014).

Meanwhile, there has been a decline in Porter's market share of seats offered (from Pearson and Toronto City, taken together) for travel between Toronto and some of the other cities that Porter serves (CAPA, 'Porter Airlines outlook grows more difficult in the fast-changing Canadian landscape', 10 July 2014). Both Air Canada and (particularly) WestJet increased their market shares. CAPA argues that as WestJet's Encore develops its eastern Canada network, then that too may reduce Porter's share. In general, CAPA saw an uncertain future for Porter, thanks to the need for a political decision on airport development as well as the prospect of increasing airline competition.

2 Deregulation and new airlines in Europe

2.1 The early history

2.1.1 Regulation and ownership by national governments

In the early days of commercial aviation, sovereign governments in Europe were keen to develop national airlines. While some smaller countries (notably Belgium and the Netherlands) had little or nothing by way of domestic routes, most governments made policy for domestic as well as international services.

At the end of World War II, the UK government established two national carriers, British European Airways and British Overseas Airways Corporation (later merged as British Airways). While most other European countries opted for a single national carrier, the governments of the Scandinavian countries co-operated to establish a single airline, SAS, serving routes within and beyond Scandinavia.

In general, the national carrier belonged to the state, and sometimes received government subsidy. On *domestic* routes, it usually received state protection by means of a system of route licensing, which served to exclude other companies – even others domiciled in the country in question. Access to each *international* route was determined by a bilateral agreement made between the two involved governments. Such agreements usually excluded all but the two national carriers, stipulated how much capacity each could operate, and sometimes provided for pooling and sharing of the passenger revenues received by the two airlines.

Following World War II, air travel remained expensive, and most passengers travelled on commercial or government business. National capitals became hubs for international services, and most domestic routes were spokes connecting provincial cities to the national capital. Where European railways were sufficiently well developed to accommodate most domestic travel, domestic flights served largely as feeders to international services, some of which also faced railway competition.

As the years passed, engineering developments brought larger aircraft, with lower per-seat operating costs. Incomes rose, as did demand for holidays spent in other European countries. The restrictive governmental airline regulation became increasingly inappropriate for leisure travel.

2.1.2 Deregulation: the first step

During the 1950s, *some* national governments relaxed their controls in an important respect. 'Tour operators' wanted to sell modestly priced holiday packages, which bundled together flights and hotel accommodation, and often included minor items such as coach transfers between destination airport and hotel. The 'low-cost airlines' of that era could sell the aircraft flights to the tour operator at prices that were well below the cost levels of the national carriers.

The tour operator aimed to sell every seat on each flight, and the consequent very high load factors helped the tour operator to sell the entire package at a low price – often one that was well below the round-trip airfare charged by the national carrier. Any government that agreed to allow such airlines to carry passengers insisted that the flight could be sold only in conjunction with hotel or similar accommodation. Such flights became known as 'charter flights'; the airlines licensed *only* for such flights were called charter airlines. The market power of each national carrier was not very greatly affected; the right to offer *scheduled* air travel as a separate service remained tightly held by the national carrier.

The sale of package holidays soon gathered pace in some countries (especially Britain and Scandinavia), but made little progress in others. It was not unknown for the package-holiday traveller to encounter, on board the outward flight, the occasional business traveller, who was not seen again until boarding time for the return flight.

The tour operators also took an innovative approach in regard to both origin and destination ports. The charter flight might travel to a holiday destination that was not served well (or at all) by the scheduled airlines. And in Britain, at least, charter flights soon started departing from provincial airports, to allow a direct flight to the holiday destination, rather than travel *via* the national capital.

As the package-holiday sector boomed, some of the national carriers sought a share of the new market. In particular, British European Airways set up a subsidiary company British Airtours, which operated a dedicated fleet of (ageing) aircraft, handed down by the parent company.

2.2 The legislative impact of the European Union

As the countries of Western Europe drew together politically – eventually to form the European Union – the new supra-national body sought to remove national barriers and other impediments to market competition. Regarding aviation, it sought to facilitate competition between airlines domiciled in different countries, and to look critically at subsidies paid by some national governments, in support of their national airlines – two issues now considered in turn.

2.2.1 Legislating for a single European aviation market

Under the general competition rules (Articles 81 and 82) of the Treaty of the European Communities, the European Community (EC) soon began to look critically at the bilateral agreements made between national governments for international flights. In December 1987, it took some modest, first steps towards deregulation. The second package (in 1990) included a right for every EC-domiciled airline to carry passengers on routes between their country of domicile and any other (EU) country.

The Community then took a large and important step in June 1992 when the Council adopted EEC Regulation No. 2408/92. Most of its provisions took effect on 1 January 1993. Subject to some qualifications (considered below), Article 3(1) of the regulation states that 'Community air carriers shall be permitted by the Member State(s) concerned to exercise traffic rights on routes within the Community' (European Commission, 2004a, p. 5). This put in place a (liberalised) *single* European aviation market: any airline company holding an air operator's certificate issued by a country within the Community could launch any scheduled or non-scheduled service within the Community area, without getting *any* governmental route authorisation (see also European Commission, 2007a, annex A3).

Of course, there were conditions. Some concerned *transitional* arrangements. In particular, there was no right of access to a *cabotage* route until 1 April 1997. (Cabotage is also known as a ninth freedom right, whereby an airline domiciled in country A may operate a route falling entirely within country B; see the glossary in European Commission, 2007a.)

The *enduring* conditions give individual Member States certain powers:

1   For a route for which the market does not provide 'sufficient' service, a state has the right to select and subsidise an airline to fulfil a so-called 'public service obligation', while prohibiting entry to that route by all other airlines (§2.2.2 below has more on 'state aid').
2   A state may (without discrimination on grounds of airline nationality) manage and determine the distribution of traffic between two or more airports serving a given metropolitan area (Article 8).
3   A state may limit access at congested airports (Article 9).

Since then, two developments have extended the geographical scope of the single European *aviation* market. First, the EU has taken in further member countries (mainly in Eastern Europe), with the EU aviation legislation applying from the date of accession. This enabled some EU carriers, notably Ryanair and EasyJet, to prepare in advance for operation in the new member States. Similar opportunities were available for airlines domiciled in those new countries; there, the main anticipating airline was WizzAir. (The major advantage seems to have gone to the long-established airlines of Western Europe.)

Second, the EU has negotiated aviation-specific agreements with certain countries *outside* the Union (initially Norway, Iceland and Switzerland, and then Morocco, the Western Balkans, Georgia, Jordan, Moldova and Israel) for the establishment of 'Common Aviation Areas', in which (in the main) EU aviation rules apply.

A later case concerned a *provisional* agreement made between the EU and the Ukraine in November 2013 ('EU and Ukraine skies to join forces', EC Press Release IP-13-1181, 28 November 2013, and 'EU and Ukraine for a Common Aviation Area Agreement', EC Memo 13/1065, 28 November 2013, both accessed on 29 November 2013, at europa-eu/rapid). However, that step soon proved to be a factor in the political confrontation which resulted in a challenge to Ukrainian sovereignty.

2.2.2 'State aid' under the European Community Treaty

Article 87(1) of the Treaty of the European Communities is based on the principle that State aid is incompatible with a common market. Accordingly, it prohibits a transfer of State resources that would give an economic advantage to any firm or other economic undertaking in a manner that (i) would not arise in the normal course of business, *and* (ii) has the potential to affect adversely competition between firms. In particular, that second condition rules out State aid that offers an advantage to one firm but not to actual or potential competitors domiciled within the EU.

Articles 87(2) and 87(3) of the Treaty set out some exemptions from the prohibition. In particular, Article 87(3) (a) exempts 'aid to promote the economic development of areas where the standard of living is abnormally low or where there is serious unemployment'. Article 87(3) (c) exempts 'aid to facilitate the development of certain economic activities or certain economic areas, where such aid does not adversely affect trading conditions [in a manner that is] contrary to the public interest'.

In the course of its consideration of the many instances where (purported) state aid had been proposed or offered, the Commission developed guidelines to help it to achieve consistency in its decision making (European Commission, 2007c).

In regard to aviation, 'state aid' issues have arisen in two specific contexts:

1   contracts between airlines and public-sector airports (a detailed consideration of an example is given in §12.3.4);
2   financial grants from governments to airlines in support of the launching and/ or continuing operation of specific individual routes, especially those serving areas that are deemed to be deserving of regional aid (this is considered in depth in §11.2).

2.3 Company outcomes in the single aviation market

2.3.1 Airline entry encouraged by the progressive deregulation in Europe

The establishment of a single European market encouraged the establishment of new airlines, attracted especially by the opportunities to provide scheduled services on routes not then served by the national carriers. Noting the success of

Southwest Airlines, most of the new companies adopted a low-cost business model. In addition some small, older carriers converted to that model.

In keeping with the phased process of deregulation, the new low-cost carriers began their *international* services by flying between the home country and other EU countries. Early movers were the Dublin-based Ryanair – which had been allowed to operate services from Ireland to Britain for some years before the EU legislation allowed it to fly to other countries – and EasyJet, which started flights from its base at London Luton.

Ryanair

Ryanair was founded in 1985 by the Ryan family, apparently without previous business experience in aviation, and with relatively modest available capital. Its first route was from Waterford (in Eire) to London (Gatwick), using a 15-seat Bandeirante. Though soon moving to lease some smallish jets, it encountered severe price competition from established airlines, and, by 1990, it had accumulated losses of £20 million. The family then invested another £20 million, and restructured the business – abandoning business class and a frequent flyer programme, and adopting low-cost operation. This soon proved to be the turning point. Indeed, Ryanair earned its first profit in 1991 ('History of Ryanair', accessed at www.ryanair.com, 29 November 2007).

EasyJet

EasyJet launched in November 1995. It was the brainchild of a young Greek, Stelios Haji-Ioannou, who had commercial experience in shipping, where his father had amassed a personal fortune in oil tankers. The father invested £5 million after judging his son's plans, which were based largely on the strategy of Southwest Airlines (Sull, 1999, especially pp. 22–3). While the business model was well considered, its initial implementation was relatively weak. (The appointment of an experienced manager from Air New Zealand was to lift standards.) Initially, EasyJet contracted out most aspects of its operations. It even relied on another airline (Air Foyle) for the organisation of its flying operations, until it secured its own Air Operating Certificate in October 1997. It then grew rapidly, and seems to have avoided making any further major mistakes.

Somewhat later, both Ryanair and EasyJet established airline bases in other European countries, and soon became large and important airlines. Inevitably the early steps in network expansion require the establishment of airline staffs at a considerable number of new stations (ports), with relatively few routes served at each station. Despite the substantial costs of station operation, both Ryanair and EasyJet successfully passed through that stage, and soon were well placed to engage in a long, continuing expansion, in which they were able to reap network economies by increasing the average number of routes served *per station*.

On the other hand, there are practical limits to the *rate* of expansion that new airlines can achieve while maintaining tight managerial control. (The earlier US example of People Express – which grew at a remarkable rate before plunging into financial difficulties – served as a warning to airline managements around the world.) Such limits on growth-rates, when taken together with the very considerable size of the EU aviation market, made it inevitable that the early movers were unable to serve *all* the European market regions in the short term. Thus there were opportunities for further well-managed entrants to become securely established in their own regions, and then perhaps go on to expand elsewhere in Europe.

On 1 May 2004, eight central and eastern European countries – the Czech Republic, Estonia, Latvia, Lithuania, Hungary, Poland, Slovenia and Slovakia – became members of the EU. (Bulgaria and Romania joined later, on 1 January 2007.) These new member-countries offered distinctive opportunities for EU airlines to begin new intra-EU services to/from these countries, without having to surmount any regulatory hurdles. Though both Ryanair and EasyJet started new services to some of the new member countries on 1 May 2004, the extent of their initial penetration was sufficiently modest to leave room for the expansion of a few locally based low-cost carriers, notably WizzAir, which launched in both Hungary and Poland.

2.3.2 Low-cost airlines in Europe in 2007

By 2007, there were a dozen or so *significant* low-cost airlines domiciled in the EU, and these are listed in Tables 2.1 and 2.2. Significance was judged here by the presence of favourable signs, such as operation of *new* aircraft (usually A320 or B737-700/800 models), location of the initial base (sometimes in a region that had been *relatively* poorly served by the traditional, national carriers), and good growth since the launch.

The *annual* passenger totals (Table 2.2) reveal the strength of Ryanair and EasyJet. The growth of Air Berlin and TUI fly owed more to take-overs than did the growth of Ryanair and EasyJet. (And TUI fly still carried a considerable number of passengers on charter flights.)

Though Vueling had quickly reached almost 6 million passengers annually, the lack of profitability stressed its board and (no doubt) its management. The underlying issue was the very competitive presence at Barcelona of *two* LCCs, the other being Clickair. And Barcelona was served also by the legacy carrier Iberia.

2.3.3 Airline exits since 2008

That Barcelona issue was addressed in 2008 when Clickair was merged into Vueling (Table 2.3), and their joint capacity reduced. Also shown in Table 2.3 is the *closure* of three other airlines. Sky Europe was said to have costs that were not

Table 2.1 Selected low-cost airlines[1] operating in Europe, mid-2007

Airline	Founded[2]	First base	Ownership and other information
Air Berlin	1991	Berlin	In 2006, listed as a UK public company; later took over dba and LTU; the former merged into Air Berlin in October 2008
Clickair	2006	Barcelona	Not a listed company; Iberia owned 20%
EasyJet	1995	London Luton	Listed as a public company in 2000
Flybe	1979	Jersey (Channel Is.)	When Flybe took over BA Connect, British Airways acquired 15% of Flybe's shares
Germanwings	2002	Cologne–Bonn	Lufthansa
Meridiana	1963	Olbia (Sardinia)	Owned by Meridiana Group; adopted LCC strategy in 2003
Monarch	1968	London Luton	Began as charter operator (for package-holidays); started scheduled services in 1986; offered one-way fares from 1993; adopted other low-cost features 1994
Norwegian	1993	Oslo	Public company listed in Oslo; became a LCC in 2002; bought FlyNordic in 2007
Ryanair	1985	Dublin	Re-launched as LCC in 1990; listed as (Irish) public company in 1997
Sky Europe	2002	Bratislava	Listed as public company, 2005
Sterling	1994	Copenhagen	Since 2006, owned by FL Group (Iceland); adopted low-fare strategy in 2002; purchased Maersk Air in 2005
TUIfly	2002	Hanover	The low-cost airline Hapag-Lloyd Express became part of TUI AG group in 2007
Vueling	2004	Barcelona	At first, investor and management owned; became a listed company in 2006
Wind Jet	2003	Catania (Sicily)	Owned by Finaria Group
WizzAir	2004	Budapest and Katowice	Indigo (US) and other private investors

Sources: Airline web sites, and Centre for Aviation (CAPA)

Notes
1 The table excludes the smallest companies, and also some larger ones that served mainly package-holiday travellers.
2 Some of the older airlines had antecedents. And some of the stated dates refer to the year in which a traditional airline adopted a low-cost/low-fare strategy.

low enough to make their low fares profitable (anna.aero, 4 September 2009). Sterling was based at Copenhagen, and faced competition from another LCC, Norwegian, as well as the legacy carrier, SAS. Though based in under-served Sicily, Wind Jet did not manage to reach a sufficient scale in the face of competition from Alitalia.

Table 2.2 Operations of the selected low-cost airlines in Europe, 2007[1]

Airline	Annual passengers[1] (millions)	Load factor[2] (%)	Ports served	Routes	Flights per day	Fleet size	Aircraft type[3]
Air Berlin	28	77	135		600	124	A320 and B737-800
Clickair	4		49			14	A320
EasyJet	38	84	89	360	810	137	A319
Flybe	7		53	162	470	76	Q400
Germanwings	7	82	69			24	A319
Meridiana	4		42			22	MD82
Monarch	4		17			31	A321
Norwegian	7	80	74	132	220	33	B737-300
Ryanair	49	82	139	606	900	148	B737-800
Sky Europe	4	80	39	92	90	14	B737-700
Sterling	5	75	60	124	140	25	B737-700
TUIfly	14	84				56	B737
Vueling	6		25	60	150	21	A320
Wind Jet	2	67	18		60	10	A320
WizzAir	4	84	36	70	90	13	A320

Sources: European Low Fares Airline Association, Members' Statistics December 2007 (www.elfaa.com); Air Berlin, Annual Report 2008 (www.airberlin.com); Germanwings (www.germanwings.com).

Notes:
1 Passengers and load factors are generally for the year to December 2007 – but to December 2006 for Germanwings. For Monarch, pax and fleet are total, ports are scheduled services only.
2 These are the claimed/reported load factors, as shown in the source documents. The data often refer to seats sold rather than seats occupied.
3 This records the predominant type(s) in each airline's fleet. Only clickair, Norwegian, Ryanair, Vueling and WizzAir had homogeneous fleets.

2.4 Recent airline developments, mainly in Eastern Europe and Russia

In countries in Eastern Europe and Russia, recent years have seen the foundation of some new airlines, and the successful rejuvenation of some old ones, together with the demise of some national carriers. Those events have been an important complement to the changes in Western Europe.

2.4.1 In Greece, the launch of Aegean Airlines – which eventually bought Olympic

In 1994, the Vassilakis Group acquired Aegean Aviation (founded in 1987) and began to operate executive charter flights. The 1999 deregulation of the Greek airline industry allowed the Group to establish Aegean Airlines, which began scheduled services by flying two new CRJ100 jets on domestic routes. By April 2001, Aegean served 11 Greek and 7 international ports. In 2003, Aegean earned a first (marginal) profit (Aegean Airlines, Annual Report 2008, p.14).

Table 2.3 Airlines shown in Table 2.1 that had disappeared by September 2014

Airline	Base	Outcome	Comments
clickair	Barcelona	July 2008: merged into Vueling	Both LCCs hubbed in Barcelona, same aircraft type (A320, with 180 seats), and many routes in common. After the merger, Iberia held 46% of the shares.
Sterling	Copenhagen	October 2008: ceased operations	Blamed financial crisis in Iceland for ultimate financial problem. At the close, poignant *mea culpa* on its website: 'We made mistakes over the years. But [we hope] we have done more right than wrong; at least we have made the market more competitive to the benefit of our customers.'
Sky Europe	Bratislava (Slovakia)	September 2009: ceased operations	While growing rapidly, up-front revenue from future bookings offset the lack of profits. Then growth slowed . . .
Wind Jet	Catania (Sicily)	August 2012: ceased operations	The end came when Alitalia reversed its decision to take over Wind Jet.

Sources: 'Merged clickair + Vueling will fly to 50 airports; 17 routes to lose a competitor', anna.aero, 11 July 2008; 'Slovakian LCC SkyEurope finally goes under'. anna.aero, 4 September 2009; 'Sterling collapse leaves opportunities at Copenhagen', anna.aero, 7 November 2008; 'Wind Jet collapse bad news for Catania', anna.aero, 16 August 2012

In December 2005, Aegean began to order *new* A320 aircraft. The first three of these arrived in 2007; further firm orders in that year took the *planned* fleet to 25 such aircraft. Aegean soon carried more passengers than Olympic Airways, the legacy national carrier (Aegean Airlines, Annual Report 2008, p. 15).

The advent of the general financial crisis increased concerns that Greece could not sustain two major airlines. Aegean made an offer to the Greek state to buy Olympic (press release, 6 March 2009). The government preferred to sell to the Marfin Investment Group, which then launched a smaller 'Olympic Air' on 1 October 2009.

Aegean soon returned to the battle – by announcing (press release, 22 February 2010) a binding agreement between Marfin and Aegean for a merger of the two airlines, subject to European Commission approval.

It was 26 January 2011 before the EC said 'No'. It refused approval mainly because it feared the merged airline might abuse its (very) dominant position in the domestic market. Yet, many other EU domestic markets were dominated by a single carrier ('Aegean/Olympic merger denied due to domestic dominance', anna.aero, 2 February 2011).

Aegean soon tried again. It announced (press release, 22 October 2012) that it had agreed with Marfin to buy all the shares of Olympic Air, again subject to approval by the European competition authorities.

The networks of the two airlines were already differentiated: Aegean had focussed on the (high-growth) routes to Western Europe, while Olympic had retreated – and become a regional airline serving domestic routes and some ports in Eastern Europe (CAPA, 'Aegean, Olympic Air try once again to combine forces', 25 October 2012).

By then, Aegean's fleet comprised 22 A320s, together with 4 A321s and 3 A319s. Olympic had invested in turboprops, and operated 10 Q400s and 4 Dash 8-100s, together with a small and diminishing number of jets (Aegean, press release, 22 October 2012).

In the very depressed state of the Greek economy, both airlines were recording financial losses. This time, the EC said 'Yes' ('Mergers: Commission approves acquisition of Greek airline Olympic Air by Aegean Airlines', IP/13/927, European Commission, 9 October 2013). It said that 'Olympic Air would be forced to exit the market in the near future due to financial difficulties if not acquired by Aegean . . . so the merger causes no harm to competition that would not have occurred anyway.'

On 14 January 2014, an Aegean press release noted the same-day announcement that Ryanair was to establish two bases in Greece. Aegean also remarked that Aegean had introduced new, low domestic fares in October 2013.

2.4.2 A more recent launch: Volotea

Nowadays, Western Europe sees few launches of a new low-cost carrier. An interesting exception is Volotea, which launched in April 2012, just before Easter. Its two founders were formerly senior managers at Vueling. Initial funding (reported to be about €50 million) came from three venture-capital firms (Manuel Baigorri, 'New carrier Volotea sets up in Barcelona', *Bloomberg*, 16 February 2012).

Volotea chose Venice Marco Polo Airport (VCE) for its first base. Its general plan was to serve routes between smaller cities in Europe, usually offering between one and three flights weekly. It flew pre-loved B717 aircraft, leased from Boeing and each having 125 seats in the modest-sized cabin (Boeing news release, 'Boeing, new European airline Volotea agree to 717 leasing deal', 15 February 2012).

In 2012, Volotea had a busy summer. After starting at Venice with 14 routes mainly to ports in Italy and Spain (anna.aero, 29 February 2012), it opened a base at Ibiza, initially serving nine new routes (anna.aero, 20 June 2012). On many of its routes, Volotea had no competition.

Two years later, its website (volotea.com, accessed 24 October 2014) named no fewer than 64 destinations, listed alphabetically: Ajaccio, Alghero, Alicante, Ancona . . . Milan, Montpellier, Munich, Mykonos . . . Venice, Verona, Zakynthos, Zaragoza. Some routes were served only in the summer, some only in the winter, and others were served all year round. Volotea's fleet then comprised 15 B717s (ch-aviation.com, accessed 25 October 2014).

The most important elements in Volotea's start-up strategy were its choice of minor routes, generally serving small cities, and mostly without direct competition from other airlines.

2.4.3 The rise and rise of Turkish Airlines

In contrast to the Olympic Airways case, some legacy national carriers *have* flourished in the more competitive conditions of recent years. An outstanding example is the full-service carrier, Turkish Airlines. Founded in 1933, it remained in government ownership until a partial privatisation in 2004 saw 25 per cent of the shares pass to private hands. In 2013, some 49.1 per cent of the shares remained in government hands (Turkish Airlines, Consolidated Financial Statements 2013, p. 7).

After operational and financial troubles in the 1970s and 1980s, Turkish began a remarkable ascent. Growth was especially strong after 2006, and proved to be reasonably rewarding, though profits have varied significantly from year to year.

From its hub in Istanbul, Turkish Airlines served 107 ports at the end of 2005, then 196 in 2011, and 264 in 2014 (Annual Report, 2014, p. 28). Though its route access depends on conventional bilateral negotiations between governments, it has little or no competition on some routes, especially on those between Turkey and Africa.

The 2014 (passenger) fleet of Turkish Airlines comprised 252 aircraft. There were no less than 10 different aircraft types, mainly B737-800, A330, A321 and A320 models (Annual Report 2014, p. 30). The adverse effect of aircraft variety on operating costs was moderated by the presence of large numbers of most types.

Its hub location is especially advantageous. There is no other significant airline hub in the immediate region. Furthermore, when serving passengers travelling to or from Europe, Istanbul is close enough to allow Turkish to deploy on its European sectors short-haul aircraft, notably the A320 and the B737-800. This helps Turkish to offer high flight frequencies to many European ports. In contrast, Emirates and other Arabian Peninsula competitors hub at greater distances from Europe, and operate wide-body aircraft less frequently (for given route density).

The total revenue passenger kilometres sold by Turkish Airlines increased from 30 billion in 2007 to 107 billion in 2014; its revenue passenger load factors rose from 72 per cent (in 2011) to 78.9 per cent in 2014 (Annual Report 2014, p. 28). In a 2011 ranking of world airlines based on RPKs, Turkish came twenty-third, only a little below EasyJet which was twentieth (EU Memo/12/714).

Low-fare services

With Turkey attracting increasing numbers of tourists, there has been a growing role for low-cost airlines. Besides western European carriers such as EasyJet, Turkish Airlines has faced competition from Pegasus, a carrier based at the *other* airport in Istanbul.

In April 2008, Turkish Airlines started its own low-cost subsidiary, Anadolu Jet, based at Ankara. In 2011, Anadolu's sold output was 4.0 billion RPK; that rose to 6.5 billion RPK in 2014. The major part was on domestic routes (Turkish Airlines, Annual Report 2011, pp. 68–9; Annual Report 2014, p. 55).

2.4.4 The privatisation of TAP, the Portuguese national airline

In June 2015, a Portuguese government offer of a 61 per cent stake in the national carrier, TAP, resulted in a deal with a joint venture comprising David Neeleman (the founder and CEO of the Brazilian airline Azul) and the Portuguese bus company, Barranquiro Group (Kurt Hofmann 'Portugal sells 61% stake in TAP to JetBlue founder', *Air Transport World*, 12 June 2015). (What will these colonials get up to next?)

The presence of a bus company mirrors a partnership established earlier in Mexico, where VivaAerobus was founded by a joint venture between Irelandia and IAMSA (a large bus group in Mexico). In that case, air travellers are offered feeder road-bus travel at discounted fares (§5.1).

The purchase of the controlling interest in TAP required approval by the European Commission. The part-ownership by a bus company may raise EC eyebrows. On the other hand, the joint venture is taking on TAP's estimated debt (exceeding US$1 billion), and competition in Portuguese airline markets is likely to be enhanced by the privatisation.

2.4.5 Legacy carriers and new airlines in Eastern Europe

The state airlines of the former Communist era had some time in which to prepare for the deregulation that came with membership of the European Union. Yet changes did not always come easily. The national airlines of Romania, Hungary, the Czech Republic and Poland remained quite small, relative to the sizes of most Western European national carriers. And the low-cost EU entrants have taken market share from such national airlines.

Hungary

Founded in 1956, the national flag carrier Malév was included in the privatisation programme of the Hungarian government in 1999, but was not sold until 2007. The airline gradually abandoned its long-haul routes, became a regional carrier, and was renationalised in 2010. On 9 January 2012, the EC announced a long-awaited ruling that Malév had received illegal state aid in the years 2007 to 2010 ('illegal' because Malév 'would not have been able to obtain similar financing from the market on the terms conceded by the Hungarian authorities'). Accordingly, the Hungarian government was required to recover some large sums from Malév (Kerry Reals, 'EC orders struggling Malev to pay back "illegal" state aid', *Flight Global*, 9 January 2012). The ruling was the immediate cause of the closure of the airline on 3 February 2012.

The success of both WizzAir and Ryanair, in Hungary and in nearby countries, seems to have been a significant factor in the decline of Malév. When Malév closed, Ryanair took only two weeks to establish a base at Budapest; it then started 13 *new* routes.

Romania

Though TAROM is another state-owned carrier with a history of financial deficits, it has made recent efforts to become profitable. In the years 2000 to 2003, it abandoned its loss-making long-haul routes, and then expanded within the EU and other European countries ('Central European carriers abandon many long-haul routes', anna.aero, 23 March 2010).

The airline website (tarom.ro, accessed on 26 May 2015) reported that the jet fleet comprised four B737-700, four B737-300 and four A318 aircraft – together with two A310 long-haul aircraft intended to be withdrawn. There were also nine ATR turboprops, used on domestic routes.

While still owned by the state, Tarom was placed under private management at the end of 2012, with a consequent reduction of the annual loss in 2013, to about €30 million (Mirabela Tiron 'After more than a year under private management, Tarom Still In The Red, But Losses Narrow', *Ziarul Financiar*, 6 November 2014, English version accessed at zfenglish.com).

By March 2015, in terms of seats offered on routes from Romanian ports, WizzAir had become marginally larger than Tarom ('Romania sees traffic grow by 11% (CAGR) in 10 years; WizzAir is #1 carrier', anna.aero, 6 March 2015).

It remained to be seen whether the airline *can* become profitable, given the competition from low-cost carriers.

Czech Republic

Following a history of financial deficits, a restructured Czech Airlines (CSA) – still owned by the government – had a fleet comprising one A330, 6 A320s, and 9 A319s, as well as 4 ATR72 and 3 ATR42 turboprops (airline website, 20 October 2014). In September 2012, the airline became a member of the Czech Aeroholding Group, a government-owned joint-stock company, which also owns Prague Airport (airline website, accessed 20 October 2014).

An announcement (Czech Aeroholding, 13 March 2013) said that the government had approved the sale of 44 per cent of the CSA shares to Korean Air (the privately owned flag carrier of South Korea). The intention was for Korean Air to hub at Prague, with CSA carrying transfer passengers within Europe.

A few months later, Czech Aeroholding announced (press release, 5 December 2013) that Korean Air would exercise an option to buy a further 34 per cent of CSA, for immediate on-sale to Travel Service, a privately owned Czech airline, which operates both charter flights, and low-fare scheduled services under the SmartWings brand name, flying mainly B737-800s (189 seats) and -700s (148 seats).

Although not mentioned in those documents, it seems that the underlying aim of Korean Air was to gain as much influence over CSA as possible, while keeping a majority of the CSA shares in Czech hands, to ensure that CSA can still gain entry to EU and other international routes as a Czech company. It remained to be seen whether the EU will find the arrangement acceptable.

Poland

For many years, the usual annual outcome for the Polish national carrier, LOT, was one of financial deficit, notwithstanding the various attempts to restructure the operation. Though LOT became a joint-stock company in December 1992, a 'privatisation' in 1999 saw about 68 per cent of the shares still in the hands of the State Treasury, with 25 per cent held by a regional investment fund and seven per cent by the company's employees. Talks with Turkish Airlines about that company taking a financial interest in LOT came to nothing, reportedly because EU regulations prevented Turkish from taking a majority share in an airline registered in an EU country.

In January 2013, LOT received an emergency government loan of US$127 million, with the government insisting that the airline reduce its size. Poland's Prime minister was reported as saying that if the airline did not change its ways, then it would not survive (Kurt Hofmann, 'Polish president: LOT must change to survive', *Air Transport World*, 15 February 2013). The airline adjusted its summer flight schedule, to offer fewer flights on loss-making routes, while trying out more flights on profitable routes.

In May 2013, the European Commission approved the government's financial assistance, subject to the airline submitting an acceptable restructuring plan. Among other changes, the company then reduced its ground staff by about 35 per cent, phased out its older aircraft, and introduced B787 jets on its longer routes, to Toronto, New York and Chicago. For 2013, the company came close to financial break-even.

In July 2014, the EC 'formally approved the Restructuring Plan of LOT and found the state aid granted to the carrier lawful in terms of the provisions of EU legislation' (LOT press release, 'The European Commission says official "yes" to LOT!', lot.com, 29 July 2014). In September, the airline reported it had *not* drawn on the second tranche of government aid, made available to it in the previous year. (LOT press release, 'LOT brings profits from flying after nine months of 2014', 2 October 2014).

More good news came in April 2015, when LOT announced that its 2014 profit exceeded the profit target in the Restructuring Plan by more than 40 per cent (LOT press release 'More than PLN 99 million profit on core business – LOT is in black for the first time in seven years' 16 April 2015). On the other hand, the press release concluded by saying that in 2016, when the Restructuring Plan formally ended, LOT would start flying to new short- and long-haul destinations. That prompts a question: with such expansion, will the profits continue?

Eurolot was a wholly owned subsidiary of LOT when it launched as a turbo-prop operator in 1996. Later it became a separate joint-stock company, with 62.1 per cent of its shares held by the State Treasury.

Until 2011, Eurolot served only Polish domestic routes. In the following year, it began to serve international routes to more than a dozen ports, mainly in northern Europe. By then, it operated a fleet of twelve Q400s, each with 72 seats (eurolot. com, accessed 22 October 2014).

However, it seems the regional expansion was unprofitable. In February 2015, Eurolot announced it would cease trading (Kurt Hofmann, 'Eurolot to be liquidated April 1', *Air Transport World*, 9 February 2015).

Those brief accounts of legacy carriers suggest that the closure of Malév may have influenced airline and government attitudes elsewhere in the region.

2.4.6 Airlines of the Baltic states

We now travel further east. The Baltic countries, listed from north to south, are Estonia (capital, Tallinn), Latvia (Riga) and Lithuania (Vilnius). All have small land areas, and small populations (about 1.4, 2.4 and 3.7 million, respectively). To the south, there lies Belarus (10 million people), and further south, Ukraine (50 million). To the east is the Russian Federation.

After recovering their independence, the Baltic countries found themselves without *native* airlines. The new governments in Estonia and Lithuania soon established new companies; in Latvia, the main story began later, in 1995.

Estonia

Estonian Air began operations in 1991 as a state-owned public limited company, using the Tallinn-based aircraft of the former branch of Aeroflot. It soon abandoned many of its initial routes to Russian ports. In 1995, it started a switch to western-built aircraft, when it leased two *new* B737-500 aircraft ('History of Estonian Air', accessed at estonian-air.ee, 4 November 2012).

In 1999, Estonian started code-sharing with SAS on routes to Copenhagen, Stockholm and Oslo. While Estonian expanded over the next several years, financial problems were never far away. In 2011, SAS declined to invest further funds, and the Estonian government provided a capital injection of €30 million, thereby increasing its share ownership to 97.34 per cent of the total, with the balance still held by SAS (Estonian Air, Annual Report 2013, p.11).

On 1 July 2011, the airline appointed a new CEO. At the end of that year, it announced it would introduce Embraer jets. Efforts to develop Tallinn as a hub during 2011 resulted in passenger numbers growing by 16 per cent, compared with 2010. Yet revenue rose only 12 per cent, the load factor declined marginally to 65 per cent, and the net loss increased from €2.6 million to €17.3 million.

Responding to those financial results, the government appointed a (further) new CEO, Jan Palmér (formerly CEO of Cimber Sterling), who took up the position in November 2012. The hubbing plans were abandoned (CAPA, 'Estonian Air is aiming to survive by rapidly downsizing its operations', 8 November 2012).

Accordingly, by the end of 2013, it was offering year-round services to ten ports mainly in northern Europe. For 2014, it also planned a winter route to Munich, and summer routes to Nice, Split and Paris ('Estonian Air carried 551 169 passengers last year', Estonian media release, 8 January 2014).

Writing in May 2014, CEO Palmér gave an unusually explicit analysis: 'there is no direct competition to Estonian Air as the geographical location and [market] size does not attract other airlines to invest in a regular operation suiting both business and leisure travellers'. So, a niche airline can 'create a profitable traffic system with non-stop operations to nine to twelve destinations . . . We have downsized our operations to develop Estonian Air into an efficient niche player focused on the Nordic . . . markets' (Annual Report 2013, p. 2).

In 2013, it carried considerably fewer passengers. By the end of the year, its smaller fleet comprised 4 × E170 (with 76 seats) and 3 × CRJ900 (88 seats). The load factor fell to 67 per cent (from about 71 per cent in 2012), because of the use of regional jets instead of smaller turbo-props. Punctuality improved considerably, to 91.4 per cent of flights. Net operating income increased to €7.4 million (previously a loss of €15.8 million). The overall net loss was greatly reduced at €8.1 million.

However, the outcomes during 2014 were not so favourable. While the scale of operations was much the same as in 2013, total revenue declined by 4 per cent and the net loss increased to €10.4 million. In accounting for that situation, Estonian quoted a December 2014 IATA report: 'Breakeven load factors are highest in Europe, caused by a combination of low yields due to the highly competitive open aviation area, and high regulatory costs' (Estonian, Annual Report 2014, pp. 5–6).

For its smaller flight schedule, Estonian concluded it needed only five of its seven aircraft. In March 2015, the airline said it was establishing a new subsidiary, to be called Nordic Flyways, that would operate additional 'white label' services for other carriers – that is, flights operated in the name of other carriers who would take the financial risks on those flights (Alan Dron, 'Estonian Air sets up outsourcing subsidiary', *Air Transport World*, 25 March 2015).

Potentially the most important news concerned the EC and a new private investor. In October 2014, the airline submitted to the EC a modified Restructuring Plan. And in November, the government identified Infortar (a private company with the largest shareholding in the Scandinavian passenger ferry operator, Tallink) as a new investor in Estonian Air. Infortar's participation was conditional on approval by the EC of the Restructuring Plan (Estonian, Annual Report 2014, p. 10). With Infortar as an investor, the aim would be to exploit operational synergies between the airline and the ferry group.

Latvia

On 28 August 1995, the Latvian government and SAS Airlines signed a joint venture agreement that established *AirBaltic*; the government took 51 per cent of the shares, and SAS held most of the rest. AirBaltic's first flight came on 1 October, flown by a Saab 340 turboprop ('Company history', www.airbaltic.com, accessed 2 November 2012). Since then, AirBaltic has enjoyed interesting times.

Despite diverse profit and loss results, the company grew in most years. Before 2009, the airline operated a point-to-point network: besides its home base at Riga, there were several aircraft based at Vilnius (in Lithuania). However, when the financial recession arrived, AirBaltic changed its style to that of a hub-and-spoke airline, with a large increase in transfer traffic at Riga (Victoria Moores, 'AirBaltic chief Bertolt Flick on the Baltic meltdown', *Airline Business*, 18 May 2009). The only remaining direct services *from Vilnius* were to Riga and Brussels. Yet the airline retained some routes *within* Finland and Scandinavia, and later re-launched a number of routes from Vilnius (anna.aero, 9 March 2010).

In the spring of 2010, the airline announced a number of direct routes from Tallinn, but cancelled most of them in the September. The Estonian Consumer Protection Department then offered advice to Estonians thinking of travelling on AirBaltic ('Estonians warned to be careful with AirBaltic', *Baltic News Network*, 15 October 2010).

The very rapid expansion of AirBaltic in 2010 and 2011 prompted concerns about the airline's financial situation – especially because on new routes, profitability may lag behind growth. In press releases issued on 21 and 23 September 2011, AirBaltic vigorously criticised the Latvian government for not making decisions concerning extra funding for the airline. It said it was seeking 'legal protection' (for a new business plan); if approved by the court, this would prevent the government from blocking extra investment offered by the major private shareholder, BAS. However, the court refused approval.

While the Latvian government held 52 per cent of the shares, the major *hands-on* private investor, BAS, was believed to be controlled by a Russian billionaire (anna.aero, 22 September 2011). One of AirBaltic's strengths was its Riga hub, which connected EU ports with ports in Russia. While the airline's access to the EU ports depended on EU nationals having control of the airline, Russian investment in the airline *might* help it to win and retain entry to the Russian market.

On 29 September 2011, AirBaltic announced that the government of Latvia and BAS had 'reached agreement' and would jointly inject the capital into AirBaltic: 'The Latvian government will secure €81.9 million (LVL 57.6 million), while the private investor BAS will secure €71.1 million (approximately LVL 50 million).'

On 4 October, CEO Bertolt Flick said 'I have agreed to step down, as the agreement between the shareholders does so require.' On 21 October, the airline announced that, starting on 1 November, the new CEO would be Martin Gauss, previously CEO of Malév.

AirBaltic reported (13 December 2011) 'Today the Latvian government agreed to a capital increase [of LVL 57.6 million] for AirBaltic to enable the future development of the Latvian national carrier and fleet modernisation.' Yet the company history (website, accessed 2 November 2012) records that in December 2011, the Latvian government increased its shareholding to 99.8 per cent. That record does not make it clear whether the airline also got the previous planned funding of LVL 50 million from BAS, and if it did, what financial and ownership terms were agreed with BAS.

A later press release ('AirBaltic reshapes for profit', 6 March 2012) quoted the new CEO as saying:

> In the past few years AirBaltic achieved unprecedented growth that turned Riga into the only functioning transit hub in the Baltic region. However, it

came at a cost to the airline. AirBaltic has now been stabilised. Currently, we are focusing on reshaping our business, to achieve improvements of LVL 330 million in the next five years, and return to profitability in 2014.

Some two years later, the airline announced:

AirBaltic has surpassed by far its original plans and has turned around the FY2012 *loss* of €27 million, converting it into a net *profit* of +€1 million for 2013. AirBaltic has achieved profitability one year ahead of the initial schedule.

('AirBaltic Profits and Annual Report Approved'
press release, 16 April 2014).

Yet there were some modest outcomes in the course of 2014. In August, the airline operated 4 per cent fewer flights that in the previous August ('AirBaltic serves 283,914 passengers in August', press release, 8 August 2014). Then, early in 2015, AirBaltic was forced to make further changes. The fighting in Ukraine had reduced the number of transfer passengers at Riga, and that reduced the company's revenues. Accordingly, it again planned to emphasise point-to-point services (Victoria Moores, 'Baltic Remodeling', *Air Transport World*, 2 March 2015).

Lithuania

In 1991, the Lithuanian government founded *FlyLAL*, which began by deploying the Vilnius-based fleet of Aeroflot. After FlyLAL had experienced many years of financial losses, the government privatised the airline in 2005, soon after Lithuania had joined the EU. In 2008, the company suffered from the general financial crisis, and from a battle with AirBaltic for passengers at Vilnius. The government declined to give financial assistance. FlyLAL closed On 17 January 2009.

Lithuania was then without a local (scheduled) airline until the July 2013 launch of *Air Lituanica.* Though a private company, the principal owner was the Vilnius municipal enterprise *Start Vilnius*, which held 83 per cent of the shares (media release, 'Air Lituanica keeps attracting new shareholders', 6 August 2013). Its main aim was to improve air connections, to support local business and tourism.

Air Lituanica leased one E175 aircraft from Embraer; and (initially) Estonian Air provided one Embraer E170 (76 seats) on a wet lease (media release 'Air Lituanica and Estonian Air signed a lease agreement for E170 aircraft' 6 June 2013). A modest route strategy seemed carefully considered ('Interview with Simonas Bartkus, CCO, Air Lituanica', anna.aero, 26 June 2013). While it gradually increased its flight schedule during 2014, a question remained: were demand levels on the chosen routes high enough to make the new company financially viable?

An answer came when Ait Lituanica ceased flying (media release, 'Air Lituanica stops flight operations', 22 May 2015).

On the same day, Estonian said it would increase its daily frequency on the Tallinn–Vilnius route from six to 11 flights, starting on the following Monday. And AirBaltic said it intended to launch, in September, services from Vilnius to six European destinations previously served by Air Lituanica. Its CEO added 'Today's event in Vilnius is a strong signal that the three Baltic countries should take a common approach to their aviation, to best support travelers, new economic activity and new jobs.' (Alan Dron, 'Air Lituanica halts services', *Air Transport World*, 22 May 2015).

2.4.7 The Russian revolution

When the Soviet Union dissolved at the beginning of the 1990s, there were major consequences for the national carrier, Aeroflot. Upon the establishment of the Commonwealth of Independent States (CIS), Aeroflot survived in Russia itself, while most of the other states soon established their own airlines. It was often convenient to arrange for new carriers to grow out of the (previous) local Aeroflot branches.

Aeroflot

Aeroflot is now an open Joint Stock Company, formally renamed *Aeroflot – Russian Airlines*. The Russian government owns 51 per cent of the shares, with the balance held by institutions and individuals ('About us', aeroflot.ru/cms/en/about/company_profile, accessed 26 October 2014). Nowadays, Aeroflot JSC (that is, Aeroflot itself, and excluding other smaller airlines that are now members of the Aeroflot Group; see below) is heavily weighted towards international routes, where entry is governed by bilateral agreements between governments. Aeroflot has mirrored the other major Russian airlines in various ways: using aircraft made in the Americas and Western Europe, and improving punctuality and other service features. These initiatives were rewarded by considerable growth; it became the largest airline by sold output.

In addition, recent developments have made the Aeroflot Group much more than just Aeroflot JSC. Pursuant to a government decision, the Group became the owner, in November 2011, of majority shareholdings in five Joint Stock Companies: Rossiya Airlines, Vladivostok Avia, SAT Airlines, Saratov Airlines, and Orenburg Airlines (Aeroflot Group Consolidated Financials 2011, p. 3). While each of those companies was fairly small, one effect of the mergers was to increase the RPK market-share of the Aeroflot Group by about 11 percentage points (Aeroflot Group Consolidated Financials 2011, p. 6).

The ostensible government purpose of the ownership transfers seems to have been to strengthen the overall air services in some of the Russian regions, especially in the Far East, where – in late 2013 – Vladivostok Avia and SAT Airlines were merged, to form *Aurora Airlines*. In January 2014, Aeroflot transferred 49 per cent of the shares of the new company to the Sakhalin Regional Administration. The plan was to greatly increase the output of the company (Aeroflot, Annual Report 2013, p. 48).

Meanwhile, *Rossiya Airlines* 'is developing as a regional airline based . . . in St Petersburg', with 'an increase in flight frequency to popular destinations in the North-West and South of Russia, and to Europe and the CIS'. An older subsidiary, *Donavia* (based at Rostov-on-Don) was tasked with serving the southern part of European Russia. *OrenAir* 'is focused on charter flights to the most popular international tourist destinations (Annual Report 2013, pp. 46–7).

For 2014, Aeroflot JSC reported considerable growth in passenger traffic. It increased capacity (ASKs) by 14.0 per cent (compared with 2013); sold output (RPKs) rose by 12.2 per cent. The load factor declined by 1.2 percentage points, to 72.2 per cent (media release 'Aeroflot Group Announces Traffic Statistics for December and 12 months 2014' 29 January 2015).

For the Aeroflot Group, perhaps the most interesting event of 2014 was the planned launch of a low-cost subsidiary, *Dobrolet* (Aeroflot, Annual Report 2013, p. 48). In recent times, two foreign low-cost airlines (EasyJet and WizzAir) had entered routes to Moscow. Then the Russian parliament passed legislation allowing Russian carriers to offer different fare classes and to sell non-refundable tickets (CAPA 'Dobrolet nears take-off, but can Aeroflot's LCC subsidiary achieve the required cost structure?' 8 April 2014).

The new airline launched on 10 June, on the Moscow–Simferopol route, but closed on 4 August, because of sanctions imposed by the EU (Polina Borodina, 'Russia's Dobrolet ceases operations due to EU sanctions', *Air Transport World*, 4 August 2014).

Aeroflot then registered a new LCC, *Pobeda*, which launched on 1 December 2014 from its base at Moscow Vnukovo airport. By June 2015, its fleet of eleven B737-800s had carried one million passengers on domestic routes (Polina Montag-Girmes, 'Aeroflot's new LCC Pobeda carries its one-millionth passenger', *Air Transport World*, 4 June 2015). Yet, when Pobeda sought to fly internationally notwithstanding a government requirement that requires two years' prior experience on domestic routes, the federal regulator withheld permission (Polina Montag-Girmes, 'Russia denies international status to Aeroflot LCC Pobeda', *Air Transport World*, 24 September 2015).

Transaero

This Joint Stock Company was established in 1990, and was the first privately owned airline in Russia. Its *scheduled* services began in 1993. It too has some emphasis on international routes, for which it has a considerable number of wide-body aircraft. In recent years it has been the second largest Russian airline, measured by RPK (see Table 2.4 below). It still operates charter flights (recently accounting for about one-fifth of its RPK output). In May 2015, it operated a remarkably heterogeneous fleet of 94 aircraft, of 10 different types, including 14 Boeing 747, 12 Boeing 777, 13 B737-500, 18 Boeing 767, 7 Boeing 737-700 and 5 B737-800 aircraft (ch-aviation.ch, accessed 28 May 2015).

One interesting Transaero innovation was the launch, on 14 January 2014 of a low-fare ticket type, 'Discount Class', available on a wide range of domestic and

Table 2.4 Sold output (billion RPK) of major Russian airlines, 2010–13

Airlines/groups	Total sold output (billion RPK)				Domestic RPK as % of total RPK			
	2010	2011	2012	2013	2010	2011	2012	2013
Aeroflot Group	39.2	46.1	74.6	85.3	28	29	33	34
Transaero	26.3	33.2	41.0	47.1	22	22	21	
S7 Group	13.0	14.0	17.6		72	71	66	
UT Air	8.0	12.4	16.0	18.6	81	58	51	51
Ural Airlines	4.8	6.8	9.5	11.8				
All Russian airlines	147	167	196	225	40	40	36	35

Sources: Aeroflot Group, Consolidated Financials 2010, p. 9; Consolidated Financials 2011, p. 6; Annual Report 2013, p. 41. (For the five companies merged into Aeroflot in November 2011, the 2011 data include only their November and December outputs.) Transaero Annual Report 2011, p. 3; Annual Report 2012, p. 20; press release, 'Transaero Airlines Announces Its Operational Results for 2013', 21 January 2014. (The Transaero Annual Reports also include data for the other major airlines, sourced from the Transport Clearing House, Ministry of Transport.) UTair, Annual Report 2011, p. 14; Annual Report 2012, pp. 26–7; press release, 'UTair Reports Results of Annual General Meeting', 30 June 2014.

international routes. On that first day, there were much higher load factors on many of the flights, even approaching 100 per cent in several cases. The Discount Class ticket conditions followed the (then) Aviation Rules of the Russian Federation; accordingly, passengers receive 'free drinks and food or meals depending on flight length'. Note also that 'Passengers acquiring a ticket at Y tariff [full economy fare] will be seated in the business class cabin' (airline press release, 'Transaero Airlines launched low cost service', 16 January 2014). Transaero also has a first-class cabin in some of its aircraft; understandably, this is called 'Imperial Class'.

Despite its size, Transaero was much troubled by the downturn in the Russian economy in 2015. On those events, see the discussion at the end of this section.

S7 Airlines

In May 1992, a directive from the Ministry of Transport established a state-run enterprise, S7 Airlines, based in Novosibirsk (Siberia) and formed from the local branch of Aeroflot. Eventually, the airline was privatised; yet it retains its eastern focus. While also serving routes to CIS, Europe, the Near East, South-East Asia and some countries in the Asia-Pacific region, it claims to be the largest *domestic* carrier in Russia, with its main hubs at Moscow (Domodedovo) and Novosibirsk (Tolmachevo).

Its fleet comprises mainly A319, A320 and A321 aircraft. S7 also operates some charter flights. The S7 Group includes Globus Airlines, established in March 2008, and based at Moscow Domodedovo, where it deploys various Boeing 737 aircraft, including -800s. The Group carried 9.2 million passengers in 2013 ('About S7', accessed at.*s7.ru*, 29 October 2014).

UTair

UTair had its origins in Tyumen (just to the east of the Ural Mountains, and not far from the border with Kazakhstan) where the local Aeroflot branch was converted to a joint stock company in 1991 (UTair, Annual Report 2011, p. 4). The company was renamed UTair in 2002, and the group now has helicopter and other subsidiaries in Russia and elsewhere (including UTair–Ukraine) At 31 December 2011, the largest shareholder was a non-state (oil company) pension fund, with about 61 per cent of the shares. Other institutions had about 28 per cent (including foreign investors with 4 per cent), and individuals had 11.5 per cent (Annual Report 2011, pp. 78–9).

As seen in Table 2.4 below, domestic routes accounted for almost 60 per cent of its total RPK in 2011. However that percentage was lower in 2012 and 2013. And in the first 9 months of 2014, while the total RPK figure grew to 17.8 billion, this total reflected a mere 3.5 per cent increase in domestic travel, coupled with a 46 per cent increase in international travel, compared with the corresponding period of the previous year (press release, 'UTair shows stable monthly growth of main performance indicators', 20 October 2014).

While UT Air initially served eastern parts of Russia, the airline has spread its wings, and now describes Moscow (Vnukovo) as its 'principal hub' (Annual Report, 2011, p. 18). Its jet aircraft *were* predominantly B737s, with eight new 737-800 aircraft added in 2011. More recently, however, it started taking delivery of A321s (220 seats), and on 29 October 2014, the website utair.ru recorded eight such aircraft. Also of interest are its two B767-300 aircraft, each in a single-class layout (no less than 336 seats, in rows of 2 + 4 + 2 seats).

Besides its taste for high-density layouts, UTair has recently introduced a Premium Class on its A321 aircraft (news release, 'UTair introduces PREMIUM service class on three more routes', 2 October 2014).

Ural Airlines

Ural Airlines is yet another company that grew out of (the old) Aeroflot. Ural was founded as a separate joint stock company in December 1993, after it had been legally separated from Yekaterinburg Airport, where it still has its base. (When Aeroflot was the monopoly Soviet carrier, it was customary for a local branch to comprise both air carrier and home port.) In May 2015, Ural operated six A319 aircraft, 18 A320s and ten A321s (ch-aviation.ch, accessed 28 May 2015).

Ural Airlines has grown vigorously in recent years, serving not only its home region in eastern Russia, but also introducing international services. In the year 2014, it carried 5.16 million passengers (some 17 per cent more than in 2013), and those passengers travelled 13.3 billion RPKs (press release, 'Ural Airlines carried more than 5 million passengers in 2014', 19 January 2015).

2.4.8 The Russian aviation sector as a whole

In addition to the five major entities listed in Table 2.4, the sector includes many smaller companies, some of whom are based in remote, underpopulated or peripheral regions – for example *Omskavia* (at Omsk, east of the Urals and just north of the border with Kazakhstan) and *Ak Bars Aero* (in the republic of Tatarstan).

Since 1990, the sector as a whole has exhibited some remarkable volatility. From 1970, two decades of steady growth led to an output of 159 billion RPK in 1990.

Following the dramatic political changes in Russia, the (recorded) sector output was only 72 billion RPK in 1995, and then shrank further to 53 billion in 2000. The new century saw a period of new growth, to 94 billion in 2005 and then 147 billion in 2010 (data from Federal Air Transport Agency of the Russian Federation, as quoted in Transaero, Annual Report 2011, p. 19. On that p. 19, which deals with the Russian Air Transport Market, Transaero remarks 'The number of *dishonest airlines* [italics added] continued to decline. Their number has shrunk from 296 to126 since 2000. Thirty-seven certificates were cancelled last year.' The last reference seems to be to air operator certificates. But Transaero gives no elucidation of 'dishonest airlines'.)

From 2010, the sector continued to grow strongly, as seen in Table 2.4. Most of the larger airlines have also grown strongly. On the other hand, some smaller companies have failed – thanks to misconceived entry and/or the forces of competition. For example, *KD Avia* built a hub for east-west travel in the Russian enclave of Kaliningrad, which lies to the *west* of the three Baltic States. The company closed in September 2009 (anna.aero 2 October 2009).

A dramatic life-history concerns *Avianova*, an avowed low-cost carrier funded by a Russian investment firm, together with Indigo Partners (the US venture-capital fund) as a junior partner. Based in Moscow, Avianova launched in September 2009 ('New Russian LCC launches: Avianova starts domestic flights from Moscow Vnukovo', anna.aero, 4 September 2009). Growing rapidly, the airline switched its Moscow operations to Sheremetyevo, and opened a second base at St Petersburg (anna.aero, 25 May 2010). After a further year of growth, Avianova was flying six A320s, reportedly with a load factor around 80 per cent, on a domestic network of some 20 domestic routes, and one international route (to Ukraine).

However, Avianova was setting very low fares, in order to attract those not previously flying. While the business plan anticipated that the company would be in the black in the following year (2012), it needed considerable additional funding in 2011. It seems the company's Russian investor did not wish to supply further funds, and sought to sell its 51 per cent stake. Thus the airline was unable to fund additions to its fleet (Anastasia Dagayeva and Grigory Milov, '51% of discount airline Avianova up for sale', *The Moscow Times*, 8 July 2011; see also Wikipedia on Avianova, accessed 1 November 2014).

Because Russian law did not allow a foreigner to be an airline general manager, the incumbent CEO was formally an officer of another company, which provided consulting services to Avianova. At a time when the two investors had divergent views regarding the future of the company, the CEO was removed from his post, and the airline apparently ceased operations (reports in *Flight*

Global, 14 July and 3 October 2011, by (respectively) Kerry Reals and David Kaminski-Morrow).

More recent is the closure in December 2012 of *Kuban Airlines*, which was then the twentieth largest airline, measured by seats offered. Based at Krasnodar (immediately to the east of the Black Sea) and at Moscow Vnukovo, where it offered many domestic services, the low-fare airline had struggled financially. It also failed to meet a new regulation for scheduled airlines (set by the Federal Air Transport Agency) that required a minimum operating fleet of eight aircraft, each with at least 55 seats; Kuban had seven (CAPA, 'Kuban Airlines ceases operations, the last vestige of LCC SkyExpress? UTair gains most', 19 December 2012).

While Aeroflot flies many international routes, it is not surprising that some of the other major airlines have a greater emphasis on domestic routes (that is, routes within Russia alone). The right-hand portion of Table 2.4 reveals some preference for expansion on international routes. For Aeroflot, the *increase* from 2011 to 2012 in the output proportion for domestic routes is a consequence of its acquisition of the five smaller carriers. Transaero is exceptional: it has the smallest domestic proportion of domestic routes, notwithstanding its relatively recent (initial) foundation. Otherwise, the table shows the domestic proportion declining, even for the sector a whole.

In regard to airline networks, competition in domestic services has encouraged individual carriers to inaugurate direct (non-stop) routes that bypass Moscow. In summer 2009, Oren Air launched flights between Düsseldorf (Germany) and Orenburg, which is about 1200 km *east* of Moscow, and close to the Kazakhstan border (anna.aero, 22 May 2009). In 2010, Ural Airlines launched flights between Novosibirsk and St Petersburg ('About us', accessed at www.uralairlines.com, 22 November 2012). In 2012, Ural started flying between Ekaterinburg in the Ural Mountains and the Hungarian capital, Budapest, a sector distance of about 3000 km (anna.aero, 10 October 2012). Also in 2012, Rossiya Airlines launched direct service (anna.aero, 10 October 2012) on the (international) route between St Petersburg and Nukus, which is in Uzbekistan (and hence not within the Russian Federation).

Since 1990, when the aviation sector was opened up to some degree, the government has remained active in shaping aviation policy, sometimes making very detailed interventions. In particular, it sought to enlarge the provision of airline services to remote and disadvantaged regions (as does the EU, of course). It also limits foreign ownership of Russian airlines, and deploys governmental bilateral agreements to control airline entry to international routes.

Towards the end of 2014, the Russian economy suffered a downturn, which reduced the demand for air travel. When taken together with a change in currency exchange rates, the situation created major financial problems for many Russian airlines, including the very largest.

By May 2015, Transaero, UTair, Ural Airlines and Red Wings had all requested financial help from the Russian government. In January 2015, Transaero received a loan on advantageous terms. Other airlines then sought similar treatment (Polina

Montag-Girmes, 'Russia's Ural Airlines seeks government help', *Air Transport World*, 16 March 2015; 'Ural Airlines applies for $32mn in Russian state aid', ch-aviation.ch, 17 March 2015).

Unsurprisingly, the loan to Transaero did not solve all its problems. In September 2015, Aeroflot announced it planned to acquire Transaero with its debts for the nominal sum of one ruble (Polina Montag-Girmes, 'Aeroflot to buy 75%, plus one share, of Transaero', *Air Transport World*, 2 September 2015). The deal would add to the debt burden already facing Aeroflot (Germain Moyon, 'Aeroflot-Transaero deal, bigger but not better: analysts', *Agence France Presse*, 6 September 2015). There were also reported concerns about the senior management of Transaero (Polina Montag-Girmes, 'Transaero reshuffles management; Pleshakova resigns as CEO', *Air Transport World*, 3 September 2015; Polina Montag-Girmes, 'Aeroflot agrees to lead Transaero restructuring', *Air Transport World*, 4 September 2015).

However, when the agreed deadline of 28 September 2015 passed without the establishment of financial arrangements for dealing with the very large debt, Aeroflot withdrew from the proposed deal, and the Russian government apparently decided to allow Transaero to go into bankruptcy (Polina Montag-Girmes, 'Aeroflot drops plans to acquire Transaero; bankruptcy imminent' *Air Transport World* 1 October 2015; 'Transaero to file for bankruptcy shortly?', ch-aviation.ch, 2 October 2015).

2.5 Traditional and low-cost airlines: traffic growth and market shares

The growth of EasyJet and Ryanair, and then (later) the success of some of the other new airlines, all reflect the various ways in which European travellers have been attracted by the offerings of the new carriers. Besides the obvious appeal of lower fares, several non-price factors seem to have encouraged travel with the new companies:

1   The LCCs offer the convenience of direct, non-stop flights. Furthermore, some of those flights serve ports not served at all by legacy carriers.
2   Many of the major LCCs have superior *punctuality* records. Having adopted point-to-point operation, they do not usually offer connections between flights. In contrast, the late arrival of a legacy-carrier flight may oblige the airline to hold up connecting flights, thereby transmitting delays from one aircraft to another.
3   In addition, superior management of the new airline may help to reduce the incidence of delays arising in aircraft turn-around at ports.
4   The major LCCs sometimes claim lower rates of lost baggage – and this too may be a result of superior management.

Within the EU, besides the adoption of point-to-point networks, the growth in the number of direct routes has been helped by the single-market legislation, which makes route entry simpler than before. For EU–27 (the 27-country grouping prevailing at the end of 2006), the number of city pairs directly connected by intra-EU routes (that is, excluding domestic routes) increased by 170 per cent, from about 850 city-pairs in 1990 to about 2,300 in 2006. In contrast, the number of domestic routes rose by no more than about 15 per cent (EU Flying Together 2007, p. 5).

In Europe, the dichotomy between the new and traditional carriers is reflected in the existence of two industry associations – the Association of European Airlines which, at the end of 2013, had 30 airline members, and the European Low Fares Airline Association, which then had 10 airline members.

Summary data published by the two associations form the basis of Table 2.5, which gives a rudimentary comparison of the two industry sub-sectors. Despite some qualifications reported in the table notes, one message is clear: for the nine years shown, the low-fare airlines have carried an increased number of passengers each year; over that period, the passenger number have more than doubled. In contrast, those of the traditional airlines that are members of the European Airline Association have fluctuating annual passenger numbers, with a total increase over the same nine years of about 5 per cent. The traditional airlines also have a somewhat lower passenger load factor, though this may be regarded as reasonable given that they target business travel (to a greater degree than do the low-fare airlines).

Table 2.5 Passenger numbers and load factors, European airlines, 2006–14

Year	ELFAA members (low-fare airlines)		AEA members	
	Passengers boarded[1] (millions)	*Passenger load factor (per cent)*	*Passengers boarded[1] (millions)*	*Passenger load factor (per cent)*
2006	106	83	346	76
2007	121	82	363	77
2008	149	81	350	76
2009	162	82	326	76
2010	172	82	338	78
2011	189	83	399	78
2012	202	83	402	79
2013	216	84	373	80
2014[2]	236	86	369	77

Sources: European Low Fares Airlines Association, Members' Statistics (published annually), accessed at elfaa.com, 28 May 2015; Association of European Airlines, AEA Traffic and Capacity Data, accessed at aea.be, 28 May 2015

Notes
1 For the ELFAA airlines, the passenger counts refer to the intra-European and other short/medium haul routes served by such airlines. For the AEA members, the counts are of all passengers carried by those airlines; of those totals, about 20 per cent travel on long haul routes to/from Europe. The table serves to demonstrate the differing growth records of the two airline categories, but does not accurately portray European short/medium haul market shares.
2 For the AEA members, the 2014 totals come from the AEA table of *monthly* data.

3 The Arabian Peninsula

3.1 Introduction

In the last decade or two, local entrepreneurs in many of the other regions of the world have observed the changes in aviation in the USA and Europe, and sensed that a combination of rising real incomes and an offer of lower airfares (based on the new lower-cost modes of operation) would allow them to launch and develop successful local airlines, mainly serving short-haul networks. In the outcome, many such companies have had successful launches; and some have prospered to such a degree as to suggest a secure future.

Even when income levels remain low, the introduction of lower fares has often resulted in substantial increases in air travel, thereby giving an opportunity for a new airline to flourish *alongside* an old national carrier, even where the latter was government-owned or belonged to affluent and powerful individuals close to government. While quite a number of governments have been willing to license new airlines, often in the hope of promoting tourism and other economic development, only a few have engaged in full economic deregulation.

The Arabian Peninsula has several long-established national airlines, belonging to various governments of the region. And in recent times, two governments and a royal family have established airlines that (mainly) fly long-haul routes: Emirates (Dubai, established 1985), Qatar Airways (Doha, 1993) and Etihad Airways (Abu Dhabi, 2003). The first and third of those carriers are located within the United Arab Emirates, a federation of spatially small, contiguous states. Given the scope of the present study, those 'national carriers' are not featured here. Rather, this chapter looks particularly at the entrepreneurial origins of the new *short-haul* airlines, and at their fundamental decisions on which routes to serve and what aircraft to fly.

Until recently, the prevailing practice in the region was that aviation properly belonged to the public sector. However, the aviation developments in some other world regions seem to have stimulated fresh thinking in the region about a role for privately owned airlines.

Indeed, in 2003, the Kuwait government offered two licences allowing the establishment of Kuwait-based private airlines. In due course, this led to the founding of a low-cost carrier, which was the first *privately owned* airline in the region. In the same year, in Sharjah (one of the United Arab Emirates), the government itself launched the region's first *low-cost* airline. The history of that company begins this account of the more important events in the region.

3.2 Air Arabia (Sharjah)

It was October 2003 when Air Arabia started flying from its base in Sharjah. Though the airline began as a government enterprise, its legal form changed in June 2007 – from a limited liability company to a public joint stock company (PJSC) – following a successful IPO in which the government offered 55 per cent of the shares to UAE and other investors (Air Arabia, Annual Report 2008). The shares trade on the Dubai Financial Market.

Though now majority-owned by private investors, the board of directors (listed in successive annual reports – see also press release, 'Profiles of Air Arabia board nominees 2014', 24 February 2014) typically includes some individuals who have public-sector roles – in the Sharjah Executive Council, the Sharjah Airport Authority and the Sharjah Directorate of Civil Aviation. Adel Ali (the airline's CEO from 2003, and still the CEO in 2015) and other senior managers have had prior experience with airlines such as British Airways, Gulf Air and Ryanair ('About Air Arabia – management team', airarabia.com, accessed 2 April 2009).

From 2003 onwards, a number of local factors assisted the birth and growth of the airline. The airport at Sharjah had speedy check-in procedures, little by way of runway congestion, and a style that favoured the operation of a low-cost carrier. Sharjah is *very* close to Dubai, and so can readily serve much of the travel to and from the home countries of the many expatriates working in Dubai.

With (initially) limited competition from other low-cost airlines, Air Arabia was able to set fares at levels that were low enough to attract new travellers, yet high enough to make the company profitable. Indeed the company reports it earned a profit even in its first year, and has been profitable every year so far (up to 2014) – though profit has *not* always increased from one year to the next (Air Arabia Investor Presentation FY 2014, p. 18). Like leading newcomers on other continents, the airline emphasises the importance of good staff performance, and the need to provide good employment conditions (see, for example, 'Our greatest asset', Annual Report 2008, p. 29).

Air Arabia chose to fly (new) A320 aircraft with a (favourable) 31/32 inch seat pitch, allowing 162 seats in a single-class cabin ('Air Arabia expands its Egyptian network', anna.aero, 8 January 2011). By mid- 2015, the fleet had grown to a total of 42 (leased and owned) aircraft. Recognised by Airbus for the reliability of its A320 operation, the airline has attained very high daily utilisation rates, up to 13 block hours per aircraft.

By the end of 2014, Air Arabia was flying 101 routes and serving 100 ports. Besides its routes in the immediate region, the company flew non-stop services from Sharjah to more-distant ports such as Nairobi, Kiev, Moscow (Domodedovo), Kathmandu and Colombo. On local routes, frequencies were once or twice daily; some longer routes were served only two or three times weekly.

To promote further expansion of the company, Air Arabia has established hubs in other countries, as well as expanding the list of ports it serves from Sharjah. In 2008, it made a modest start in Nepal, but within months it closed that operation, because of 'the political uncertainty and on-going opaque regulatory environment' (Annual Report 2008, p. 19).

In the same year, Air Arabia established a joint venture with Regional Airlines, a privately owned Moroccan carrier (Air Arabia media release, 3 November 2008); Air Arabia holds 41 per cent of the shares. With Regional as the majority owner, *Air Arabia Maroc* is recognised as a Moroccan company. The new airline launched in May 2009 (Annual Report 2009, p. 19), and by the end of the year there were three aircraft based at Casablanca. Under an open-sky agreement between Morocco and the EU, flights began to ports in Western Europe. In 2014, Air Arabia Maroc served eleven such ports (including London Gatwick and Amsterdam), as well as Istanbul.

In 2009, Air Arabia established a joint venture with Travco (a large Egyptian travel and hospitality group) to launch a new low-cost carrier, *Air Arabia Egypt,* based at Alexandria (Annual Report 2009, p. 26). The first route, to Amman, was launched in June 2010 (Air Arabia media release 22 May 2010).

In its 2012 Annual Report (p. 38), however, Air Arabia sounded a note of caution: *Air Arabia Egypt* 'maintained its regular operations, and will further invest in increasing its reach at the right time.' Then the Air Arabia *Annual Report* 2013 notes that 'Air Arabia Egypt maintained its existing operations, which is considered a great achievement considering the transition that Egypt is still going through.'

Yet another joint venture was under consideration on 7 June 2010 when Air Arabia issued a press release 'Air Arabia and Tantash Group to launch Jordan's first low-cost carrier'. However, Air Arabia later wrote (in its 2011 Annual Report p. 9) 'we have weathered 2011 with all its surprises cautiously and consciously – dealing with the changing circumstances on [a] daily basis . . . We have decided that under the current circumstances we will freeze our plans to open a new hub in Jordan'.

Almost four years later, Air Arabia chose another partner when it took a 49 per cent stake in a Jordanian carrier, Petra Airlines (Alan Dron 'Air Arabia takes major stake in Jordanian carrier', *Air Transport World*, 6 January 2015). The prior owner, the RUM Group, was to retain ownership of the balance of the shares. Air Arabia would manage the new airline. (CAPA 'Air Arabia prepares to launch a new Jordan-based airline . . .' 23 April 2015; Alan Dron 'Air Arabia Jordan launches services' *Air Transport World,* 29 April 2015).

And in May 2015, Air Arabia launched a small base (with two A320s) in the neighbouring emirate of Ras Al Khaimah, where the airport is less than 100 km from Sharjah (Air Arabia press release, 6 May 2014). The ports to be served from RAK were already well served from Sharjah and Dubai. However, the new arrangement would make Ras Al Khaimah more accessible for international passengers, and was expected to increase the flow of tourists visiting RAK.

Although the *proportionate* expansion of the Air Arabia Group may have slowed somewhat after the first few years, profits are still being earned and passenger numbers have continued to grow strongly, reaching 5.3 million in 2012, then 6.1 million in 2013, and 6.8 million in 2014, when sold output reached 13.8 billion RPK (up from 9.2 billion in 2011) (Air Arabia Investor Presentation, 2014 Full Year, p. 26).

3.3 Jazeera Airways and Wataniya Airways (Kuwait)

When the Kuwait government announced that it was prepared to license two new privately-owned airlines, a local entrepreneur Marwan Boodai joined with other investors to develop a hybrid business model for a new airline, to be called *Jazeera Airways*. After concluding that the airline would need US$34 million for its initial capitalisation, the investors themselves staked US$10 million for 30 per cent of the shares, and raised the further US$24 million from a greatly over-subscribed IPO in June 2004. The transactions were structured to conform to Islamic banking practices. Shares were allocated on a *pro rata* basis; Jazeera claims that one in every 25 Kuwaitis bought shares in the company (*From IPO to Take-off*, pp. 3–5, accessed 3 April 2009 at jazeeraairways.com).

Besides Mr Boodai as chairman, the initial senior management group included Andrew Cowen as CEO and Steven Greenway as Chief Commercial Officer; each previously held the same position at (respectively) Sama and SkyEurope. The government approved the funding and ownership arrangements, and the airline began flying on 30 October 2005.

Jazeera decided to buy (new) A320 aircraft, each with 165 seats in a *dual-cabin* layout, chosen with an eye to the affluence of Kuwaitis and others in the region. By the end of 2008, it had eight such aircraft, and daily utilisation reached 13.2 block hours per aircraft. At that time, Jazeera served 25 ports; the more distant of these were Khartoum, Istanbul, Delhi, Mumbai and Kochi. In 2008, Jazeera carried 1.4 million passengers, at a load factor of 67 per cent (down from 74 per cent in the previous year); net profit was about nine per cent of revenue (FY 2008 Presentation, 24 March 2009).

However, in 2009, the financial crisis led to overcapacity in the market. Jazeera recorded a net loss equivalent to almost 18 per cent of revenue. Although passenger numbers rose to 1.8 million, the larger fleet (10 aircraft at year-end) had a load factor of only 61 per cent, and the average fare dropped to KD 25, from KD 35 in the previous year (FY 2009 Presentation, issued 29 March 2010). The resolve for 2010 was to increase the yield, while containing fleet growth to one extra aircraft that year, and none in 2011.

In the outcome, 2010 brought unexpected political events, and market conditions that were worse than anticipated. The Jazeera management then reduced the overall level of activity, dropped the most unprofitable routes and focussed on those that were potentially profitable. The total number of passengers boarded fell to 1.3 million, average yield increased markedly, and the net loss fell to about 34 per cent of the 2009 level (Jazeera Airways, Annual Report 2010).

That strategy reduced the amount of *needed* aircraft capacity. In February 2010, Jazeera purchased a (small) aircraft-leasing company, and then managed to lease four of its A320s to Virgin America, and one to another carrier, thereby reducing its own fleet to six aircraft.

In 2011, the pursuit of profit rather than size continued: the number of passengers boarded fell slightly to 1.2 million, the load factor recovered to 65 per cent, and there was a net *profit*, of KD 10.6 million (Jazeera Airways, 2011 Full Year Results and Presentation). Over the next several years, the profits continued *every quarter*, occasionally setting new records for the company.

In 2013, Jazeera carried 1.14 million passengers (still much fewer than in 2009), and recorded an outstanding on-time performance of 94 per cent (pp. 5–7, Jazeera Airways Group, Annual Report 2013). During that year, it received its fourteenth new A320. (The final delivery from its order for 15 aircraft arrived in May 2014.) It continued to lease out un-needed aircraft, with one aircraft placed with *Nas Air* in November 2013.

The importance of the leasing initiative is illustrated by the profits earned by its subsidiary, Sahaab Aircraft Leasing, which contributed 50 per cent of the Group's total profit in 2011. Of course, as the airline operation recovered from the general financial crisis, the proportionate profit contribution from Sahaab declined to 41 per cent in 2012, and to 25 per cent in 2013 (Annual Report 2013, p. 9).

Also important was the decision about the nature and size of Jazeera's network. After 27 ports in 2009, the airline served only 19 ports in 2013. Those remaining ports were more closely grouped around Kuwait. 'As our peers boast about flights to Dallas and Guangzhou, we remain focused on our home market of Kuwait and point-to-point regional travel. Kuwait is one of the most active travel markets in the Gulf and Levant, with 9 million travelers passing through Kuwait International Airport in 2013. Our growth opportunity is at home.' (Jazeera Airways Group, Annual Report 2013, p. 4).While that report (pp. 7–9) boasted of the benefits of the Group having both a leasing company that owns the aircraft, and an airline that flies many of them, the financial thinking soon changed.

With the airline carrying more passengers and earning larger profits, *without* network expansion, the Board decided to sell the aircraft and focus on the airline. At the beginning of 2015, the Group announced the sale (media release, 'Jazeera Airways Group signs agreement to sell 15 Airbus A320s for USD 507 million', 15 January 2015). The profitable Jazeera Airways 'will eventually become an asset-light, debt free and cash-rich business . . . [which] will deliver higher return on equity for shareholders for the years to come'. The proceeds from the sale 'will be used to finance exceptional dividends payment to shareholders and invested in new customer experience-enhancing investments and initiatives to support medium and long term growth plans'.

The second Kuwait government licence went to *Wataniya Airways*, which had some major Kuwaiti companies among its founders, and launched an IPO in 2006, in order to fund much of its start-up costs. It too opted for (new) A320 aircraft, and chose to become a premium airline: each aircraft had 22 seats in First

Class and 96 seats in Premium Economy (media release, 5 March 2009, accessed at wataniyaairways.com).

It launched service to Dubai in January 2009. Upon the March arrival of its second A320, it started flights to Cairo, Beirut and Bahrain. Other ports soon added were Amman, Damascus, Jeddah and Sharm el Sheikh. By mid-2010, it operated 6 A320s (with a seventh to arrive in October 2010), and had started routes that summer to Istanbul, Alexandria, Vienna and Rome (news release, 17 May 2010).

It experienced a large loss in its first half-year (news release, 5 August 2009) – as was to be expected, especially when the start-up coincided with the financial crisis. However, by late 2010 the situation had become worse, leading to a decision to reduce the network, and take out of service some of its aircraft (Cathy Buyck 'Wataniya Airways drastically cuts its network', *Air Transport World*, 1 December 2010). Financial losses continued, and the airline ceased operation in March 2011 (Ivan Gale, 'Wataniya Airways shuts down', *The National* (Abu Dhabi), 18 March 2011).

As a full-service carrier, Wataniya was in a crowded market place, with Kuwait Airways (Kuwait's 'national airline', founded in 1954) also based at the port. A government licence to start an airline was a chance to compete, but not a guarantee of success.

3.4 Flynas and Sama Airlines (Saudi Arabia)

In Saudi Arabia, following promulgation of the Air Traffic Privatisation Act, the General Authority of Civil Aviation granted airline licences to two new companies, and mandated destinations that each *must* serve (Nas Air media release, 18 September 2007, accessed at flynas.com). The two airlines, *Nas Air* (later called *Flynas*) and *Sama*, launched in February and March 2007, respectively.

Nas Air

Nas Air, based in the Saudi capital, Riyadh, is a business unit of National Air Services, an aviation services company founded in 1999 and owned privately by Saudi investors (flynas.com accessed 12 January 2009, and media report 12 December 2006 at ameinfo.com). It built up a fleet of almost 20 *new* aircraft – Airbus A320 and A319 models, and Embraer E190 and E195 models, all operated *initially* with single-class cabins.

An unusual feature of the airline's role was a government requirement for it to take over a number of PSO (public service obligation) domestic routes previously operated by the national carrier, Saudi Arabian Airlines. The process began in October 2007 ('Nas Air moves in on national routes', ArabianBusiness. com, 30 October 2007). For some years, the airline managed to increase the scale of its operations.

Following the March 2012 arrival of a new CEO, the company introduced a new fare structure, with three distinct ticket types that offered an orthodox trade-off between fare level and ticket flexibility (Nas Air press release, April 2012).

Other changes in the operation of the airline came in the second half of 2013. Yet another new CEO announced (press release 30 July 2013) that it had already received four new A320s in 2013.

The first day of 2014 saw the introduction of business class (press release 'Flynas launches business class service starting next Wednesday', 28 December 2013). As the airline website subsequently confirmed, while some of the A320s remained equipped with 180 economy seats, others had eight business class seats, together with 156 economy seats.

Meanwhile, a most dramatic announcement came in November: Flynas was to fly long-haul routes to ports in Europe, North Africa and the (Indian) sub-continent, using A330 aircraft (press release, 'Flynas spreads its wings to expand into long-haul sectors', 18 November 2013). A later announcement (press release, 26 February 2014) identified the long-haul destinations as Kuala Lumpur, Jakarta, Karachi, Casablanca, Paris, London Gatwick and Manchester.

Later that year, however, an airline press release (15 October 2014) said that 'flynas has suspended all long-haul flight services ... including all flights to London Gatwick', and went on to explain: 'As the load factors on the above routes have not met the company's commercial expectations, flynas is concentrating on enhancing its performance by focusing strongly on its successful domestic and regional services.'

Soon after, the airline appointed yet another CEO (*Air Transport World*, 19 November 2014). With air travel growing strongly in its home region, flynas put emphasis on domestic routes when it announced it would add two A320s to its fleet in 2015 (media release, 'Flynas adds 2 Airbus A320s in 2015', 15 April 2015).

Sama Airlines

Sama Airlines was incorporated in 2005, with a plan to operate as a low-cost airline, owned by private and institutional Saudi investors. In 2006, the General Authority of Civil Aviation granted Sama a national carrier licence that *required* the recipient airline to be based in Dammam, in the east of the country (Sama media release, 'Sama awarded national air carrier licence . . .', December 2006, flysama.com).

Having recruited senior managers with experience at major US airlines (flysama.com, accessed 28 June 2010), Sama assembled a fleet of six (ageing) B737-300 aircraft (ch-aviation.ch, accessed 28 June 2010), and launched its first flight in March 2007. When faced with early operating difficulties and increased fuel prices, the private shareholders put in a further US$53 million ('Shareholders strengthen Sama Airlines with additional SR200 million of financing', Centre for Asia Pacific Aviation, 14 July 2008).

Bruce Ashby (previously CEO of IndiGo, and earlier a senior manager at US Airways) was appointed as CEO from 1 December 2008 (Sama press release, 26 November 2008.) The airline then sought growth by developing international rather than domestic routes. According to its website booking engine (accessed 28 June 2010), Sama served only three ports in Saudi Arabia (Riyadh, Jeddah and Dammam), while operating international flights (from Riyadh and/or Jeddah, but not from its Dammam base) to eight ports in Egypt, UAE and Syria.

Despite these efforts, Sama was unable to earn enough revenue to cover its costs. Being also unable to get financial support from government or further funding from its investors, it closed on 23 August 2010 ('Saudi Arabia's Sama ceases services', anna.aero, 26 August 2010; 'Sama to cease operations', Centre for Asia Pacific Aviation, 23 August 2010).

3.5 Bahrain Air

With buoyant expectations for aviation in the region, a private, closed Bahraini Shareholding Company (whose shareholders all had Bahraini or Saudi nationality) founded this low-fare airline in 2007. Bahrain Air started flying in February 2008, and carried 400,000 passengers in its first year of operation. However, being a new start-up, the airline was particularly vulnerable to the adverse financial events of 2008. The shareholders agreed unanimously to double both its authorised and paid-up share capital (news release, 14 September 2008).

By mid-2010, it had introduced business class as well as economy. It then operated eight Airbus aircraft, some new from Airbus, and all with dual cabins: A320s with 12 Premium Class and 150 Economy Class seats, and A319s with 12/120 seats, at respective pitches of 35/36 and (a generous) 32/33 inches (bahrainair.org and ch-aviation.ch, both accessed on 29 June 2010).

From its Bahrain island base, the airline then served 21 ports. Besides some Persian Gulf neighbours, these included capital and major cities in Lebanon, Syria, Iraq, Iran, Egypt, Bangladesh, India and Nepal. The timetable showed about 200 flight sectors per week. In a news release (14 March 2010), the company said 'Bahrain Air hopes to break even next year [2011] as it shakes off the recession and expands its operations'.

However, on 1 April 2011, the company announced that it had been forced to suspend flights to Najaf, Baghdad, Beirut and Mashhad, and to reduce frequency on the services to Damascus and Amman. The principal new problems were the local and regional 'unfortunate political events' together with a 35 per cent increase in operating costs thanks largely to higher fuel prices and increased insurance premiums.

Better news came in a press release (12 April 2012): in June it would begin direct flights from Dammam (in the eastern province of Saudi Arabia), to Beirut (Lebanon) and to Khartoum (Sudan). 'Our thanks and appreciation goes to the Civil Aviation Authorities in the Kingdom of Saudi Arabia for their far sighted support in this venture.'

(The airports at Bahrain and Dammam are about 100 km apart. The Saudi government's liberalisation of traffic rights may have been due in part to the willingness of Saudi passengers to drive across the recently constructed (and already congested) Saudi–Bahrain causeway, in order to access flights from Bahrain to Beirut and Khartoum. Also relevant, no doubt, was the earlier closure of Sama, the Saudi Arabian airline that had been designated as the company that would be based in Dammam.)

For the second quarter of 2012, Bahrain Air reported (press release, 24 July 2012) that, compared with the corresponding period of the previous year, passenger numbers increased by 57 per cent, the load factor was 78 per cent (59 per cent previously), and average aircraft utilisation had increased by 45 per cent, to reach 13.1 hours per aircraft per day.

On 15 August 2012, CEO Richard Nuttall announced a return to profitability for June and July, while acknowledging that those months are the best of the year for the airline. He went on to say: 'We are currently putting [in] every effort to reach an agreement with our creditors for the restructuring of our debts that accumulated as a result of the unfortunate events that took place in Bahrain and the region.'

The outcome became clear on 12 February 2013: the company's shareholders held an Extraordinary General Meeting. A statement from the Board of Directors (bahrainair.net) said that the shareholders had made the decision 'to announce the company's immediate suspension of operations and to file for voluntary liquidation'.

The statement went on to offer several specific criticisms of the conduct of the government of Bahrain. It summarised the general situation in these terms:

> The airline is now being required to make immediate payments on past government debts or face closure at the same time as having its scheduled operations, both destinations and frequencies, being reduced considerably by the Civil Aviation Affairs in the Ministry of Transportation. This effectively strangles the airline by simultaneously requesting payments and reducing its ability to generate the necessary revenues both to make these payments and to sustain long term profitability.

The other major airline based in Bahrain is the long-established Gulf Air, which had started as a cooperative venture between several governments in the region. As those countries established or expanded their 'own' airlines, there was progressive withdrawal of their governments from Gulf Air ('History', gulfair. com). With the last to go being the Sultanate of Oman, Gulf Air became wholly owned by the Bahrain government in 2007. In February 2013, the Deputy Prime Minister of Bahrain was the chairman of Gulf Air's Board of Directors, and three other ministers (including the Minister of Transport) served as members of the Board (gulfair.com, accessed 22 February 2013).

3.6 Felix Airways (Yemen)

Yemenia, the incumbent national flag carrier of Yemen, traces its history back to the late 1940s. In recent times, it has operated large aircraft (Airbus A310, A320 and A330) on long-haul services as well as some regional routes. Since 1978, the Yemen government has owned 51 per cent of the shares, and the government of Saudi Arabia has owned the other 49 per cent ('About Yemenia', yemenia.com, accessed 14 December 2012).

In March 2008, the Yemen government decided to start a new airline, *Felix Airways*, with initial emphasis on domestic routes. Yemenia owns 25 per cent of the Felix shares, and a manager from Yemenia became the CEO of Felix.

Felix soon built a small jet fleet comprising two CRJ200 aircraft and two CRJ700s. From its base at Sana, the company launched flights in October 2008, and carried about 640,000 passengers during the period to December 2010 (airline magazine, date not ascertained, accessed at felixairways.com on 14 December 2012).

By 2011, the airline had begun thinking about A320s or similar, to enable it to develop regional services. Late in 2014, Felix took delivery of its first ever B737-300, wet-leased from an Egyptian airline ('Yemen's Felix Airways takes delivery of first B737', ch-aviation.ch, 8 December 2014). Three months later, however, the airport runway at Sana was damaged in the course of military fighting ('Yemenia suspends operations indefinitely; Sana airport damaged', ch-aviation.ch, 30 March 2015). When accessed on 30 May 2015, the Yemenia website reported that its flights were suspended until further notice, while the Felix website did not give such notice.

3.7 Flydubai

On 19 March 2008, the government of Dubai announced it was starting a new, *low-cost* carrier that would be independent of Emirates Airline (also government-owned). However Emirates would provide some start-up assistance, and the first CEO, Ghaith al Ghaith, was to come from Emirates' management. On 14 July 2008, Boeing and the new airline (named Flydubai) announced an order for no less than 50 B737-800 aircraft, which aircraft it would operates in a dense, single-class layout with 189 seats. However all aircraft delivered since August 2013 have been configured with a business class cabin; most of the other aircraft have been retrofitted with business class seats (flydubai.com, accessed 30 May 2015).

Flydubai launched on 1 June 2009. By 9 June, it was flying to Beirut, Amman, Damascus and Alexandria. As pointed out by anna.aero ('Dubai launches new LCC . . .' 5 June 2009), Emirates, the national carrier launched by the Dubai government in 1985, already served the first three of those routes.

At the end of 2012, the Flydubai fleet (by then, some 28 aircraft) served a network of just over 50 ports, each linked to the Dubai hub by non-stop flights. Besides many nearby ports in the Arabian Peninsula, the network included ports at more distant cities such as Addis Ababa, Khartoum, Alexandria, Beirut, Istanbul, Belgrade, Kiev, Yekaterinburg, Kabul, Kathmandu, Dhaka, Chittagong, Hyderabad and Colombo.

That list helps to identify a major distinction between Flydubai and Emirates. At the end of 2012, Emirates operated a fleet of wide-body aircraft, serving 120 destinations, including many very large cities. Of course, Emirates is also a full-service airline, whereas Flydubai may now be described as a hybrid airline.

According to its airline website, accessed on 30 May 2015, Flydubai then operated more than 45 B737-800 aircraft, and flew to more than 90 destinations.

Ports added to the network in the three months of March to May 2015 were Quetta (Pakistan), Lar (Iran), Novosibirsk and Nizhniy Novgorod (Russia), Chennai (India), and Sylhet (Bangladesh). New ports in 2014 included Moscow Vnukovo, Bratislava, Prague and Sofia, and – in east Africa – Dar es Salaam and Zanzibar (Tanzania), Entebbe (Uganda) and Kigali (Rwanda).

Rapid expansion of a new airline usually requires owner-investors with deep pockets, able to fund the operating losses commonly experienced when starting each new route, and to finance the purchase of any fully-owned aircraft. As in the case of most start-up airlines, Flydubai seems to have incurred substantial initial financial deficits. However, in late 2011, its CEO was telling the media that it hoped to turn a profit in 2012 (Asa Fitch, 'Flydubai on course for profit', *The National* (Abu Dhabi), 28 October 2011; 'Flydubai edging towards profitability . . .', anna.aero, 23 April 2012). For 2014, Flydubai carried 7.25 million passengers, and 'reported a net profit of AED 250 million (US$68 million) an increase of 12.3% compared to 2013'; thus 2014 was 'the third consecutive full year' of profitability ('2014 sees flydubai achieve increased revenues of AED 4.4 billion up 19.1% and profits of AED 250 million', media release, flydubai.com, 3 March 2015).

3.8 Some conclusions

Most flights from and to ports within the region are on international routes; as such, each service requires bilateral agreement between the involved governments. While there are domestic routes within the larger countries, notably Saudi Arabia and Yemen, no government in the Arabian Peninsula has deregulated airline entry to its domestic air services market.

Nevertheless, the regulatory positions of the governments have not prevented considerable growth in airline services in the region (as summarised in Table 3.1 below). In granting new-airline licences, however, governments of the region have sometimes attempted to steer that growth –by offer of incentives and/or by direct administrative requirement.

In Kuwait, while Jazeera took up a role as a low-cost airline, the other entrant Wataniya was awarded exclusive passenger terminal facilities at The Sheikh Saad Terminal, Kuwait International Airport. This provided 'personalized check-in services, fast-track immigration procedures and exclusive lounges serving all our guests', to help Wataniya in its role as a full-service airline ('Our story', watinyaairways.com, accessed 30 March 2009).

Similarly, when Saudi Arabia granted licences for two airlines, it *required* that one company fly certain 'public service obligation' routes previously operated by the national carrier, and *required* that the other company (Sama) establish its base at Dammam. When Sama encountered financial troubles and ceased flying, the Saudi government then allowed the neighbouring carrier Bahrain Air to fly (Saudi) domestic routes from Dammam, and later allowed Felix Airways (owned by Yemen and Saudi investors) to take on that role.

Table 3.1 New airlines of the Arabian Peninsula: a summary

Airline	Domicile	Launch	Ownership	Cabin
Air Arabia	Sharjah emirate	Oct 2003	government, then private 2007	single
Jazeera	Kuwait	Oct 2005	private	dual
Flynas	Saudi Arabia	Feb 2007	private (initially Nas Air)	single, then dual in 2014
Sama	Saudi Arabia	Mar 2007	private, *closed* Aug 2010	single
Bahrain Air	Bahrain	Feb 2008	private; *closed* Feb 2013	single, dual from 2010
Felix	Yemen	Oct 2008	mainly private	single, apparently
Wataniya	Kuwait	Jan 2009	private; *closed* Mar 2011	dual
Flydubai	Dubai emirate	Jun 2009	government	single, dual from 2013

Sources: airline and other sources, as cited in the preceding sections

While most of the new carriers began with single (economy-class) aircraft cabins, they later sought to sell more expensive tickets to business travellers, by creating a second cabin.

Also noteworthy is how the general financial crisis greatly stressed the newly founded airlines. Sama, Wataniya and Bahrain Air all succumbed; Jazeera managed to survive by halving the size of the airline.

In contrast, the larger new airlines, Air Arabia (private, and launched well before the crisis) and Flydubai (government-owned, and launched towards the end of the crisis period), expanded at a great rate, and needed considerable capital injections to support their fast growth. Such a path is not available if the owners cannot or will not invest on that scale.

4   Asia

4.1 Introduction

Many Asian countries have long-established national carriers, and some of those companies have a considerable international presence. Besides India and China with their large surface areas and very large populations, some of the smaller states have sizeable domestic airline networks. Furthermore, in many parts of the region, neighbouring countries are close enough together to allow an airline equipped with modern short-haul aircraft – such as the Airbus A320 or the Boeing 737-700 or -800 – to operate non-stop services to many foreign ports. This has led many of the new airlines to develop *international* point-to-point networks.

While most of the old national carriers were government-owned, nearly all the new airlines have been started by private entrepreneurs. Where the initiative comes from an individual, it has been common in Asia (as elsewhere) for the new company to seek further capital, usually by listing on the national stock exchange. On the other hand, some of the largest and most important of the new airlines have been initiated (or befriended) by long-established conglomerates, who may supply start-up and expansion capital from their own (group) resources.

This chapter looks in turn at the more interesting developments in various countries, without attempting to catalogue all the new airlines.

4.2 Major budget carriers in the ASEAN countries

Of the ten countries in the Association of Southeast Asian Nations, six have notable levels of civil aviation activity; and there is budget-carrier presence in each of those six. In respect of *domestic* services, Indonesia has the largest number of passengers, though Malaysia is not far behind despite its *much* smaller population. Inbound tourism helps to give Thailand and the city-state of Singapore large numbers of *international* passengers. The following sub-sections look at major budget carriers domiciled in four of the ASEAN countries. As will be seen, some of those carriers have affiliated airlines domiciled in other ASEAN countries.

4.2.1 AirAsia in Malaysia, and its affiliates in other countries

In 2001, private investors bought a loss-making (Malaysian) company, and re-launched it as *AirAsia*; it claims to be the first *low-cost* airline in Asia. Having

Table 4.1 Operating statistics for the AirAsia group, 2014

Airlines	Launched	Passengers (millions)	ASK (billions)	RPK (billions)	Load factor[1] %	Number of aircraft[2]
AirAsia (Malaysia)	2001	22.1	34.6	27.3	78	81
Thai AirAsia	Feb 2004	12.2	15.4	12.4	80	40
Indonesia AirAsia	Dec 2004	7.9	11.7	9.2	78	30
Philippines AirAsia	Mar 2012	3.0	4.6	3.1	70	15
AirAsia India[3]	Jun 2014	0.3	0.3	0.2	80	3
AirAsia Group[4,5]		45.6	66.6	52.2	79	172

Source: Preliminary Operating Statistics, 2014, accessed at airasia.com

Notes
1 Revenue passenger load factors
2 Fleets generally comprise A320s only, and are counted at end of 2014.
3 For 2014, the data for AirAsia India are disclosed only for the third and fourth quarters.
4 The passenger total reveals a small rounding discrepancy, which is present in the source document.
5 The Group totals refer to the operations of the five airlines listed here.

inherited ageing B737-300 aircraft, the new management built up a fleet of 30 such aircraft, but then decided to switch to *new* A320s, almost all of which it has purchased directly from Airbus. Each is operated with a single cabin, of 180 seats.

The first A320 was delivered in December 2005. As further A320s arrived, the B737s were gradually withdrawn. AirAsia operated its A320s with an airport 'turn' of only 25 minutes, which supported aircraft utilisation of some 12 block hours per day; yet the airline also claims a good punctuality record ('About us', accessed at airasia.com, 8 March 2013).

Following early successful growth in Malaysia, AirAsia joined with local investors in Thailand and in Indonesia, to launch (respectively) *Thai AirAsia* and *Indonesia AirAsia*. In both cases, the local investors held 51 per cent of the shares, while the Malaysian company had 49 per cent. In each case, majority local owner-ship secured government acceptance of the company as being locally domiciled, and so permitted the airline to fly on both domestic and international routes of the country of domicile. Both airlines launched in 2004 (Table 4.1).

In 2012, AirAsia established two further affiliates. The first, *Philippines AirAsia*, launched at Manila (Clark) on 28 March. In general, the routes it entered were already served by other low-cost carriers. Its first two services were to domestic tourist destinations, and faced competition from AirPhil Express. Later in the year, it started international routes, and again faced competition. For example, when it launched a daily flight to Hong Kong on 19 July, the route was served by Dragonair (daily), Cebu Pacific (daily), SEAir/Tiger Airways (nine weekly) and AirPhil Express (four weekly) (anna.aero, 4 April and 26 July 2012).

Subsequent events suggest that the initial marketing by Philippines AirAsia may have lacked local insights. In March 2013, the company acquired a 49 per cent stake in Zest Air, a company with a strong domestic presence that complemented the regional links that AirAsia brought to the alliance. The new ownership structure and the ensuing hub and route rationalisation helped to increase passenger numbers and load factors for Philippines AirAsia (AirAsia, Annual Report 2013, pp. 119–20).

The second new affiliate, *AirAsia Japan*, launched on 1 August 2012, as a joint venture with the long-established All Nippon Airways (ANA). Again, this company was not a first mover. Rather, it entered the Japanese low-fare market at about the same time as a few other low-cost carriers. Its initial modest load-factors and sizeable financial deficits exposed some differences between the two owners in their policy judgements. The joint venture was dissolved in 2013. (ANA then relaunched the company as a subsidiary, on which see §4.4.2 below.) 'Despite this setback, we remain confident of the Japanese market and would like to be able to return here again in future' (AirAsia, Annual Report 2013, p. 101).

On 1 July 2014, AirAsia announced plans to form a new joint venture with no less than four Japanese companies in order to launch a new AirAsia Japan (media release 'AirAsia to re-enter Japan's low cost carrier market' 1 July 2014). Later news said the launch would be in 2016 (Jeremy Torr, 'AirAsia to restart services to Japan with revamped LCC', *Air Transport World*, 24 July 2015).

Meanwhile, in April 2013, the Foreign Investment Promotion Board of India approved the formation of *AirAsia India* as a tripartite joint venture with Tata Sons Limited together with another Indian investor. The details of the government permissions and the eventual launch are given in §4.3.5 below.

Growth of the AirAsia group

By 2008, AirAsia had become the largest domestic operator in Malaysia, then carrying 58 per cent of all domestic passengers. The group also did well in Thailand, where its domestic passenger share was 57 per cent in 2011. With three Thailand hubs, the airline increased connectivity in the local network, and so enabled many Thai passengers to make direct journeys, without change of aircraft in Bangkok (AirAsia, Annual Report 2011, pp. 112–14).

Initial difficulties in the much larger Indonesian market – where it carried only 8 per cent of domestic passengers in 2008 – resulted in a decision 'to refocus the business from mostly domestic to mostly international routes' (AirAsia, Annual Report 2009, p. 40). However, the Indonesian affiliate resumed domestic growth in 2011 (AirAsia, Annual Report 2011, pp. 116–18). In 2014, the unchanged fleet number was worked a little less than in 2013; the RPK total reduced marginally, and the load factor went up by two percentage points.

In the Philippines, early financial deficits discouraged further investment there. However, the merger with Zest allowed some decision-making that improved the situation. Three aircraft were taken from the fleet, RPKs increased more than the ASKs and the load factor increased by seven points.

While the Malaysian operation has been the most profitable, there has been some volatility in profits even there. In the ASEAN countries generally, the entry of other LCCs (considered below) is likely to make it harder for AirAsia to earn the high profit rates previously attained (CAPA, 'AirAsia's 2013 outlook marred by intensifying competition and continued losses at new affiliates', 5 March 2013).

On the other hand, AirAsia itself, and to some extent its affiliates, had the opportunity to benefit from the passenger transfer facilities included in the new (somewhat low-cost) KLIA2 terminal, opened at Kuala Lumpur in 2014 (and reported below in §12.4.4). At p. 101 of the *AirAsia Annual Report 2013*, the chairman noted the prospective move of AirAsia into that terminal, and commented that it 'will afford us the space and infrastructure to offer better and more exciting service'. (That may be a Delphic reference to AirAsia's prospects for building up the number of its *transfer* passengers at KL!)

4.2.2 Tiger Airways/Tigerair (Singapore)

Tiger Airways' founding shareholders were Singapore Airlines, Dahlia Investments Private Ltd (a subsidiary of Temasek Holdings), Indigo Partners LLC and Irelandia Investments. Singapore Airlines is government-owned, and Temasek is an investment vehicle of the Singapore government; Indigo is an American investment company, while Irelandia represents Tony Ryan (founder of Ryanair).

Because Singapore is a city-state, Tiger was unable to fly at all without route permissions granted by the governments of other countries. Its inaugural flight (in September 2004) was from Singapore to Bangkok (Thailand). Thereafter, the airline quickly established a Singapore-based network. By June 2015, the number of ports served from Singapore had reached 37 ('Tigerair story', accessed at tigerair.com, 1 June 2015).

Throughout, the overall Tiger strategy has been to seek *very* low operating costs to support its low fares. In particular, it chose to operate new A320s, acquired directly from Airbus, and configured in a one-class layout of 180 seats.

In January 2010, the parent company, Tiger Airways Holdings Limited, went to the market with an Initial Purchase Offer, and its shares became traded on the Singapore stock exchange. Following the IPO, the (reduced) holdings of the main shareholders were Singapore Airlines (34.4 per cent), Indigo Singapore Partners (15), RyanAsia (11.2), and Dahlia Investment Pte (7.7) ('Company overview' and 'Investor information', accessed at tigerairways.com, 23 December 2009 and 18 June 2010).

In the following years, Tiger encountered serious difficulties. In the year to 31 March 2011, it grew considerably in Singapore, with capacity (ASK) up 22 per cent and revenue up 28 per cent; this resulted in a modest profit before tax. However, the pilots in Singapore became unhappy with their situation, and in the next financial year, the pilot exodus was so great as to disrupt the intended flying programme. In addition, the subsidiary company in Australia (on which see §7.11) was grounded for a while by the safety regulator. The overall result was a large financial deficit for the holding company.

A new CEO was rewarded by *some* improvement in the Singapore operation in the financial year 2013. The trading name was then changed to Tigerair (Chairman's Statement, p. 3 of each of the Tiger Airways Holdings Limited Annual Reports for 2011, 2012 and 2013.

In the financial year ending 31 March 2014, Tigerair Singapore carried 5.1 million passengers, for a total of 9.3 billion RPK, both figures being about 16 per cent higher than in the previous year. However, the ASK rose about 25 per cent, and so the load factor declined from 84 to 78 per cent (Tiger Airways Holdings – Operating Statistics, issued 11 April 2014). The yield declined to 6.74 (Singapore) cents per RPK (from 7.47 cents in 2013), and the operating profit of SGD7 million in 2013 turned into an operating *loss* of SGD52 million in 2014.

Part of the Group's financial problem arose from an increase in the number of aircraft held in Singapore, thanks to delivery of five new A320s, and the return of two A319s from the Philippines' operation (considered below). This resulted in a Singapore fleet of 27 aircraft at the end of the 2014 year, compared with 20 in the previous year (Tiger Airways Holdings Limited, Annual Report 2014, p. 2 and pp. 6–8).

For the 2015 financial year, the operating loss was reduced to SGD40 million. In the fourth quarter of that year, the operating loss fell to SGD2.3 million, from SGD24.2 million in the previous fourth quarter (media release 'Turnaround efforts continue to bear fruit' 5 May 2015, tigerair.com).

Tigerair affiliates in other countries

After operating flights from Singapore to a few ports in *Australia*, the holding company sought permission from the Australian government to fly *domestic* routes. This was granted in 2007, when Tiger Airways established a separate operating company domiciled in Australia. The Australian operation became a major financial burden on the Singapore parent; for the details, see §7.11. Eventually, it was sold to Virgin Australia.

In the *Philippines*, the Tiger group took a 40 per cent share in a local airline, which took on the brand name Tigerair Philippines. This too brought Tiger some financial problems. In March 2014, Tiger sold that stake to Cebu Pacific (Tiger Airways Holdings Limited, Annual Report 2014, p. 9). (Cebu Pacific is a successful LCC domiciled in the Philippines; see §4.2.4 below.)

In *Indonesia*, the Tiger holding group invested some funds in helping Mandala Airlines to resume flying in 2012. However this too led to some financial difficulties. The details are reported below in the next section.

4.2.3 Some new airlines in Indonesia

With its very large population, spread over several large and some other islands, Indonesia has a large and important aviation sector. Yet, at one stage, its poor safety record resulted in the EC banning *all* Indonesian airlines from EU airspace. When the EC revisited that issue, it exempted from the ban just two Indonesian (passenger) airlines: the national flag-carrier *Garuda*, and *Mandala Airlines* (European Commission, 'List of airlines banned from EU airspace', 30 March 2010). This section looks at Mandala and also at a very large newcomer, *Lion Air*.

Mandala Airlines

Founded in 1967 (with military origins), Mandala acquired new owners in 2006, when an Indonesian aviation enterprise Cardig International bought the company outright, and then sold 49 per cent of the shares to the American investment firm Indigo Partners. The new management (with Warwick Brady, formerly of Ryanair, as the first CEO) emphasised safety and on-time operation, and switched to A319 and A320 aircraft, with 144 and 180 seats respectively ('About Mandala', Mandala Airlines website, accessed 31 March 2009).

At that stage, Mandala flew eight Airbus aircraft. A year later, it became 'the first privately owned Indonesian airline to achieve IOSA registration', a safety certification awarded by IATA (Mandala media release, 'Mandala receives IOSA safety registration', 26 March 2010).

Mandala's continuing expansion exposed the company to considerable competition on some dense routes. In August 2010, on its busiest domestic route, Jakarta to Surabaya, Mandala offered 20 flights weekly in each direction, but faced competition from *five* other airlines who offered a total of 257 weekly flights each way. On a busy international route, Jakarta – Singapore, Mandala flew once daily, while *eight* other airlines offered a total of 220 weekly flights ('Indonesia's Mandala goes international to Singapore, Hong Kong and Macau', anna.aero, 1 September 2010).

On 13 January 2011, being unable to pay debts, the company ceased flying, and sought court protection (akin to the Chapter 11 provisions in the US), while it tried to find new investors. Eight months later Mandala announced a conditional arrangement: an Indonesian investment firm, Saratoga Group, was to hold 51 per cent of the shares as the financial investor, while Tiger Airways (Singapore) was to have 33 per cent as the strategic investor (that is, the owner managing the company's operations); the previous investors were to hold the rest (Esther Samboh, 'Mandala aims to fly as soon as acquisition is finally closed', *The Jakarta Post*, 26 September 2011).

Even then, another seven months passed before Tiger Airways Holdings announced in Singapore (media release, 'Revitalised Mandala takes to the skies!') that Mandala would resume flying on 5 April 2012. While the Mandala name would remain, bookings were to be handled on the Tiger Airways website; in effect, Mandala was to become Tiger's affiliate in Indonesia (Centre for Asia Pacific Aviation, 'Tiger-backed Mandala resumes operations with focus on Indonesia's largest routes', 5 April, 2012).

Further financial troubles became manifest early in 2014. In response to excessive capacity in the Indonesian market, Tigerair Mandala cut about 30 per cent from its ASKs flown, leaving its (then) nine A320s flying for less than nine hours per day (CAPA, 'Tigerair Mandala slashes capacity and aircraft utilisation levels: will other Asian LCCs follow?', 19 February 2014).

Evidently that response proved to be an insufficient. In June, the Tigerair Mandala board announced that the company would suspend operations from 1 July 2014 (CAPA, 'Tigerair Mandala suspension begins needed consolidation to

Indonesian & Southeast Asian LCC sectors', 20 June 2014). Thus Mandala's superior safety standards did not secure it a place in the Indonesian aviation sector.

Lion Air and its affiliates

This privately owned carrier began service in 2000, and has become by far the largest low-fare operator on domestic routes in Indonesia. It was the launch customer for the B737-900 model, which can carry up to 220 passengers in a single-class layout. After receiving a first B737-900 in April 2007, the Lion fleet in mid-2015 included 71 such aircraft, together with 30 B737-800s (ch-aviation. ch, accessed 1 June 2015).

As the fleet numbers imply, Lion's passenger numbers grew at a remarkable rate, often exceeding ten per cent per annum, and sometimes considerably exceeding that figure. The company's growth has been driven by its low fares, supported by a determined drive for low costs in general. Lion was rated as the fifth-largest LCC in the world, measured by the number of passengers carried ('Fast-growing Lion Air close to offering 1m seats per week', anna.aero, 23 July 2014; the four larger carriers were Southwest Airlines, Ryanair, EasyJet and GOL. That last is a new Brazilian airline, introduced here in §5.6.2.) Lion then served about 50 domestic ports, and also operated several international routes.

The very great success enjoyed by Lion Air has come notwithstanding some blemishes on its safety record. The 11 December 2014 revision of the EU list (published in accordance with Regulation (EC) No 2111/2005) shows that Lion Mentari Airlines was then still among the Indonesian airlines banned from flying in European airspace.

In addition, in March 2015, the Indonesian Director General of Civil Aviation was reported to have reprimanded Lion for extensive flight delays during a few days in February 2015, and to have imposed a ban on granting any further route permits to Lion until that company met certain conditions ('Indonesian regulator reprimands Lion Air for excess flight delays', ch-aviation.ch, 2 March 2015).

Lion has also begun to explore what has become the common strategy of a successful new carrier in Asia, namely the establishment of affiliated airlines. With AirAsia operating an affiliate in Indonesia, Lion took a 49 per cent stake in a joint venture with a Malaysian company (National Aerospace and Defence Industries) to establish a new hybrid airline, *Malindo Air*, based in Kuala Lumpur and launched in March 2013.

Malindo operates both turboprops and jets; by June 2015, its rapidly growing fleet comprised 11 × ATR 72-600s, 2 × B737-800s and 6 × B737-900s. Unusually, its base is dispersed over two airports. The jets fly (mostly) international routes from Kuala Lumpur International Airport. The turboprops fly local (mainly domestic) routes from the old Subang Airport, which is relatively close to the Kuala Lumpur downtown and gives less costly access. On the routes flown by jet aircraft, Malindo offers both economy and business class.

Lion's other initiative has been to start a wholly owned full-service carrier in Indonesia. *Batik Air* launched in May 2013, operating B737-900s sourced from an order placed by Lion. While initially focussing on domestic routes, especially the longer routes from Jakarta to eastern Indonesia, Batik was intended later to fly international services as well (CAPA, 'Lion Air full-service subsidiary Batik Air to expand with A320s, 787s and new base at Jakarta Halim', 23 September 2013).

In late 2014, the Lion group received the first three A320s from its order for a very large number of A320 family aircraft, and these were assigned to Batik (Linda Blachly, 'Lion Group takes delivery of first three A320s', *Air Transport World*, 12 November 2014). The pace of Batik's expansion is strikingly indicated by its further fleet growth. In June 2015, Batik operated $7 \times$ A320s, $13 \times$ B737-800s and $6 \times$ B737-900s (ch-aviation.ch, accessed on 2 June 2015).

4.2.4 Cebu Pacific (Philippines)

Though incorporated in 1988, it was only in 1991 that Cebu Pacific received government permission to operate international and domestic air transport services. It began scheduled (domestic) passenger services in 1996, with an inaugural flight between Manila and Cebu, its first base. Official status as a Philippines carrier – giving it permission to fly international routes – came in 1997. After its modest beginnings, the airline was purchased by J G Summit Holdings, an important Philippines conglomerate. It began international services in November 2001 (Cebu Air Inc., Annual Report 2010, p. 1). In 2005, it formally adopted a LCC business model.

In 2010, an Initial Purchase Offer for about 30 per cent of the outstanding shares resulted in J G Summit Holdings retaining ownership of about 68 per cent of the shares; a majority of the other shares passed into foreign ownership; Philippines' law requires that Filipino citizens hold at least 60 per cent of the shares (Annual Report 2010, pp. 17 and 40).

Cebu Pacific gradually acquired (new) Airbus jets to replace the initial fleet of ageing and thirsty DC9 aircraft. By March 2009, the jet fleet comprised 10 A319s and 11 A320s (Cebu media release, 10 March 2009). It had also built up a fleet of eight ATR72-500 turboprops, which operate on the modest runways found at many domestic ports that attract tourist travel (media release, 3 March 2009).

After a pause occasioned by the difficult general economic conditions, Cebu announced (media release, 22 April 2010) it had ordered 22 more A320s, for delivery between October 2010 and the end of 2014. Besides its eight turboprops, the Cebu fleet in June 2015 comprised 10 A319 aircraft, 31 A320s and also 6 (leased) A330s, each with more than 400 seats in an all-economy layout (!) (cebupacificair.com, accessed 3 June 2015; Annual Report 2014, p. 1).

At the end of 2014, Cebu Pacific served 57 domestic and 37 international routes, and operated some 2650 flights per week (Annual Report 2014, p. 1). While the airline still has an important hub at Cebu, its main base is now at the Ninoy Aquino International Airport (Manila), where it moved all its flights into the (then) new Terminal 3 (media release, 9 September 2008).

Cebu's passenger numbers have grown remarkably. In 2014, it carried some 11.1 million domestic and 3.2 million international passengers. On domestic routes, it then carried about 54 per cent of all the passengers (Philippines Civil Aeronautics Board, 'Domestic scheduled passenger traffic', cab.gov.ph, accessed 3 June 2015).

Of course, traffic increases do not guarantee profitability. Indeed, for 2008, Cebu incurred a deficit of P$3.3 billion in net income after tax. Yet, in the next five years, it earned profits of (respectively) P$3.3, 6.9, 3.6, 3.6 and 0.5 billion.

That last figure, for 2013, reflects a difficult year for domestic airline service in the Philippines. At one stage there were six airlines flying on Philippines domestic routes: Zest, AirAsia, Cebu Pacific, Tigerair Philippines, Philippines Airlines (the long-serving national carrier) and PAL Express (a subsidiary of the national carrier).

There followed a marked consolidation: as reported above, AirAsia merged its Philippines affiliate with Zest; in March 2014, Cebu Pacific purchased all the shares in Tigerair Philippines (including the 40 per cent stake of Tiger Airways Holdings) (Cebu Pacific, 1Q2014 Investor Presentation, 20 May 2014); and PAL Express became a full-service airline, and took over almost all the domestic routes previously flown by its owner, Philippines Airlines (CAPA, 'Cebu Pacific domestic outlook brightens . . .' 30 April 2015).

The consolidation reduced the competitive pressures. In particular, Cebu Pacific soon secured benefits from its purchase of Tigerair Philippines, after a fleet rationalisation that reduced costs, and some route network adjustments. In the 2014 outcome (compared with 2013), the passenger total increased 17.5 per cent, and the load factor rose three percentage points to 83.9 per cent. The domestic-market passenger share increased to 60.8 per cent, though on-time performance was only 73 per cent. Net income rose 67 per cent, though the net income margin was only 1.6 per cent (Cebu Air, Annual Stockholders' Briefing, 24 June 2015).

Looking to the future, Cebu ordered sixteen ATR 72-600 turboprops, with delivery staring in 2016. Earlier it had ordered no fewer than 30 Airbus A321neo aircraft, for delivery between 2017 and 2021. Fitted with 220 seats, these longer-range aircraft 'will enable the Company to serve cities in Australia, India and Northern Japan, places the A320 cannot reach' (Annual Report 2012, p. 3). (Older UK readers may recall an advertising campaign for a boutique beer.)

4.2.5 The Jetstar Group (outside Australia)

In Australia, Qantas launched Jetstar in 2004 as a low-fare fighting brand, intended to curb the domestic expansion of Virgin Blue; for the details, see §7.9. Qantas soon arranged for Jetstar to start serving routes between Australia and Asia. It also set up a joint-venture airline in Singapore.

Indeed, in 2004, Singapore hosted the launch of no less than three budget carriers: Valuair in May, Tiger Airways in September, and Jetstar Asia in December (Civil Aviation Authority of Singapore, media release, 13 December 2004; Ng Boon Yian, 'Clearing Asia's crowded skies', *Asia Times*, 27 July 2005). (The Singapore government required majority Singaporean ownership for each such airline.)

Jetstar Asia

At the outset, Qantas held 49 per cent of the shares, the Singapore government's Temasek investment company held 19 per cent, and two local businessmen held the balance between them. (Later, the 51 per cent of shares owned in Singapore were redistributed, as shown in Table 4.2, below.) Jetstar Asia started with services to distant ports, including Hong Kong, Taipei and Manila. Its (new) A320s each had 180 seats.

In its early years, Jetstar Asia struggled to make profits. The outcomes improved after a 2009 adjustment in which Qantas increased its share-holding to 49 per cent, and Newstar Investment bought out the other Singaporean owners, aiming to strengthen the management (Matt O'Sullivan, 'Budget airline reverses losses', *Sydney Morning Herald*, 7 February 2011).

Valuair

Valuair chose to offer a relatively high service quality (for a budget airline): it had a seat pitch of 30 inches, included meal service in the price of the ticket and assigned seats before boarding. It received Indonesian government permission to fly to Indonesian ports, including Jakarta; it also started routes to other ports, including Bangkok. However, it was soon in financial trouble, and its founders apparently did not have deep pockets.

Table 4.2 Company ownership and fleet numbers, Jetstar group, November 2014

Airline:	Jetstar[1]	Jetstar Asia[2]	Jetstar Pacific	Jetstar Japan	Jetstar HK[3]
Launch date	May 2004	Dec 2004	May 2008	Jul 2012	(stalled)
Qantas-owned shares (%)	100	49	30	45.7	24.5
Other share-holders (%)	–	Newstar 51	Vietnam Airlines	JAL & others	Shun Tak 51 China Eastern 24.5
Aircraft types and fleet numbers					
A320 (180 seats)	54	18	5	18	
A321 (220 seats)	6				
A330 (c. 300 seats[4])	4				
B787-8 (21 bus./ 314 Y)	7				

Sources: Jetstar 'Our fleet', accessed at *www.jetstar.com* 18 November 2014; Jamie Freed 'Qantas moves closer to Hong Kong Jetstar remedy' *Sydney Morning Herald* August 31, 2014

Notes
1 Though domiciled in Australia, Jetstar also serves domestic routes in New Zealand.
2 These share holdings in place from March 2009, after a change intended to strengthen management.
3 The ownership figures are those applying *after* the partners had adjusted their shares, in an attempt to assure all that control of the airline would rest with the parties domiciled in Hong Kong and China. In November 2014, the HK government had yet to decide whether to give regulatory approval.
4 Each A330 has a business-class cabin, with about 40 seats.

Seeking help, Valuair started talks with Jetstar Asia, and in July 2005, the two airlines merged. Because Jetstar Asia had not received government permission to serve Indonesian ports, the Indonesian services were still branded as Valuair flights ('Jetstar and Valuair merge as fuel prices, competition bite', *Straits Times*, 25 July 2005). The Indonesian flights were operated by Jetstar crews, and the Jetstar Asia service standards applied, rather than the more generous standards previously offered by Valuair.

The nominal branding arrangement persisted for many years, with Jetstar Asia increasing the number of ports it served in Indonesia, and increasing some flight frequencies. Finally, the Indonesian government relaxed some restrictions on the operation of further LCCs ('Jetstar Asia takes over Valuair flights to Indonesia', Channel NewsAsia (Singapore), 24 October 2014). On 26 October 2014, Jetstar Asia began operating Indonesian flights under its own name.

Jetstar Pacific Airlines

In 2008, a Vietnamese company Pacific Airlines (founded in 1991) held talks with Qantas, resulting in the establishment of a new company, with the shares held by State Capital Investment Corporation, Qantas, Saigon Tourist and Mr Luong Hoai Nam (the CEO of the company). Initially Qantas held 18 per cent of the shares, with this set to increase to 30 per cent in 2010. Qantas took two positions on the six-person board, and also arranged for a number of its managers to take senior positions in the new company (Jetstar media release, 14 April 2008).

Under a new brand name – *Jetstar Pacific Airlines* – the new company launched on 23 May 2008, still using the previous fleet of four ageing B737-400 aircraft. By 2010, the company had made only limited progress; and there were reports suggesting that relations between the Vietnamese government and the company management had become strained (Tom Allard and Matt O'Sullivan, 'Vietnam promise turns to mayhem', *Sydney Morning Herald*, 15 January 2010; 'Vietnam's airports see traffic quadruple in last 10 years; few European airlines present', anna.aero, 15 January 2010).

Eventually, the locally held shares passed to Vietnam Airlines. By 2013, the company fortunes had improved sufficiently to permit Jetstar Pacific to retire its ageing Boeings, and operate an A320 fleet of five aircraft (Table 4.2).

Qantas launched *Jetstar Japan* in 2012; for some details, see §4.4.2 below. Also in 2012, Qantas announced it planned to launch *Jetstar Hong Kong*, for which it acquired some new A320s before the company had obtained an air operator certificate from the Hong Kong government. In its initial form, the airline was reported to be an equal-shares joint venture between Qantas and China Eastern. In June that year, Hong Kong investor Shun Tak Holdings took a one-third share. After reading the tea leaves, the joint venture partners later agreed that Shun Tak would become the majority investor, as shown in Table 4.2.

As early as September 2012, Cathay Pacific Airways and Hong Kong Airlines had filed objections to the Jetstar Hong Kong application for an operator certificate.

In the outcome, it was June 2015 before the HK Air Transport Licensing Authority announced its decision, which was to refuse the application, apparently because it considered that control of the airline would be exercised from Australia and mainland China, while the Hong Kong legislation required that the principal place of business be in Hong Kong itself (Jamie Freed, 'Jetstar Hong Kong shows signs of stalling as new aircraft selloff considered', *Sydney Morning Herald*, 7 July 2014; Karen Walker, 'Hong Kong denies Qantas' LCC Jetstar application', *Air Transport World*, 25 June 2015). Qantas then announced it would not provide any further funding for Jetstar Hong Kong (Jeremy Torr, 'Qantas to pull out of Jetstar Hong Kong', *Air Transport World*, 25 August 2015).

4.3 The rapid growth of air travel in India

4.3.1 Introduction

For several decades, strict government control of civil aviation resulted in a rather limited development of domestic airline services. The two significant carriers were both government-owned: Air India, long designated as the national flag carrier on international routes; and Indian Airlines, a domestic airline formed in 1953 by nationalisation of eight small domestic carriers. Besides the usual issues of low labour productivity, high costs and high fares, the two airlines faced bureaucratic delays in getting permission to purchase and import new aircraft. Further, the government required Indian Airlines to provide service on some regional routes where there was insufficient traffic to allow that company to cover its costs. Supposedly, those routes were to be cross-subsidised by the profits earned on routes between the major cities such as Bombay, New Delhi, Madras and Calcutta.

Those handicaps resulted in serious shortcomings in the industry's performance (O'Connell and Williams, 2006). Travel on the domestic airline network grew slowly; and foreign airlines carried rather more than half the travel on international routes. Despite the obstacles, however, the 1990s saw entry by two significant privately owned airlines, Air Sahara (launched in 1991) and Jet Airways (1993).

Later still, in 2003, the Ministry of Civil Aviation commissioned an in-house report, which proposed several changes:

- liberalisation of entry and operational requirements;
- reform of taxes and government charges;
- subsidies for the operation of non-commercial regional routes;
- privatisation of the two national carriers;
- privatisation of airports; and
- economic regulation to deal especially with improper use of airline market power.

The government accepted *some* of these proposals, and the aviation sector became better able to serve the increasing numbers of people who wanted to travel by air and who had the financial means to do so when the airlines offered efficient services at reasonable prices.

4.3.2 The new privately owned airlines

Several privately owned airlines launched on Indian domestic routes, mainly within the five year period ending in 2010. Some of the new airlines were initiated by conglomerates. With no market for *direct* investment in such airlines, there is little or no legal obligation for a conglomerate to publish disaggregated data for its airline; that handicaps public discussion of the performance of those airlines.

Jet Airways

After private investors had funded its launch in May 1993, *Jet Airways* became a public company in March 2005, through an Initial Purchase Offer for its shares. In 2007, it bought the long-established Air Sahara. That subsidiary was then renamed *Jet Lite*, to signal a (separate) low-fare operation. At the end of March 2014, the company operated nine A330s, 49 B 737-700/800/900 aircraft and five B777s, together with 15 ATR-500 and three ATR-600 turboprops (Jet Airways, Annual Report 2014, p. 16). Its network then comprised 56 domestic ports (including those served only by Jet Lite), and 20 international ports. Yet the company incurred a substantial financial loss in 2013, and a much larger loss in 2014 (Jet Airways, Annual Report 2014, p. 53).

Air Deccan

Founded by G R Gopinath, *Air Deccan* began operations in 2003. It was the first of a number of low-cost carriers that sought to encourage middle-class travellers to switch from Indian Railways. It began with a single turbo-prop aircraft (an ATR42) and very modest funding, relative to the needs of start-up airlines. Nevertheless, it expanded very rapidly, with early funding from private equity firms, and (later) the proceeds from an Initial Purchase Offer of company shares. It also secured improved managerial performance following a recruitment drive that brought in experienced European managers (Pandit, 2007). Even so, profitability proved to be elusive, and this led to a merger, as noted below.

Kingfisher Airlines

Founded by Dr Vijay Mallya, Chairman of the UB Group (Kingfisher media release, 25 April 2005), *Kingfisher Airlines* launched from a base in Mumbai, as a wholly owned subsidiary of United Breweries Holdings Limited (a very large Indian conglomerate that sells Kingfisher beer among its other brands).

For the inaugural flight in May 2005, it operated a brand-new A320, configured with 174 seats. In a remarkably rapid expansion, Kingfisher acquired various A320 family aircraft, mostly configured with two cabins to accommodate

Kingfisher First and Kingfisher Class (economy) passengers, and some turboprop aircraft for its minor routes. The independent airline monitor Skytrax awarded Kingfisher five-star status for its customer service (Kingfisher media release, 4 March 2008).

Despite all these successes, Kingfisher too was not making profits. Mallya and Air Deccan's Gopinath eventually agreed to merge the two airlines, albeit with two brands: Kingfisher, for the principal two-class services, and Kingfisher Red for a budget operation, based mainly on what had previously been the Air Deccan services to smaller ports (Pandit, 2008; Kingfisher Airlines, Annual Report 2007–08).

By September 2009, Kingfisher operated 24 A320 aircraft, each with either 180 seats (Kingfisher Red) or 134 seats, and eight A321s (199 or 151 seats), together with 27 ATR 72 turboprops (66/72 seats) which it deployed on regional routes. Another sizeable operation, and yet . . .

SpiceJet

Offering low fare services from the time of its launch in May 2005 ('About us', spicejet.com, accessed 15 June 2009), *SpiceJet* is a publicly listed company, whose shares are widely held. It chose to use high-density seating in its Boeing NG aircraft, namely the B737-900 with 212 seats and the B737-800 with 189 seats. In March 2014, it operated 58 aircraft.

Given its low-cost approach, the airline had the common experience of losing money for several years after its start. Worse still, after a small profit in the financial year to March 2011, it reported losses in 2012, 2013 and 2014. Although operating revenue increased each year, the net losses were (about) 15 per cent, 3 per cent and 15 per cent of the respective operating revenues (SpiceJet, Annual Report 2013–14, pp. 32 and 44).

The management responded by increasing the number of premium seats (with 35 inch seat pitch), adjusting the list of routes flown, making other marketing changes, and postponing the purchase of further aircraft, while seeking to get more ASK (available seat kilometres) from the existing fleet (Annual Report 2013–14, pp. 31 and 36–7).

In the first quarter of the following financial year, it claimed unchanged revenue despite an eight per cent reduction in offered capacity, thanks to a higher load factor and improved yield (SpiceJet Q1 – FY15 Investor Presentation, p. 13). For the second quarter, there seems to have been a change in the capacity strategy: 'SpiceJet's revenue increased 15% year-over-year, well ahead of capacity (ASK) increase of 7%' (SpiceJet Announces Q2FY15 Results, 15 November 2014, p. 1).

However, the airline was still losing money. In the financial year ending 31 March 2015, the net loss was reduced by about 31 per cent from that of the previous year, but remained substantial (SpiceJet, 'Statement of audited financial results for the quarter and year ended March 31 2015', 28 May 2015).

In mid-January 2015, SpiceJet was reported as saying that Ajay Singh (who helped found SpiceJet) had agreed, subject to regulatory approval, to buy a controlling stake in SpiceJet from Sun Group. Singh's stated intention was to dispose of the turboprop fleet, use a reduced B737 fleet to serve only the routes between major cities, and maintain only a lean workforce. He thought SpiceJet could return to profitability in the following financial year. That report lifted SpiceJet's share price quite significantly (Reuters, 'India carrier SpiceJet's new owners plan to cut fleet, shrink network', 16 January 2015).

Three months later, JP Morgan Chase was reported as offering an equity-led buyout. Singh rebuffed the approach, reportedly saying that if further capital were needed, that could come from local investors, once the stock-market valuation of the airline had recovered (Jeremy Torr, 'Indian LCC SpiceJet cool on bailout', *Air Transport World*, 28 April 2015).

IndiGo Airlines

Launched in August 2006, *IndiGo Airlines* is a part of InterGlobe Enterprises, a privately owned Indian conglomerate that was established in 1989, and is focused on travel and hospitality. The airline was funded by internal group equity and external debt financing. The first CEO was Bruce Ashby, who came to the airline (for a three-year term) after serving as a senior manager at US Airways. It offers a single fare type, though it recently introduced a Family Fare at lower rates, available on selected routes and flights, for a family booking (made on a single passenger number (PNR) for a group of four to nine people.

IndiGo operates a fleet of new A320s, each with 180 seats. By November 2014, it had 84 aircraft, served 31 domestic ports and 5 international destinations, and operated almost 550 flights daily. It particularly emphasises on-time performance. IndiGo has grown very quickly, with annual growth rates (in the usual metrics) in excess of 20 per cent, though the *percentage* rate has begun to slow as the airline has become larger. IndiGo began service on international routes in 2011, after the five years of domestic operation required by the Indian government (see media release, 17 November 2014, goindigo.in; 'About' statements there and at interglobe.com, both accessed 20 November 2014; 'IndiGo passes 70 million passengers; India's #1 domestic airline still growing at 20% per annum', anna.aero, 5 February 2014).

GoAir

GoAir is owned by the Wadia Group, a conglomerate dating from the nineteenth century. It too flies A320 aircraft, each with 180 seats, and serves both major cities and leisure destinations in India. After launching in November 2005, it grew at a modest pace, operating only nine aircraft four years later. In May 2014, its fleet of 19 aircraft averaged about 140 flights daily, and served some 22 ports in India. (At that date, GoAir still had not taken up the opportunity to serve international routes.)

GoAir offers spacious business class in the first three rows of its cabins; for such travel, the fare is generally about twice the lowest economy class fare.

It claims that its on-time performance and its reliability have helped it to obtain reasonable load factors ('About us', accessed at goair.in, 20 November 2014).

Paramount Airways

Based in Chennai (the home of Paramount Textiles), *Paramount Airways* began operations in October 2005, flying several (leased) Embraer jets in south and east India. It earned *operating* profits starting in 2006–7. The company became involved in a legal dispute with its aircraft lessors, who repossessed the aircraft. Flying operations ceased in August 2010 (Wikipedia entry on Paramount Airways, accessed 19 November 2014; Directorate General of Civil Aviation, 'Air Transport Statistics for the year 2010–11', Tables 2.11 and 2.52, accessed 25 February 2013).

4.3.3 The performance of scheduled domestic services

Since 2001, the number of passengers flown on Indian domestic scheduled services has increased very markedly. In that year, the group of government-owned airlines and the (then) set of privately owned airlines each carried about 6.5 million passengers. Thereafter the passenger total for the government airlines increased modestly, reaching 9 million in 2011. In contrast, the privately owned airlines carried 51 million passengers in 2011 – though there was then a small decline in the following two years (Directorate General of Civil Aviation, Indian Air Transport Statistics, accessed at dgca.nic.in).

For the more recent years, Table 4.3 reports the passenger numbers and load factors of the individual airlines. While most of the private airlines grew strongly, there is considerable variation between them in the extent – and, even, in the timing – of that growth. Furthermore, the load factors differed significantly between airlines. After the difficult year of 2009, most of the load factors increased, but still were not very high by international standards. Initially, the government-owned airlines had low load factors but these increased over the period. (Of course, airlines that target business travel usually have lower load factors; and for minor routes, the case for reasonable frequency often lowers the load factor.) The private airlines also had the better record for flight cancellations and punctuality, according to fragmentary data in the DGCA Indian Air Transport Statistics (accessed on 2 March 2013).

However, the privately owned airlines companies did have their troubles. One remarkable feature of the domestic market is the large number of airlines competing on major routes. In its report 'Is India's domestic market too competitive to be profitable?' (14 December 2011), anna.aero notes that, if you count Jet Airways and Jet Lite as separate carriers, the seven domestic carriers each carried between 6 and 20 per cent of the passengers flying on domestic routes in October 2011. After analysing Official Airline Guide data for early December, anna.aero noted six major routes on which all seven carriers competed. While many thin routes were served only by a single airline, it found only five city-pair monopoly routes having two flights per day.

Table 4.3 Outputs of individual Indian airlines, scheduled domestic services, 2009–14

(a) Number of passengers carried per year (millions)

Airline	2009	2010	2011	2012	2013	2014
GoAir	2.06	3.09	3.72	4.21	4.39	6.20
IndiGo	6.10	8.50	11.83	14.77	15.69	21.43
Jet Airways	7.79	9.72	11.06	11.76	11.35	11.71
Jet Lite	3.28	3.86	4.63	4.06	3.83	2.92
Kingfisher (closed Sep 2013)	10.51	10.66	10.92	2.61	1.21	–
Paramount (closed Aug 2010)	0.83	0.24	–	–	–	–
SpiceJet	5.45	6.72	8.76	10.61	11.11	11.75
Total for private airlines	36.02	42.79	50.91	48.02	47.57	54.60
Air India (and other national airlines)	7.20	8.62	8.98	9.76	10.68	11.84
All airlines	43.34	51.64	59.87	57.78	58.25	66.44

(b) Revenue passenger load factors (per cent)

	2009	2010	2011	2012	2013	2014
GoAir	77.1	77.9	77.7	75.7	75.1	76.9
IndiGo	78.8	83.8	83.3	80.5	80.8	76.9
Jet Airways	69.5	75.2	73.8	73.2	72.6	74.0
Jet Lite	73.1	78.8	77.6	75.8	74.7	76.5
Kingfisher (closed Sep 2013)	70.6	80.7	81.1	68.4	64.0	–
Paramount (closed Aug 2010)	85.8	86.3	–	–	–	–
SpiceJet	74.8	81.3	75.8	73.8	74.4	78.4
Air India (and other national airlines[1])	57.1	63.7	62.2	66.4	71.1	74.9

Source: Directorate General of Civil Aviation (India), Air Transport Statistics (dgca.nic.in)

Note
1 Estimated from DGCA data.

Besides the fare competition on dense routes, fuel costs have been a particular financial burden in India, especially because of a sales tax on Air Turbine Fuel, levied by the individual states, at rates that range between 4 and 32 per cent. In 2012, the (Indian) government granted permission to four airlines – SpiceJet, IndiGo, Air India and Kingfisher Airlines – to directly import fuel, a remarkably discriminatory arrangement intended to allow those companies to avoid paying the sales tax. However, none of those airlines was able to set up a physical distribution network ('Economic survey 2013: rationalise taxes, introduce fair pricing regime on ATF', *The Times of India*, 27 February 2013).

4.3.4 *The demise of Kingfisher Airlines*

Given that many of the airlines were so recently established, it is unsurprising that not all have survived. That Kingfisher succumbed was perhaps less foreseeable, especially because it had one of the larger fleets, and a few years' more experience than some of the other companies. As seen in Table 4.3 (which reports Jet Airways and Jet Lite as two separate carriers), Kingfisher carried more domestic passengers in 2009 than any of the other airlines, though that lead diminished in 2010. In 2011, with total Indian traffic growing, Kingfisher still managed a small increase in passenger numbers; but by then it was no longer the largest on that (or any other) metric.

Kingfisher's problem was that successive unprofitable years had left the airline in debt, while (seemingly) its conglomerate owner was unwilling to give more support. At times, some Kingfisher staff went unpaid, resulting in some not reporting for work, and flights being cancelled (Airwise/Reuters, 'Kingfisher cancels 41 flights on staff absence', 14 July 2012).

On 20 October 2012, the company acknowledged that the DGCA had suspended the airline's operating licence, thereby grounding the airline (which in fact had already stopped flying). And *The Times of India* ('Government withdraws all international flying rights and domestic slots from Kingfisher Airlines', 26 February 2013) said that the government had 'decided to take away these rights to free them up for use by other carriers'. The newspaper judged that this action signalled the end for Kingfisher Airlines.

4.3.5 Foreign direct investment in airlines in India

In 2009, when the general financial crisis had severely damaged the financial position of the local carriers, the Indian government gave thought to relaxing the constraints on foreign investment in Indian airlines. At that time, foreign *financial* investors were allowed to hold up to 49 per cent of the shares, but foreign *airlines* were not allowed to take direct stakes that might give them effective managerial control (Nitin Luthra, 'India looks to ease airline investment limits', *Wall Street Journal*, 28 May 2009; Cuckoo Paul, 'LCC dogfight over India', *Air Transport World*, 1 May 2010). Legislative change did not come until September 2012, when the Indian government decided to allow foreign airlines to take a direct stake not exceeding 49 per cent of the shares.

Soon, Etihad began negotiations with Jet Airways (Centre for Asia-Pacific Aviation, 'Etihad's potential investment in Jet Airways to be a game-changer for India', 2 February 2013). In the outcome, the government granted approval for Etihad to acquire a 24 per cent equity stake in Jet Airways, whose chairman noted (Jet Airways, Annual Report 2014, p. 2) 'This partnership between the two airlines will be mutually beneficial across all areas, including network growth, revenue enhancement, operational synergies and cost improvement.'

The new government policy also had the effect of encouraging foreign airlines to consider setting up *new* airlines in India, which the foreigners might effectively manage and control notwithstanding the shareholding limit. The Malaysian-based AirAsia soon proposed to join with Tata Sons and another Indian investor to establish yet another of its airline affiliates (Anirban Chowdhury, 'Tata Group charts return to the skies', *Wall Street Journal India*, 21 February 2013). (Tata is a famous and important Indian conglomerate, now returning to aviation after an earlier era. In 1932, J D Tata launched Tata Aviation, the first airline in India. In 1953, that company was taken over by the government, and renamed Air India.)

The new venture received the approval of the (Indian) Foreign Investment Promotion Board in April 2013. However, winning the other needed approvals took a further thirteen months. While the Ministry of Civil Aviation issued a No Objection Certificate in September, it was 7 May 2014 before the Director General of Civil Aviation granted an Air Operator Permit (Bursa (bourse) announcements of 27 September 2013 and 8 May 2014, accessed at airasia.com on 23 November 2014).

The delays in granting the various government permissions were thought to reflect opposition from incumbent Indian airlines (CAPA, 'AirAsia India to launch on 12-Jun-2014. The LCC's greatest test or its most lucrative opportunity?', 30 May 2014). Nevertheless, the eventual granting of the AOP indicated that the earlier change of government policy *did* permit foreign investment in *new* airlines, as well as allowing additional funding sources for incumbent airlines.

The new airline began service on 12 June 2014, only *five weeks* after receiving its Air Operator Permit. From its initial base at Bangalore, the new airline's first route was to Goa. That short (480 km) sector already had service from GoAir and Jet Airways (each with daily flights), SpiceJet and IndiGo (each six flights weekly), and Air India (four weekly flights) (anna.aero, 19 June 2014). Clearly, the AirAsia India choice of route depended on self-confidence regarding cost levels and service quality rather than on finding under-served routes!

The Tata group also wanted a second airline! In September 2013, Singapore Airlines announced it had signed a Memorandum of Understanding with Tata Sons to launch a *full-service* carrier to be based in New Delhi (Karamjit Kaur, 'SIA partners Tata group to set up new airline in India', *The Straits Times* (Singapore), 19 September 2013). Subject to approval by the Indian government, Tata Sons would hold 51 per cent of the shares, with the balance to be held by Singapore Airlines.

In September 2014, while the government administrative processes were still incomplete, the airline, now named as *Vistara*, announced the arrival of the first (of 20) brand new A320s (media release, 'Vistara takes delivery of its first Airbus A320 aircraft', airvistara.com, 25 September 2014). While that announcement also referred to an 'operational launch in October 2014', the Air Operator Permit was not issued until mid-December (media release, 'Vistara gets "AOP"; all set for the take off', 15 December 2014). A few days later, Vistara said it would start flight from New Delhi to Mumbai and Ahmedabad on 9 January 2015 (Anne Paylor, 'Vistara secures AOP, to launch commercial operations Jan. 9', *Air Transport World*, 22 December 2014).

Early in February 2015, Vistara was able to announce the arrival of its fifth A320, each with 148 seats, comprising Business class (16 seats), Premium Economy (36) and Economy (96) (media release, 'Vistara's fleet grows to five', 6 February 2015). After starting with 68 flights weekly, Vistara expected to operate 164 flights weekly in early March.

On 18 April, the one hundredth day since the launch, Vistara was operating 197 flights daily (media release, 'Vistara completes 100 days in skies', 19 April 2015).

On 18 May (media release, 'Vistara adds Lucknow to its route network') the airline claimed on-time performance of 90 per cent in January, 98 per cent in February, 96 per cent in March and 97 per cent in April.

It also noted that Vistara had flown more than 200,000 passengers in the four months since its launch. Using the fragmentary (and sometimes obscure) data in the Vistara media releases, a ball-park calculation of the load factor for the period up to 18 May suggests an estimated overall passenger load factor in the range of 75 to 80 per cent. If that estimate is broadly sound, then Vistara seems to have had a decent start. However, those airline media releases had nothing to say about financial outcomes.

4.4 New carriers in China, Japan and South Korea

4.4.1 China

In earlier days, the Civil Aviation Administration of China was both the aviation regulator and the operator of the state airline. In 1987, the government removed the airline from CAAC control, and divided it along regional lines, to form six separate, state-owned airlines. Three of them – Air China, China Eastern and China Southern – remain as large and important players.

In addition, the government started to allow entry to the domestic market by new companies. However, the deregulation was not total: while airlines put forward route proposals, it is the CAAC that decides who flies where. After a decade or so, some 100 companies were offering scheduled airline services (anna.aero, 4 September 2009). CAAC then closed off further airline entry, except for joint ventures involving existing airlines (CAPA, 'Aviation changes in China: an airline and airport review Part 2', 10 December 2012).

Total passenger traffic on *domestic* routes has grown rapidly in most recent years ('Chinese domestic air travel growth . . .', anna.aero, 27 July 2011 – which is based on CAAC data). Factors contributing to this growth include China's very large population and the initially limited market penetration, rising income levels, the entry of new airlines and the consequent increased connectivity of the overall airline network.

An interesting feature of the sector is the prevalence of ownership and other links *between* the various airlines, with Air China and China Eastern having very important positions in the web of influences. (For a very striking diagram of these connections, again see CAPA, 'Aviation changes in China'). Indeed, at that date, there were only two large *independent* new carriers – Spring Airlines and Juneyao Airlines.

The three large legacy carriers together now have more than 800 aircraft. Table 4.4 lists eight significant new airlines, selected essentially on fleet capacity ('Sichuan Airlines now China's sixth biggest carrier', anna.aero, 20 March 2013). As the table shows, the domestic market is so large that an enterprising airline can soon become quite sizeable. Even the smaller fleets of the very newest of the airlines are impressive. Note however that in a few cases (notably Hainan Airlines, which operates a number of wide-body aircraft), a significant portion of the capacity is deployed on international routes. Two of the new carriers, (Hainan Airlines and Shenzhen Airlines) were launched in 'special economic zones', which are areas chosen by the government for rapid economic development.

- *Shanghai Airlines* started in 1985, and is described as China's first local airline. At one stage, the Shanghai government owned 35 per cent of its shares. Later it became a wholly owned subsidiary of China Eastern ('Airlines in China', airlineupdate.com, accessed 20 April 2013).
- Launched in 1988, *Sichuan Airlines* has its base at Chengdu, in the western province of Sichuan. Though the Sichuan Airlines Group is (just) the largest shareholder, China Southern holds 39 per cent of the shares, while Shandong and Shanghai Airlines each hold 10 per cent!
- *Xiamen Airlines* launched in 1992 by China Southern, which has retained 51 per cent of the shares; it is based at Xiamen (Fujian).
- *Hainan Airlines* launched in 1993 and is based at Haikou in the special economic zone of Hainan. Although most of its shares are privately owned, the ultimate effective control of 51 per cent of the shares rests with the Hainan Provincial Government (Hainan Airlines, Annual Report 2008, p. 105). In a media release (2 December 2009), Hainan Airlines announced it had become the first airline in China to receive a four-star classification from Skytrax.
- *Shenzhen Airlines* launched in 1993; its base is at Shenzhen, in a special economic zone adjacent to Hong Kong. It was founded by the state-owned Guangdong Development Bank, with assistance from Air China. In 2005, the bank sold 65 per cent of the shares to two private companies, making the company the largest privately controlled airline in China. However, in 2010, Air China increased its holding to 51 per cent. Though Shenzhen retained its identity, Air China gained a southern hub to help it compete with China Southern ('Air China wins Shenzhen air control for southern hub', *Bloomberg News* 22 March 2010; 'Air China says Shenzhen Airlines to retain brand', *China Daily*, 23 March 2010).
- *Shandong Airlines* was launched in 1994 by China Eastern; but now the largest shareholder is Air China. It is based at Jinan, which is about 400 km SSE of Beijing.
- *Spring Airlines* is privately owned and independent, being without ownership links to any other airline. Launched in 2005, it is a budget carrier, based in Shanghai, and was established by a travel company, Spring Travel. The airline takes a strict low-cost approach, flies A320s (with 186 seats each), and averages nearly six sectors per aircraft per day (Cantle, 2008). No doubt the travel-company parentage helps it to attract passengers.
- *Juneyao Airlines* is the other independent airline in the list. Launched in 2006, it too is based in Shanghai, a location with a significant amount of business travel.
- Not shown in Table 4.4 is *Tianjin Airlines*. Launched in 2007, and based in Tianjin, this is the only new airline that focuses on regional routes, where it operates smaller aircraft. At April 2013, the fleet comprised 50 Embraer190 jets, 23 ERJ145s and 17 Dornier328 turbo-props.

Table 4.4 Fleets of major new airlines in China, April 2013

	Shanghai	Sichuan	Xiamen	Hainan	Shenzhen	Shandong	Spring	Juneyao
Established	1985	1988	1992	1993	1993	1994	2005	2006
Aircraft types								
A319		18			5			
A320		31			56		35	29
A321		23						
A330		4		14				
B737								
− 700	8		15		4	3		
− 800	40		64	82	48	49		
− 900					5			
Other	19		6	15		13		
Total	67	79	85	111	118	65	35	29

Sources: Aircraft numbers are estimates, based on ch-aviation.ch and 'Airlines in China' at airlineupdate.com, both accessed on 13 April 2013.

In 2012 CAAC began to make important changes in its thinking about airline entry and airline performance. Perhaps because Spring Airlines had demonstrated markedly superior productive efficiency, CAAC sought to put more emphasis on airline productivity, rather than making mere growth the main consideration. To that end, it again started to encourage LCC entry, and it expected private investment to be an important driver. Rather than having more airlines based in Shanghai or other very large cities, CAAC was expected to prefer airlines based in other regions, perhaps with fare-levels set in light of regional differences in income levels (CAPA, 'China may allow LCCs and new entrants in airline sector reforms, but no deregulation for now', 10 October 2013; CAPA, 'China's aviation reforms match frugality with low-cost airline innovation as a new script unfolds', 19 February 2014).

In short, despite a major role for private company initiatives, individual airlines would still be constrained or, at least, 'guided' by the government acting through its aviation agency. The general style of such an approach seems not unlike that prevailing in Russia, in some countries in the Arabian Peninsula, and elsewhere in Asia.

4.4.2 Japan

Until recent times, Japan's domestic routes saw little entry by low-cost carriers. This seems to have been due to several, diverse factors: the lack of buoyant economic growth in Japan; the presence of the high-speed *shinkanzen* rail services that link quite a number of important city-pairs; and the dominant position of the two legacy carriers, All Nippon Airways (ANA) and Japanese Airlines (JAL).

On the other hand, low fares might be especially attractive to travellers in hard economic times; and travel by *shinkanzen* between a city to the north of Tokyo and a city to the south requires a transfer between Tokyo railway stations.

Thus it is not surprising that both ANA and JAL themselves made some low-fare moves, albeit limited. In 1998, the latter launched JAL Express, based in Osaka and flying older aircraft. And in 2005 ANA launched Air Next, which was based at Fukuoka, and also deployed older aircraft, namely B737-500s. In 2010, ANA merged Air Next with some of its other subsidiaries. There were also two small independent start-ups, Air Do (see Table 4.5) and Ibex (launched 2000) (CAPA, 'LCCs in Japan, Korea and China', 27 November 2009).

Among several other entries during that period (Table 4.5), that of *Skymark Airlines* has been particularly important. After a modest beginning, that company prospered and grew, and established a base at Kobe as well as its first base at Haneda Airport, Tokyo. It flew a homogeneous fleet of A320s, with high-density seating. However, in 2013, it withdrew from the Osaka (Kansai) market, in the face of increasing competition from some LCC entrants that had launched in 2012, and are discussed below (CAPA, 'Skymark Airlines withdraws from Osaka Kansai market indefinitely as LCC competition intensifies', 3 April 2013).

In January 2015, Skymark entered into formal bankruptcy, but continued flying. Given that the company had already set a less ambitious course, there were several parties interested in giving commercial assistance; these included ANA.

In April, ANA Holdings and Skymark agreed a deal in which ANA would take 19.9 per cent of Skymark's shares. Other investors were to be Integral (a Tokyo-based investment fund, that would take 50.1 per cent), together with the Development Bank of Japan and Sumitomo Mitsui Banking Corporation ('ANA All Nippon to assume Skymark's A330s', ch-aviation.ch, 23 April 2015). (The ANA stake was capped at less than 20 per cent, in order to allow Skymark to retain the use of its thirty-six slots at Tokyo Haneda airport.)

However, Airbus was among the creditors of Skymark, and was thought likely to block the deal – because it was not satisfied that the deal sufficiently protected its interests (Jeremy Torr, 'Airbus likely to block ANA-Skymark deal', *Air Transport World*, 1 June 2015).

The next interesting entrant was *Fuji Dream Airlines* which launched in July 2009. This company belongs to Suzuyo, a group which engages in freight for-warding and other transport activities. Fuji Dream operates (new) smaller, Embraer jets, and is based at a new airport which opened at Shizuoka, near Mount Fuji, in June 2009. Though less than 200 km from both Tokyo and Nagoya, the port is said to have a catchment area with about 4 million people ('New Japanese airport serving Mount Fuji', anna.aero, 5 June 2009).

Both ANA and JAL started services there on the day the new port opened. From 1 April 2010, however, JAL withdrew its flights to Fukuoka and Sapporo, and instead code-shared on Fuji Dream services ('JAL/Fuji Dream Airlines to start code-sharing', airlineroute.net, 25 February 2010).

Then, in 2012, both ANA and JAL vigorously embraced the low-cost concept. Even then, much of the initiative came from outside Japan (Table 4.5). As seen earlier, the rival airlines AirAsia and (the Qantas-owned) Jetstar had become serial joint-venturers; their engagements with local partners led to the establishment of both *Jetstar Japan* and *AirAsia Japan*. In addition, ANA joined with other

Table 4.5 Major new airlines in Japan, May 2015

Airline	Launched	Owners	Base(s)	Aircraft	No of seats
Skymark (then in bankruptcy)	Sep 1998	Skymark CEO & a travel agency	Tokyo (Haneda) Osaka (Kobe) & Sendai	27 × B737-800	177
Air Do	December 1998	Local investors in Hokkaido	Tokyo (Haneda)	3 × B737-500 6 × B737-700 4 × B767-300	
Fuji Dream	Jul 2009	Suzuyo (transport conglomerate)	Shizuoka (Mt Fuji)	3 × E170 6 × E175	76 and 84, respectively
Peach	Mar 2012	ANA, and two investors	Osaka	14 × A320	180
Jetstar Japan	Jul 2012	JAL, Qantas and financiers	Tokyo (Narita) & Osaka Kansai	20 × A320	180
AirAsia Japan	Aug 2012; closed June 2013	ANA and AirAsia	Tokyo (Narita)	4 × A320	180
Vanilla	Dec 2013	ANA subsidiary	Tokyo (Narita)	9 × A320	180
Spring Airlines Japan	July 2014?	Japanese partners & Spring (China)	Sapporo (Chitose)	3 × B737-800	189

Sources: Fleet numbers from: ch-aviation.ch; 'About us', www.skymark.co.jp/en/company; www.flypeach.com; 'Jetstar Japan joins the new breed of Japanese low cost carriers (three in 2012!)' anna.aero 11 July 2012. All websites accessed on 1–2 May 2013 and/or 19 May 2015

investors to found *Peach Aviation*, which is based at Osaka Kansai ('Peach wins Japanese LCC race to launch flights', anna.aero, 7 March 2012). After the years of inaction in Japan, these three new airlines battled to be the first to enter.

As already noted (§4.2.1 above), the ANA–AirAsia joint venture was soon dissolved. ANA re-launched the airline as a wholly owned subsidiary, Vanilla Air, which offered two regular fare types, one basic at a low fare and the other more flexible (vanilla-air.com/en and Wikipedia entry for Vanilla Air, both accessed 26 November 2014).

The next entry was that of *Spring Airlines Japan*, a joint venture between the Chinese private company Spring Airlines (said to have 33 per cent of the shares in the Japanese company) and Japanese partners, including the very large travel company JTB. The Japanese affiliate launched at the end of July 2014, deploying B737-800s configured with 189 seats, and having the first three rows (18 seats) curtained off to form a premium cabin.

The airline began with three aircraft flying on three routes – to Hiroshima, Saga and Takamatsu ('Spring Airlines Japan launches operations from Tokyo Narita', anna.aero, 5 August 2014; 'Spring Airlines finally gets domestic flights off ground after training delays', *The Japan Times*, 1 August 2014; Wikipedia entry on Spring Airlines Japan, accessed 26 November 2014). Those route choices suggest a desire to avoid the most-dense routes.

While the individual newcomers are very much smaller than the long-established incumbents, they are winning as much as half the extra traffic (CAPA, 'Japan's expanding LCCs drive growth but need cultivating', 5 April 2014). However, as usual, profitability is more elusive than growth. It remains to be seen whether all the newcomers will survive.

4.4.3 South Korea

As in Japan, budget carriers have arrived only recently. Indeed, though Korea now has a population of about 50 million, the national carrier Korean Air had no significant (domestic) competitor of *any* kind until the entry in 1988 of the full-service Asiana Airlines – which belongs to a Korean conglomerate, the Kumho Asiana Group, and has built a strong reputation for customer service. Its diverse fleet of about 60 aircraft serves both domestic and international routes. Both airlines are based primarily in the national capital, Seoul, in the north-west of the country.

The next significant airline entry (Table 4.6) came in 2005 when local interests established Hansung Airlines (as it was then named) as a local carrier operating large turbo-prop aircraft from its base in Cheong Ju (Jeonju), a city of about 650,000 residents, a little inland from the west coast, and a major tourist attraction. After financial problems had twice led to its closure, the airline re-emerged in 2010 as a jet operator, under a new name, T'Way, but still based in Jeonju.

In 2006, a provincial government partnered with a private company to establish Jeju Air, based on the island of Jeju that lies well off the south-west coast of Korea.

Table 4.6 Major new airlines in South Korea, November 2014

Airline	Launched	Owners	Base	Fleet	Seats
T'Way Airlines	2005; re-launch 2010	Cheong Ju City and Univ. of Chungcheong	Cheong Ju	8 × B737-800	189
Jeju Air	Jun 2006	Aekyung Group	Jeju	16 × B737-800	186/189
Jin Air	Jul 2008	Korean Air	Seoul (Gimpo)	13 × B737-800	189
Air Busan	Oct 2008	Asiana, City of Busan and commercial enterprises	Busan (Gimhae)	3 × B737-400	162
				3 × B737-500	147
				2 × A320	162
				4 × A321	191/195
Eastar Jet	Jan 2009	Eastar Group	Seoul (Gimpo)	5 × B737-700	149
				5 × B737-800	186

Sources: ch-aviation.ch; airbusan.com; jejuair.net/jejuair/ko;jinair.com; all accessed 7 May 2013 and/or 26 November 2014

Only in 2008 did the two legacy carriers respond to the budget-airline entry. With other investors, Asiana established Air Busan, based at Gimhae, near Busan, where the metropolitan population is about 4.5 million. And Korean Air created a wholly owned subsidiary, Jin Air, based (like the parent) at Seoul.

For all but Air Busan, the high-density cabin layouts, seen in Table 4.6, indicate low-fare intentions. Late in 2014, the entire low-fare sector comprised five airlines. Only three of those were independent companies. The other two are effectively controlled by the two full-service incumbents. While none of the new carriers had reached economical scale, three of them operated B737-800s only, and a fourth had that model and some B737-700s as well. In the 18-month period to November 2014, each of the five had increased the size of its fleet. In particular, Air Busan had increased the number of Airbus planes, and may be intending to phase out its ageing Boeing aircraft. Given the size of the population of Korea, having five separate low-fare carriers does not seem excessive, especially when three of them are not based in the capital, Seoul. Of course, continuing presence depends also on having good management.

5   Latin America

Developments in Latin America are of especial interest: increases in income levels have afforded major opportunities for airline growth and entry; some of the legacy carriers have cast off accustomed ways and embarked on new business models; and some of the new airlines have offered business class as well as economy class services. Moreover, growth in the demand for international travel has encouraged airline ownership arrangements that seek to sidestep the protectionist regulatory regimes of individual countries. Accordingly, this chapter reports on legacy carriers as well as new airlines. The account starts in the north of the region and works south.

5.1 New airlines in Mexico: Volaris, VivaAerobus and Interjet

The Mexican population of about 110 million people yields a sizeable domestic market. Until recent years, two airlines dominated: Mexicana which launched in 1923, and Aeroméxico which started in 1934. However, following deregulation in 2005, a number of new, low-cost airlines entered the industry. The ensuing lively competition saw the early exit of some of them.

It also caused problems for both legacy carriers. Aeroméxico was said to have considerable debts – and insufficient profits and capital to repay those debts (Wikipedia on Aeroméxico, accessed 16 July 2013). In October 2007, its owners sold out to a banking group, which successfully kept the airline in business. Mexicana too encountered grave financial problems. It ceased flying in August 2010, and its subsidiaries closed soon after.

Besides Aeroméxico, there remain three significant new airlines, Interjet, Volaris and VivaAerobus. All three were funded by private investors, with airlines in other countries holding shares in two of them.

Volaris

Though planning for *Volaris* started in 2003, the inaugural flight came only in March 2006. The initial investors were a Mexican investment fund and TACA (an airline initially based in El Salvador, but now with a presence in several Latin

American countries). Further funding came in July 2006 when the World Bank made a loan of US$40 million. Subsequent share transactions left TACA with an increased holding, and saw Indigo Partners investing in the airline. In the second half of 2013, Volaris made an Initial Purchase Offer of stock sufficient to raise US$398 million, to help fund acquisition of further Airbus aircraft (ch-aviaion.ch, accessed 13 July 2013).

Volaris started with A319 aircraft, later added A320s, and then began to dispose of some A319s. In 2015, it received its first two A321s, each with 220 seats. At the end of 2015, it planned to operate 53 *other* aircraft: thirty-six A320s (each with 179 seats, after retrofit where needed); and 17 A319s (144 seats) (Volaris, Investor Presentation, May 2015, p. 16; Annual Report 2013, pp. 12, 14).

The airline's initial base was at Toluca, about 50 km to the west of Mexico City and having lower airline operating costs than the Mexico City International Airport (MEX). In March 2010, however, Volaris did start a few flights at MEX, perhaps anticipating the collapse of *Mexicana*. When Mexicana closed, Volaris *immediately* entered six MEX routes previously served by Mexicana (anna.aero, 29 September 2010). A year later, Mexico City had become the largest port in the Volaris network ('Mexico City replaces Tijuana as Volaris' biggest base', anna. aero, 22 September 2011).

Volaris has become a profitable airline with low costs and a good reputation. It has claimed to have lower unit costs 'than any [other] publicly traded airline in Latin America', thanks to having an efficient uniform fleet, high asset utilisation (passenger load factor usually above 80 per cent, and about 12 flight hours per aircraft per day), direct sales distribution and a variable, performance-based compensation structure for staff.

In June 2009, Volaris launched international services, flying to Los Angeles (LAX) daily from Toluca and twice daily from Guadalajara (Volaris media release, 30 June 2009). In 2014, Volaris carried 9.8 million (domestic and international) passengers (up 9.7 per cent on 2013), who travelled 9.7 billion miles (RPM) (media release, 'Volaris reports December 2014 traffic results . . .', 7 January 2015).

VivaAerobus

Also launched in 2006, *VivaAerobus* is a joint venture of IAMSA (the largest road-bus group in Mexico) and Irelandia, an investment vehicle of the Ryan family (the founders of Ryanair). Its first CEO was a former Chief Operating Officer of EasyJet ('About us', vivaaerobus.com, accessed 19 April 2009).

Based in Monterrey, in northern Mexico, VivaAerobus launched with a fleet of ageing B737-300 aircraft, each with a single-class cabin of 148 seats. By mid-2013, it operated 22 such aircraft, with an average age of 22 years (planespotters. net, accessed 15 July 2013).

In October 2013, the airline placed an order for new A320s – 12 current A320s and 40 A320neos. In the meanwhile, it leased six A320s, configured with 180 seats, and these entered the fleet from March 2014. Although progressive withdrawal of the (smaller) Boeings began at the same time, the total fleet capacity increased. VivaAerobus planned to complete the withdrawal of the older Boeings in 2016 ('VivaAerobus starts operations of its new Airbus A320', press release, 13 March 2014).

While initially shunning the major, competitive route between Monterrey and Mexico City, VivaAerobus soon developed a sizeable domestic network, with feeder road-bus travel offered to airline passengers at discounted fares. Like Volaris, VivaAerobus started some flights from Mexico City in 2010, and subsequently developed its network in southern Mexico. It carried almost 3 million passengers in 2009, and in January 2012 it carried its 10 millionth passenger since start-up ('VivaAerobus celebrates 10 millionth passenger', anna. aero, 14 March 2012).

After an unsuccessful attempt in 2008 to establish service from Monterrey to Austin (Texas), VivaAerobus started routes from Monterrey to other US cities in 2010. It also began flights from Guadalajara to Ciudad Juarez (at the Mexican border), together with a local connecting bus service going just across the US border to the bus terminal in El Paso, Texas (VivaAerobus, news release, 2 March 2010).

Regarding its flights from Monterrey to Houston, the airline alleged that Continental Airlines (which flew the route daily) responded to entry by greatly reducing its fares – but only for travel *on the two days each week on which VivaAerobus flew the route* (VivaAerobus news release, 10 June 2010; such targeted pricing is assessed in §15.3).

After earlier talk of an IPO, to help fund the acquisition of newer aircraft, VivaAerobus announced (news release, 11 February 2014) that it had:

> decided to postpone its initial public offering due to volatile market conditions . . . The company is in a strong financial position and has the support of world-class investors and partners. We will continue to monitor market conditions and look forward to taking the company public in the future.

In May 2015, VivaAerobus brought into service the first of the brand-new A320s. The second aircraft soon followed (ch-aviation.ch, 7 June 2015). Being still privately held, it seems that VivaAerobus was *not* publishing passenger numbers and financial results.

Interjet

The other surviving entrant, *Interjet*, launched at the end of 2005, flying A320s from its first base at Toluca. At mid-2013, its fleet comprised no less than 39 such aircraft, each with a single-cabin layout of 150 seats, at a comfortable 34-inch pitch; the average age of the fleet was 6.7 years (*planespotters.net*, accessed 15 July 2013).

Like Volaris and VivaAerobus, it later began flights from Mexico City, which became its second base and eventually its largest port. While building a very large domestic network, Interjet developed international services only to San Antonio and Guatemala ('About Interjet', accessed at www.interjet.com.mx, 15 July 2013).

The initial funding for Interjet came from the Aleman Group, which is owned by one of Mexico's wealthiest families. In 2011, Interjet initiated an IPO for a minority stake in the airline, but cancelled the float at the last moment, because of conditions then prevailing in financial markets. The intention had been to raise funds for the purchase of 40 A320neos.

Interjet then decided to take into its fleet a smaller jet, the new Russia-built Sukhoi Superjet 100. As an early customer, Interjet presumably got a low price on its order of 20 aircraft. No doubt, the aircraft's smaller capacity (93 seats, again at a generous 34-inch pitch) has helped Interjet enter quite a number of thin routes, beginning in September 2013. (On the early routes flown by the Superjet 100, see CAPA, 'Interjet's new Superjets are featured in the latest competitive roll-out from Mexico City', 22 October 2013.)

Growth of the market and changes in market shares

When Mexicana and its subsidiaries closed on 28 August 2010, the market lost a significant amount of airline capacity. Indeed, in July, the Mexicana group had carried almost 27 per cent of the domestic passengers.

Yet the impact on total traffic was fleeting. As Table 5.1 shows, the number of domestic passengers in September 2010 *was* markedly smaller than in July. Yet it was only slightly lower than in September 2009 (not shown in the table); and the December 2010 total was much the same as in December 2009. And the

Table 5.1 Passengers on scheduled domestic services, major airlines, Mexico 2010–14

	2010				2010	2011	2012	2013	2014
	July	*Sept*	*Oct*	*Dec*					
Monthly total passengers[1,2] (millions)	2.50	1.74	1.96	2.10	2.04	2.12	2.34	2.54	2.74
Airline shares of total passengers (%)									
Aeroméxico	13.7	22.6	23.0	20.9	16.9	19.7	18.0	16.6	15.5
Aeroméxico Connect	15.5	22.9	22.6	20.1	18.7	20.4	19.8	19.1	20.6
Interjet	13.9	21.2	20.1	24.8	16.3	24.9	23.9	24.5	23.8
VivaAerobus	10.3	8.4	10.4	10.8	8.8	11.5	12.5	12.2	11.9
Volaris	13.7	18.0	16.7	17.7	14.8	18.1	20.5	23.1	23.3
Total market share for the five named airlines	67.2	93.1	92.7	94.4	75.8	94.6	94.7	95.6	95.1

Source: Dirección General de Aeronáutica Civil, México: Resumen 2010–14

Notes
1 For the months in 2010, total number of passengers travelling on all airlines.
2 For full years 2010 and later, average monthly number of passengers travelling on all airlines.

passenger figures for 2011 and later years continue to demonstrate further growth in the domestic market taken as a whole.

The lower part of Table 5.1 shows the varying outcomes for the proportionate shares of the individual airlines. Particularly striking is the rise and later decline of the mainline Aeroméxico; perhaps its prevailing relatively low load factors gave it an immediate ability to take more passengers, while the three new airlines were increasing their capacity. Later, it lost that increase in market share, while Aeroméxico Connect, which serves regional routes and flies smaller aircraft, broadly held its gain. In 2011, as the three *new* airlines added to their fleets, their market shares increased greatly. Volaris stood out when it scored further increases in the following years.

5.2 Two important airlines in Central America: Copa and TACA

Central America, the narrow strip of land that connects Mexico and South America, comprises no less than seven countries, with a combined population of about 40 million people. The region has two important carriers – both long established, and both with notable influence in South America.

Copa Airlines

Copa Airlines (Panama) was launched in 1947, by Pan American Airlines and other private investors. Copa eventually withdrew from Panama's (limited) domestic routes, in order to focus on international services. It was 2005 before Copa launched its IPO and listed on the New York Stock Exchange. In recent years, the company has been *very* profitable, and has expanded very rapidly (Copa Form 20-F 2012, pp. 2–3, 51–7; Copa Presentation (to investors), 28 May 2015).

Copa is a full service airline, with business- and economy-class cabins. Important to its success is its punctuality – in most years, it claims to have about 90 per cent of flights on-time. Also important is the operational efficiency of its Panama City hub, which serves well for travel between any of Copa's ports in the US and Mexico and any of the many ports it serves in South America, especially because all the spoke distances are within the range of most modern *short-haul* aircraft.

In 2015, Copa served 73 cities in 30 countries in the Americas. In recent years, its load factor of around 76 per cent serves well enough for a full-service carrier that competes by offering service frequency through its hub. In the five years 2010 to 2014, its operating margin was around 20 to 21 per cent of operating revenue, except for 2012 when the margin was 'only' 17.9 per cent. However, changes in exchange rates clouded its financial situation in 2015 (Copa Presentation 2015, pp. 17, 18).

At April 2015, its fleet comprised 23 Embraer 190s (10/84 passengers), 12 Boeing 737-700s (12/112) and 63 B737-800s (16/144). In the following two years, it envisaged a further increase in the B737-800 numbers, and further small reductions in the numbers of the other two aircraft types. It has firm orders for 61 B737-MAX 8 and 9 aircraft, with deliveries commencing in 2018 (Copa Presentation 2015, pp. 24, 36).

TACA

TACA (El Salvador) In the 1930s, an entrepreneur set up a group of TACA airlines each domiciled in a distinct Latin American country ('Business: first papers for Taca', *Time Magazine*, 18 October 1943, accessed at taca.com, 13 July 2010). Of those companies, the sole survivor was the El Salvador carrier, later called Taca International.

Over the years 1989–95, TACA built strategic alliances with the flag airlines of Guatemala (Aviateca), Nicaragua (NICA) and Costa Rica (LACSA), and consolidated these Central American operations under the name of Grupo TACA. In 2001, it established a new airline TACA Peru, which hubbed from the capital city, Lima. (By 2006, TACA also held a major stake in the Mexican airline Volaris, which it helped to found.)

By 2004, the TACA group was serving Mexico City, Toronto and 10 ports in the US, as well as some countries in Central America and many important destinations in South America and the Caribbean. It claimed on-time departure levels exceeding 90 per cent ('Our history', accessed at www.taca.com, 13 July 2010). The group airlines offered both executive and economy class travel, with meals served in both. Again, the emphasis was on high quality rather than low fares.

In 1998, TACA ordered new Airbus A319 and A320 aircraft, to re-equip its airlines; later it similarly purchased Embraer E190s. TACA International held the pooled fleet, and leased aircraft to the other airlines. (Some of the airlines also operated other, usually small, aircraft.)

At July 2010, the pooled fleet comprised 8 E190s (96 seats), 11 A319s, 16 A320s (150 seats) and 5 A321s (194 seats) (aircraft data, ch-aviation.ch; seat numbers, taca.com; both accessed 13 July 2010). As is usual in aircraft with two cabins, those seat-numbers are modest – as are the numbers of each aircraft-type. However, at that stage, there was – in the offing – a merger with another group, on which see §5.5 below.

5.3 Colombia, the home of Avianca and other carriers

Going south from Central America, a land-bound traveller comes first to Colombia, whose population of almost 50 million makes it the third most populous country in Latin America (after Brazil and Mexico).

Avianca

Avianca, the flag-carrier of Colombia, has roots going back to 1919, and has always been owned by private investors. Notable events in recent times include: an alliance formed in 1994 between Avianca and a Colombian regional carrier,

SAM; the establishment in 1998 of Avianca's major new hub at Bogotá; the 2004 purchase of SAM by Avianca; and the integration of the small Brazilian carrier Oceanair, renamed as Avianca Brasil in 2010.

Avianca has long operated as a full-service carrier, offering business and economy class cabins. In mid-2010, it still had a somewhat mixed fleet. A later merger with TACA is taken up in §5.5 below.

Aero República

Also in Colombia is Aero República, founded in 1992. Copa acquired the company in 2005 ('History' aerorepublica.com, accessed 19 July 2010). In its early years, Aero República flew domestic routes, operated old aircraft, and earned a poor reputation on punctuality. In December 2006, Copa started to replace the entire fleet with new E190s, and this process was completed in January 2010. On 6 October 2010, Copa announced (media release 'Aero República is now Copa Airlines Colombia' copaair.com) that following the airline's re-equipment, its entry to international routes and its improved punctuality, the airline was to trade as *Copa Airlines Colombia*.

VivaColombia

VivaColombia is a newcomer, which claims to be the first 'true' low-cost carrier in Colombia. It was founded by local investors (Grupo Fast and Grupo Bolivar), together with the two parties that founded VivaAerobus – Grupo IAMSA and Irelandia Aviation.

VivaColombia launched in May 2012, flying A320s, each with 180 seats. At the end of 2014 its (then) six aircraft served a network of 22 routes serving Medellin (its base), Bogota and ten other domestic ports, and also international flights to Lima (Peru), Panama and Quito (Ecuador) (vivacolombia.co and ch-aviation.ch, both accessed 2 December 2014).

In 2010 the Chilean airline, LAN purchased a majority stake in a small Colombian airline, which (in 2011) it re-branded as *LAN Colombia*. Section 5.7 below reports some later details.

5.4 Airlines in Ecuador

To serve its population of about 15 million, Ecuador has three airlines of note. *Tame* was founded in 1962, and remains a state enterprise. It operates a considerable domestic network together with international services from (the capital) Quito to various ports in South America, the US and Cuba. At end-2014, its fleet (mainly) comprised 4 A319s, 5 A320s and one A330, together with 4 Embraer 190s and 3 ATR42s (tame.com.ec, accessed 2 December 2014). *Avianca Ecuador* launched in 1986 as AeroGal. It merged with VIP of Ecuador in 2012, and is now branded as part of the Avianca group. It flies Airbus A319s and A320s (aerogal.com.ec, accessed 6 September 2013). The third airline, *LAN Ecuador,* appears below in §5.7.

5.5 The merger of TACA and Avianca

The word of merger intentions came in a joint media release 'Avianca and TACA will form the leading airline network in Latin America', 7 October 2009). The respective holding companies said that each of them 'will contribute its respective controlling ownership participations in the operations of [Avianca and TACA] to a newly formed holding company'.

On the same day, a joint presentation 'Creating a Leading Latin American Airline' stated that the individual airlines would (initially?) fly under their individual air operator certificates. The presentation also put emphasis on the common service culture of the two groups, on the great size of the operations of the combined group, and on the need for regulatory approval for the transaction.

That approval came within a few months. In a media release ('AVIANCA and TACA officially close their shareholders agreement', 2 February 2010), the two groups explained that Synergy Aerospace Corp, majority shareholder of Avianca, and Kingsland Holding Limited, owner of Grupo TACA were placing their investments in those groups into a new company, AVIANCA-TACA Limited (later named Avianca Holdings). Synergy owned 67 per cent of the shares, with the remaining 33 per cent held by Kingsland.

The government approvals allowed the various constituent airlines to continue with their prevailing operating rights for domestic and international routes. Viewed as a whole, AVIANCA-TACA was to fly from four hub ports in four countries, namely Bogotá (Colombia), San Salvador (El Salvador), San José (Costa Rica) and Lima (Peru).

After three years of very considerable growth in passenger numbers, achieved even while the holding company integrated the operations of the constituent airlines, (the new) Avianca announced (in two distinct media releases issued on 28 May 2013) that all its airlines would now trade under the single brand 'Avianca', with all flights designated under the one airline code, AV. However, the individual airlines would still fly under separate AOCs.

From 2009, Avianca had withdrawn its ageing B737, B757, MD83 and F100 jet aircraft. At 30 September 2014, the *group* fleet comprised 15 × A330s, 109 × A320 family (mainly A320s), 12 × E190s and 28 turboprops (ATR 42 and other types). Its jet orders were for the A320neo and the B787 (Avianca Holdings Corporate Presentation 2014, p.15, accessed 8 June 2015 at aviancaholdings.com).

In 2014, the Avianca group carried 26.2 million passengers (up 6.5 per cent on the previous year), and enjoyed an overall passenger load factor of 79.4 per cent (down one percentage point), while increasing the total RPK to 32.6 billion. However, net profit was greatly reduced at US$128 million (previous year US$249 million; Annual Report Form 20-F, 2014, pp. 3–4).

Despite some profit concerns, it was clear that the Avianca group had become an important force in South American aviation.

5.6 Aviation in Brazil

Serving almost 200 million people occupying a very large land area, Brazil's market for domestic air travel is regarded as the fourth largest in the world. Yet its aviation sector since 1995 has seen considerable turbulence, arising from competition within the sector, and from external factors such as increased aircraft fuel prices, variations in the currency exchange rate, and fluctuations in the overall level of economic activity.

This section looks first at the major airlines and the significant newcomers, notes some change in airline shares in the domestic market, considers the roles of the government's aviation regulator and its general-purpose industry regulator, and reports on recent mergers that have left Brazil with only four (perhaps five) large airlines.

5.6.1 Two venerable airlines: Varig and TAM

The oldest Brazilian airline, *Varig*, was founded in 1927. By 1960, it had become a well-recognised national flag-carrier, operating both international and domestic services. However, its fortunes waned as domestic routes became more competitive. The eventual outcome is reported below.

Another long-established airline, *TAM*, began as an air taxi service in 1961. It soon became a public company; and eventually it listed in the US. During a gradual process of expansion and development, TAM first operated regional flights, and then introduced its first jets in the early 1990s. By 1996 it was serving all the country's regions; and it then introduced its first A320 aircraft. Its first international flight came in 1998. After a period of aggressive growth, it became the largest *domestic* carrier (by market share) in 2003 ('TAM's history', tam.com. br accessed 27 October 2009).

By December 2009, TAM's narrow-body fleet comprised 21 A319s, 81 A320s and 5 A321s, all with single-class cabins (Annual Report Form 20-F, 2009). On its domestic network (serving 42 ports) it made intensive use of its aircraft – though in the depressed market of 2009, daily block hours per aircraft declined to 11.8, after being 12.2 hours in 2007 and 2008. In 2009, TAM's sold output (RPKs) was up 6.4 per cent on the previous year, though its increased capacity resulted in a lower overall load factor. Moreover, both domestic yield per RPK and total revenue declined from the 2008 levels. The later years are taken up below.

5.6.2 GOL: a low-cost newcomer

In 2001, while TAM was growing into a very substantial company, a Brazilian road coach company Grupo Auréa started a new, low-cost airline, *GOL*, which became a publicly listed company in 2004. From the outset, GOL was *very* successful in attracting passengers, in part because – on GOL's own account (GOL, Form 20-F for 2009, p. 39) – its fares were in general somewhat lower than those set by TAM. By the end of 2007, GOL's fleet comprised: 36 B737-800, 30 B737-700 and 12 B737-300 aircraft (GOL, Form 20-F, 2007, p. 33).

5.6.3 The demise of Varig

To some extent, the entry and growth of GOL and the expansion of TAM was at the expense of Varig. Furthermore, because the Brazilian economy had become depressed, the aviation regulator, ANAC, embarked on a measure of temporary re-regulation in 2003–04, in response to perceived 'excess' capacity (Bettini and Oliveira, 2008).

In February 2003, Varig and TAM agreed to code-share, 'as a preliminary stage in a possible merger between the two companies' (TAM, Form 20-F, 2009, p. 19). However, CADE (the Administrative Council for Economic Defence – an anti-trust unit within the Finance Ministry) saw the code-sharing as amounting to cartel conduct, and started legal action against the two airlines (Bettini and Oliveira, 2008, p. 290). By February 2005, 'it became clear that the proposed merger would not take place', and the code-share deal was cancelled (TAM, Form 20-F, 2009, p. 20).

In June 2005, Varig sought bankruptcy protection. Many of its assets (notably airport and route operating rights that stemmed from Varig's role as a flag-carrier) were then vested in a new company called VRG. In April 2007, however, it was GOL rather than TAM which bought VRG (GOL, Form 20-F, 2008, p. 18).

5.6.4 The further growth of GOL

At first, the enlarged GOL operated two distinct brands: GOL itself, continuing as a low-fare carrier; and Varig, providing services for business travellers, with some of its aircraft configured for two cabin classes (GOL, Form 20-F, 2007, p. 19). In June 2008, GOL's purchase of VRG was approved by the economic regulator (CADE), and GOL began to integrate the two airlines and their networks. The process was completed by the beginning of 2009, and the integration helped to reduce unit costs. Also, GOL ended the Varig intercontinental flights to Europe, to concentrate on domestic services and regional flights (GOL Form 20-F 2009, p.45; 'FAQ', voegol.com.br accessed 6 July 2010). Although GOL's prospects seemed rosy, the onset of the global financial crisis helped to put the operating account into significant deficit in 2008 (GOL, Consolidated Financial Statements Year ending 31 December 2008, p. F5).

Since then, the airline sector in Brazil has seen significant fluctuations around a rising trend in the traffic level. While GOL was growing overall, those changes together with fluctuations in the price of fuel put a premium on nimble management.

At the end of 2014, the company was operating 35 × B737-700 (144 seats), 9 × B737-800 (177 seats) and 95 × B737-800SFP 'short field performance' (also 177 seats), for a fleet total of 139 aircraft, each with a single cabin. (GOL valued the 'short field performance' because it enabled the airline to use the airport of Santos Dumont in Rio de Janeiro.) Almost all those aircraft were leased, and their average age was 7.2 years. In 2014, the airline secured, on average, 11.5 block hours per aircraft per day, up from 11.2 hours in 2013, but down from levels of up to 13.0 hours in previous years (Form 20-F 2014, p. 24).

The fleet plan was to have 142 B737NG aircraft in 2017, and then increase the total fleet to 148 aircraft in 2018 and to 157 in 2019, as B737-MAX aircraft were delivered from 2018 onwards (Form 20-F 2014, p. 25).

5.6.5 Other newcomers: TRIP, Avianca Brasil and Webjet

In 1998, the Caprioli Group (a travel conglomerate based in Campinas) launched *TRIP Airlines*, with Viracopos-Campinas airport as its headquarters and initial base. TRIP began by focussing on regional routes, often providing airline connections where none existed before. Another Brazilian transport conglomerate, White Eagle Group, became an investor in 2006; and in September 2008, the United States holding company, SkyWest Inc. (parent of SkyWest Airlines) also invested in TRIP ('about us', *voetrip.com.br* accessed 11 July 2010).

By mid-2010, TRIP served 70 Brazilian ports, using a fleet composed mainly of turbo props, namely 14 × ATR42s (each with 45 to 48 seats) and 14 × ATR72s (66 to 68 seats). It had also begun to operate Embraer jets, which suggested an intention to enter major routes, in competition with the established airlines.

Avianca Brasil

Launched in 1998 as an air taxi operator, and at that time called Oceanair, *Avianca Brasil* grew as it began to operate jets on some major domestic routes. Despite already being a subsidiary of Synergy, Oceanair was re-branded as Avianca Brasil only in 2010, when it began to acquire A319s, as part of the Avianca group (avianca.com.br and Wikipedia on Avianca Brasil, both accessed 11 July 2010).

Webjet

Another low-fare newcomer, *Webjet*, started flying in May 2005 (with but a single aircraft). Initially, it had very low load factors, and suspended operations in November. After two new investors bought the company, it resumed flying in January 2006. A year later the company was taken over by CVC Viagens, a large travel wholesaler which sought lower airline prices than it had been paying to the major airlines ('About us' webjet.com.br, and Wikipedia on Webjet, both accessed 4 July 2010). Thereafter Webjet grew quickly, offering scheduled services on weekdays, and charter flights at weekends. By July 2010, it was operating 20 ageing B737-300s (www.ch-aviation.ch, accessed 4 July 2010).

5.6.6 Regulation of the domestic market

Despite those airline entries, and the more recent entry of Azul (reported in the next section), TAM and GOL still dominated the domestic market in 2009. Given that dominance, it was particularly important that the government aviation regulator, ANAC, took a pro-competition stance on many issues.

In particular, in reaching a decision on an airline application for permission to enter any particular route, ANAC takes into account the availability of airport capacity as well as the presence of competing airline services and any increase in demand (TAM Form 20-F, 2009, p. 43). (For a detailed account of ANAC's powers, see 'Aeronautical services' in the English-language section of anac.gov. br, accessed 10 July 2010.)

At certain times, a few of the busiest ports (for example, the Congonhas at São Paulo, and Santos Dumont in Rio de Janeiro) are slot-restricted. Although ANAC does allocate runway slots, these do *not* become the property of the airline. Furthermore, the ANAC rules for the allocation of new or other available slots give some preference to new airlines (TAM Form 20-F, 2009, p. 44; GOL Form 20-F, 2009, p. 33).

5.6.7 The entry and rapid growth of Azul

The growth of GOL and TAM did not deter David Neeleman (founder and former CEO of JetBlue) from starting a Brazilian low-cost airline, *Azul.* Though Neeleman came from an American family, he was born in Brazil, and so had Brazilian citizenship. This made him eligible to become the chairman and dominant investor of the new airline. The investors put in US$200 million before its December 2008 launch ('About us', viajemais.voeazul.com.br, accessed 3 July 2010).

For its headquarters and first base, Azul followed TRIP by choosing Viracopos-Campinas International Airport (VCP). In the industrialised state of São Paulo, the Campinas metropolitan area has a population of about three million. Its airport is about 85 km from each of the two main airports at São Paulo (anna.aero, 19 December 2008; Wikipedia, accessed 4 July 2010). No doubt, one reason for the choice of Campinas was the availability of uncongested facilities. Also favourable were prospects of high rates of economic growth in the Campinas area.

Azul launched with Embraer 190 and 195 aircraft in a one-class layout (106 and 118 seats, respectively), with a minimum 32-inch seat pitch (Embraer media release, 12 December 2008). By mid-2010, the airline operated 18 such aircraft (ch-aviation.ch, accessed 4 July 2010); all came new from Embraer, except for a few E190s leased from JetBlue. Initial plans to acquire (on average) one extra aircraft every month were *not* cut back despite the impact of the general financial crisis.

Azul's aim was to undercut the fares of rival airlines by about 15 per cent (CAPA 'Brazil's LCCs and start-ups gaining market share', 23 September 2009). Azul's smaller aircraft made it commercially viable to serve thinner routes that did not attract GOL or TAM. No doubt, those factors helped the considerable growth in the airline's passenger numbers: Azul reached the million-passenger total after only eight months, and the next million took only a further four months (Azul news release, 30 April 2010). As seen in Table 5.2, Azul attracted 3.8 per cent of the total RPKs flown on domestic routes in 2009. This was well ahead of its initial plans.

Some 18 months after its launch, Azul was serving 19 ports from its Campinas hub. It also had two or three non-spoke routes at each of Rio de Janeiro, Belo Horizonte, Porto Seguro and (the Brazilian city of) Salvador.

Table 5.2 Airline performance, domestic routes in Brazil, 2009 and 2013

Airline	Calendar year 2009				Calendar year 2013			
	RPK (billion)	Load factor %	Market share %		RPK (billion)	Load factor %	Market share %	
			ASK	RPK			ASK	RPK
TAM	25.7	65.8	46.3	45.6	34.9	79.1	40.4	40.8
GOL	23.3	66.9	41.3	41.4	31.2	70.7	35.1	33.9
Avianca[1]	1.4	71.2	2.4	2.5	6.3	77.8	4.9	5.4
Azul	2.1	79.7	3.2	3.8	11.6	83.5	9.2	10.0
TRIP	0.8	60.5	1.7	1.5	3.3	72.4	4.8	4.5
Webjet	2.5	67.1	4.4	4.5	–	–	–	–
Others	0.4	–	0.7	0.7	0.9	75.0	0.8	0.6
All	56.3	66.8	100.0	100.0	88.2	76.0	100.0	100.0

Source: ANAC (National Civil Aviation Agency, Brazil) Dados Comparitavos Avançados (www2. anac.gov.br)

Note
1 In 2009, Avianca Brasil traded as Oceanair.

5.6.8 Some consolidation in the domestic market

In July 2011, GOL purchased Webjet, and at first continued to operate Webjet's fleet of 20 fuel-thirsty B737-300 aircraft. Despite the soft state of the economy, it was November 2012 before GOL grounded Webjet's fleet, and flew the passengers on its own aircraft. It then 'began the process of winding up Webjet's activities and the consequent discontinuation of its brand' (GOL, Annual Report 2012, p. 46).

In the second quarter of 2013, GOL sub-leased five of its B737-800 aircraft to a European airline (Transavia) for the European summer (GOL, 2Q13 Results Conference Call, August 2013, p. 17). That helped GOL deal with the reduced demand levels then prevailing in Brazil.

In 2012, the two airlines headquartered in Campinas, Azul and TRIP, agreed to a merger in which Azul would lead. Given the regulatory regime, the initial step was an all-embracing code-share deal ('Acordo de codeshare entre Azul e Trip leva cliente a 100 destinos', *Brasilturis Journal*, 20 September 2012).

CADE considered the merger to be pro-competitive because 'Azul and Trip together are in a better position to compete with the market leaders of national civil aviation, TAM and GOL.' However, CADE imposed two conditions.

First, Azul had to phase out the prevailing code-share agreement between TRIP and TAM. Second, with effect from 30 days after the decision, the company had to ensure that it used not less than 85 per cent of the slots assigned to it at (the congested) Santos Dumont Airport. The company's slot utilisation 'will be measured quarterly. If [the condition is] breached, a pair of the merged company's slots will be returned to ANAC for redistribution' ('CADE approves merger of Azul and Trip', cade.gov.br, accessed 6 September 2013). (Was the penalty to be applied for each and every quarter in which the utilisation rate was too low?)

5.6.9 Growth in the domestic market after 2009

Though market conditions were changing from year to year, and there was a demand decline in 2012, the cumulative picture over the four-year period to 2013 is one of considerable growth. Indeed, total RPK increased by 57 per cent (Table 5.2), accommodated in part by a large increase in the overall load factor, from 67 to 76 per cent. Azul, TRIP and Avianca increased their market shares, while both TAM and GOL *lost* market share, though both had substantial increases in RPK. In both 2009 and 2013, Azul had much the highest load factor.

For the calendar year 2013, the combined domestic RPK share of Azul and TRIP was about 14.5 per cent (Table 5.2). With TRIP also operating Embraer jets, the joint fleet in August 2013 comprised only two aircraft families, E190/195 jets and the (ex-TRIP) ATR 72 turboprops used on the thinner regional routes. The total fleet was about 75 aircraft, with a further 40 E195 aircraft on order. Thus, within five years of its launch, Azul served about 100 ports, all in Brazil, and operated about 220 routes (ch-aviation.ch, accessed 20 August 2013).

In May 2013, Azul announced an IPO for shares, intended to raise about BRL 1 billion. Much of that sum was to be used for aircraft purchases for the airline's intended growth. Because of adverse financial-market conditions, however, the IPO was cancelled in August (Julia Leite, 'JetBlue founder Neeleman's Azul pulls IPO as Ibovespa slumps', *Bloomberg*, 20 August 2013).

Late in 2014, Azul again filed IPO papers with the (US) SEC and the Brazilian securities regulator. However, this too was cancelled when the financial markets changed unfavourably. The company's funding problems were accentuated by the subdued demand conditions in Brazil, and by a currency depreciation of the Brazilian real (CAPA, 'Azul faces challenges in funding growth as investors shy away from Brazilian companies', 13 April 2015).

5.7 LAN branches out from its base in Chile

Situated on the Pacific coast of South America, Chile has a population of about 18 million people. Back in 1929, the government launched an airline, *LAN*, as a state-owned enterprise. After privatisation in 1989, the present majority shareholders took control in 1994. The company listed on the New York Stock Exchange in 1997.

Despite (or perhaps because of) its longevity, LAN adopted a new (low-cost) business model for domestic routes in Chile and for some other routes within South America. It also launched three subsidiary operating companies: *LAN Peru* in 1999, *LAN Ecuador* in 2003, and *LAN Argentina* in 2005, each domiciled in the respective country. Upon acquiring the Colombian airline *Aires* in November 2010, LAN restructured that company's operations, secured for it the award of the IOSA safety certificate, and began to introduce A320s. It then rebranded the airline as *LAN Colombia,* at the end of 2011 (LAN Airlines, Form 20-F for 2011, pp. 67, 78).

Besides the usual inter-governmental agreements for regional and other international routes, LAN obtained government permissions to operate *domestic*

Table 5.3 LAN's domestic market shares (per cent) in five countries, 2009 and 2014

% shares	Chile	Peru	Argentina	Ecuador	Colombia
2009	81	77	30	15	–
2014	78	63	27	36	19

Sources: LAN Annual Report 2009, p. 48; Latam Annual Report 2014, pp. 63–70

Note
Though the source texts are not fully explicit, it seems the shares are of passenger numbers.

services within those four countries (as well as in Chile, of course). LAN Argentina won such permission at a time when the government was unhappy with the performance of (the, then, privately owned) Aerolineas Argentinas (CAPA 'Aerolineas Argentinas to focus on expansion in protected domestic market following 737-800 order' 29 October 2013). In contrast, LAN Ecuador started with international routes, and began domestic services only in April 2009.

The extent of LAN's penetration of the domestic markets is reported in Table 5.3. Most notable is its domestic share in Peru, where however the share has declined. Yet LAN has done well in both Ecuador and Colombia.

For its domestic and regional services in all five countries, LAN re-equipped with the Airbus A320 family. On some routes, it offered a Premium Economy cabin as well as the main cabin. The company used its new aircraft intensively: it increased some route frequencies, redesigned check-in procedures, started new routes (to increase connectivity), and (last, but not least) introduced lower fares – especially on off-peak flights (LAN, Annual Report 2007, p. 39).

These initiatives resulted in some dramatic increases in passenger numbers (Table 5.4). Indeed, over the five years to 2009, almost all the output measures went up, despite the effects of the general financial crisis. The single important exception concerns the year 2009: although LAN operated more capacity than in the previous year, and had both a higher RPK total and a slightly higher load

Table 5.4 Operating statistics for all passenger services,[1] LAN group airlines,[2] 2005–11

	2005	2006	2007	2008	2009	2010	2011[3]
Passengers (millions)	8.0	8.9	11.1	13.2	15.4	17.3	22.5
ASK (billions)	23.7	26.4	31.6	35.2	38.8	42.3	48.1
RPK (billions)	17.5	19.5	24.0	27.0	29.8	33.1	38.4
Load factor (%)	73.8	73.8	76.1	76.6	76.9	78.3	79.8
Yield (US cents/RPK)	8.4	9.3	9.2	10.5	8.8	9.4	10.4
Revenue (US cents/ASK)	6.2	6.9	7.0	8.0	6.8	7.3	8.3

Source: LAN, Annual Report 2009, p. 9; LAN, Annual Report 2011, p. 52; LAN, Form 20-F 2011, p. 72; LATAM Merger Presentation, 2012, p. 4

Notes
1 Includes international as well as domestic routes.
2 The data are for the years preceding the merger with TAM.
3 The operations of LAN Colombia and its predecessor are included here only for the year 2011.

factor, those gains rested on lower average fares, resulting in reduced yield and reduced unit revenue per ASK.

At 29 February 2012, the LAN group deployed 136 passenger aircraft, including 77 A318/319/320 and 9 B737-700 narrow-body jets used on domestic and regional services, and 31 B767-700 jets for longer routes (LAN, Form 20-F 2011, p. 89). Clearly LAN was a formidable entity when it entered into negotiations with TAM regarding a merger – which is the subject of the next section.

5.8 Latam Airlines Group, the merger of LAN and TAM

Among South American airlines, LAN based in Chile and TAM in Brazil stood out as two of the largest; indeed, each of LAN and TAM was about as big as Avianca *after* its merger with TACA. Furthermore, there was little overlap of the route networks of LAN and TAM. Thus, in the event of a merger proposal, national governments would be likely to grant permission, provided detailed proposals did not have significant adverse consequences for individual national interests.

The two airlines revealed merger plans on 13 August 2010. The two companies signed a binding and final agreement in January 2011, the Chilean antitrust court gave its approval in September, and the Brazilian antitrust agency (CADE) did likewise in December. The very complex process for a public offer for the exchange of shares concluded successfully in June 2012 (Latam Airlines Group, undated brochure, p. 1, accessed on 18 August 2013 at the Media Center, www.latamairlinesgroup.net).

Of course, the structure of the new company had to comply with foreign-ownership conditions. In particular, Brazil required that foreign interests hold no more than 20 per cent of the shares of an airline flying domestic routes in Brazil (Latam Merger Presentation, May 2012, p. 21, which displays a telling diagram of the proposed corporate structure for the merger). Under the proposal, LAN and TAM were to continue to fly under their separate brands, and (no doubt) under their separate AOCs.

Upon merging in December 2012, the *passenger* fleet of the Group numbered just over *300 aircraft*. The Airbus short-haul family dominated: 5 × A318, 57 × A319, 141 × A320, and 9 × A321 (Latam Annual Report 2012, pp.14–15). Also notable was a total of 41 × B767s, which included recent acquisitions of the -300 model. Few airlines in the world had significantly larger fleets than Latam.

Of course, the sold output was also very large. In 2012, counting regional and other international flights as well as domestic flights in the seven countries in which Latam had operating rights, the group carried 65 million passengers flying a total of 104 billion RPK, at a passenger load factor of 78.2 per cent.

However, the consolidated *financial* results have not been very good: in 2011, there was a very small total profit, and in 2012 a substantial total loss of about US$500 million (Latam Consolidated Proforma Income Statement and Operating Statistics, 2011 and 2012, accessed at latamgroupairlines.net). The integrated accounts for the next two years record net losses of US$264 million for 2013, and US$227 million for 2014 (LATAM, Form 20F for 2014, p. 5). Of course these results have been adversely affected by generally poor economic conditions in several South American countries.

5.9 Other airlines in the south of the continent

Argentina

In Argentina (population over 40 million), another of South America's venerable airlines, *Aerolíneas Argentinas* has had a chequered history. Established in 1950, as a State Company (www.austral.com.ar, accessed 12 July 2010), the airline was sold in 1990 to a consortium led by Iberia (the Spanish airline). In 2001, another private owner, the Marsans Group, took control. Later that decade, when the airline experienced very severe financial difficulties, the Argentine government recovered possession of almost all the shares, and then installed a new board of directors in February 2009 (media release, www.aerolineas.com, 5 February 2009).

In an attempt to restore the fortunes of the company, the new board ordered 20 new Embraer E190s, for use on domestic routes flown by the airline's subsidiary, Austral. It also started leasing and buying B737-700 and -800 aircraft for Aerolíneas Argentinas itself. The last of the E190s arrived in March 2011, and in the same month, the airline re-joined the IATA Clearing House (after a suspension of 10 years). In 2012, the airline retired the last of its ageing MD80s and B737-500s. Following disposal of its B747s, the company's only long-range aircraft were A340s ('Our history', www.aerolineas.com, accessed 26 August 2013).

The airline closed unprofitable routes, redesigned its domestic route-network, launched some new international routes, and cut some of its labour costs. In the outcome, the company carried more passengers and increased its market shares. In particular, by mid-2013, Aerolíneas Argentinas (together with Austral) was offering about 52 per cent of the seats being flown on domestic routes ('Aerolineas Argentinas growing by 30%; new domestic routes spearhead this year's surge', anna.aero, 7 August 2013).

In October 2013, while benefiting from the prevailing protectionist attitude of the Argentine government, the company ordered 26 additional B737-800s from Boeing, to enable the airline to further increase its domestic and regional services (CAPA, 'Aerolineas Argentinas to focus on expansion in protected domestic market following 737-800 order', 29 October 2013).

It was not clear, however, whether the rejuvenated airline could earn sufficient profits.

Uruguay

Uruguay (population about 3.3 million) is one of the smaller countries in South America. Besides its coastline on the South Atlantic, its land borders are with Brazil and Argentina. Its capital Montevideo is about 200 km east from Buenos Aires. The 50-minute flight from Montevideo crosses from the north side of the mouth of the River Plata to the south side of the river at Buenos Aires.

In 1936, the Uruguayan government established the airline *PLUNA,* which remained a government-owned flag carrier until serious financial difficulties led to partial privatisation in 1994, involving a consortium led by Varig, which provided the management. After Varig itself sought bankruptcy protection in 2005, the Uruguayan government resumed control of PLUNA, but later sold 75 per cent of the shares to individual Uruguayan investors and to a German-based investment consortium, Leadgate, which took the managerial role.

The new management closed the loss-making service to Madrid, and replaced the ageing Boeing 737-200 aircraft with a single-model fleet of new Bombardier CRJ 900 regional jets, each seating 90 passengers in a single-class cabin. In developing its hub at Montevideo, PLUNA used these smaller aircraft to operate frequent services (usually, seven flights daily) to Buenos Aires' city port (Aeroparque Jorge Newbery).

It also started several new services to meet perceived traveller wants. It began a daily flight from Montevideo to Buenos Aires' international airport (Ezeiza), timed to connect there with overnight flights to Europe and to the US (PLUNA news release 13 January 2010, and a report by anna.aero, 9 March 2010). It began to build traffic on long and/or thin routes to various Brazilian ports, including Brasilia, Belo Horizonte, Rio de Janeiro, Campinas Viracopos, Sao Paulo Guarulhos, Curitiba and Porto Alegre. (On some of those thin routes, PLUNA was the only airline offering *non-stop* service to/from Montevideo.)

Besides aiming to serve passengers wishing to fly to/from Uruguay, it sought also to win patronage from travellers willing to hub at Montevideo while flying between ports in other countries. In that regard, PLUNA itself flew to Santiago (Chile) and to Asuncion (Paraguay). However, besides Buenos Aires, the only other port it was permitted to serve in Argentina was Cordoba, the second most populous metropolitan area. In its bid to help Aerolíneas Argentinas, the Argentine government seemingly did not want PLUNA to capture traffic that could hub at Buenos Aires (CAPA, 'Uruguay's Pluna warns . . .', 8 June 2012).

By December 2008, PLUNA had received seven of its new jets. In the calendar year 2009, it carried some 37 per cent more passengers than in 2008. After several years of financial losses, it earned a small profit in 2009 (media release, flypluna. com, 4 February 2010). In the early months of 2010, it flew more passenger than in the early months of 2009 (news release, 26 May 2010). By early 2012, the fleet numbered 13 CRJ 900s.

Despite winning substantial *transit* traffic to its hub – said to be about 40 per cent of all its passengers – PLUNA did not reach comfortable profitability. Besides the conduct of the Argentinean government, there were other problems, of course. PLUNA was said to be carrying debts of about US$380 million. Furthermore, the mergers of the larger South American airlines suggested that in the near future PLUNA might find it even harder to compete.

A crisis in available working capital came in July 2012. After failing to obtain further funding from private investors or from the Uruguayan government, Leadgate closed the airline (CAPA, 'Aerolineas Argentinas, BQB, GOL and LAN-TAM poised to benefit from demise of Uruguay's Pluna', 13 July 2012).

The immediate consequence was a dramatic reduction in the number of passengers at Montevideo Airport. A recently started Uruguayan airline, *BQB* (owned by a Uruguayan bus operator, Buquebús) expanded its services on the route to Buenos Aires, using ATR72-500 turboprops – which are well suited to such a short route. Initially, PLUNA's longer (international) routes were left unserved; later, airlines domiciled in other countries entered some of them.

In the second half of 2014, BQB planned to deploy an A319 on the busy Montevideo–Buenos Aires route, with the agreement of the Uruguayan regulator. But the Argentine regulator would not allow BQB to substitute the jet for the on-going turbo-prop service. BQB was reported as returning the jet to the leasing company. Soon after, BQB terminated its services to Brazilian ports, and abandoned plans to start flying to some ports in Chile. Then, BQB was reported as further reducing its operations, and removing two ATR 72 turbo-props from its fleet of four (see reports at ch-aviation.ch, dated 5 August, 4 and 8 September, and 11 October 2014).

With BQB known to be in financial trouble, its founder/CEO suspended operations on 10 April 2015 (with the agreement of the Uruguayan regulator), separated the airline from the bus company, and sold the airline to Amaszonas (a small scheduled carrier domiciled in Bolivia).

At the time, Amaszonas was seeking to expand into Paraguay, and was expected to relaunch service on 4 May 2015 on the routes from Montevideo to Buenos Aires and Montevideo to Asuncion (Paraguay) (reports at ch-aviation.ch dated 11 April, 19 April and 4 May). However, on 26 October 2015, the airline website (amaszonas. com) showed only a single route (to Asunción), where Montevideo passengers could transfer to/from other Amaszonas flights on that company's growing network.

For that Monday (26 October), flightradar24.com recorded five E 190 flights (operated by Austral for its parent, Aerolíneas Argentinas) from Montevideo to Buenos Aires. Of these, three went to Ezeiza (to connect with long-haul flights), while the other two were in the morning and evening peak periods, and flew to Aeroparque. The list did not include any flights by an airline domiciled in Uruguay. The Argentine government regulator had won the first battle.

5.10 Market concentration in Latin America

While agreements between governments in Latin America have supported growth in international travel, the pursuit of (perceived) national interests has sometimes resulted in obstacles to airline entry. *In general*, access to a country's *domestic* routes is open only to airlines domiciled in that country; usually, there are limits on the extent of foreign ownership of an airline that flies domestic routes.

Despite those requirements, each of three holding companies – Latam, Avianca and Copa – has at least one subsidiary or affiliate domiciled in a country other than that of the holding company. For the large South American continent, Table 5.5 shows the presence of one or more of the three groups in *all* of the countries other than Bolivia, Uruguay and Venezuela.

In the case of Asia, the ability to launch subsidiary airlines in other countries, while meeting the regulatory requirements of those host countries, helped the

Table 5.5 Airline groups and other significant airlines possessing rights to operate domestic services in Latin American countries,[1,2] 2014

Countries	LATAM group	Avianca group	Copa	other airlines
Mexico				Aeroméxico, Volaris*, Interjet*, VivaAerobus*
El Salvador		Avianca		
Honduras		Taca de Honduras		
Panama			Copa	
Guatemala		Avianca (Aviateca)		
Costa Rica		Avianca (LACSA)		
Colombia	LAN Colombia	Avianca	Copa Colombia	VivaColombia*
Venezuela				Conviasa
Ecuador	LAN Ecuador	Avianca Ecuador		Tame
Brazil	TAM	Avianca Brasil		GOL*, Azul*
Peru	LAN Peru	Avianca Peru		
Bolivia				Amaszonas
Paraguay	TAM Paraguay			
Chile	LAN			Sky Airline Chile
Uruguay				BQB
Argentina	LAN Argentina			Aerolíneas Argentinas (and *subsidiary* Austral)

Notes

An asterisk denotes an airline that may be classified as a low-cost carrier.

1 Rows are for countries, listed (broadly) in order by geographical location, from north to south.
2 In each row, the cell entries identify airlines that are domiciled in the country.

growth of the more successful, new low-cost carriers. While that cross-border model has been important in South America too, such growth initiatives have come not from *new* airlines but from long-established legacy carriers.

In contrast, most of the six *low-cost* Latin-American airlines (identified by asterisks in Table 5.5) have (so far) concentrated on providing domestic services within the country where the airline is domiciled. The principal exception has been GOL, which has continued to fly some of the international routes it inherited when it took over Varig. However, the establishment of VivaColombia – whose ownership is related to that of VivaAerobus in Mexico – may signal the beginning of a trend for the cross-border expansion of low-cost airlines in Latin America.

Despite the earlier entry by LAN Argentina, the Argentine government presently seems to be intent on protecting Aerolíneas Argentinas, and may be unwilling to welcome an airline based elsewhere. However, in South America in general, locally domiciled LCCs that are affiliated with LCCs established in other countries may receive a reasonable welcome.

6 Africa

6.1 Introduction

Among all the continents, Africa is regarded as the one where airline services are the least developed. There are several factors at work. Most parts of Africa have very modest income levels; many independent countries have small populations, and some of those are small in spatial extent; in most cases, a 'national' carrier has only a small domestic market; and those who have tried to support *regional* carriers often find it difficult to secure and maintain the needed degree of cooperation between the governments of the countries in the region.

Furthermore, because of the earlier extensive colonisation by European powers, a significant proportion of international commercial and trade links may *still* be those between the African country and its former ruler. In consequence, airlines such as Air France and British Airways commonly fly daily to the capital cities of their former colonies.

In part because of that colonial heritage, there is some lack of *direct* air links *between* African countries, even sometimes between adjacent countries. Instead, a business traveller (for example) may have to travel via an airline hub in a third country; and that hub may be distant. And, where one or more sectors in an indirect journey are monopoly routes, the fare can be very high.

Usually, the only alternative is travel by road, with journeys often taking many hours, even in the case of adjacent countries.

For the future, there remains the possibility of designing a well-considered hub-and-spoke network for the entire continent. Ssamula and Venter (2013) suggest a network with four hub ports. In proposing the use of low-cost smaller aircraft on some spokes, they recognise one turbo-prop, the F50, but neglect the newer fuel-thrifty types, the Q400 and the ATR 72. This *may* compromise their conclusions.

Of course, a hub-and-spoke network can give monopoly power to its operator. Securing effective regulation of such a network in Africa would require effective cooperation between independent states. Section 6.2 looks briefly at the modest record of governmental attempts to agree on the introduction of Pan-African open skies.

Few African countries have seen much competition between airlines in the provision of *domestic* services; the major exception is the Republic of South Africa, whose domestic market is considered here in §6.3.

In large regions such as East Africa and West Africa, governments have sought to provide airline services on a collaborative basis. Unfortunately the history is often of financial difficulties and airline closures. In very recent years, however, some private airlines have entered and sought to establish pan-African networks. And in one case, an inter-governmental initiative has established a commercial company. For the various regions, those issues are discussed in §§6.4–10.

6.2 Inter-governmental talks on African open skies

In the Yamoussoukro Declaration of 1988, African governments gave in-principle support to having a single African airspace that would give (eligible) African airlines access to all routes within Africa. Recognising the lack of progress, African ministers in charge of civil aviation met again in Yamoussoukro (Côte d'Ivoire), in November 1999, and adopted the Yamoussoukro Decision (Economic Commission for Africa, 1999). This established arrangements for the gradual liberalization of intra-Africa air transport services, with the Decision to take precedence over any multilateral or bilateral agreements on such services. By the Decision, the states were to grant to each other free exercise of the rights of the first, second, third, fourth and fifth freedoms of the air, and in effect gave up most powers to regulate fares.

Although implementation has been hesitant, the attempts are on-going (Africa Union presentation 'Economic integration in Africa: experience in air transport liberalisation: the Yamoussoukro Decision', EU-AU Aviation Seminar, Brussels, 2006, accessed at www.africa-union.org, 4 April 2009; ICAO/ATAG/WB Development Forum, 2006). In April 2009, the first-ever EU–Africa aviation conference (European Commission, 2009) was held in Windhoek, Namibia.

Despite governmental sloth, recent years have seen the entry of several carriers, and prolonged (though usually successful) negotiation of bilateral access to international routes. Some such entries in North African countries have been noted in §3.2. The discussion here concerns new-carrier initiatives in sub-Saharan Africa.

6.3 Competition on domestic routes in the Republic of South Africa

For some years, the government-owned flag carrier South African Airways (SAA) has faced a significant full-service rival, the privately owned Comair. After modest beginnings in 1946, Comair started flying jets in 1992, and became a British Airways franchisee in 1996 ('about us', comair.co.za, accessed 4 April 2009). Some details for SAA and Comair appear in Table 6.1.

In 2001, Comair started a wholly-owned subsidiary, *Kulula*, a low-cost airline which emphasised on-line booking at kulula.com. The new company also branched out into other on-line retailing, even including the marketing of cell phones, and soon claimed to be the largest on-line retailer in South Africa.

After launching on South Africa's main routes, Kulula started flying also from Lanseria, a low-cost secondary port, a little north of Johannesburg and well located

Table 6.1 Significant airlines in the Republic of South Africa, at end of 2014

Airline	Launch year	Owner	Fleet	Further information
South African Airways (SAA)	1934	Govt. of South Africa	short-haul fleet: 11 × A319 4 × A320 13 × B737-800	National flag carrier
Comair	1946	private investors	7 × B737-300 10 × B737-400	Operates local British Airways flights under franchise; also owns Kulula.
South African Express	1994	Govt. of South Africa	10 × Q400 12 × CRJ-200 4 × CRJ-700	Besides domestic ports, serves ports in Botswana, Namibia, Mozambique
Airlink	1995	private investors	12 × ERJ-85 14 × ERJ-135 2 × ERJ145 8 × Jetstream 41	Franchisee of SAA. Small-town feeder network
Kulula	2001	Comair	9 × B737-800 (189 seats) and one B737-400 (162 seats)	Serves: Johannesburg, Lanseria, Cape Town, Durban, East London, George
1time (closed 2012)	2004	private investors	at time of closure: 11 × MD80 family	Domestic and a few international routes
Mango	2006	South African Airways	6 × B737-800 (186 seats) some wet-leased aircraft	Serves: Johannesburg, Cape Town, Durban, Lanseria, Bloemfontein
FlySafair	2014	established aviation co.	4 × B737-400	

Sources: fleet information from South African Airways, Integrated Report 2013; Comair, Integrated Annual Report 2014 and ch-aviation.ch, accessed 12 December 2014; port information from airline websites and Wikipedia, accessed 13 September 2013 and 11 December 2014

to serve the country's administrative capital, Pretoria. Though Kulula initially operated some early-model B737 aircraft, the parent Comair began to acquire B737-800 aircraft, and gave priority to re-equipping Kulula (see Table 6.1).

In 2004, local investors with limited funds launched a new airline *1time* with MD80 aircraft. After building up a domestic network, 1time operated the most frequent LCC service on most of its routes. However, as fuel prices rose, 1time was increasingly handicapped by the thirst of its old aircraft. It closed in November 2012.

Seeking to recover some of the market share it had lost to the new low cost airlines, South African Airways (SAA) launched its own budget airline, *Mango*, in 2006, and equipped it with new B737-800 aircraft (Table 6.1).

Competition between airlines on South African domestic routes

Table 6.1 also shows two regional airlines, *South African Express* and *Airlink*, both closely related to South African Airways. In 2014, the privately owned Airlink was in the course of disposing of its Jetstream 41s (ch.aviation.ch, 11 November 2014). And the government-owned South African Express was deemed insolvent ('South African Express admits insolvency', ch.aviation.ch, 30 November 2014) but was still flying.

Thus when 1time withdrew, competition in the South African market reduced (for a while, at least) to rivalry between SAA and Comair for full-service customers, and between their respective LCCs for budget travel.

In 2012–13, South African Airways carried 7.0 million passengers, including those flying on long-haul services, while Mango carried 1.8 million passengers (South African Airways Integrated Report 2013, p. 8). In 2013–14, Comair and Kulula together carried 5.2 million passengers, on domestic and regional routes (Comair Integrated Annual Report 2014, p. 8). Though that passenger total is not disaggregated, it is clear that Kulula had a larger fleet and carried more passengers than did Mango.

Legal actions under competition legislation

As in other industries, some airline marketing strategies can contravene competition laws. Responding to a complaint from Nationwide (a small airline no longer in business), the (South African) Competition Tribunal examined two SAA incentive schemes that were in force during 2000–2001. These gave override commissions to travel agent companies, and paid rewards to travel-agent employees, to encourage them to sell tickets for domestic travel on SAA. In its deliberations, the Tribunal noted that, for the period in question, SAA received almost 66 per cent of the total ticket revenue for domestic airline travel, while Comair had 27 per cent.

In its decision (*Competition Commission and South African Airways (Pty) Ltd* [2005] ZACT 50, 28 July 2005, accessed at saflii.org, 21 July 2010) the Tribunal found that the schemes constituted anti-competitive conduct and contravened §8(d)(i) of the South Africa Competition Act 1998. (The Act says a dominant firm shall not require or induce a supplier or customer not to deal with a competitor *unless* the firm concerned 'can show technological, efficiency or other pro-competitive gains which outweigh the anti-competitive effect of its act'.)

The next legal joust, which started in 2006, concerned a similar matter, namely the SAA incentive schemes for travel agents that were in force from 1 June 2001 until 31 March 2005. Complaints came from both Nationwide and Comair. According to the Competition Tribunal (*Nationwide and Comair v South African Airways (Pty) Ltd* [2010] ZACT 13, 17 February 2010, §§16 and 20):

> what Comair and Nationwide effectively seek in these proceedings is a declaration by the Tribunal . . . that [the] incentive schemes . . . were exclusionary and amounted to prohibited practices in terms . . . of the Act. . . .

The practical utility to Comair and Nationwide . . . is that such a declaration is a prerequisite . . . to the institution of an action in the High Court for damages flowing from the anticompetitive conduct ruled by the Tribunal.

The Tribunal found that the agreements resulted in 'foreclosure of rivals in the domestic airline market [that] was likely to be substantial' (§224 of its report), and declared (§254) that the override incentive agreements and the trust agreements/payments contravened §8 (d) (i) of the Act.

Comair noted later (Annual Report 2012, p. 6), 'We also won the appeal which SAA [then] lodged, and have issued a multi-million Rand summons against SAA for damages related to this claim.' At p. 9 of the Integrated Annual Report for 2014, Comair noted it was waiting for a hearing date in the High Court of South Africa.

Government funding for the South African Airways group

The main public-policy issue concerning SAA is the long-running financial support given by the South African government, and intended to fund restructuring of the airline, in order to make it efficient and profitable. Such funding raises two issues.

The *first issue* arises in any market economy in which airlines are intended to earn their keep by selling their services to customers. Unless there are exceptional circumstances (preferably with prior definition thereof in general-purpose legislation), the general principle is that taxpayers' funds should not be given to an airline. As already seen in Chapter 2, the European Union *does* have such legislation. This has been applied to the restructuring of loss-making government-owned airlines. In some instances, the EU has approved – and in others the EU has disallowed – the actions of member states. (See, in particular, §2.4.5 on government funding of 'national carriers' in Hungary and Poland. In the former case, the airline became legally obliged to repay the funding, and the immediate consequence was closure of the airline.) In regard to this first issue, the situation of SAA is considered below.

The *second issue* arises when a government-supported airline competes with one or more other airlines. Financial aid for one airline but not for the other(s) results in a playing field that is not level. This adversely effects economic efficiency, and is generally regarded as being inequitable.

In South Africa, Comair's assertion (Annual Report 2009, p. 3) was that 'SAA and its subsidiary, Mango, our main competitors, continued to sell tickets at well below their operating costs and received another bailout of R1.6 billion during the year. The total taxpayer bill for these airlines over the past five years is now in excess of R17 billion, with no clear indications that this trend will change.'

Under a heading 'State funding of SAA' (Integrated Annual Report 2014, p. 9), Comair remarks that in entering the main South African routes, it relied on government commitments to create a pro-competitive aviation industry. It claims that the state aid to SAA has resulted in a 'disruptive challenge to the sustainability of the domestic industry'. Accordingly, the Comair Group has 'found it necessary to challenge, by way of an action before the South African High Court, the R5 billion State guarantee provided by government to SAA.' The basis of the challenge is that 'such funding is contrary to government's domestic aviation policy, the Constitution, the Public Finance Management Act, the Promotion of Administrative Justice Act and the SAA Act. The Group is awaiting a court date . . . but sincerely hopes that the matter will be amicably settled with government.'

The performance of South African Airways

SAA acknowledged its financial problems in June 2007, when it started to restructure its operations in order to try to attain profitability within about 18 months, albeit at the cost of considerable one-off restructuring expenses. The results for the financial year ending 31 March 2009 were reported to be much improved compared with the previous year; indeed, the accounts stated a small but positive operating surplus in 2009 (SAA, Annual Report 2009, p. 28).

Since that time, however, there have been further losses, further subsidies and further proposals for restructuring. In the 2012 financial year, SAA incurred an operating loss of R1.3 billion, and looked forward to renewing the entire short-haul fleet by 'replacing the current B737-800s with more fuel-efficient A320s' (Annual Report 2012, pp. 19, 20). (As already noted, Comair was then *acquiring* the very same Boeing model, to update its fleet!)

On a healthier note, SAA *did* turn its attention to developing new regional routes in Africa (Annual Report 2012, p.18), to offset declining fortunes on several long-haul routes to other continents. Given the limited network connectivity in Africa, this *might* prove to be a worthwhile initiative, in both social and financial terms.

SAA also experienced a remarkable instability in senior management, and a troubled relationship with 'the Shareholder' (the South African government). CEOs have come and gone. In September 2012, the board members resigned when the board found itself at loggerheads with the responsible Minister. In the following month, the then CEO and some other senior managers went too.

Following the board resignation, the government required that SAA prepare a Long-Term Turn-Around Strategy before the government would authorise major capital expenditures. In the meanwhile, the government did promise a guarantee of ZAR 5 billion (then, about USD 550 million), to enable the airline to borrow on financial markets (CAPA, *World Aviation Yearbook 2013 – Africa*, pp. 12 and 13).

In addressing a parliamentary committee on 10 September 2013 (text accessed at the website of South African Express), the Minister of Public Enterprises introduced a new CEO of SAA, and noted that a Long-Term Strategy document had been presented to him in April. He went on to welcome the airline's recent success in beginning to reduce cost levels, and in developing new network strategies.

On the very same day, Comair announced a significant improvement in its profits (media release, 10 September 2013). In commenting on this ('Comair profit recovers on the back of reduced competition and successful transformation programme',16 September, 2013), CAPA observed that the closure of 1time allowed Comair and SAA to add fewer seats in total than 1time had withdrawn from the budget market, and raise their fares. (Operating results have to be interpreted carefully!)

By December 2014, the SAA headlines were becoming more urgent. The acting CEO Nico Bezuidenhout (serving in that role for the second time) announced a 90-day action plan to resuscitate the 'long-term turnaround strategy' (Victoria Moores, 'South African Airways unveils urgent 90-day strategy', *Air Transport World*, 9 December 2014). Earlier news (Alan Dron, 'Etihad, South African Airways to create partnership', *Air Transport World*, 7 May 2013) prompted the thought that the South African government might seek another airline as an equity partner. Perhaps this was in mind when the government announced that oversight of SAA was to be transferred from the Department of Public Enterprises to the National Treasury ('South African treasury to oversee SAA's operations', ch-aviation.ch, 13 December 2014).

A further airline entry

The established South African cargo company, Safair, set up a subsidiary, FlySafair, which intended to enter the domestic (RSA) market as a low-fare passenger airline in October 2013. After it obtained the appropriate government licence, the High Court of South Africa granted an interim injunction – upon application by Comair (and another party), who argued that the FlySafair share ownership did not satisfy the nationality requirements for classification as a South African airline (CAPA, 'FlySafair's wings are clipped by South Africa's High Court at the point of take-off', 11 October 2013).

FlySafair modified its share ownership in April 2014 (Victoria Moores, 'South African start-up FlySafair secures license', *Air Transport World*, 16 April 2014). It launched services on 16 October 2014, and soon was flying to Johannesburg, George and Port Elizabeth from Cape Town. The website ch-aviation.ch (accessed 13 December 2014 and 10 May 2015) showed it started with two B737-400s; by the later date, the fleet had grown to four such aircraft.

The airline website (flysafair.com, accessed 10 May 2015) stated (in various undated news releases) that it set very low fares for travel without checked bags, and served all the direct links between Johannesburg, Cape Town, George and Port Elizabeth, *except* for George–Port Elizabeth. It operated with a 25-minute turn-round, and yet had an outstanding on-time departure record, and carried its first 250,000 passengers in less than six months from start-up.

It seemed that the domestic market in South Africa had become even more competitive than before.

6.4 Domestic and regional airline services in East Africa

When some countries in East Africa formed the East African Community, this led to the establishment of *East African Airways*. Upon the demise of that Community in the 1970s, however, that airline was disbanded. Some of the countries then established individual government-owned carriers, whose fortunes have varied markedly, as have the mechanisms of control. There has also been some entry by private investors.

Uganda

Following the disbandment of East Africa Airways, a successor airline Uganda Airways itself went out of business in 2001. *Air Uganda* was launched in 2007. Owned by the Aga Khan Development Fund, and based at Entebbe, the company served routes to eight ports in Kenya, Tanzania, Rwanda, Burundi and South Sudan. It flew three CRJ200 jets (each 50 seats), offering both economy and premium economy classes ('About us', www.air-uganda.com, accessed 25 September 2013).

At times, it had a code-share agreement with *RwandAir* (another 'national airline', launched in 2002) for the route between Entebbe and Kigali. RwandAir also flew a CRJ200 on the route, and set the same fares as Air Uganda. Passengers could choose flight times irrespective of which airline operated the flight.

In July 2014, Air Uganda suspended its operations indefinitely, upon revocation of its Air Operator Certificate by the (Uganda) Civil Aviation Authority. That decision followed a visit to Uganda by ICAO officers, who inspected the work of the Authority (Samuel Sanya, 'Air Uganda suspends operations', *New Vision* (Uganda), 17 July 2014).

Kenya

The government established *Kenya Airways* in 1977, to serve as its national flag carrier. The new airline soon received a commercial brief; and later it was privatised. After an IPO in 1996, KLM held 26 per cent of the shares, and the Government of Kenya 23 per cent (Kenya Airways, Annual Report 2007–08). At the end of 2013–14, the government held almost 30 per cent of the shares, KLM had 27 per cent, and the balance was widely held (Annual Report 2013–14, p. 61). Other *foreign* shareholders had about 16 per cent of the shares.

Reflecting its diverse market ambitions, the airline built up jet fleets of both wide- and narrow-body aircraft. At 31 March 2014, the latter comprised five B737-800, four B737-700, four B737-300, fifteen E190 and five E170 aircraft (Annual Report 2013–14, p. 36). Even though that fleet is from only two aircraft families, the small aircraft numbers are insufficient to secure some of the economies of scale in fleet operation.

In recent years, the airline has struggled financially. In the year 2013–14, the passenger load factor fell two percentage points to 66 per cent.

Besides its own operation, Kenya Airways holds about 40 per cent of the shares of *Precision Air*, a local airline based in Dar es Salaam, in Tanzania. At 31 March 2013, the Precision fleet comprised five ATR72-500 aircraft, four ATR42s, and two ageing B737-300s ('Directors' Report and Financial Statistics 31 March 2013', pp. 5, 10, accessed at precisionairtz.com, 15 December 2014).

The turbo-props (with about 70 and 40 seats, respectively) complemented the short-haul fleet of Kenya Airways.

A potentially important development is the launch in April 2014 of *Jambojet*, a subsidiary of Kenya Airways. As a low-cost carrier, it is intended to promote regional travel within Kenya, and so flies both jets and turboprops. The fleet soon comprised three B737-300 and two Q400 aircraft (ch-aviation.ch, accessed 10 May 2015). From Nairobi, it then served Mombasa (five flights daily) and five other ports in Kenya.

By then, the number of passengers flying on domestic routes had increased by about 30 per cent. Indeed, in its first year it claimed to have flown about 500,000 passengers (Jambojet news releases, 23 April and 29 April 2015). It also claimed a good on-time performance for departures: 85 per cent over the first 6 months, reaching 92 per cent in October 2014 (news release, 'Jambojet records high on-time performance', 18 November 2014).

While the airline seems to have started well, a definitive judgement awaits publication of financial data. Because Jambojet is a wholly-owned subsidiary, Kenya Airways may choose not to disclose.

The Fly540 venture

A privately owned airline, Fly540, began domestic flights in Kenya in November 2006, initially operating ATR-42 turboprops. Soon after that launch, a long-established conglomerate, Lonrho, bought 49 per cent of the shares of FiveForty Aviation Limited, a company registered in Kenya (fly540.com, accessed 20 June 2008, and the Lonrho Annual Report 2009).

Lonrho wanted Fly540 to become the first *regional* African airline of an international standard (Lonrho, Interim Report 2010, pp. 5–6). There were to be three hubs: the already-established East African base in Nairobi (Kenya), serving ports in Kenya, Uganda, Tanzania, Southern Sudan and Burundi; in Angola (on the *west* coast of Central Africa), a base in Luanda for *Fly540 Angola*; and in Ghana (West Africa) a base for *Fly540 Ghana*. Lonrho held 60 per cent of the shares of each of the Angola and Ghana airlines, which were established as locally domiciled companies – no doubt to help obtain AOCs from the respective governments.

Although *Fly540 Kenya* was carrying about 200,000 passengers annually, (fly540.com, accessed 22 July 2010), Lonrho reported an operating loss on its transport segment (comprising that airline mainly) of about 25 per cent of that segment's external revenues (Lonrho, Annual Report 2009, pp. 7, 32).

The interests of Lonrho in the fly540 group were soon to be taken over by a new company, *Fastjet*. That history continues below in §6.5.

Mozambique

In 1936, the Mozambique government launched *LAM Mozambique*, a national carrier based in the capital city, Maputo. Although the airline became a limited company in 1998, the government still held most of the shares (91 per cent in 2014); company employees held the balance.

In recent times, it acquired three E190s (two cabins, 9/85 seats). However, one of these was destroyed in an unusual flight incident; it seems not to have been replaced. Its other jets are one B737-500 (99/14 seats), and one B737-700 (12/120 seats). Its subsidiary *MEX-Mozambique Express* flies two Q400 turboprops (72 seats) on local routes. Like many other airlines in Africa (and elsewhere), LAM appeared on the EU list (published 11 December 2014, under Regulation (EC) No 474/2006) of carriers whose aircraft are banned from EU airspace.

Among LAM's routes are interesting examples of regional connectivity. In 2002, it started flying from Maputo to Dar es Salaam (Tanzania). No doubt reflecting a common Portuguese heritage, it opened a route in 2009 (with three E190 flights weekly) to Luanda (Angola), a sector distance of about 2900 km, ('LAM company history and fleet', and media releases issued 28 August 2012, 28 April 2013 and 13 June 2014, all accessed at lam.co.mz).

6.5 The entry of Fastjet, with plans to become a pan-African carrier

The company *Fastjet plc* was registered in the UK in 2011; its shares trade on the London Stock Exchange's Alternative Investment Market (AIM). Two founding senior managers, CEO, Ed Winter, and Chief Financial Officer, Angus Saunders, each had prior airline experience in senior management positions in companies such as British Airways, Go, and easyJet as well as in airlines based in other countries ('About us', fastjet.com, accessed 26 September 2013).

As a hybrid low-cost airline, Fastjet aimed for high operating standards while flying within and between several African countries. To accelerate its plans, it agreed to take over the aviation interests of Lonrho, including a 49.98 per cent holding of the shares in the separate company Fly540 Kenya. On 2 July 2012, Fastjet paid by issuing to Lonrho ordinary shares in Fastjet. At 13 May 2013, Lonrho held 49.14 per cent of the Fastjet shares, and two of the Fastjet directors were nominated by Lonrho (Fastjet, Annual Report for the period ending in 31 December 2012, pp. 5, 12).

Fastjet chose to operate the smaller Airbus A319 aircraft. The upward trend in the price of aviation fuel had reduced the scope for profitable operation of the A319. Several major airlines sold-off a sizeable number of A319s, and that resulted in low second-hand prices. Evidently, Fastjet thought the low leasing costs of the A319 made it economical for deployment on the (thin) routes it planned to serve.

Given the acquisition from Lonrho, the Fastjet management chose Tanzania for its first base, because:

- the Tanzania Fly540 operation was relatively new, and as such, was expected to have the least number of legacy issues;
- the Tanzanian government and Civil Aviation Authority were very positive and welcoming;

- the Airbus A319 aircraft had already been approved on the Tanzanian register;
- the competitive environment was more benign than in Kenya where Kenya Airways dominates the market and has considerable influence over the Kenyan Government and the Civil Aviation Authority.

(Fastjet, Annual Report 2012, p. 7)

For the launch, three A319s were flown to the Fastjet base at Dar es Salaam; each had between 145 and 156 seats. The (Tanzanian) Fly540 operation was closed early in November. As planned, Fastjet started two domestic routes on 29 November 2012 – between Dar es Salaam and Kilimanjaro, and between Dar es Salaam and Mwanza. Its twice-daily flights faced competition from the incumbent turbo-prop operator, Precision Air.

Further domestic routes followed, though not promptly. In March 2013, Fastjet started flying from Kilimanjaro to each of Zanzibar and Mwanza. In November, it launched a route from Dar es Salaam to Mbeya, where the airport had been re-built to accommodate jet aircraft. Besides Mbeya itself, Fastjet could thereby serve the densely populated areas across the borders with Malawi and northern Zambia (media release, 'Fastjet launches new domestic route in Tanzania', 28 August 2013).

International routes were even slower to materialise. Though the Government of Tanzania had promised Fastjet it would grant rights to fly international routes from Tanzania, Fastjet still had to overcome any protectionist attitudes in other countries. Eventually Fastjet announced flights between Dar es Salaam and Johannesburg, to begin on 27 September 2013, initially with three flights per week. It expected its entry to reduce the average fare on the route, and so encourage more travel (media release, 'Update on fastjet's international route', 29 July 2013). (The media release did not mention that the only route-competitor was South African Airways.)

On the day before the intended launch, however, Fastjet announced (media release 'Update on first international route' 26 September 2013) that the first flight to Johannesburg had been postponed

> ... due to unexpected administrative delays caused by the South African Department of Transport which this week made a very late request for additional documentation. Although [the airline] delivered these documents without delay, the South African Department of Transport has said it will take several days to process these documents.

The media release goes on to quote the Fastjet CEO as saying that 'administrative delays of this nature are not unusual in the markets in which we operate'. In the outcome, it was 18 October before Fastjet operated its first scheduled flight to Johannesburg.

Gradually thereafter, Fastjet launched flights to other countries. The route to Lusaka (in Zambia) started on 1 February 2014, initially with two flights weekly.

Fastjet added a third flight, starting on 15 April. The launch of flights to Harare (Zimbabwe) came on 5 August. Fastjet pointed out (media release 6 August 2014) that previously travellers could fly between Harare and Dar es Salaam only via Nairobi (Kenya) or Johannesburg, or go by road for a distance of about 2,200 km. Fastjet soon added a third weekly flight.

Service to Entebbe (Uganda) started on 16 September, initially two flights weekly but increasing to four on 29 September. In announcing the service (on 1 September), Fastjet remarked 'Since Air Uganda ceased flying, the fares offered by other carriers for flights in and out of the country [Uganda] have risen steadily'. It again anticipated that the introduction of Fastjet low fares would stimulate more travel.

At the end of November 2014, Fastjet completed its second year, in the course of which it had sold 569,000 one-way tickets, compared with 358,000 tickets in its first 12 months. By comparing seats sold with seats flown (without regard for distance travelled), Fastjet claimed a load factor of 77 per cent, up five points on the first year. It also claimed high rates for on time-performance, with monthly averages often reaching or exceeding 90 per cent. Yet it incurred vary large financial deficits during those first two years, in part because it was unable to enter international routes as readily as it had hoped.

Continuing losses incurred by the fly540 units were ended during 2014 when Fastjet disposed of the Kenya operation and closed the companies in Ghana and Angola.

Nevertheless, the losses on Fastjet Tanzania itself were a major concern. However, good news came in December 2014: compared with the previous December, passenger numbers were about 75 per cent higher, the load factor was 76 per cent (up two points), the yield per passenger rose about 20 per cent, and total revenue doubled. Helped also by the fall in the price of aircraft fuel, Fastjet Tanzania posted its first profitable trading month, as measured by Earnings before Interest and Tax (media release, 'Passenger statistics and operating update', 12 January 2015).

On the other hand, an AOC for an affiliate to be based in Zambia – previously expected in 2014 – had been delayed, though Fastjet said in December that it *did* expect to get the AOC in 2015 (CAPA, 'Fastjet 2015 outlook', 30 December 2014).

Nevertheless, there was *some* good news. In March, the company was granted an Air Service Permit by the Government of Zimbabwe (media release, 'Fastjet announces Zimbabwe Air Service Permit granted', 25 March 2015). The company described that as 'a significant step towards ... obtaining an Air Operating Certificate' for (the planned) Fastjet Zimbabwe, which would operate domestic flights within, and international flights from, Zimbabwe. In emphasising potential route opportunities, the Fastjet CEO was quoted as saying 'For example there are as many as 100 buses a day travelling the 1,100km between Harare and Johannesburg at fares up to $120 – return.'

In April came some very good news: Fastjet plc announced it had placed 5 billion shares, at one penny per share, to new and existing investors and to Fastjet management. The placing raised GBP 50 million, which would increase working capital, fund launching of operations in Kenya, South Africa, Uganda, Zambia and Zimbabwe, and begin acquisition of further used A319 aircraft.

The placing also demonstrated investor faith in the prospects for Fastjet plc. Much then depended in getting access in other countries in the region. In anticipation of early growth, Fastjet signed a letter of intent for a lease on a fourth A319, to enter service in the third quarter of 2105 (Fastjet media release, 'Planned fleet expansion', 18 May 2015). Two more A319s were expected to arrive by the end of September (Victoria Moores, 'Fastjet signs LOI for its sixth Airbus A319', *Air Transport World*, 26 August 2015).

Having received its Air Operator Certificate from the government of Zimbabwe, Fastjet Zimbabwe launched with a flight from Harare to Victoria Falls on 28 October 2015, a route it planned to serve three times weekly (media release, 'Today we are flying our inaugural flight from Harare to Victoria Falls!', 28 October 2015).

6.6 Enter Flyafrica, another pan-African aspirant

Flyafrica is a joint venture of a Zimbabwean infrastructure company and a private-equity aviation investment group. Its aim is to establish low-cost airlines in each of several African countries. Flyafrica chose to start in Harare, where the initial fleet of Zimbabwe Flyafrica comprised two B737-500s (114 seats, including a small separate business-class cabin), with another three such aircraft stored in Prague in the care of the previous owner, ČSA (ch-aviation.ch and Wikipedia article on Zimbabwe Flyafrica, both accessed 11 May 2015).

The intention was to launch on 23 July 2014 with a first flight on the tourist route from Johannesburg to Victoria Falls. At the last moment, the Civil Aviation Authority of Zimbabwe insisted on the pilots being licensed in Zimbabwe (rather than South Africa). In the outcome, the first flight was postponed for one week ('Fly Africa flights to start this week after pilot licencing delay', *New Zimbabwe*, 26 July 2014). The initial frequency was three flights per week, with a fourth flight to start in September as a result of a high level of advance bookings (media release, 'There Is No Such Thing As Africa Time!', flyafrica.com, 17 July 2014).

By the end of 2014, Zimbabwe Flyafrica was flying on two further routes: it started Harare–Johannesburg on 1 November; and on 1 December, it began Harare–Victoria Falls, in competition with Air Zimbabwe (CAPA, 'Flyafrica.com 2015 outlook', 7 January 2015).

For the Flyafrica group, the next move was the founding of Namibia Flyafrica, in which it had Nomad Aviation as its local partner. The first route was from Windhoek to Johannesburg, flown twice daily (media release, 'Flyafrica.com expands into Namibia', 20 October 2014). (That route was already served by SAA, Comair and Air Namibia.)

By March 2015, Namibia Flyafrica was also serving Windhoek to Cape Town (daily), while Zimbabwe Flyafrica had added Bulawayo–Johannesburg (daily), in competition with Air Zimbabwe. By then, the Flyafrica group was flying all five of the B737-500 aircraft ('Flyafrica.com serves six airports', anna. aero, 11 March 2015).

6.7 ASKY Airlines, a new community airline in West Africa

In West Africa, there was an early *community* regional airline, *Air Afrique*. Founded in 1961, and headquartered in Abidjan (Côte d'Ivoire), it served 11 franco-phone countries of West Africa, and was owned by the governments of those countries; Air France also played a role. Air Afrique had heterogeneous fleets of both narrow- and wide-body aircraft. Besides flying routes between West Africa's regional capitals, it also operated routes to Europe (especially France) (Wikipedia, 'Air Afrique', accessed 24 July 2010).

Though once well regarded among African airlines, Air Afrique suffered from government interference, even in regard to daily operations. After a long period of decline, the owning governments decided to close the (bankrupt) airline (David Bamford, 'Air Afrique wound up', *BBC News*, 15 August 2001, accessed 25 July 2010).

A plan to start a new airline, again under the auspices of Air France, came to naught. Eventually the Economic Community of West African States established (in September 2005) the Regional Airline Promotion Company, charged with the task of planning for and setting up a *private-company* airline. In turn, that led to the founding of *ASKY Airlines,* with a capitalisation of USD200 million. Shareholders were to provide USD120 million, with 80 per cent of those shares to be sold to (local) private shareholders, and the balance to come from 'institutional partners'. The remaining amount of USD80 million was to be borrowed.

The flourishing *Ethiopian Airlines* then signed a Memorandum of Understanding with ASKY in June 2008, for a partnership in which Ethiopian took the remaining 20 per cent equity share and became the manager. A contract was signed in January 2009 ('Milestones' accessed at *flyasky.com* 24 July 2010). ASKY obtained an AOC from the government of Togo, and established its headquarters in the capital, Lomé.

ASKY launched in January 2010, with two B737-700 aircraft belonging to and operated by Ethiopian Airlines. By June, ASKY was flying short-haul routes between 15 ports in 14 countries in West and Central Africa. Remarkably, its timetable showed services continuing *throughout the night*. For example, on Tuesdays and Saturdays, flight KP12 left Lomé at five minutes past midnight, headed west to visit five ports in five different countries before returning to Lomé some 12 hours later.

Over a week, the two aircraft together flew 10 circuits departing Lomé between midnight and 02.30, and 13 others leaving Lomé at around 13.00 hours. (This must have yielded remarkable average daily block hours per aircraft.) Clearly, many passengers experienced stops at intermediate ports. The services were not very frequent: the 15 ports had an average of 7.6 ASKY departures per *week*. Of course, the ASKY routes also served to extend the Ethiopian Airlines network, to which passengers could transfer at Lomé.

By September 2013, the ASKY fleet had grown to three B737-700s together with four Q400 turboprops; even the latter had a small business-class cabin (seven seats) as well the main cabin of 60 seats. ASKY then served 23 ports, located in 20 countries, and it had abandoned its all-night flying. It was operating 174 flights weekly, carrying about 10,000 passengers. Lomé had become an orthodox hub, though some flights still served one or two intermediate ports, and there were two routes that by-passed Lomé (flyasky.com, accessed 30 September 2013).

6.8 Airline difficulties in Central Africa

After Air Afrique closed, the member states of the Economic and Monetary Community of Central Africa (CEMAC), namely Cameroon, Chad, Central African Republic, Equatorial Guinea and Democratic Republic of the Congo, together with the island country of São Tomé and Príncipe, *eventually* sought to establish *another* community airline, provisionally called Air CEMAC.

After failed negotiations with three airlines, CEMAC turned to Air France, which was reported as wanting a 33 per cent stake in the joint venture, and a monopoly for Air CEMAC on future CEMAC regional routes (CAPA, 'Air CEMAC moves closer to launch in partnership with Air France', 7 August 2013). However, after further talks ('Air CEMAC's launch delayed 'til 2014 over protracted Air France talks', ch-aviation.ch, 24 September 2013), CEMAC eventually abandoned the proposal ('Central African trade bloc calls quits on Air CEMAC project', ch-aviation.ch, 8 May 2015).

In the years after the closure of Air Afrique, there were also some attempts to establish national airlines in Central Africa. In particular, the Cameroon government launched its own airline, *Camair-Co*, in 2011. The initial fleet comprised one B767-300ER and two B737-700. By 2013, it served five ports in Cameroon and six ports in other Central and West African countries (camair-co.com, accessed 4 October 2013).

On its (monopoly) domestic routes, it pursued rapid capacity growth, and in consequence sustained low load factors and financial losses (CAPA, 'Cameroon's aviation market experiences strong growth driven by Camair-Co and regional competitors', 23 September 2013). Camair later added two Chinese-built turboprops, MA60s, to be used on domestic routes instead of a B737-700, 'which has thus far proven to be excessive' ('Camair-Co takes delivery of two MA-60s', ch-aviation.ch, 30 March 2015).

In 2014, upon arrival at Paris CDG airport, one of its B737-700s was seized by its lessor, and was later released when the airline paid up some money owed ('Camair-Co pays . . . $1.9mn in outstanding B737 lease fees', ch-aviation. ch, 24 July 2014).

Later, Camair-Co announced it would acquire one further B767 and three early-model B737s, either -300s or -400s ('Camair to acquire B737 Classics as part of fleet expansion drive', ch-aviation.ch, 20 April 2015). It remained to be seen whether the older Boeings were to serve *instead* of the newer ones.

6.9 National airline problems in West Africa

Following the closure of Air Afrique, two significant West African national carriers in *anglophone* countries were soon wound up by their government owners. Nigerian Airways closed in 2003, and Ghana Airways in 2005. The resulting diminution in airline services in that part of West Africa encouraged entry by a new airline in Nigeria, as reported in the next section.

Since those closures, there have been problems for some other national carriers in the region. Of particular interest here is *Sénégal Airlines*, a company which launched only in 2011. Private Sénégal interests subscribed for 64 per cent of its shares, while the Sénégal government and its agencies held the balance. The country's capital, Dakar, is the most westerly capital city in Africa. It is located about 2300 km to the west of Lomé (the base for ASKY Airlines). In its early days, the Sénégal fleet comprised two A320s, one A330 and one CRJ100, serving 16 ports, mostly within and around Sénégal, but extending east as far as Douala and Libreville (both to the east of Lomé; 'about us', senegalairlines.aero, and ch-aviation.ch, both accessed on 4 October 2013).

And yet, at 17 December 2014 (and again on 14 May 2015), the website ch-aviation.ch reported Sénégal Airlines had a smaller fleet, namely one A320 and one Q400. Then, in March 2015, the government said it was to nationalise the airline 'to stave off its imminent collapse' under the weight of a debt of USD 75 million ('Dakar to nationalize Senegal Airlines', ch-aviation.ch, 28 March 2015). Once the airline's financial position had been stabilised, the government hoped to sell a 49 per cent stake to a strategic private investor.

6.10 The rise of Arik Air in Nigeria and in the region

Following the 2003 closure of Nigerian Airways, there was an opportunity for another airline to fill the gap. A new, privately owned company, *Arik Air*, took possession of some of the Lagos ground facilities formerly used by Nigerian Airways, and launched its first services in 2006. In 2007 it carried about 650,000 passengers, and the annual total reached two million passengers as early as 2009. After that date, the *proportionate* growth was more modest ('Arik Air's traffic grows by 19% in 2013', anna.aero, 30 July 2014)!

By 2015, Arik had a fleet of 23 aircraft comprising two A330s, eight B737-800 aircraft and four B737-700s, one CRJ1000, four CRJ900s and four Q400s. Its domestic and regional network centred on Lagos and on the Nigerian capital, Abuja. The most frequent service was that between those two cities, of course. Notable among the long-haul routes was Lagos–Dubai via Abuja. The network as a whole comprised 42 routes serving 29 ports in 12 countries (ch-aviation.ch, accessed 15 May 2015).

In 2015, at the ceremonial launch of a new regional service from Lagos via Cotonou (Benin) to Abidjan (Côte d'Ivoire), Arik's Deputy Managing Director said the airline was thinking about developing Cotonou as a regional hub, to rival that of Lomé, the hub for ASKY Airlines. He went on to say:

> We are not flying through Lomé Airport for strategic reasons. Besides, we want to build Cotonou as another hub because Lomé is being developed by one of our competitors and so we want to do the same thing with Cotonou.
>
> ('Nigeria's Arik Air eyes potential regional hub in Cotonou',
> ch-aviation.ch, 2 March 2015)

An Arik Air hub at Cotonou could certainly promote regional connectivity. But Cotonou and Lomé are close to each other – little more than 100 km by air – even though in different countries. Perhaps regional connectivity might be even better served if both airlines hubbed at the same port. (Of course, in the US, separate *rival* hubs were chosen to enhance airline profitability. Perhaps it is unreasonable to blame Arik Air for putting profits ahead of public benefit.)

From March 2015, Arik Air was also flying from each of Abuja and Lagos to Dakar (Sénégal); both routes also served Accra (Ghana) as an intermediate port, and both services had an overnight transit in one direction. At the time, there was no rival non-stop service between Accra and Sénégal (media release, 'Arik Air strengthens Dakar route with Abuja plus Accra connections', arikair.com, 25 March 2015).

One interesting feature of these Arik Air initiatives was the introduction of some links between francophone and anglophone cities.

7 Australia

Airline interactions in a small market

Following the survey, in Chapters 1–6, of short-haul airline services around the world, this chapter takes a *close-up* look at the processes of airline competition in a single country, Australia. Being much the same size and shape as the 48 contiguous states of the USA, Australia has non-stop domestic jet flight sectors of up to five hours in flying time. While having a population approaching 25 million persons, Australia has very little long-distance travel by rail. Outside the major cities, there are very few roads of motorway/inter-state highway standard. (Even so, leisure travellers sometimes take long road journeys for the *en-route* experience.) Thus, for most journeys outside the metropolitan areas, air travel takes on particular importance.

7.1 The structure of the airline sector: a brief historical overview

During the regulation era, which began in 1952 – when the population of Australia was about nine million people – and ended in 1990, the structure of the Australian domestic airline industry was very simple. With one very minor exception, only two companies – the privately owned Ansett and the government-owned TAA – were allowed to fly jet aircraft on domestic mainline routes. Both were full-service airlines.

Government legislation ensured that almost everything was tightly controlled. The detailed scheme of regulation (known as the 'two-airline policy') even ensured that the two companies had the same fleet capacity.

The two companies served virtually the same list of routes. On most of them, they engaged in 'parallel scheduling' – that is, on each route they operated equal numbers of flights, with matched departure times. They set the same fares; and, thanks to the regulatory capacity constraints, the aggregate *sold* outputs of the two companies were always closely similar. In popular, sarcastic parlance, the two carriers were known as the 'heavenly twins'. Fun-loving economists use the term 'a symmetrical duopoly'.

For many decades, the Australian *international* carrier, Qantas, was also owned by the government. Following deregulation of domestic airline services in 1990, the government merged Australian Airlines (a later name for TAA) into Qantas, and in 1995 it privatised the enlarged Qantas. Ansett and Qantas then continued to dominate the deregulated domestic airline sector.

There were two minor jet-airline entrants during the 1990s. On each occasion, Ansett and Qantas soon restored the mainline domestic duopoly, which encountered serious challenge only in July 2000, when Virgin entered as a low-cost operator, offering economy-class service. By then, the Ansett market share had declined a little, and so the company was struggling financially. It ceased trading in 2001, leaving Qantas racing to expand its fleet in an attempt to hold on to its new-found route monopolies. However, Virgin steadily increased its fleet, and eventually entered all the Qantas routes. There followed an era of vigorous competition between those two companies.

To gain market share, Virgin used its cost advantage to undercut the Qantas fares. By 2004, Virgin had won almost one third of the domestic market. In response, a worried Qantas launched Jetstar, an in-house low-cost carrier serving domestic routes initially, and later some regional international routes as well. That competition gave Virgin additional incentive to move up-market, to attempt to capture some of the business travel, which Qantas found to be very remunerative.

Besides the Qantas and Virgin services on the mainline domestic routes, there remained only three regional carriers of significant size. In the main, these flew turbo-prop aircraft. However, most of the interior of the continent is sparsely populated, resulting in some very long regional routes with small passenger flows. On some of the longer routes, smaller jets are deployed.

Following the exit of Ansett, two of the regional carriers became independently owned: in Western Australia, Skywest operated turboprops and a few F100 jets from its base in Perth; Rex used a homogeneous fleet of Saab 340 turboprops to serve local routes in Victoria and New South Wales. The third regional was a Qantas subsidiary, called QantasLink, which flew turboprops and a few smaller jets in most of the Australian states.

In 2007, the Singapore low-cost airline Tiger Airways established a subsidiary, Tiger Airways Australia, which entered several Australian mainline domestic routes. The structure of the Australian industry then remained largely unchanged until 2013, when some dramatic changes made the industry even more concentrated.

In short, the Australian airline sector is important enough to be of interest, and simple enough to allow some informal analysis of the competitive battles between two airline camps. This chapter looks only at the mainline jet operations. (There is a brief discussion of Australia's regional/local services in Chapter 11.)

7.2 The airline network and passenger numbers in the regulation era

The (right-wing) Australian government of the day (1952) may be forgiven for fearing that the government-owned domestic airline, just created by its left-wing predecessor, would drive out the very few private companies offering inter-state airline services, and so establish a monopoly. Accordingly it introduced a scheme of regulation to control the provision of *domestic* airline services.

Two domestic airlines – the government carrier (TAA) and a chosen private airline (Ansett Airlines) – were given exclusive access to the 'trunk routes', defined as non-stop *interstate* service between any pair of ports included in a list of eighteen ports (Independent Review of Economic Regulation of Domestic Aviation, 1986, Table 6.1). That list included the capitals of the six states and two territories, together with other ports of importance, especially for business travel. Other airlines could fly between such a port pair but only if the aircraft stopped at one or more intermediate ports and carried mainly passengers travelling to or from those intermediate ports. The concentration of the Australian population in a small number of large cities made it very difficult for any third airline to meet the qualifying condition.

In order to control fleet capacities, the government used its general powers to control imports, in order to prevent other companies from acquiring jet aircraft. And to balance the operations of the two major airlines, it put the same limit on the *aggregate* seat-kilometres flown by each.

While the air-fare control mechanisms did change a little over time, the enduring basic outcome was that each airline charged the same *regular* fare for a particular route. Discounting of those fares was discouraged by the upper limit placed on the total available seat kilometres (ASKs) offered by each. The overall fare level was reset periodically to provide that neither airline lost money. In practice, that meant that the government airline 'got by' financially, while the owners of the private company enjoyed an attractive rate of profit in a low-risk business environment.

In the 1980s, increasing public criticism of the two-airline policy led the (left-wing) government of the day to set up an independent public inquiry. Following publication of its report (Independent Review of Economic Regulation of Domestic Aviation, 1986), the Australian government ended all aviation-specific economic regulation. From 31 October 1990, the economic conduct of airlines became subject only to Australia's general trade-practices (anti-trust) legislation (then, the Trade Practices Act 1974) (Bureau of Transport and Communications Economics, 1991b, p. 11).

During the (nearly) 40 years of airline regulation, the Australian population almost doubled, reaching about 17 million in 1990. Also stimulating the amount of domestic air travel were rising living standards, the introduction of jet aircraft, and later the development of longer-range short-haul jets. Total domestic air travel increased from 1.2 billion revenue passenger kilometres (RPK) in 1952 to 13.9 billion in 1988 (Bureau of Infrastructure, Transport and Regional Economics, domestic airline performance indicators, Canberra, various years).

Under regulation, the number of city-pairs enjoying non-stop service was rather small. And in some cases, the non-stop flights were infrequent. Accordingly, the journeys of many passengers involved intermediate stops, often with change of aircraft. For example, a Sunday journey in 1975 between two state capitals, Brisbane and Adelaide – both among the five largest cities in Australia – required the passenger to hastily change aircraft at both Sydney and Melbourne. The passenger in question vividly recalls the complete lack of airline food in economy class during the five-hour journey (now flown non-stop in about 2½ hours). In effect, both Ansett and TAA had adopted domestic hub-and-spoke networks *before* they were invented in the USA. One difference, however, was that each of the several Australian hubs had very large numbers of passengers who began and/ or terminated their journeys at a hub port.

The regulated fare structure did not particularly encourage the introduction of non-stop hub-busting flights. A passenger travelling via a hub city *never* paid a lower fare than that which would have applied if direct service had been made available. In some cases, the indirect fare was the same as the direct fare would have been; in many cases, the indirect fare was larger, reflecting the greater distance actually travelled (Independent Review of Economic Regulation of Domestic Aviation, 1986, table 13.2).

The scheme of regulation had the effect of restricting the output of the airline sector, in a manner not unlike that adopted by a profit-seeking monopolist. No doubt this was what the owners of Ansett wanted. And the managers of TAA also seemed to find the situation congenial.

Nevertheless, during the later part of the regulation era, the growth in the number of passenger journeys did encourage the two airlines to increase the number of trunk-route city pairs for which they offered (some) non-stop service. For the mid-year weeks including 30 June, that number increased from 35 in 1975 to 44 in 1980 and to 52 in 1985 (Independent Review of Economic Regulation of Domestic Aviation, 1986, table 26.1).

7.3 With deregulation pending, the incumbents strengthen the castle walls

Removal of a potential rival

In July 1987, Ansett's owners (TNT and News Ltd) bought a small, third company, East-West Airlines, which held grandfathered rights to fly on a few minor trunk routes, and otherwise operated some intra-state services, mainly in New South Wales. It seemed that Ansett sought to ensure that East-West did not become a competitor under the anticipated deregulation. The (then) all-industries Trade Practices Act prohibited mergers that would result, or be likely to result, in the merged entity being in a position to dominate the market. However, because Ansett and Australian had approximately equal market shares, the regulator (the Trade Practices Commission) could not claim that Ansett (plus East-West) would dominate the interstate market. So the Commission was unable to prevent the take-over (Mills, 1989, pp. 212–14).

Airline access to passenger terminals

The two incumbents exploited access to passenger terminals as a barrier to entry. At many of the major ports, they owned their own terminals, which were built on land they leased from the airport operator. Usually the port had no (significant) common-user facilities.

Although the Department of Aviation had long administered those ports, the Australian government established, in June 1986, the Federal Airports Corporation, which was to manage the ports from 1 January 1988. Clearly Ansett and Australian Airlines (the new name for TAA) did not relish the prospect of dealing with a more commercially-oriented manager. At the very end of 1987, the government was persuaded to grant both airlines extended 20-year leases on their existing terminals.

As part of the deal, the new leases required *each* airline to grant to any entrant access to two gates at each of Sydney and Melbourne and one gate at each of the other major ports (Minister for Transport and Communications, 1987; Bureau of Transport and Communications Economics, 1991a, pp. 23–4). Perhaps this was intended merely as a fig-leaf. As later events were to show, the provision was insufficient to support significant airline entry.

There was, however, one major port exception: in 1987, the Department of Aviation was constructing a new domestic terminal at Brisbane. While most of its gates were to be leased to Ansett and Australian, the terminal was also to have several common-user gates. At the planning stage, Ansett and Australian had objected to the cost of the 'excessive' size of the proposed terminal. With hindsight, it seems their main aim was to try to prevent the creation of terminal space that would become available to an airline entrant.

The airlines' dispute with the pilots: an exercise in reducing excessive costs

The pilots' contracts with Australian and Ansett provided for each pilot to work rather few stick hours. In calculating efficient cost levels, the airline regulator accepted 400 hours per annum (Independent Review of Economic Regulation of Domestic Aviation, 1986, §3.6), while the world-wide standard practice for short-haul operations was then around 600 to 700 hours. In the absence of any increase in the work-load, the two incumbents would face a material cost handicap in competing with any entrant.

The ensuing industrial dispute with the pilots concerned stick hours only. Ansett threatened legal action against the pilots' association in the event of a strike. To avoid that risk, the association asked all its members to resign their positions; almost all of them did so. (So, Ansett won that round!)

In August 1989, the pilots closed down the inter-state route network. For about three weeks, the closure was total. Then the two majors began a few flights flown by staff pilots. Gradually other pilots were recruited (mainly from other countries), and the number of services increased. Those who had resigned were unable to recover their jobs.

The pilots' association had made a grave error. Its position had been undermined by three factors. Despite the very great disruption caused, the government declined to intervene. The other employees of Australian and Ansett *were* willing to work alongside the newcomer pilots. And around the world there was a sufficient pool of qualified and experienced jet pilots, able and willing to fly for Ansett and Australian.

7.4 The first decade of deregulation: growth without (successful) entry

7.4.1 Attempted airline entries

When the two-airline policy ended at midnight on 30 October 1990, there was early optimism about entry (Bureau of Transport and Communications Economics, 1991a). In the event, the firm grip of the two incumbents was not to be significantly disturbed for almost 10 years. However, two new companies did try.

After securing A$65 million from a public fund-raising, *Compass Airlines* launched on 1 December 1990, in time for the summer holiday travel. It built up a fleet of four A300-600R aircraft, averaging 277 seats each, together with one A310 with 212 seats, all in single-class layouts. Besides seeking low operating costs per passenger, its choice of *wide-body* aircraft served to increase the number of passengers it could handle at the limited number of gates available to it. Yet deploying such large aircraft at those gates was physically awkward.

Compass began to serve most of the major routes between seven ports: five state capitals (Adelaide, Brisbane, Melbourne, Perth and Sydney), together with two major tourist destinations (Cairns and the Gold Coast) which (arguably) had been somewhat neglected by the incumbent airlines. Compass undercut the incumbents' standard fares, while relying on its low cost-base to make that financially viable.

The incumbents responded by offering special discount fares. These were available on remarkably lax conditions (unlike their standard advance-purchase fares) but often only for flights at times corresponding to the times of the (few) Compass flights on the route. For an example, see Mills (2002, p. 211), which also recounts the role of travel agents in encouraging travel on the incumbents' services. No doubt, those actions contributed materially to the entrant's problems.

Other difficulties facing Compass included the 1991 economic recession, which reduced the level of demand for air travel, and managerial shortcomings in the way Compass used its accounting and revenue management systems (Trade Practices Commission, 1992).

Compass ceased trading on 20 December 1991. For travellers, it had brought lower fares, which increased the amount of travel. Yet it left many holding paid tickets that the company could not honour. Its venture had also drawn attention to the possibility of expanding airline services in Australia beyond the scope traditionally envisaged by Ansett and Australian.

Undeterred by the financial failure of Compass, another company, *Southern Cross Airlines*, went ahead with its long-planned capital raising – which fell short of the A$50 million it sought. It chose a much smaller aircraft, the MD80 (with 20 Executive Class seats, and 122 economy seats), and deployed five of them on east-coast routes between Adelaide, Melbourne, Sydney, Brisbane, Townsville and Cairns.

The company launched on 31 August 1992, again trading as Compass Airlines. As before, the incumbents offered targeted discounts for economy travel;

and again many travel agents did not enthuse about the entrant's services. The newcomer soon experienced a liquidity crisis, and ceased trading on 12 March 1993.

In its report (Bureau of Transport and Communications Economics, 1993, pp. 65–72), the Bureau judged the operating costs were probably at the budgeted level. However, the airline did not manage to attract as many high-yield passengers as planned, perhaps because its flight frequency was insufficient for business travellers.

For the remainder of the 1990s, the two incumbents were not troubled by any further entry by companies seeking to fly jet aircraft on Australia's major routes.

7.4.2 Air-travel growth and fare-structure changes

In the 1990s, the two incumbents continued to match each other on fares and service quality, and (generally) in regard to routes flown and flight frequencies. Nevertheless, the domestic airline market continued to grow strongly, with total RPK reaching 27.8 billion in 1999 – a doubling in the 11 years since 1988. Some of the increase was due to a *cautious* expansion in fare discounting, offered especially for weekend leisure trips. Population increase and rising income levels continued to play important roles.

Over the years 1991–9, the aggregate revenue-passenger load factor averaged 75.6 per cent, noticeably higher than the 72.5 per cent recorded over the (regulated) period of 1980–8 (Bureau of Transport and Regional Economics, Domestic Airline Performance Indicators 1944–2002). (That comparison excludes the years 1989 and 1990, which were affected by the immediate and lasting consequences of the close-down in 1989.)

There were further increases in the number of port pairs connected by direct, non-stop flights. Some of the new non-stops were for capital-city routes such as Sydney–Hobart, Brisbane–Canberra and Brisbane–Perth. Others served tourist travel on major interstate routes such as Melbourne–Cairns and Sydney–Launceston. Yet, there remained many routes for which the traveller had to combine a flight between state capitals with a separate flight between a capital city and a regional port in that state.

Over the six years from October 1993, the airlines increased their *full* fares in real terms – by some 20 per cent in business class, and by about 7 per cent in economy class (Bureau of Transport and Regional Economics, 2006). Both airlines also increased the proportion of discount tickets, and offered larger discounts, thereby reducing the overall fare averages.

For the years 1991 and 1992, some econometric modelling (Bureau of Transport and Communications Economics, 1993, ch. 9) suggests that those fare changes transferred about A$700 million per annum from the airlines to their passengers. (For about 18 million journeys per annum, that averages about A$40 per one-way journey.)

The *net* public gain depended principally on savings in airline costs, and on three types of benefits for passengers: extra travel induced by lower fares; journey-time savings stemming from the introduction of more direct flights; and time savings arising from greater flight frequencies, which resulted in reduced 'schedule delay' (with actual departure time becoming closer to preferred departure time). The BTCE modelling puts the *net* annual value of all those elements at about A$120 million, representing on average about A$7 per one-way journey.

7.4.3 The ageing aircraft fleets of the duopolists

There may have been tacit collaboration between the airlines on *not* replacing their aircraft fleets. Ansett had been one of the very first operators of B767 aircraft. By the end of 2000, its B767-200 models were on average about 16 years old (Australian Transport Safety Bureau, 2002, p. 50). Ansett also then had 20 A320 aircraft, purchased from 1989 onwards, and 24 B737-300 models, dating mainly from the late 1980s (Bureau of Transport and Communications Economics, 1993). In contrast to the regulation era (when frequent fleet renewal was encouraged by the regulator's generous financial approach), it seems that Ansett's owners may have become unwilling to invest in new aircraft.

Qantas transferred some of its ageing Boeing 767 aircraft from international to domestic routes, where they flew alongside B737-300 and -400s purchased mainly in the 1980s and 1990s. No doubt comforted by the Ansett parsimony, Qantas may well have thought that it too could postpone investment without suffering any competitive disadvantage.

7.5 The unregulated duopoly: an unstable equilibrium?

In the regulation era, the restrictive provisions of the two-airline policy ensured the stability of a symmetrical market-sharing equilibrium. In particular, an airline offering superior service – and so attracting more than half the passengers – could not add capacity unilaterally; thus its load factors would increase, and this would eventually bring a halt to further traffic growth. While it might then enjoy superior profits, the solvency of the less successful airline was assured by the regulatory arrangements.

Upon deregulation, if one airline became more successful than the other, it *could* take the extra profits without increasing capacity; and the equal-shares equilibrium might persist. *Or*, if aggressive, it could increase capacity (and possibly lower its fares) to win an even larger share of the market, and perhaps drive the other airline from the market.

Those observations prompt consideration of differences between the situations of the two airlines.

Management issues at Ansett

Upon deregulation, the Ansett owners (TNT and News) became keen to sell out, and both eventually did so. In the meanwhile, the Ansett managers faced uncertainty about the eventual ownership structure, in particular about the prospect of a take-over by Air New Zealand. And when that airline did buy in, it may have found the managerial task more challenging than it expected. There was also one specific issue: in the 1990s: Ansett acquired small jet aircraft to serve some thin regional routes; these services incurred major losses, and this affected the company's general financial situation.

International services

Once Australian Airlines was merged into Qantas, international travellers flying on Qantas could be steered towards Qantas domestic flights for their travel within Australia. Realising the importance of this factor, Ansett took prompt advantage of the government liberalisation of international air routes; in 1993, it began to develop services within Asia. But the few services it started still left the company well behind Qantas in regard to passenger feed.

Asymmetry in market outcomes

Both in the regulation era and in the 1990s, Ansett was thought to offer slightly better service than its rival, and this seems to have given it a larger share of business travellers paying full fares. However, after deregulation, this may have come at the cost of significantly lower load factors. Certainly, over the years 1994–5 to 2000–1, Ansett's domestic revenue-passenger load factor averaged 6.1 percentage points below that attained by Qantas. (That figure and the following calculations are based on operating data published in Qantas Annual Reports and Bureau of Transport Economics data for domestic airline aggregates.) Was Ansett's advantage in fare yield large enough to outweigh its much higher proportion of empty seats?

In 1994–5, Ansett operated 18.1 billion available seat-kilometres (ASK), compared with 13.5 billion by Qantas. As both companies moved to increase capacity, the difference between them gradually diminished, becoming only 0.9 billion ASK in 2000–1. In 1994–5, Qantas had the smaller sold output; but the difference gradually diminished, until Qantas went slightly ahead of Ansett in 2000–1. In short, Qantas overtook Ansett on several measures, and gradually became the more successful airline.

7.6 Enter two more new airlines

The Qantas–Ansett duopoly on the mainline routes came under significant challenge in the year 2000, which was a propitious time for launching new services, because of the extra traffic arising from the Olympic Games (held in Sydney in September).

A local, regional airline (Impulse) acquired some B717 jets, and entered the Melbourne–Sydney route on 5 June. And on 3 August a new company (then called Virgin Blue) launched on the Brisbane–Sydney route.

7.6.1 The fleeting ambition of Impulse Airlines – and the aftermath

For its launch as a low-fare airline, Impulse had the benefit of local experience, acquired while serving regional routes in New South Wales since 1994. With a reputation for competent organisation, Impulse attracted investment from two major Australian financial institutions (McGowan, 2000) and also from overseas sources.

It then leased five *new* 717-200 aircraft (Boeing Company press release, 11 April 2000), and entered the Melbourne–Sydney route. By early 2001, it was operating 19 flights each way on weekdays. Impulse also mounted a limited Brisbane–Sydney service, attempted services from Canberra, and in March 2001 announced it would fly between Melbourne and Hobart (*Airline Industry Information*, 6 March 2001).

As usual, both Qantas and Ansett introduced some discounted fares in a selective manner (Mills, 2002, pp. 206–7.) Impulse's financial position soon became untenable, especially because a key overseas institutional investor was not prepared to subscribe to a further $50 million share issue (*Australian Financial Review*, 2 May 2001).

On 1 May 2001, Qantas agreed to pay Impulse A$50 million to allow the latter to buy out its institutional shareholders. In return, Qantas took an exclusive wet-lease of the Impulse aircraft, giving Qantas effective control, subject to regulatory approval.

From its examination, the ACCC concluded that a Qantas take-over would create less damage to competition than having Impulse going into receivership ('ACCC not to oppose Qantas/Impulse merger ACCC', media release 116/01, 18 May 2001) – *provided* that Qantas gave certain undertakings, including handing back some peak-period runway-access 'slots' at Sydney Airport, to allow more access for Virgin Blue and any other entrants (Undertaking to the ACCC Pursuant to Section 87B of the Trade Practices Act 1974 by Qantas Airways Limited, 17 May 2001).

Upon the immediate removal of the Impulse services from the Sydney–Melbourne route, Qantas transferred the major part of the Impulse B717 fleet to thin routes not then served by Qantas. Some of these new direct services helped passengers to avoid change of aircraft at major ports such as Brisbane, Sydney or Melbourne; and the initiative may also have helped Qantas to forestall or limit route entry by Virgin.

In November 2001, when Qantas became the outright owner of Impulse, the B717 flights were introduced under the existing QantasLink brand name, no doubt in part to prevent Impulse pilots and cabin crew from accessing the superior pay and conditions of Qantas mainline crews. As became clear later, Qantas thereby also had the makings of a new in-house low-fare airline.

7.6.2 The entry of Virgin Blue

This new company chose Brisbane city for its headquarters, with good gates available at the new passenger terminal at Brisbane Airport. Backed by the Virgin airline group, the company start-up was managed parsimoniously. In particular, the initial aircraft were older B737-400 models, reported to have been little wanted at the Brussels base of Virgin Express.

The Virgin route strategy was to grasp opportunities available on routes that were *relatively* neglected by the incumbents, who seemed still to have a preference for carrying passengers between adjacent capitals on the eastern seaboard, rather than flying them directly to their destination ports. However, in starting with Brisbane–Sydney, Virgin chose a route on which Qantas and Ansett offered a frequent service, and provided a reasonable amount of capacity. (For the 12 months immediately preceding the Virgin entry, the revenue passenger load factor on that route was 76.5 per cent, while for all domestic routes – including many thinner ones – it was 75.3 per cent; Bureau of Infrastructure, Transport and Regional Economics, Canberra.)

Unlike Impulse, Virgin did not bet the company on a single route. Indeed, Virgin entered the Brisbane–Melbourne route (prior load factor of 80 per cent) only a month later. Two months after that, it launched on Brisbane–Adelaide (prior load factor of 85 per cent, though it must be noted this was then a very thin route, averaging only 18,000 monthly passengers). In the first seven months of 2001, Virgin entered a further six routes.

On its first three routes, Virgin's entry resulted in very large increases in the total (all airlines) passenger numbers, thanks to lower (average) fares and, on the Adelaide route, increased convenience arising from the greater frequency of non-stop flights. In consequence, there were only modest reductions in load factors. Even on the Adelaide route, where capacity had more than doubled, the reduced load factor stood at a reasonable 75 per cent.

At first, Virgin did not enter the densest route of all, Melbourne–Sydney. The lower fares there, following the Impulse entry, had resulted in many extra passengers; this left the route load factor broadly unchanged. However, when Qantas removed the Impulse aircraft from the route, Virgin entered very promptly. The route outcomes were affected by the problems encountered by Ansett, reported in §7.7 below.

7.6.3 An allegation of predatory conduct by Qantas

Just a few weeks after entering the Brisbane–Adelaide route, Virgin Blue lodged a formal complaint with the Australian Competition and Consumer Commission (ACCC), saying (media release, 23 January 2001) it believed that 'Qantas Airways Ltd. is engaging in illegal predatory pricing practices'. (Under Australian legislation, predation *may* be considered an 'abuse of market power', which was outlawed by §46 of the (then) Trade Practices Act.)

Eventually, the ACCC announced (media release, 7 May 2002) it had instituted legal proceedings against Qantas, and alleged that 'Qantas misused its market power by substantially increasing the number of seats available on the Brisbane–Adelaide route in an anti-competitive manner and matching or undercutting air fares in response to Virgin Blue's entry in an anti-competitive manner'. It also said that 'the effect of Qantas' conduct was that each of Qantas, Virgin Blue and Ansett were forced into operating at losses' for certain periods.

Notwithstanding the determined tone of that statement, the ACCC (under a new chairman) later announced (media release, 21 November 2003) it had decided to discontinue the legal action. It noted that: cases alleging misuse of market power are difficult to resolve in a court; since the date of that Brisbane–Adelaide dispute, consumers had benefited from competition between Qantas and Virgin Blue; and Virgin Blue continued to operate on the Brisbane–Adelaide route.

In effect, the ACCC was saying that any predatory intent on the part of Qantas had failed to drive Virgin from the industry or even from the route, and so the case was unimportant. However, as is argued later (§15.3), predatory tactics remain a significant issue in aviation; it is not always the case that everyone lives happily ever after.

7.7 The demise of Ansett

In December 2000, Ansett announced it was temporarily grounding some (old) B767 aircraft, because of maintenance problems. Safety concerns caught public attention again on 12 April 2001 when the Civil Aviation Safety Authority grounded all ten aircraft in Ansett's B767 fleet.

The beginning of the end came on 12 September 2001: the company went into voluntary administration, and two days later halted all flights. The government did not respond to populist pleas for a rescue. Hoping to sell the company to new owners, the administrator resumed limited services on 29 September, initially flying five A320s between Sydney and Melbourne, and later using five further A320s on other major routes. However, attempts to sell the airline were unsuccessful, and Ansett closed permanently on 5 March 2002.

Though Ansett's regional subsidiaries, Skywest, Kendell and Hazelton, also closed in September 2001, all three resumed operations later that month. Skywest was sold in February 2002, and continued to fly (in Western Australia) under the same name. When Kendell and Hazelton were sold on 1 August 2002, the new owner merged the two non-overlapping operations (both flying SAAB 340 aircraft) to form Regional Express (trading as Rex).

Though Ansett's demise did come *after* the arrival of Impulse and Virgin, its difficulties had grown over several years. It is likely that those airline entries played only a minor role.

7.8 Virgin grows strongly

However, Ansett's exit certainly helped Virgin. With Ansett in administration and operating on a reduced scale, Virgin entered eight more routes in the last three months of 2001. After Ansett's final exit in March 2002, Virgin launched service on nine further city-pair routes that year. All but two of those were 'trunk routes' which had been reserved for the two incumbents during the regulation era. The exceptions were tourist routes from Sydney to Coffs Harbour (New South Wales) and Sydney to Maroochydore (Queensland). Noting the limited ambition of the Qantas turbo-prop services, Virgin introduced its B737 jets to both routes. (In this section, all the factual details are sourced from Virgin media releases.)

In the next years, Virgin's (domestic) expansion continued apace: 11 more routes in 2003, and 12 more in 2004.

Upon Ansett's closure, high-quality passenger terminals owned or used by Ansett became available at many major ports, notably Melbourne, Adelaide, Perth and Sydney. After using make-shift arrangements at those and some other ports in order to secure early entry, Virgin was keen to have better accommodation. Yet, with some airport owners jockeying for terminal ownership and control, there were delays before Virgin secured access to the superior facilities: Cairns came first (May 2002) followed by Canberra, Melbourne, and Adelaide; and it was December that year before Virgin entered the vacant terminals at Perth and at Sydney.

Virgin also greatly increased its market share. In April 2002 (the first calendar month after the *final* closure of Ansett), Virgin had a sold output (RPKs) of roughly 20 per cent of the domestic total. Over the next two years, Virgin steadily increased its share, reaching 36 per cent in the first few months of 2004. In absolute terms, Virgin increased from about 0.45 billion monthly RPKs when Ansett closed, to about 1.1 billion in the early months of 2004.

Of course, when Ansett faltered and finally expired, Qantas made extraordinary efforts to increase its capacity, in order to replace as much of the Ansett service as it could. Thus, while Virgin took market share, Qantas still increased the absolute amount of traffic it carried.

7.9 Qantas creates Jetstar, its own 'low-cost' airline

7.9.1 The big-bang launch of Jetstar

On 17 October 2003, a Qantas media release announced a plan to establish 'a domestic low cost carrier'. The Qantas CEO Geoff Dixon explained:

> low cost, point-to-point, airlines ... are able to perform profitably at fare levels which traditional network carriers find unsustainable ... Of course this does not mean that the full service model is no longer needed. Consumers need both high value network and no frills point-to-point services for different trips and different purposes.
>
> (Sir Reginald Ansett Memorial Lecture, 17 September 2003,
> accessed at qantas.com)

In the outcome, Qantas launched a wholly owned subsidiary airline, *Jetstar*, on 25 May 2004. This deployed the 14 Boeing 717s previously operated by Impulse, each now with 125 seats in a single-class layout. Though these aircraft were adequate for regional routes, Qantas recognised that early replacement would be desirable, and soon announced it had ordered 23 *new* A320 aircraft, for use by Jetstar (Qantas media releases, 1 December 2003 and 25 February 2004).

On its very first day, Jetstar began service on a total of 18 city-pair routes from Brisbane, Melbourne and Sydney to regional cities and tourist destinations (media release, 'Jetstar takes to Australian skies', 25 May 2004).

On nearly all the launch routes, Qantas had previously offered (nonstop) service operated mainly or solely by the B717 aircraft (Qantas PDF timetable, published 10 May 2004). From 25 May, Qantas itself continued to operate non-stop service, usually with B737 aircraft, on 11 of the denser routes. On some other routes, Qantas continued to fly (QantasLink) turboprop services, alongside the Jetstar B717s. Virgin already flew 14 of the 18 initial Jetstar routes.

Jetstar claimed its launch was a great success. Of course, to a considerable extent, the change was nominal. In particular, Qantas had announced ('Jetstar announcement of route network and fares'. 25 February 2004, qantas.com) that it would transfer, to Jetstar's B717 flights, passengers previously booked for travel on or after 25 May on full-service Qantas flights.

7.9.2 Separate management for Jetstar

Qantas decided on separate management for Jetstar, with little or no input from the Qantas hierarchy on day-to-day operating decisions. No doubt, this encouraged 'local' managerial initiative. The separation also helped to ensure that Jetstar remained a low-cost carrier. In particular, pilots and cabin crew could not access Qantas pay rates.

The engineering base for the B717 fleet remained at Newcastle (and, later, Jetstar's A320 fleet was maintained there). Jetstar generally employed its own passenger handling staff, even at ports also served by Qantas. However Jetstar sometimes relied on apron crews employed by Qantas. For such shared services, the accounting methods used to apportion costs inevitably influenced the reported profitability of Jetstar. Even so, Qantas claimed (media release, 'Qantas results for the year ended 30 June 2004', 19 August 2004) that Jetstar 'recorded a small operating profit in its first full month of operation'.

To keep costs at a very low level, aircraft were based in only a few ports, and were not stationed overnight at other ports. Jetstar sought to speed up boarding by not pre-assigning seats to passengers. Passengers were not allowed to check baggage through from one flight to another. And to aid punctuality, each flight was closed *strictly* 30 minutes before the departure time (Jetstar media release 22 July 2004).

7.9.3 But Qantas itself keeps control of Jetstar route entries

Earlier experience of legacy airlines starting in-house low-cost airlines conveys a cautionary tale: without parental control, junior could easily cannibalise parts of the family's business, with adverse effects on *overall* family profitability; on the other hand, if junior was *too* restricted, she would lose physical condition – and then lose money.

Initially, Jetstar was to take over some routes on which Qantas itself could not turn a profit. Otherwise, on a few shared routes, Qantas flew at peak times while

Jetstar served departure times that did not generally interest business travellers; one example was Brisbane–Cairns (Qantas media release, 15 October 2004). On a few other shared routes (such as Sydney–Gold Coast), Qantas eventually operated just one or two flights daily to attract travellers who wanted full service, while Jetstar offered as many as six or eight flights. Initially, Jetstar found inter-capital routes were out of bounds.

Later, however, the Qantas board became more relaxed about any downside to Jetstar taking passengers from Qantas. Indeed, in the battle with Virgin Blue, it seems the board may have come to the view that it did not matter greatly which airline name appeared on the aircraft, as long as the revenue accrued to the Qantas group and not to Virgin. Eventually Jetstar was allowed to fly inter-capital routes too.

Among the underlying factors at work that may account for the change in Qantas thinking, the most interesting is that the differences in service quality and in flight time-of-day, may be better-than-expected *discriminators*, that serve to encourage Qantas customers themselves to choose flight-times and service levels in a manner that is profitable for the Qantas group.

7.9.4 Jetstar: fares and marketing

For its economy-class service, Jetstar offered just two ticket types: a heavily constrained JetSaver, and a flexible but (generally) *much* more expensive JetFlex. To compete with Virgin, Jetstar emphasised low fares right from the outset. For example, on 13 May 2004 the Jetstar website featured 'everyday' low fares from as little as A\$59 for many of the routes in the initial network. However, where Jetstar had a monopoly on a route, the lowest available fare was often much higher – for example, A\$179 on the (longish) route between Sydney and Hamilton Island.

Its marketing included a great deal of newspaper and television advertising, both at the time of the launch and subsequently. Also helping to attract passengers to Jetstar was its Qantas affiliation, which gave it a respectability that could not be gained immediately by an independent start-up airline.

Initially, the Qantas website informed its visitors whenever Jetstar served the route of interest. Later, Qantas began to offer Jetstar bookings on its own website – but did not draw attention to its practice of charging a few dollars more than the corresponding fare offered on the Jetstar site.

7.10 Ongoing competition between Virgin and the Qantas group

7.10.1 Virgin re-thinks its role

In launching Jetstar, Qantas did well in the immediate battle. In the longer term, however, the Qantas strategy had a downside too. With Jetstar competing successfully for low-fare travellers, Virgin was encouraged to try harder to attract business travellers, whose preponderant preference for Qantas was giving the latter a handsome advantage in *average* yield (revenue) per passenger-kilometre.

Among Virgin's changes were: provision of improved airport lounges; superior (2 + 2) seating (in the first three rows of its Boeing 737s), for which it charged a 'Premium Economy' fare (introduced on 14 March and upgraded on 27 November 2008 (media release, 26 November 2008); and in late 2005, a frequent-flyer programme, which was redesigned later to focus more on those who travel very frequently (media releases, 15 November 2005 and 23 August 2007).

Other changes included: the introduction of fare types that could be *fully* refunded (without penalty), even in the event of a no-show rather than prior cancellation of travel; and direct computer access to Virgin's back-office for the travel departments of larger businesses. Finally, Virgin tried to overcome some institutional practices of the Australian government that (in their effect) greatly favoured Qantas for travel by government employees, a matter of particular importance on routes from Canberra.

7.10.2 Changes in aircraft fleets for domestic routes

Jetstar made a gradual transition to a homogeneous fleet of A320s. It farewelled its last B717 in July 2006, at which time it had 23 A320s, each with 177 seats (Jetstar media release, 27 July 2006). By 2014, Jetstar (together with a subsidiary, Jetstar Asia) flew about 90 aircraft on domestic, New Zealand and other international routes (Qantas Data Book 2014, accessed at *qantas.com.au*). That fleet number includes four B787-8 aircraft, and seven A330-200s, all generally flown on international routes.

As Jetstar started to release its B717 aircraft, *Qantas* needed to replace its old BAe147s. Accordingly, Qantas retained eleven of the B717s, for use on thin regional and tourist routes, mostly in Western Australia and the Northern Territory. That fleet (by 2014, grown to some eighteen aircraft) flew under the QantasLink brand (Qantas Data Book).

Qantas also acquired some *new* small aircraft. In 2006, it started taking delivery of the (recently launched) Bombardier Q400 turboprop (72 seats), which it chose for passenger comfort and cruising speed (360 knots) (Qantas media release, 12 January 2006). No doubt the rising price of fuel also encouraged its preference for turboprops for shorter regional routes. By late 2014, QantasLink operated 31 such aircraft.

After launching with early-model Boeing 737s, *Virgin* soon phased out those aircraft, and introduced B737-700s with 144 seats and B737-800s (180 seats). Eventually, as Virgin expanded its fleet by focussing on the -800 model, the number of -700s was progressively reduced; in June 2013, only three such aircraft remained.

In an earlier change of strategy, Virgin had announced (media release, 20 February 2007) it would acquire some smaller jets, specifically six Embraer E170s (78 seats) and 14 E190s (104 seats), in order to serve thin routes that could not be flown economically by its B737s. The initial deliveries were three E170s, which flew the 200 km Sydney–Canberra route in a bid to attract government and other business travellers. However, the main growth was in the E190 fleet, which soon reached 18 aircraft.

With hindsight, subsequent rises in the price of jet fuel suggest that introducing the E170s was a mistake. Qantas did better with its deployment of the Q400 turboprops, one of whose many roles was to provide off-peak flights between Sydney and Canberra.

7.10.3 Further route entries

Following the 2004 launch of Jetstar, both that airline and Virgin Blue entered many further city-pair routes, many with daily flights. Several of those routes had not previously enjoyed *non-stop* service by any airline.

In building up its domestic network over its first five years, Jetstar added about 30 further routes. About half of these carried tourists from a state capital to a resort in *another* state. Nearly all those routes already had (or were to gain) competing service from Virgin.

A further one quarter of the Jetstar entries were *off-peak* flights on inter-capital routes, intended to attract low-fare travellers without diverting business travellers from Qantas services. Most of these were not begun until 2009, perhaps because Qantas needed to be convinced that such market segmentation was feasible and profitable. On such routes, the willingness of Virgin to offer low off-peak fares no doubt helped to stimulate the Jetstar entry.

During those years, Virgin Blue continued to extend *its* network. Between August 2004 and August 2010, it too entered some 30 routes. Its Embraer aircraft allowed it to offer jet service on thin routes that had rarely if ever seen such service before. In particular, Virgin entered two interstate routes from Sydney – to Mackay and to Rockhampton, both coastal cities in Queensland – after Jetstar had pioneered non-stop services but then withdrawn upon finding that its A320 aircraft were too large for the traffic offering.

7.11 The arrival of Tiger Airways Australia

Tiger Airways launched its Singapore-based network in September 2004 (already reported, in §4.2.2), and started flights to Darwin in December 2006. Seemingly in anticipation of that entry, Qantas had handed over that route to its Singapore-based subsidiary, Jetstar Asia, which began a daily A320 service in October 2006, flying Singapore–Darwin–Cairns. Tiger's next Australian port was Perth: service from Singapore started on 23 March 2007, increasing to daily service on 1 May 2007.

Meanwhile, Tiger sought Australian government approval to start a new *domestic* Australian airline. In March 2007, the government's Foreign Investment Review Board gave permission for Tiger to establish a *wholly owned* (!) subsidiary. Tiger Airways Australia was incorporated in the (Australian) Northern Territory ('Tiger Airways About us – Milestones' tigerairways.com accessed on 19 August 2010). Like its parent, the Australian subsidiary was to operate A320s, and was to offer very low fares.

Tiger Airways Australia became the anchor tenant of the new (low-cost) Terminal 4 at Melbourne Airport. In November 2007 and early 2008, it launched flights from Melbourne to the Gold Coast resort area, to the Queensland regional ports of Mackay and Rockhampton, and also to Launceston, Maroochydore and Newcastle. Many of those routes had little or no non-stop service from other airlines. It also started flights from Melbourne to Darwin and to Perth; these connected with services from Singapore, and so allowed easy rotation of aircraft for maintenance in Singapore.

In 2008, Tiger opened a base at Adelaide, and started flying to Melbourne and Hobart. However, it was 2009 before it flew from Melbourne and Adelaide to Sydney, where high airport charges had deterred earlier entry. (Perhaps Tiger then negotiated lower charges.) On 30 August 2010, its website showed services on 17 routes.

In July 2011, however, the (Australian) Civil Aviation Safety Authority (CASA) became concerned about Tiger's safety standards, and grounded the entire airline for several weeks. In August, Tiger was allowed to resume on a small scale, and was then permitted to build up its flying gradually. The later story is taken up in §7.13.

7.12 Market growth and airline traffic shares

As already seen, the fall of Ansett led to significant disruption of the domestic market. While the passenger traffic carried by Australian-registered airlines operating domestic flights amounted to 33.7 billion RPK in the financial year to 30 June 2001, the corresponding total in the next year was only 31.2 billion. As seen in Table 7.1, that decline was soon recovered. Indeed subsequent growth in *every* financial year up to June 2014 brought the total market to some 67 billion RPK, more than twice the 2002 figure. In that basic sense, the market entries of Virgin and Tiger, and the Qantas establishment of Jetstar, have (belatedly) demonstrated a success for deregulation.

In many countries, it is easy to trace the fortunes of the individual airlines. In Australia, however, the government has long neglected to publish data for individual airlines, a practice that no doubt reflects the influence of the regulation-era duopoly, which wanted as much secrecy as it could get away with. Thus, even at the *aggregate* (network) level, the only data on passenger numbers and RPKs *of the individual airlines* are those published by the airlines themselves. Some of those records are incomplete; others bring complications arising from differences in the definitions employed. For those reasons, Table 7.1 has some estimated figures.

Despite those limitations, the table readily conveys some important points. As Qantas handed to Jetstar more and more route opportunities, the total sold output (RPKs) of Qantas mainline (jet) services has remained broadly steady; the continued (domestic) growth of the company has stemmed (almost entirely) from the expansion of Jetstar. However, traffic on the regional routes served by QantasLink has also grown, in part because the B717 jets released by Jetstar were used to increase the jet capacity of QantasLink.

Meanwhile, Virgin's RPK total has also grown each year (except for a small downturn in 2010). However, after its initial breakneck expansion, its share

Table 7.1 Passenger travel (in billions of RPKs) on scheduled domestic services[1] of Australian-domiciled airlines, 2002–14

Year to 30 June	Total	Qantas domestic	Jetstar domestic	Qantas Link	Virgin domestic	Skywest	Tigerair	Rex
2002	31.2	20.17	–	2.36	*7.90		–	
2003	34.0	22.50	–	2.33	8.33	*0.10	–	*0.27
2004	39.2	23.71	0.28	1.93	12.59	0.14	–	*0.31
2005	43.8	22.47	4.35	1.88	*14.38	0.24	–	0.40
2006	46.7	22.45	6.41	2.09	*14.95	0.24	–	0.45
2007	51.3	23.71	7.75	2.51	*16.43	0.25	–	0.50
2008	55.4	24.83	8.60	2.90	16.67	0.28	*1.51	0.54
2009	56.4	23.78	9.06	2.92	17.47	0.28	*2.26	0.48
2010	57.7	24.09	9.46	2.94	17.23	0.29		0.46
2011	61.8	24.72	11.37	3.22	17.76			0.45
2012	63.8	24.77	12.80	3.40	19.22			0.44
2013	66.3	24.94	13.96	3.41	19.43	–	*3.15	0.41
2014	*67.2	24.16	14.58	3.56	*20.51	–	*3.99	0.39

Sources and estimation methods

Total traffic: Australian Domestic Airline Activity (traffic on domestic and regional services, excluding domestic passengers on sectors of international flights), Bureau of Infrastructure, Transport and Regional Economics, Canberra; this series not published after 2013 – estimate for 2014 supposes increase since 2013 is same as increase when domestic passengers on domestic sectors of international flights are included.

Qantas domestic, Jetstar domestic and QantasLink: Qantas Annual Reports/Preliminary Final Reports.

Virgin: Virgin monthly traffic reports, except for the estimated figures, which are derived by subtracting from the total the traffic carried by other airlines; from May 2013, total includes the traffic of Virgin Australia Regional Airlines.

Rex and Skywest: airline monthly traffic reports, with estimated figures based on miscellaneous information in airline press releases; from May 2013, Skywest RPKs are included in Virgin totals.

Tigerair Australia: the estimated 2008 figure is for seven months starting December 2007; from 2013, Tigerair data come from Virgin Australia monthly statistics, except for (estimated) June figures.

Notes

Travel amounts preceded by asterisks have been estimated from limited published data. For Jetstar, Skywest and Tigerair, cells containing a dash indicate that the airline concerned did not fly in the years so marked.

1 The data do not include the very small amount of travel on domestic sectors of international flights.

of the total domestic market declined slightly, from 32.1 per cent in 2004 to 29.3 per cent in 2013. The 2004 entry of Jetstar was undoubtedly the major factor in the halt to the earlier growth in Virgin's market share. Previously, Qantas had *not* gone all out to attract leisure travellers wanting to fly at low fares.

The other significant message from Table 7.1 is the dominance of the Qantas and Virgin camps. In the financial year 2011–12, the other players together attracted only *approximately* six per cent of the RPK total. As the Table implies, Tigerair was by far the largest airline (then) outside the Qantas and Virgin groups. Yet, that independence was soon to end, as is reported next.

7.13 Further changes in airline style and ownership

The successful establishment of Jetstar gave the Qantas camp an obvious advantage over Virgin. However, the consequent fiercer airline competition for leisure travel, sold at low fares, encouraged Virgin to compete more vigorously for the custom of business travellers. Towards the end of his 10-year reign as the founding CEO of Virgin, Brett Godfrey introduced a 'Premium Economy' class. This offered somewhat superior cabin conditions and some other advantages. However, the introduction of an all-out Business Class awaited the arrival of a new CEO.

Meanwhile there was a management change at Qantas. Upon the retirement of *its* CEO in 2009, the Qantas board appointed as the new CEO the (relatively young) manager, Alan Joyce, who had successfully led Jetstar since its inception in 2004. This appointment had the effect of sidelining a long-established and very senior Qantas manager, John Borghetti, who then left Qantas.

In May 2010, when Godfrey retired from Virgin, Borghetti became Virgin's new CEO. Among the early changes that he introduced was the fleet-wide inception of a fully-styled Business Class. Other moves included: withdrawal of the (small) E170 jets; and introduction of several A330-200 wide-bodies, to be used on the non-stop sectors of 4+ hours between Perth (in Western Australia) and each of the east-coast ports of Melbourne, Sydney and Brisbane.

While these moves helped Virgin Australia (as it was now called) to compete for more business travel, the company still had no *direct* competitive response to the Qantas in-house low-cost carrier, Jetstar. That situation changed in dramatic fashion in November 2012, when Virgin announced (in three media releases of 30 November 2012) that it proposed, subject to some conditions, to acquire 60 per cent of the shares in Tigerair Australia (as *it* had become called), and to buy outright the Perth-based regional carrier, Skywest.

In due course, these plans received the needed approvals of the (Australian) Foreign Investment Review Board, the ACCC (Australian Competition and Consumer Commission) and the Securities Industry Council of Singapore. The Skywest purchase completed in April 2013, and the Tigerair transaction was finalised in July 2013 (Virgin Australia media release 11 April 2013; Annual Report 2013, p. 3).

While the Virgin board favoured the Tiger acquisition as an important counter to the Qantas ownership of Jetstar, the purchase brought immediate challenges, notably a need to turn Tiger's financial deficits into profitability.

After starting on that task, Virgin announced (media release, 'Proposed acquisition of remaining 40% of Tigerair Australia', 17 October 2014) an intention to buy the remaining Tiger shares for A$1. That would allow cost savings arising from closer integration of the operations of the two airlines. The proposed agreement would also bring to Virgin certain brand rights allowing Tigerair Australia to fly under that name on routes to various short-haul *international* destinations.

On the same date, the Board of Tiger Airways Holdings Limited issued a lengthy announcement on 'The Proposed Sale of the Company's Entire 40% Shareholding Interest in Tiger Airways Australia Pty Ltd', noting that (1) the

Australian company had incurred operating losses ever since it launched in 2007, (2) the Board considered that divestment was in the best interests of the Company's shareholders', and (3) the Australian Competition and Consumer Commission, upon being advised of the intended transaction, had not taken steps to oppose it. For its part, Virgin said it hoped that the proposal would get Foreign Investment Review Board approval by the end of 2014. In February 2015, Virgin announced that it had just completed the Tigerair acquisition (ASX release, 'Virgin Australia Holdings Limited announces completion of the remaining 40% of Tigerair Australia', 6 February 2015).

Qantas and Virgin dominate the airline sector

Upon that completion, the Qantas and Virgin camps each owned a mainline jet operator *and* a low-cost jet carrier, together with a regional airline equipped wholly or largely with turboprop aircraft. Between them, the two groups owned/controlled almost the entire Australian airline sector. Of the companies listed in Table 7.1, only Rex remained independent. Its share of the RPK total in the 2014 financial year was only about 0.6 per cent.

Australia has *very* few other scheduled airlines. One carrier of note is *Airnorth*, based in Darwin (in northern Australia) and founded in 1978 to serve nearby small communities. By July 2013, Airnorth had grown large enough to operate four E170 jets (76 seats) as well as some small turboprops (media release, 5 July 2013). It used the jets to serve a few lengthy domestic routes, and also some regional routes that include the international route between Darwin and Dili (the capital of East Timor). Airnorth is an unlisted public company – and has a marketing agreement with Qantas!

7.14 Other developments since 2012

Upon arriving at Virgin, Borghetti instituted a review of the airline's activities. Besides the intensified pursuit of business travellers, Virgin claimed progress in reducing cost levels by winning greater productive efficiency, boosting its loyalty (frequent flyer) program, and again targeting yield and profit margins rather than market share (presentation, Citi Australian Investment Conference, 23 October 2012).

The airline also stepped up moves to establish code-shares and other liaisons with various overseas airlines. An important purpose there was to increase *international* passenger-feed to/from Virgin domestic services, a matter of importance because Virgin's own international services were slight compared with those of Qantas.

In keeping with that objective, Virgin welcomed to its share register three overseas airlines: Air New Zealand, Singapore Airlines and Etihad. Soon, those companies subscribed additional share capital when Virgin Australia experienced sizeable domestic operating losses, which arose mainly from a capacity and fare battle with Qantas.

For its part, Qantas reasonably complained that share-holding restrictions in the Qantas Sale Act 1992 (the legislation that effected the privatisation of Qantas) prevented Qantas from obtaining comparable investment from overseas airlines (such as Emirates, with whom it was collaborating in code-share and other arrangements). To respond to that concern, the Australian government secured parliamentary passage of the Qantas Sale Amendment Act 2014, which repealed certain prohibitions on foreign ownership of Qantas shares.

In regard to competition with Virgin on domestic routes, Qantas publicly drew a 'line in the sand', in effect seeking to retain (for Qantas and Jetstar combined) a two thirds share of the domestic market. This was to be achieved by adding twice as much capacity in any period in which Virgin increased *its* capacity on domestic routes.

The problem for Qantas was that at fare levels that might cover its (lowered, but still high) operating costs, Qantas could not attract enough passengers to support its desired market share. Thus Qantas too was recording operating losses, thanks in part to the reduced yields that resulted from the increased domestic capacity operated by both airline camps.

By mid-2014, there were signs that the ongoing financial losses might encourage domestic capacity restraint by both airlines (Jamie Freed, 'Qantas blinks first in Virgin battle, with domestic capacity freeze', *Sydney Morning Herald*, 22 May 2014). Yet that did not discourage further capacity increases on some selected routes.

Both groups also sought to operate their fleets more flexibly, in order to increase aircraft utilisation. In particular, Virgin reconsidered its use of A330s, each with 24 lie-flat business-class seats, on the domestic transcontinental routes to Perth. After finding that the A330 was too big for weekend services, Virgin re-assigned some such flights to B737-800 aircraft. Later, and without any impact on its Perth services, it deployed otherwise idle A330s on Saturday international flights to Fiji at peak seasons of the year. It also introduced them on the short-haul route between Melbourne and Sydney at peak times, and on selected weekends when sporting events in either city resulted in unusually high demand levels (Jamie Freed, 'Virgin Australia to deploy A330 widebody on Fiji flights', *Sydney Morning Herald*, 2 March 2015).

A conclusion

During the long period in which Qantas and Virgin Australia have competed vigorously, domestic travellers have benefited greatly from route and other service innovations, and from relatively low fares (for economy-class seats, at least).

Part II
The airline industry

8 The revolution

Airline operation and outcomes

8.1 Some economic fundamentals of airline operation

8.1.1 Direct costs incurred in operating a flight

One of the important direct costs comes from the *fuel* used. A flight sector comprises three phases. Once the departing aircraft has reached its (initial) cruising height, there is a period with few if any changes in altitude, until the aircraft reaches the destination area, and begins its descent. For that period of (substantially) level flight, the rate (per unit of time) at which fuel is used is broadly uniform. Further, with the aircraft flying at a (substantially) uniform speed, the distance between the ports is a good proxy for the time-duration of that phase. Taking those two factors together, the fuel used during the cruise, and the cost of that fuel, may be taken as being proportional to the (route) distance between the ports.

For the ascent and decent phases, the rate of fuel consumption is high during the ascent, and low during the descent. The amount of fuel used in each of those two manoeuvres is not affected by the distance between the ports, nor is it materially affected by the identities of the two ports. Thus *that* part of the fuel cost may be regarded as being (broadly) the same for each flight performed by the aircraft.

In summary, the total fuel cost of a flight (by a given type of aircraft) comprises an invariant dollar amount (incurred during ascent and descent) plus a cruise component that varies in proportion to the route distance between the ports.

Engine wear during the flight brings another direct cost. Unlike the fuel cost, however, the payment is postponed to the date on which the engine undergoes heavy maintenance. The length of the period between consecutive (heavy) maintenance overhauls is determined by the numbers of hours of engine use. Thus, for the purpose of estimating the total cost of a flight, that engine cost may be regarded as being proportional to the (time) duration of the flight.

The third significant direct cost of the flight comprises the *labour costs* incurred in crewing the aircraft for the flight. Pilots and cabin crew are engaged on (usually) long-lasting contracts, under which payment is based on rates per month (or other time-period) of employment. In return the flight crew members agree to work on the flights assigned by the airline, up to a contractual maximum (often specified in terms of aggregate flight time per month (or year). Those contractual terms provide a basis for allocating shares of those labour costs to individual flights.

Last on this list of direct costs of a particular flight are the (immediate) *payments to third parties*, notably aircraft movement charges billed by the two ports, and the charges levied for the use of air traffic control services.

8.1.2 Indirect costs incurred in supporting a flight

The other costs of the airline are indirect costs, not *immediately* affected – perhaps, not at all affected – by a decision on whether or not to operate a particular flight on a particular day.

When the flight *is* operated, the passengers need to be served by airline staff (or contractors) who work inside the passenger terminals at the two ports, and/or outside on the apron. Usually, the total cost to the airline is determined by decisions on how many such posts to establish at each terminal. In turn, such decisions are based on (1) the expected total workloads that will ensue when the expected number of flights are operated, and (2) the work-rates required in the passengers terminals during (any) peak periods, having many flights arriving and departing.

Deciding on how to assign such costs to individual flights presents some tricky issues for the design of cost accounting principles. (And long manuals are written thereon.) Here it is sufficient to say that the approach should depend on the nature of the decision about the flight. If the management is considering whether or not to introduce a regular peak-period daily flight on a particular route, then there is a strong case for saying that those staff costs should be fully allocated – by assessing how many minutes of staff-time are required per passenger, and then costing that at the appropriate hourly rates (for pay and all on-costs).

On the other hand, if the aim is to shed light on how much cost would be saved if, on a particular day, the airline were to cancel a regular flight, perhaps because few passengers are expected, then there may be no consequent change in the number of employees rostered to work at the terminal on that day. In that situation, there is a strong case for recognising that *none* of those labour costs would be avoided if the flight is cancelled.

Terminal operation also incurs other costs, notably those incurred in providing and maintaining the terminal buildings and the equipment therein. To an even greater extent than in the case of labour costs, there may be situations in which such building costs are best not allocated to the overall cost of an individual flight.

One further, very important item is taken up in the next section: the cost of owning aircraft.

8.1.3 Costing of off-peak flights

When an airline schedules a regular daily flight at an *off-peak* time of day, that flight may *not* add to the airline's total costs in *all* the significant cost categories.

Perhaps the most important of those categories is the cost of *owning* long-lived assets, especially aircraft. Buying (or leasing) a sizeable jet aircraft involves very large money sums. If the airline is to avoid bankruptcy, it *must* recoup those outlays. In this simple story, we suppose that the airline (Air Utopia) buys the aircraft with funds that it borrows. (In the common situation of leasing the aircraft, the principles of the analysis are the same, even if the details differ.)

A conventional accounting approach for a newly acquired aircraft is to estimate how many years the aircraft will be retained by the airline, and how much the airline will receive when it sells the aircraft at the anticipated date of sale. On that basis, the accountant can then work out a daily 'holding charge'. The amount of that charge is such that a stream of holding-charge payments made every day (over the number of years that Air Utopia plans to use the aircraft) would match the (net) capital outlay, after allowing for interest charges incurred along the way on funds borrowed to buy the aircraft.

In the accounting framework, that charge can be regarded as an element in the cost of using the aircraft. However, that should *not* be taken as implying that the holding charge can or should be recouped *every* day. First, there are days when the aircraft is undergoing maintenance and so is not available for use. Second, there may well be days of the week where use of the aircraft earns large revenues, and other days when flying the aircraft is not so remunerative. So the financial requirement should be rephrased: to pay off the debt incurred when buying the aircraft, Air Utopia needs to earn an *average* amount of (unencumbered) daily revenues that match the daily holding charge. (Here, 'unencumbered' revenues are receipts that are *not* required to pay any other of Utopia's costs.)

The averaging approach becomes even more important when we look at the several flights that the aircraft can undertake within a single day. (So, at last, we come to the off-peak issue!) Suppose that Utopia achieves 12 block hours per aircraft per day – meaning that the aircraft spends 12 hours per day moving on the ground or in the air while performing flights. (The emphasis is on *flight* time; it is the flight that earns the money. Time spent when the aircraft is parked, or is at the gate boarding or disembarking passengers is not part of the 12 hours that is recognised in the calculation of aircraft utilisation.) On that basis, Utopia divides the daily holding charge by 12, to arrive at an hourly holding charge.

If Utopia is a full-service airline, it may well earn very handsome revenues on morning and evening peak flights, by carrying (mainly) business travellers, and filling most if not quite all the seats. However, at other times (that is, between the peaks, and after the evening peak), Utopia has to decide what to do with the aircraft. Years ago, Utopia might well have left some of its aircraft idle between the peaks. That practice seems to be less common nowadays, perhaps because of the increased pressures on airlines to earn profits. In such a profit-seeking context, how should Utopia decide on whether or not to idle an aircraft between the daily peaks (and at other off-peak times)?

First, Utopia has to recognise that flights that *are* worth operating are likely to vary significantly in their profitability. A flight with above-average profit (say, at a peak time) may result in unencumbered revenue greatly exceeding the holding charge applicable for the hours of the flight duration. Clearly operation of such a flight adds to Utopia's profits.

On the other hand, while a below-average flight may have *some* unencumbered revenue, the amount may fall short of the standard holding charge. Is such a flight worthwhile? In other words does operation of such a flight add to Utopia's profits?

To help the explanation, consider a hypothetical numerical case. Suppose that the holding charge for the time that the aircraft takes to complete the flight amounts to $2000. And suppose that for the below-average flight that is under consideration, Utopia expects to earn *unencumbered* revenue of only $1000. Even then, if the only alternative is to park the aircraft, the flight is clearly worthwhile. That conclusion follows because the holding charge is the same whether or not the flight is undertaken, and the contribution of $1000 towards meeting the aircraft's total holding charge is better than no contribution at all.

However, if the flight is financially so adverse that it makes no contribution to the holding charge, *and* if it fails to cover some of the other costs that *are* variable costs, then Utopia would be better off (on short-term considerations, at any rate) to park the aircraft rather than to operate the flight. (The long-term considerations that *may* affect that conclusion are examined in the next section.) There is one further point to note here: if Utopia finds it is parking an aircraft for quite a number of hours each week, it should do some more sums to check whether it might be more profitable to dispose of the aircraft.

To sum up: Air Utopia needs to earn enough money, in aggregate, to cover the fixed cost of aircraft ownership (as well as all its variable costs). However, that rule does not require each and every flight to meet that financial test. In particular, while peak flights should be making large contributions to the fixed cost of aircraft ownership, off-peak flights may be worthwhile even when they make only a small contribution.

The same argument applies to some of Utopia's other costs. For example, *if* the airline needs to keep a certain minimum number of staff at work in the passenger terminal even during off-peak periods, then an extra off-peak flight may be handled without extra staff. In that case, operation of the flight does not lead to extra passenger-handling costs. And such an off-peak flight should not be *required* to cover any of those costs.

Incidentally, many new airlines use their aircraft intensively throughout the day, and that may well be the most profitable strategy, especially for an airline that emphasises low fares for leisure travel. Such travellers can be induced to fly at non-peak times by an offer of (even) lower fares at such times. On the other hand, a full-service airline which (mainly) serves business travellers is more likely to find it financially preferable to park the aircraft in the period between the two daily peaks.

8.1.4 A special case: operating flights 'unprofitably' on new routes

So far, the analysis has pre-supposed that the airline seeks to establish the cost of a particular flight in order to help it to judge whether the flight is *directly/ immediately* profitable. The tacit view has been that the airline will not wish to operate unprofitable flights.

However, when an airline wishes to start a new route, it recognises that the route may not be *immediately* profitable. Even on a route with good eventual prospects, the *early* revenue-passenger load factors may be low – principally, because many prospective passengers do not immediately learn of the new direct flights, and even when they have learned, it may take a while before they have occasion to try out the new service. Despite those risks, the airline may judge there is a good prospect of eventual profitability, with those profits soon offsetting the early financial losses.

In such a case, the airline may knowingly persevere with the route, despite not being able to recover all the aircraft holding costs (and other indirect costs) during the early weeks and months. Indeed, it *may* choose to persevere even when early flights fail to cover some of the direct costs.

Such decisions are crucial for a new airline, which by definition *has* to start new routes. Bad luck or poor judgement in selecting routes can result in bankruptcy. For the established carrier, however, a single mistaken entry will often be much less of a problem.

8.1.5 Economies of scale and scope

In many industries, large firms produce at lower cost per unit of output than do small firms that make the same product. However, once an airline has become a 'major' carrier, there is little evidence of such *general* 'economies of scale' (Caves, Christensen and Tretheway, 1984; Gillen, Oum and Tretheway, 1990). In the preceding chapters, we have seen that, while there are few airlines with fleets of more than (say) 200 aircraft, quite a number of airlines operate at least (say) 60 or 80 aircraft (often of a single type). Those companies are generally quite well established, and can reasonably be regarded as 'major'.

Beyond (say) 80 aircraft, if an airline were to double in size by doubling *all* its dimensions, then its unit cost is unlikely to change much (if at all). Specifically, if such an airline were, for example, to double in size by doubling its aircraft numbers (for each of its given aircraft types) and by extending its network in a manner that doubles the number of ports served and the number of daily (non-stop) sectors flown, and if as a result the airline flies twice as many passengers in all, but over the same (average) distance per passenger, with the same (average) number of passenger *per route*, the same (average) number of passengers *per port*, and the same (average) number of passengers per flight, then the general *style* of the operation is little changed.

Because the number of passengers per route is unchanged, there is no new reason for starting to fly larger aircraft. And because ports handle much the same numbers of passengers per port as before, the style of port operations changes little if at all. Thus the unit costs of the enlarged airline – in particular, the cost per passenger flown – are much the same as before.

On the other hand, important economies can arise if the airline increases its size *in some particular dimensions, without changes in other dimensions.* To explore, we now look at some cases.

Economies of scale in respect of aircraft size

Larger aircraft generally have lower operating costs per available seat-km (ASK). The main reason is that while engine operating costs (including the cost of fuel) do increase with seat capacity, the rate of increase is less than proportional to the increase in seat capacity, other factors held the same.

That factor increases in importance as the price of fuel rises. As already reported, in recent years quite a number of airlines have introduced larger jet aircraft, and/or withdrawn smaller jets from their fleets, in order to obtain lower average operating costs per ASK. Similarly, engine maintenance costs per ASK become smaller as aircraft size increases, especially because nowadays almost every short-haul jet aircraft has just two engines.

While the number of cabin crew *does* increase more or less proportionately with passenger capacity, the number of pilots remains at two, though pilot unions often secure somewhat higher pay-rates for larger aircraft. Furthermore, airport landing charges and en-route air navigation charges often increase less than proportionately with aircraft size.

In addition, increases in the price of fuel over recent decades have encouraged the use of larger turboprop aircraft (now, up to about 80 seats) because turboprop engines use much less fuel than comparable jet engines. Similarly, few airlines now wish to buy jet aircraft with less than (say) 100 seats.

Economies of scale in respect of aircraft fleet numbers

In regard to the number of aircraft *of a single type* in the airline's fleet, scale economies arise in both maintenance and operation of aircraft. If the airline has only one aircraft type, each of its pilots can fly *any* aircraft in the fleet. If there are two distinct types, the airline needs two groups of pilots, and then scheduling and crewing of the fleet becomes more complicated. Much the same consideration applies to aircraft maintenance. By themselves, these cost circumstances encourage the airline to operate just one aircraft type.

On the other hand, an airline can benefit from flying a variety of aircraft types of differing seat capacities, in order to get reasonable matches between aircraft size and route density, and thereby secure high load factors – which in turn help to hold down the cost per passenger.

Skilled managers seek a good fleet structure, to give an appropriate balance between the opposing cost considerations. To ease that task, aircraft makers have developed aircraft *families.* For example, the Airbus A320 family includes two smaller models – the A319 and the A318 – and the larger A321. The family members span a (modest) capacity range, and yet have many common components and operating characteristics. This helps to lower inventory and maintenance costs. It may also allow pilots and cabin crew (once trained for the family) to work on any of its members, thereby increasing workforce flexibility and paring crew costs.

Also of interest is the change over time in the average airline fleet size. Over the years from (say) 1970 to 2005, as the total number of (scheduled) airlines in the world grew from less than 200 to about 800, the average airline fleet size remained at about 20 aircraft, but the average fleet size for the 50 largest airlines increased from about 60 aircraft to about 180 (larger) aircraft (Kilpi, 2007).

Many of the new, low-fare airlines fly only one aircraft family; very few fly more than two. As a result, the larger new airlines have secured most of, or almost all, the available fleet economies. For a new-start carrier, the lack of scale does matter, of course. Their aim is usually to expand quickly to a fleet of (say) fifteen or twenty aircraft of the one family, to secure a major part of the available fleet economies.

The major *legacy* airlines often have more fleet diversity, in part because they operate long-haul routes as well as short-haul. Even so, many have gained much of the benefit of fleet scale economies. However, as seen in the earlier chapters, some smaller national carriers have very diverse fleets, with only a handful of aircraft of each type. The 2015 short-haul jet fleet of the Romanian national carrier, TAROM, provides an example (see §2.4.5).

Economies of scope

On the standard definition, these arise when a firm increases the number of its different – but similar – activities. In manufacturing, such economies may be forthcoming when a firm increases its output by increasing the number of different products it makes, *and* the various product types undergo at least some of their processing on the same equipment.

For airlines, such economies are important in relation to so-called *station* costs – notably the *per-passenger* costs of passenger handling and other services carried out at the station (port). When an airline adds new routes at a port that it already serves, there may well be a reduction in its *per-passenger* station costs (at that port). To illustrate, at a station that handles (say) just six flights in the day, the airline's station crew may well be idle or under-employed at some times during the day. As other routes are added, or extra flights are started on the prior routes, the work-load can be smoothed out, so that the crews are more fully employed, and station costs *per passenger* and *per flight* are somewhat reduced.

As noted briefly in §2.3.1, after their establishment and early growth, both Ryanair and (especially) EasyJet put emphasis on launching more routes between ports already in the airline's network, in order to increase the scale of activity at those ports, and so reduce average per-passenger station costs.

Economies of route density

Airlines often find that the larger the number of passengers carried on a given route, the lower is the average cost per passenger. While still having regard for desired flight frequency, the airline may deploy larger aircraft when the number of passengers flying the route increases, thereby benefiting from economies of scale in aircraft size. In addition, dense routes generally have frequent flights, and this often helps the airline to secure a high passenger load factor, because it is then easier to match capacity to demand.

8.2 Airline choices of business model

8.2.1 Travel purposes, passenger preferences and airline scheduling

Most journeys by air are made either in the course of the traveller's business role or for a private leisure purpose. For the former, the term 'business' has to be interpreted broadly, to include not only travel by business men and women, but also travel by a wide range of professionals attending conferences or other meetings relating to their occupations. Much business travel can be completed within the one day, thereby avoiding overnight stays away from home. In contrast, leisure travel usually involves overnight absence from home, whether visiting friends and relatives or staying in a hotel.

A business traveller generally puts a high value on convenience – notably, on convenient flight departure times, and hence on flight frequency. This helps to keep to a minimum any 'schedule delay' – the difference between the passenger's most-desired departure time and the closest departure time in the airline's flight schedule. (A frequent schedule also helps whenever the business traveller wishes to switch between flights just before travel.) At the other extreme is the leisure traveller, for whom the schedule times and flight frequency are likely to be much less important; instead, securing a low fare is often the major aim.

If an airline seeks to serve both travel types, then it has to consider carefully how to shape its service. For a given route, increased flight frequency and lower load factors (which help a traveller who wishes to make a last-minute reservation) will attract business travel, but will also increase the airline's cost per seat flown. That may translate into higher fares, which will not be welcomed by most leisure travellers; indeed, if faced with high fares, those passengers may seek a more appropriate deal with another airline. To avoid that outcome, the airline can usually arrange to offer distinct, lower fares to leisure travellers, while discouraging or even preventing business travellers from buying those lower fares. (That strategy is examined in detail in Chapter 9.)

Besides fares, the profit-seeking airline chooses other service qualities with regard to the mix of travel purposes of those who want to fly the particular route. Although an airline usually maintains considerable uniformity in service qualities, it can (at the least) vary frequency and load-factor across routes.

8.2.2 Alternative network styles: hubbing and point-to-point

As noted in §1.1.3, deregulation in the US allowed and encouraged the legacy airlines to adopt hub-and-spoke (HS) networks, with hubs dispersed at major cities, but not always at the very largest cities. In contrast, in Europe the national carriers used the national capitals as hub ports, and often confined their service at regional cities to routes connecting those cities to the national capital (§2.1.1). For expository convenience, the following discussion supposes that the airline has only a single hub.

Hub-and-spoke networks

Hubbing allows the airline to bring together, on a flight *to (from)* the hub, passengers with differing origin (destination) cities. This can allow more frequent service for particular city-pairs than would otherwise be financially viable. It also allows the airline to exploit some economies of route density (Oum, Zhang and Zhang, 1995).

On the other hand, in offering travel through a hub (rather than on a direct non-stop flight), the airline carries all passengers – other than those having the hub as origin or destination – over greater distances; and each such passenger has to be boarded and disembarked on two flights. Both features incur extra costs for the airline, compared with direct, non-stop routings.

The operation of a large hub is itself somewhat costly. To avoid giving the transferring passengers a long wait before boarding their next flight, the airline can choose to organise flights in 'banks': many flights arrive within a short period, passengers and bags are sorted and re-boarded, and many flights then leave within a short period. The process is aided by the availability of two or more runways, which (after a bunched set of take-offs) may then remain little used until the arrival of the next aircraft bank. The station staff alternate similar busy and quiet periods.

Generally, no port hosts the hubbing of more than one major airline. That dispersal of hubs largely prevents a passenger transferring to another airline at the hub port. Further, the enhanced frequency of one-stop connecting flights makes it harder for another airline to compete when it offers infrequent non-stop flights between a city-pair. Indeed, the hubbing style was adopted in part to strengthen the airline's market power, and may not score well in terms of economic efficiency.

Point-to-point networks

In contrast to such hubbing practices, most *new* airlines have chosen to build point-to-point (PTP) networks, for which each flight number designates a single flight sector, and the airline serves only those routes (city-pairs) that have enough traffic to support direct, non-stop service. Of course, this reflects the fact that an entrant would need to grow for several years before it is big enough to engage in worthwhile hubbing.

Most PTP airlines do *not* seek to transfer passengers between flights at an intermediate port. Indeed, some strongly discourage such transfer. For example, Ryanair's Terms and Conditions of Carriage (website, accessed 31 December 2014) includes the following:

> ARTICLE 17 – POINT-TO-POINT AIRLINE.
> We are a 'point-to-point' airline. We therefore do not offer, and cannot facilitate, the transfer of passengers or their baggage to other flights, whether operated by ourselves or by other carriers.

In that situation, a PTP airline has no need to use a large port where many airlines congregate. Rather, it may use a secondary port in or near a large city, and thereby pay lower airport charges than those applying at the main airport in the area.

A PTP airline often secures better on-time performance than that achieved by many HS legacy carriers. Various factors contribute to that outcome. The PTP airline does not 'hold' flights to facilitate connections; any secondary ports it uses may be less congested; and the successful new airlines often have highly motivated staff.

With that emphasis on punctuality, the PTP airline often works its aircraft more intensively (that is, it secures more block hours per aircraft per day), thanks in part to shorter turn-round times between flights, and by not needing to allow time for connecting passengers to join the flight.

An airline operating a HS network will often employ at least two aircraft types: smaller jets or turboprops to fly thin and/or short spokes; and medium to large jets to fly the dense routes between major cities.

In contrast, many *entering* PTP airlines choose to operate only a single aircraft type. If it chooses to serve some thin routes (to ports that might attract spoke service from a HS carrier), it may offer only infrequent flights. However, a *surviving* PTP entrant may later add a second aircraft type, for use on thinner routes. Airlines that have added smaller *jet* aircraft include JetBlue (see §1.2.2) and Virgin Australia (§7.10.2).

8.2.3 Choosing a network style

In principle, an airline can choose between the alternative network styles. A new entrant inevitably starts with a small network, and almost all European entrants have chosen to operate a PTP network. Expansion comes most easily from choosing a number of ports to serve, and then 'joining the dots' – that is, establishing many routes between that set of ports – which enables the airline to increase the average number of routes served at each port, and thereby benefit from the economies of scale available in the operation of stations at those ports. (Later, the airline may base aircraft at the busier of those ports.) Of course that process has depended on the legal right of an EU-domiciled airline to fly between any pair of ports in the EU.

In other world regions, some *new* carriers (especially those domiciled in a country of small geographical extent that lacks much if any domestic routes) have built HS networks. The following instances are based on a scrutiny of airline websites on 20 June 2015:

- *Flydubai*, whose website listed exactly 100 ports, almost all of which were served nonstop from its hub in Dubai, UAE.
- *Peach*, the Japanese LCC (which chose Osaka (Kansai) for its base, in contrast to the other LCCs, which mainly chose Tokyo) recorded 13 *domestic* routes, of which 10 were spoke routes from Osaka, while the non-hub routes connected Tokyo (Narita) to Sapporo and to Fukuoka, and Okinawa (Naha) to Fukuoka.
- *Jetstar Asia* (the Qantas affiliate based in Singapore) recorded 20 nonstop routes to ports in 11 countries, with three of those services also going on to ports in Japan.

In contrast, a *large* incumbent has an option to build a HS network, often with several hubs. As seen in Chapter 1, upon deregulation the larger US carriers adopted that strategy. However, even those airlines have continued to operate and develop some direct flights between non-hub large cities, for routes that have sufficient traffic to support separate, direct flights at reasonable frequency. For any such route, the cost to the airline of direct carriage of the passengers will be lower than the cost of carrying them via the hub. And, flight-frequency considerations apart, direct travel is more highly valued by the passengers.

However, when an airline removes from the network 'pool' those passengers who travel on direct flights between major cities, the profitability of the hubbed network may be reduced. Even so, the direct services between the major cities may earn extra profit that readily outweighs any loss of profit on the hubbed network. And the consequent overall profit may be greater than that achievable from any other network arrangement.

As Levine (2004) points out, 'network structure is a dependent variable'; that is to say, the best option depends on the particular cost and demand circumstances that the airline faces. And the policy choice is not confined to the polar cases. A profit-seeking airline should try to judge what (if any) intermediate strategy will yield the largest profit.

For a general policy setting, Gillen and Morrison (2005) give a broad-ranging and detailed comparison of the two network styles.

8.2.4 Adapting the LCC service style to attract business travellers

Some of the service characteristics that business travellers want are an inherent part of the low-cost strategy. Many new airlines offer *punctuality*, even if only to secure high aircraft productivity and hence low costs. They also offer *reliability* – that is, operating a very high proportion of the flights they have scheduled – which requires good maintenance procedures, and is greatly helped by choosing to operate new aircraft. In those respects, many of the new airlines have performed at least as well as the old ones, and sometimes have greatly bettered the previous standards, especially in Europe.

However, other features valued by business travellers – notably, a frequent flyer scheme, airport lounges and booking arrangements that suit the travel departments of large and medium-size firms – bring extra operational complexity. Yet such extras do not conflict with the simple service style that is appropriate for leisure travellers. Even the provision of more space in the forward part of the cabin, and the service there of superior in-flight refreshments, do not create significant difficulties. And some (Virgin Australia, for example) have gone so far as to establish a separate business-class cabin.

In short, the new (low-cost) airline usually *can* adapt to attract business travel. Therefore, it becomes a matter for managerial judgement as to whether the likely extra revenues from serving business travellers will outweigh the extra costs.

8.2.5 Network competition between old and new airlines

In many competitive industries, the competing firms have the same business model. In contrast, much of the recent airline competition has pitted the approach of the point-to-point airlines (which sometimes still target customer groups somewhat selectively), against the business model of the incumbent (legacy) carriers who operate hub-and-spoke networks and seek to serve both business and leisure travellers.

Even so, some airline strategies are commonly observed in other industries. This applies especially to the practice of lowering prices selectively – that is, only on products offered by the entrants. In the airline context, the selectivity is easy to apply: simply reduce the fares on routes entered by a newcomer, and maintain high fares on other routes. Often such conduct is not in the public interest. However, in the aviation case, some details of those battles have been novel; and it is not surprising that there have been some turbulent outcomes. Those matters are considered in depth in §15.3.

For an HS incumbent facing entry by one of the new PTP airlines, one immediate and fundamental question is whether the incumbent will find it more profitable to accommodate such entry by maintaining its fares (where feasible) and thereby sharing the market, rather than reducing its fares in order to fight the entry.

Deploying some analytical modelling, Hendricks, Piccione and Tan (1997) argue that new-airline entry offering direct service between two ports already connected by an HS airline is unlikely to be successful. But their analysis is based on an assumption (p. 293) that 'individuals care only about reaching their destination at the lowest price, not how this destination is reached. In particular, they are indifferent to distance travelled, the number of stops incurred, and the airline that is flying them.' That assumption may be thought to pre-dispose the conclusion. And the authors do acknowledge (pp. 300–1), that if the entrant has a cost advantage, there can be stable outcomes in which the hub operator learns to live with the lower-cost entrant. In that case, there are efficiency gains when the newcomer displaces the incumbent on some of the routes. These gains lead to extra *net* revenue, which is shared between the two airlines.

The formal modelling undertaken by economists has generally taken as given the set of cities that is to be served in a particular region. In practice, the list of airports receiving some commercial airline service can vary, sometimes depending on the local network style(s).

In general, a PTP airline will fly a route only if the city-pair has enough local traffic, while a HS airline has an incentive to be more inclusive, because some of the traffic carried between a small port and the hub will travel also on other routes in that airline's network, and often that latter traffic too is diminished if the airline ceases to serve the small port.

On the other hand, long-established HS carriers sometimes continue to offer service *only* via a hub even when the point-to-point traffic has grown over time to a level that supports direct service. The pace of adjustment can be particularly slow in Europe: while a national carrier *may* initiate routes from its hub to regional ports in another country, it does not always readily start international direct service from regional cities in its 'home' country.

In its Annual Report for 2007 (p. 25), EasyJet noted such an instance: it operated a *direct* service between Glasgow (UK) and Malaga (Spain), which was less costly to provide than travel via a hub. (It started that service after noticing increases in the number of Glasgow–Malaga passengers it was carrying via its London ports!) Airline websites, examined in late September 2009, showed that EasyJet had direct flights on several days per week, as did Ryanair, which however used Prestwick, a secondary airport at some distance from the city of Glasgow. (The other local LCCs did not serve the route.) Neither the Spanish national carrier, Iberia, nor British Airways operated direct flights. And most of their daily connections via London were so poor as to deter use. Perhaps BA had decided to cede that Glasgow holiday route to the low-cost carriers.

8.2.6 Other aspects of the competition between legacy and new airlines

As the headlines have long made clear, most new airlines have sought cost levels below those of the legacy airlines, to support lower fares and hence make it easier to win passengers from the incumbents. To that end, the new airlines have deployed several cost-reducing policies.

Lower rates of pay

Wherever industry practice has been to offer pay scales that give higher rates for more experienced staff, all new airlines gain an automatic financial benefit from their start-up status, to the extent that they recruit people with (on average) less experience than those of the established airlines. This has applied even when recruiting pilots, though well-managed airlines recognise the wisdom of not setting pilot experience levels that are 'too low'.

In addition, for pilots and for other groups, many new airlines offer pay *scales* that are themselves lower than those of their incumbent competitors, especially where the incumbents have been paying rather more generously than was needed to attract well-qualified staff, as can happen whenever regulation or lack of competition has led to handsome profitability. Of course, some of the incumbents have responded by adjusting their pay scales, at least for new-start employees. In particular, soon after deregulation in the US, some of the large, network carriers (unwisely?) started recruiting pilots on lower scales than those available to their established pilots.

Higher labour productivity

As a historical consequence of labour bargaining in a regulatory context which allowed easy profitability, incumbent airlines have sometimes carried more staff than strictly needed. The new airlines adopted more parsimonious practices in determining the numbers of positions. They also tried to organise the work in such a way as to get more output from those staff they did employ. For example, by shortening aircraft turn-around time between flights, and by keeping aircraft employed continuously during a long day, they could increase the productivity of ground crews – and (in some situations) the productivity of pilots too.

A simpler and less costly service

As part of a strategy to focus on passengers who prefer low fares to service extras, almost all the new airlines *began* with a basic service: a single cabin class, no in-flight service of refreshments (or a very limited service offered in exchange for additional payment), and no proprietary lounges at airports. Relative to the practice of full-service incumbents, first flights of some new airlines started earlier in the day, and last flights finished later, in order to get more productivity from their most expensive assets. And some of them held fewer or no aircraft in reserve to cover for delayed flights and aircraft failures.

Subsequently, those of the low-fare airlines that sought to attract business travellers as well, introduced some of the elaborations, in the hope that the extra revenue would outweigh the extra costs. As part of the strategy, such airlines have introduced separate charges (for airport lounges, for example), reflecting a 'user pays' philosophy that allows them to continue to offer low fares for the basic service. (Further consideration appears later, in §10.4.)

The website as a sales channel

New airlines were early adopters of internet booking, which soon proved to be a low-cost mechanism for making a sale. In particular, it avoids the cost of paying commissions to travel agents. Further saving comes from *not* issuing a paper ticket/boarding pass, initially (that is, before the passenger arrives at the airport) or at all (when the passenger prints at home).

Though the incumbents were fairly quick to adopt such new practices, the cost advantage gained by the new airlines may have persisted to some extent. The legacy carriers sell a higher proportion of their seats through travel agents, while the new airlines serve those who are keen to save on fares, and who may be (on average) younger and more computer-literate.

Price discrimination

In addition, the new airlines have taken a fresh approach to segmenting the market in order to charge different fares to different kinds of passenger, in order to increase revenue. Usually the new airlines began with only one type of ticket, which had strict conditions that penalised a passenger who wished to cancel or change itinerary details. Later, nearly all of them added at least one more ticket type, with greater flexibility and a higher fare. Many legacy airlines too have adopted that new approach to market segmentation.

The new fare-setting techniques are complex, and yet so important that they merit a detailed account, which is the subject of Chapter 9.

8.3 A short history of the new-airline sector

8.3.1 Variety in genesis

The handful of US airlines that set up in Texas and California before deregulation of inter-state airline services all had impoverished births. Initial fleets comprised ageing aircraft, which were cheap to acquire, but expensive to operate and maintain. And even the outstanding survivor, Southwest Airlines, experienced initial difficulties in attracting traffic. It lacked sufficient capitalisation, and came close to bankruptcy.

The business model of the pioneers was simple: keep costs to a minimum, and compete with the established carriers by offering low fares. Without yield-management software (then in its infancy), the new airlines generally sold all tickets on a given route at the same price.

Upon seeing the success of Southwest, a number of smallish airlines of traditional style came to the view that they could do better by converting to the low-fares model. Among those who then did well are Ryanair, Norwegian and Air Asia. Others (for example, Sterling) made the switch and did well for a while before eventually failing.

In contrast, many (but certainly not all) entrants in recent years have started with new aircraft, leased or even purchased outright. They have deployed powerful computer software, often paying licence fees for the use of off-the-shelf yield-management packages. Their aim is to provide reliable, punctual service at reasonable fares, and quickly attract large passenger numbers on a growing route-network.

Yet another kind of birth arrived when some legacy carriers (notably in Europe, but also in the US) decided to respond to the low-cost challenge of new entrants by starting their own low-cost 'airlines-within-airlines'. European examples included Go (started by British Airways) and Buzz (KLM). Most such infants were subject to severe parental constraint: in particular, they were not allowed to fly on routes already served by the parent. That handicap may have been the main reason why nearly all failed, or were sold off to other companies, or were bought out by their senior management.

A later parenting style led to the outstanding early success of Jetstar, which was started by Qantas as a fighting brand in its domestic battle with a rapidly expanding Virgin Blue. Unlike the earlier cases in Europe and the US, Qantas handed over some of its own domestic routes to the new-born Jetstar, and soon purchased brand-new main-line aircraft for Jetstar to fly (as reported in §7.10.2). Upon seeing that low-cost airlines could be profitable, large-scale investors (including conglomerates from other industries) were attracted to aviation, especially in some developing countries. Even though this brings the advantage of access to in-house funding, such genesis is not always successful. Perhaps the most spectacular failure was in India, where Kingfisher Airlines became the second largest but still unprofitable domestic airline before its conglomerate owner chose not to provide further funding (§4.3.4).

8.3.2 Failure of most entrants, survival of an elite

In contemplating the low-cost airline successes, it is easy to overlook the *very* high failure rate. In the US, over the four decades following deregulation, almost all of the many start-ups soon disappeared. In Europe too, though the entrepreneurial spirit may not have been quite so vigorous, there were many new airlines, and again few have survived. In other continents, though many of the new airlines have started only in very recent years, some have already closed.

In giving an interesting judgement on the world scene in 2008, the weekly newsletter *Airline Network News and Analysis* (*anna*) gave its selection of ten leading LCCs ('10 of the best analysed: the great global LCC network strategy comparison', anna.aero, 3 October 2008). In judging success, it looked mainly for positive profits in most if not all financial years. Its ten airlines are listed in Table 8.1 where country of domicile and year of foundation have been added to the *anna* data on airline size, measured by the number of weekly departures. Some seven years later, all ten had survived – though AirTran had been taken over by Southwest.

The *anna* report emphasised the diversity of the ten airlines. WestJet and Virgin Blue flew dense routes on small networks, having (respectively) 85 routes serving

Table 8.1 anna's ten best LCCs, October 2008

Airline	Year of first flight	Country of domicile	No. of weekly departures[1]
Southwest	1971	USA	22,900
AirTran[2]	1993	USA	4,400
JetBlue	2000	USA	3,400
WestJet	1996	Canada	2,600
GOL	2001	Brazil	4,100
EasyJet	1995	UK	6,900
Ryanair[3]	1990	Ireland	7,800
Air Arabia	2003	UAE	400
Air Asia[4]	2001	Malaysia	2,900
Virgin Blue[5]	2000	Australia	2,900

Sources: Airline Network News and Analysis (*anna.aero*), '10 of the best analysed: the great global LCC network strategy comparison', 3 October 2008; 'About us' entries, airline websites

Notes
1 Data sourced by *anna* from Official Airline Guide, week beginning 29 September 2008, and here rounded to the nearest 100 departures.
2 Merged into Southwest in 2013.
3 After launching in 1985, Ryanair adopted a low-cost business model in 1990.
4 In 2001, a predecessor company was relaunched as a low-cost airline, and renamed as Air Asia.
5 Now called Virgin Australia.

37 airports and 88 routes serving 33 airports. In contrast, Ryanair had some 630 routes serving 140 airports, while Southwest operated on 430 routes connecting 64 airports. In consequence, there was wide variation in the average number of weekly flights per route: Ryanair had only about 6; yet Southwest averaged about 26; Virgin had 22, and WestJet 15. Many of Ryanair's thin routes served small holiday resorts.

The years since 2008 have seen the growth of a few more distinguished new airlines: Norwegian, which started with a different business model; WizzAir (Hungary), which first flew in 2004, and took early advantage of the extension of the European Union; and Azul (Brazil), established in 2008 by David Neeleman (who had previously started JetBlue).

Although most of the established 'national' carriers have focussed on improving their service standards and reducing their costs, a few have also shown enterprise sufficient to allow a start on new ventures. Three notable instances are: Lufthansa, which has expanded in its region by taking over Austrian Airlines and Swiss, and by taking over some low-cost carriers based in Germany; Turkish Airlines which, over many years, has gradually extended its network, and is now very large indeed; and LAN, the Chilean national carrier which has relied on bilateral governmental agreements when it established local companies to operate from Argentina, Ecuador and Peru.

8.3.3 A summary of new-airline practices

Though the business model of Southwest airlines developed out of the practices of some less successful antecedents, Southwest's outstanding performance set a precedent that has been adopted (and adapted) by many of the later entrants. For many years, Southwest stuck to its initial practices. When other, successor airlines *adapted* the approach, some purists dismissed the adapters as not being 'truly' low cost airlines. Yet well-conceived adaptation has often stemmed from adjustment of targets, notably concerning the kinds of routes selected and the passenger categories to be served.

As Levine (2004) points out, the underlying aim is to earn profits from a growing business; the lowest possible costs of production may not be an appropriate choice for the most profitable strategy. Accordingly, while still seeking economic efficiency, and aiming to offer good service at reasonable fares, some new airlines have varied the early practices to suit their circumstances, especially in regard to the passenger groups they wish to serve, and the character of the incumbent airlines in the markets they propose to enter.

Hence, there is no detailed template that new airlines 'must' adopt. The summary of practices presented in Table 8.2 identifies the issues but also recognises the (desirable) potential for diversity in managerial decision-making. Notwithstanding the fuzzy character of the generic business model, there is a very clear difference between the simplicity of the new approach and the complexity of many of the traditional practices of the legacy airlines.

Table 8.2 Practices generally adopted by new short-haul, low-fare airlines

Practices	Comments
Airline fleet	
Single aircraft family, usually A320 or B737	sometimes two aircraft types to fly diverse routes
Aircraft in the air for long hours each day	early start, late finish, quick turn-round and disciplined, punctual operation
Single cabin, at most 31 or 32 inch seat pitch	but bulkhead/exit rows may sell at premium fares
Route network	
Short-haul sectors, up to 4/5 hours flying time	non-stop, no intermediate port
Predominantly 'point-to-point'	that is, passengers start their journey at the flight origin, and complete it at the flight destination
No hubbing as such	but may allow (or even encourage) *some* passengers to book connecting flights
Routes and frequencies set to give high load-factors	
Prefer city-pairs without prior direct service	especially, avoid other *new* airlines
Promptly close new routes that don't cover costs	
Fares	
Offer only one-way fares	
Flexible pricing, with fares that vary by time/day of flight and by booking date	
For each flight, review fares frequently	in light of number of seats sold for flight
Cabin service	
Offer only limited services	
Generally charge extra for optional supplies	food and drinks, baggage in cabin, etc
Other services	
No frequent-flyer scheme, and no limited-access airport lounges	but may add these later if airline pursues business travellers
Charges for checked bags	
Airports	
May use secondary ports with lower charges	also helps avoid aircraft congestion
Seek low-cost, simple passenger terminals	
Marketing	
Sell most tickets from airline website	and avoid paying high/any fees to travel agents
May use independent reservation systems	for simplicity, and to keep costs low; but may migrate to industry standard software later
Avoid general distribution systems (GDS)	unless code-sharing becomes part of later strategy

Practices	Comments
Financial strategy	
Pursue miserly purchasing habits	e.g. bargain vigorously for aircraft purchases
Keep balance sheet in good shape	
Especially in early life, expand cautiously	
Labour policy	
Recognise importance of good staff performance	seek to maintain good morale
Seek productivity-based agreements	avoid creating too many staff positions
Aim to pay adequate but not excessive rates	some airlines prefer no unionisation
Share company profits with staff	

8.4 Traffic growth and other outcomes

8.4.1 The growth in air travel

The best single measure of the amount of air travel is the aggregate distance travelled by all the passengers – expressed as the number of revenue passenger kilometres (RPK) or revenue passenger miles (RPM). That reflects the distances travelled by passengers as well as the number of passenger journeys, and avoids a difficulty in defining a 'journey' that arises whenever a passenger transfers from one flight to another. The RPK/RPM data used in preparing the growth indices presented in Table 8.3 are adequate for the study of travel growth over time. But those data are not very suitable for comparison *across* countries.

Given our short-haul focus, the data for the large land-masses of the US and Australia relate only to domestic services in those countries. The UK data refer to *all* passengers carried by UK-domiciled airlines. Although a very large proportion of those passengers travelled on international routes, most of those passengers travelled within Europe. Some of them did not travel at all within the UK, notably those on EasyJet flights travelling between ports in other European countries. The many passengers of Ryanair travelling between UK and other ports are not included, because Ryanair is not a UK airline. Those details help to explain why the data cannot be used to compare absolute traffic levels across regions.

By 2007, US domestic travel had reached almost 2½ times the 1984 level; that multiple is smaller than the growth multiples for the other countries shown in the Table, probably because US airlines had expanded more in the years before deregulation, and because deregulation in the US was at least ten years ahead of such liberalisation elsewhere. Even in 2013, however, US travel had still not (quite) returned to the 2007 level, thanks in part to the downturn occasioned by the general financial crisis.

For UK airlines, the 2013 RPK total on *scheduled* services was rather more than five times the 1984 level. However, that multiple is enhanced by the decline

Table 8.3 Index numbers of air travel (RPK): USA, UK, Australia and world, 1984–2013

Year	US domestic[1]	UK airlines[2]		Australia domestic[3]	World all[4]
		scheduled	charter		
1984	100	100	100	100	100
1988	135	132	76	140	133
1992	143	118	94	187	151
1996	175	259	125	285	190
2000	209	353	153	327	247
2001	197	329	155	332	239
2002	193	324	148	328	241
2003	205	342	154	367	245
2004	226	360	155	424	279
2005	238	416	150	455	302
2006	240	443	147	490	321
2007	243	472	147	524	347
2008	233	482	136	564	354
2009	221	478	111	565	350
2010	227	468	106	604	378
2011	231	502	105	619	403
2012	233	519	98	650	423
2013	237	536	88	652	446

Sources

USA: press release 18-14 (11 April 2014), table 5, domestic scheduled airline travel on US airlines (Bureau of Transportation Statistics, US Department of Transport), and similar tables for earlier years.

UK: Main Outputs of UK Airlines 2013 (Civil Aviation Authority, table 0.1.4).

Australia: Domestic Airline Performance: Annual Summary (various years) (Bureau of Infrastructure, Transport and Regional Economics, Canberra). The 2013 data are estimated; publication discontinued.

World: Annual Traffic and Operations: World Airlines (Airlines for America website, airlines.org, based on data presented in the Annual Report of the Council of ICAO).

Notes
1 Scheduled domestic flights of US airlines.
2 All flights of airlines domiciled in the UK.
3 Domestic flight sectors of all Australian airlines.
4 Scheduled flights of all world airlines.

in *charter* services (carrying package-holiday travellers), a decline that stemmed mainly from the success of the low-cost scheduled airlines in attracting holiday-makers, and the consequent decisions of several of the UK charter airlines to switch wholly or in part to scheduled service.

By 2013, the Australian index was 6½ times the 1984 level. No doubt, this owes much to the quasi-monopolistic restriction of output in the base year, under the government's regulatory scheme (§7.2).

The world data bring in countries for which much of the growth is recent, because most low-cost airline entry has come only recently. Thus, it is particularly striking that world air travel increased by a multiple of (say) four, during the 30-year period.

8.4.2 Secular increases in aggregated passenger load factors

Among the changes that have supported lower fares, one that has attracted little public attention (outside the US!) is the considerable secular increase in the passenger load factor (that is, the proportion of flown seats occupied by fare-paying passengers). Table 8.4 presents data for the same years and countries as before.

For domestic services in the US, there has been an increase in the load factor over almost every interval shown.

For UK *scheduled* services, the overall increase has been a little smaller, and the series does not rise quite as steadily as in the US. The load factors for the UK *charter* (non-scheduled) airlines change little during the period. An essential feature of their business model is the need to fill a very high proportion of the seats. Thus, the lack of any significant trend is not a surprise.

The domestic services in Australia started the period at a higher load factor level than elsewhere at that time – perhaps because under the government's regulatory (two-airline) policy, there was (in effect) no competitive deployment of extra capacity. After deregulation in 1990, the load factor eventually increased to approach 80 per cent, though in some recent years, the figure has been lower than that, because of competitive pursuit of market share.

For a given aircraft type, the *per-passenger* fuel consumption decreases as the load factor increases. Thus, higher fuel prices give an airline a greater incentive to rearrange its flight schedules to increase the load factor.

Table 8.4 Revenue passenger load factors (per cent) 1984–2013

Year	USA domestic	UK airlines		Australia domestic	World all
		scheduled	charter		
1984	57.7	65.9	85.2	72.6	64.8
1988	61.4	68.9	88.8	77.4	67.6
1992	62.4	70.2	88.5	77.1	65.8
1996	67.9	72.9	88.1	73.5	68.2
2000	71.2	72.2	89.2	77.4	71.0
2001	69.1	70.4	89.5	76.5	69.2
2002	70.3	74.0	89.6	79.1	71.2
2003	72.6	74.5	88.4	80.2	71.5
2004	74.4	75.5	89.5	78.9	73.3
2005	77.0	75.5	88.5	78.7	74.9
2006	79.0	75.6	87.9	79.0	75.7
2007	79.9	76.0	87.9	80.9	76.7
2008	79.8	76.2	88.2	78.9	75.8
2009	81.1	78.9	88.1	80.8	76.6
2010	82.2	80.0	88.5	80.0	78.1
2011	82.9	79.4	88.8	79.8	78.0
2012	83.4	81.3	90.7	78.4	78.9
2013	83.5	82.6	90.9	77.4[1]	79.4

Sources and notes: As for Table 8.3.

The world markets for jet fuel are closely related, and the increases in the price of jet fuel have been much the same all round the world. However, the differences between the load-factor outcomes for the US, UK and Australia demonstrate that other factors too have been at work.

These other factors include the entry of low-cost airlines, which seek high load factors in order to reduce their cost per passenger kilometre, together with the increased importance of leisure travel. The next section looks at some details.

8.4.3 Load-factor differences across airlines

Though a high-load factor is generally good for an airline, it may be more profitable to set fares and capacity amounts at levels that result in a more modest load factor.

An airline with a high load factor faces an increased risk that on peak-period flights (in particular), it may be unable to accommodate late-booking business travellers who are willing to pay a high fare. Thus, an airline that serves mainly business travellers may prefer high fares and a moderate load factor, while a low-cost airline serving mainly leisure travellers may aim for a higher load factor. For example, UK data for 2012 (Civil Aviation Authority, table 1.7.4, 'Domestic scheduled services of all UK airlines', accessed at caa.co.uk on 25 October 2013) record load factors of 77.9 per cent for EasyJet and 72.2 per cent for British Airways.

On the other hand, the scheduled domestic services of US airlines offer some different features. For the year ending June 2013, the US Bureau of Transportation Statistics 'carrier snapshots' (accessed at www.transtats.bts.gov on 25 October 2013) show that the load factors for the (then) four legacy network airlines – American, Delta, US Airways and United – ranged between 84.6 and 86.6 per cent. Yet the very large low-cost carrier, Southwest Airlines had a load factor of only 80.2 per cent, while another low-cost carrier, Frontier reported 90.7 per cent. Two airlines in particular regions, Alaska and Hawaiian, scored 86.3 and 87.1 per cent respectively, and JetBlue was at 84.4 per cent. The low figure for Southwest may, in part, reflect continuing growth in the number of its point-to-point routes; when starting a new route, almost any airline initially experiences low load factors.

8.4.4 Load-factor differences across routes

For individual routes, the optimal load factor usually depends on the passenger types the airline seeks to attract: a low-fare airline may focus on routes between large cities and holiday resorts; an airline targeting business travellers flies routes between major cities. In the latter case, the airline often operates frequent flights to give good service for its business passengers. Any consequent reduction in the load factor helps also to reduce the incidence of occasions when the plane is full, and the airline has to turn away lucrative business travel.

Route load factors can depend also on seasonal demand variations, arising from climatic factors and institutional arrangements. While airlines often adjust route capacities seasonally, route load factors can still vary significantly with the season. (So, if possible, when analysing such data, it is wise to consider 12 consecutive months.)

For the study of inter-route differences, Australian data are of particular interest because, on almost all the routes (whether served by jets or turboprops), the Virgin camp faces competition from the Qantas camp, and there are no other competitors. This uniformity allows a focus on other factors that may explain the differences in load factors across different routes.

In providing a daily service on a thin route, an airline may need to deploy an aircraft that is on the large side, resulting in a low load factor. To avoid that complication, the following discussion of some Australian data excludes routes with less than 200,000 passengers per annum (for travel in both directions).

For calendar 2007, the set of 36 such competed 'major' routes had load factors ranging from 71.4 to 87.2 per cent. By 2013, the corresponding list had grown to 45 routes, with load factors ranging from 47.3 to 86.0 per cent.

In 2007, the route with the highest load factor was the five-hour Brisbane–Perth sector (of 3605 km). In that year, Virgin had but a single daily trip, flying west from Brisbane in the evening, arriving close to midnight (local time), and then returning overnight to Brisbane. On most days, Qantas had four RT flights, one timed to compete with Virgin for the low-fare travellers, and three day-time flights targeted mainly on business travellers. For Qantas, the absence of (day-time) competition seems to have encouraged it to operate only three such flights, notwithstanding the resultant overall load factor of 87.2 per cent. Presumably the airline judged capacity limitation was the more profitable policy.

In 2013 Virgin was competing for the patronage of business travellers by offering daytime flights on the route, and was doing so by using larger (A330) aircraft, and offering somewhat lower full fares than those of Qantas. In consequence, the flow of 603,000 route passengers in 2007 increased to a little more than one million in 2013. Despite all the extra capacity, the route load factor remained fairly high, at 80.1 per cent. That case suggests that vigorous competition *can* reduce the route load factor.

On the other hand, a second Australian situation gave a somewhat different outcome. On the important business route (sector length only 235 km) between Sydney and the national capital, Canberra, Qantas enjoyed a monopoly in 2007. Yet the load factor was the (joint) lowest that year, at 71.4 per cent. Of course, Qantas may have chosen high service frequency, to try to deter entry by Virgin, and to retain its prime position as preferred airline for travel by public servants.

Later, when Virgin entered the route, it often flew Embraer jets at times that Qantas was flying turboprops. The 2007 passenger total of 838,000 increased to 1.03 million in 2013, and the load factor *decreased* to 61.6 per cent.

8.4.5 Increase in the number of port-pairs having direct service

In most world regions, there has been a very marked increase in network connectivity, thanks in part to the focus of many new airlines on point-to-point services, to help them compete with incumbent legacy carriers.

The increase in connectivity has been particularly great in Europe. The number of direct (city-pair) services between UK ports and ports in other EU countries increased from about 120 in 1995 to about 375 in 2005 (Civil Aviation Authority, 2006, fig. 2.1). That helped to increase passenger numbers. It also helped to change some of the spatial characteristics of the passenger flows. For international short-haul passengers on scheduled airlines in 2000 and 2005, the passenger numbers in Table 8.5 demonstrate a major increase in the proportion of journeys involving a direct flight *from a regional UK airport* to a port in another European country. The alternative routings were: surface mode to a southeast England airport and then a flight; and (for passengers on scheduled flights), a regional flight connecting at a UK or other European airport.

For passengers flying on scheduled airlines, the percentage travelling on direct flights increased from 32 per cent in 2000 to 49 per cent in 2005, while those travelling by surface mode and then a scheduled flight from a port in the southeast of England decreased from 56 per cent to 44 per cent. It is very likely that those trends continued after 2005.

In Australia, the published BITRE data show that in October 1984 (before deregulation), there were 23 routes with 20 or more aircraft monthly departures; that number grew modestly to 26 in October 1990. After the Virgin Blue entry in 2000, it then grew markedly, reaching 46 in October 2007. Following further route entry by Virgin, using its smaller Embraer jets, and by Tiger Airways, the BITRE record for April 2015 identifies 64 competed routes.

In the US, the number of *direct* city-pair routes seems to have *decreased* after deregulation, as the major airlines developed their hub-and-spoke networks. Following the growth of Southwest and the entry of a few other point-to-point airlines, however, the number of direct routes increased, though it shrank again in 2008, especially when some regional services were withdrawn in response to higher fuel prices.

In other regions, notably Asia, many of the new airlines have made the introduction of new routes that increase overall network connectivity an important part of their growth strategy. Around the world, the increased convenience arising from the increasing number of city-pair direct services has been a significant factor promoting the growth in air travel.

8.4.6 Social consequences

While the increase in the *number* of passengers is well documented in many countries, information on socio-economic characteristics does *not* come as a by-product of airline administrative processes. However, the UK Civil Aviation Authority has published several reports based on special-purpose studies of travellers using UK ports.

Table 8.5 International short-haul passengers[1] departing from UK regions, 2000 and 2005

Year	Passengers (m) using scheduled airlines, and departing a UK region by:			Passengers (m) using charter airlines, and departing a UK region by:		
	Direct flights	Connecting flights	Surface mode to a SE England port	Direct flights	Connecting flights	Surface mode to a SE England port
2000	10.4	3.8	18.2	21.0	–	2.9
2005	25.6	3.4	22.9	19.7	–	2.3

Source: Civil Aviation Authority (2007, table 4.1 [CAP 775])

Note
1 Here, *international short-haul* means travel from the UK to Europe, North Africa and Turkey.

Business travel

Between 1996 and 2007, business passengers as a proportion of all those travelling on UK (domestic and international) scheduled services fell from about 42 per cent to 30 per cent, as leisure traffic grew more strongly (Civil Aviation Authority, 2009a). In 2007, domestic routes saw about 45 per cent of all passengers travelling on business. On short-haul international routes (very largely, routes between the UK and other EU countries) business travellers were about 27 per cent of the total; and 91 per cent of those business passengers flew economy class (up from 60 per cent in 1996).

It may seem surprising that only nine per cent of those business travellers opted for travel in business-class cabins. However, most airlines now set a very big difference between the discounted fare for a restricted economy class ticket and the *full* economy fare paid by most of those business travellers who opt for economy class. Thus, the proportion of business travellers buying ticket types that are targeted on business travel will have been very much greater than nine per cent.

While most no-frills carriers (as the CAA calls them) initially targeted leisure travel, many now carry business travellers as well. Indeed, in 2007, some 30 per cent of business travellers on UK short-haul international routes travelled on such airlines, compared with only three per cent in 1996, when low-cost airlines were just getting under way in Europe.

Besides somewhat lower fully flexible economy fares, low-cost airlines sometimes offer greater convenience by providing direct (non-stop) routings and by serving airports not served (or not much served) by the legacy carriers.

In the case of the UK routes, both factors are at work. Some business travellers living or working in northern parts of London find it more convenient to fly from Luton and Stansted airports, which see few flights from the European national carriers. Furthermore, business travel from or to certain UK regional cities is often better served by the direct flights of the no-frills carriers, rather than by indirect travel via London. The Civil Aviation Authority (2007) report records that the share of short-haul international business travellers using the London airports had fallen from 80 per cent in 1996 to 73 per cent in 2007. (However, the development of high-speed rail services between London and France may be responsible for part of that reduction.)

In short, the low-cost airlines have attracted UK business travellers for several reasons: lower full economy fares; more domestic services at regional UK ports, which are sometimes neglected by the legacy carriers; and increases in direct non-stop services between regional UK cities and both capital and regional cities in other EU countries.

The earlier UK report (Civil Aviation Authority, 2006, ch. 5) concludes that the business travellers who fly on low-cost airlines have lower incomes than those who pay the higher fares required for travel on the traditional airlines. Furthermore, anecdotal evidence from Australia suggests that Virgin soon attracted business travellers from smaller and less prosperous companies, while those employed by large companies (and by governments!) preferred the national carrier Qantas.

(In some countries, non-taxable frequent-flyer benefits that accrue personally to business travellers may further encourage travel on legacy carriers.)

Leisure travel

The principal distinction here is between (1) visits to stay with friends or relatives (VFR), and (2) holidays where the traveller stays in a hotel or other commercial accommodation. In regard to the latter, the recent growth of air travel permits and encourages the owners of commercial premises to increase their room prices. This may be especially important for holiday resorts, where holiday visitors generally greatly outnumber business travellers. The price rises serve to ration the limited supply of rooms.

Because it generally takes years to plan and build extra rooms, the higher prices can persist, thereby affecting the growth of holiday travel. In particular, the combination of higher room rates and lower air fares may prompt some travellers to take shorter holidays. In the more affluent countries, especially in Europe (where scheduled air fares were previously very high), there have been marked increases in the numbers of weekend breaks.

For at least some European countries, VFR visits increasingly involve air travel on *international* routes While total international passengers using UK airports grew by one-third between 2000 and 2007, VFR international travel increased by more than three-quarters (Civil Aviation Authority, 2009b); and the VFR proportion increased from 18 per cent in 2000 to an (estimated) 24 per cent in 2008. (For other European countries with larger spatial extent, notably Germany and France, the international element in VFR air travel is probably smaller.)

As that CAA report points out (p. 2), 'VFR travel occurs as a result of dispersed social networks'. In Europe, and elsewhere, such spatial dispersion arises from several factors. Thanks to EU integration, people increasingly migrate to other EU countries to take up attractive jobs. There is also increased student migration, mainly to participate in higher education. And in northern European countries, especially, some natives have bought second homes in the warmer climes of southern Europe. While the UK data generally do not classify travel *between homes* as VFR travel, those owners do offer second-home hospitality to their friends and relatives. (And, no doubt, to a greater degree than in the case of 'snowbirds' in the US, such European travel is commonly by air rather than by car.)

The numbers of international VFR passengers using the various major UK ports have grown at different rates, apparently for reasons related to airport location and to increases in the number of international routes that low-cost airlines offer at each port. Although London Heathrow still had more such passengers than any other UK port, the number at Heathrow grew only 16 per cent between 2000 and 2007, while the similar traffics at London Stansted and London Luton grew by multiples of about three and almost five, respectively. And Bristol, East Midlands and Liverpool (three regional ports with considerable low-cost airline presence) had growth rates similar to those at Luton (Civil Aviation Authority, 2009b, ch. 2).

In some other parts of the world too, the presence of migrant *workers* results in VFR air travel, especially travel on low-fare airlines. For example, in an announcement (14 April 2009) of its new route to Goa (India), the Sharjah-based Air Arabia noted that the large Indian expatriate population in the United Arab Emirates and elsewhere in the Gulf region can benefit from Air Arabia's services to Indian ports. And, like the disposition of the London ports, the low-cost airport at Sharjah is a substitute for the port at nearby Dubai, whose migrant construction workers can take a short bus ride to connect with Air Arabia's flights.

Not receiving emphasis in the CAA report is a reverse causal link: the availability of low-fare air travel may *encourage* spatial dispersion. The hesitant migrant may be reassured by the prospect of affordable return visits to family and friends, and thereby encouraged to take the foreign job. The lovelorn form a special sub-category: William Underhill ('Budget bonanza: a flotilla of low-cost airlines is redrawing the economic map of Europe', *Newsweek*, 16 March 2006) quotes a public affairs consultant as saying 'I work in Brussels and London and my girl-friend lives in Rome. I couldn't survive without Virgin Express and Ryanair.'

In case the provision of air travel that supports dispersed social networks may seem to bring only frivolous benefits, it is worth noting that the EU campaign to bring European peoples together bears sober consideration: even weekend breaks, and football specials at their worst, are to be preferred to the intra-European fighting of the two world wars.

9   Contemporary practices in fare-setting

9.1 An overview of fare-setting concepts

9.1.1 Introduction: charging different fares to different passenger groups

For a *given* flight – identified by its origin and destination ports, date of travel and time of departure – an airline *could* charge the same price for all the tickets it sells. However, airline people have long known that they can increase the total revenue earned from a flight, by charging high prices to those willing to pay such prices, and lower prices to other passengers.

Airlines also know that the purpose of the journey has a great influence on how much a traveller will pay. In particular, a business journey is usually important for the passenger, and many businesses are earning good profits; accordingly the airline can sell at high prices to such travellers.

On the other hand, many leisure travellers are keenly searching for a low fare. They will not pay the high fare that the airline charges to business travellers, because they can't afford it and/or because they don't value the trip very highly. If the airline did not offer a lower fare than the one it offers to business travellers, leisure travellers would search for another airline, or not travel at all.

However, neither of those traveller groups is homogeneous. Within each group, the highest fare that a traveller is willing to pay will vary to some degree from one person to another. On the whole, the airline is unable to identify the highest fare that each *individual* traveller is willing to pay. But it does realise that most business travellers are willing to pay a high fare that is (well) beyond the reach of most leisure travellers.

Furthermore, the airline is often unable able to identify the purpose of the journey for each individual. And even when it can identify those who are travelling on business, it is unable to *instruct* them to pay the higher of the offered fares. Instead, it (generally) offers both fares to all comers, and allows each individual to select a fare (or refrain from travel).

However, there is an important overall difference in the preferences of travellers from the two groups. As airlines have learned over the years, business travellers generally want to keep their options open until just before they travel – in case they want to change a departure time, or simply cancel the trip. In contrast, a leisure traveller usually has no need (or even any desire) for such flexibility. Often such a traveller is happy to book well beforehand. Indeed, many welcome the chance to book early, especially if they need also to reserve hotel accommodation.

After observing these general characteristics of the two groups, the airlines realised they could exploit that difference in their general attitudes, and do so in a very simple way: charge low prices for tickets sold well before the travel date, and charge high fares for tickets sold close to the date of travel. By itself, that pricing scheme might encourage some business travellers to buy early at the lower fare, and then trade in the ticket if they discover later that they need to change the date/ timing of their journeys. To discourage/prevent such conduct, an airline can specify (for example) that no changes are allowed on the cheap ticket: if the holder does not travel *exactly* as booked, then the entire amount paid for the ticket is forfeited. In contrast, when the business traveller pays the much higher price for a ticket, the airline offers great flexibility regarding when, how and (even) whether the ticket is used.

The detailed arrangements the airlines make to 'segment the market' – that is, separate the two groups – have changed materially over the years. Those matters are discussed in the next two sections.

Before turning to those fare details, however, it is important to consider a matter the airline can control *directly*, namely the number of seats it offers for purchase at each of the ticket prices. To keep the presentation simple, suppose that all the seats in the aircraft cabin are of the same standard. For weekday flights departing at the beginning or end of the business day, the airline may be confident that it will be able to sell all the seats at the high fare targeted on business travellers. In that case, it simply does not offer *any* seats at the lower fare.

In less extreme situations, the airline will place a limit on the number of seats it offers at the low fare, and choose that limit in a way that allows it to be fairly certain that it will have enough seats available to sell, at the high fare, to any prospective passenger who seeks a seat, even just before the flight departs. That limited number can differ from one flight to another. On any flight for which a large number of business travellers are expected, the airline is likely to offer, at the low fare, only a small number of seats.

On the other hand, for an off-peak flight for which the airline strongly believes it will not fill the aircraft, the most profitable early fare offer may be at a very low price. Once the airline is committed to operating the flight, there is only a modest extra cost arising from carrying an extra passenger in a seat that would otherwise remain empty. That cost may be little more than the cost of the extra fuel used to carry the (modest) increase in the payload weight. Selling the seat at *any* fare that exceeds that extra cost adds to the airline's net revenue. And provided the airline's expectation proves to be accurate, such a sale does not preclude a later sale at a higher fare.

Indeed, for an off-peak flight, as the travel date approaches, the airline may come to realise that there will very definitely be some empty seats, unless it takes a fare initiative. Shortly before the departure date for the flight, it may then offer some seats at a *very* low price (with a fare forfeit condition attached), thereby securing some extra sales – and some ongoing favourable publicity for the airline.

9.1.2 Early market segmentation approaches

Even before deregulation in the US, the airlines there (and in some other countries) employed some important techniques for segmenting the market; and they refined those techniques during the early years of deregulation (Talluri and van Ryzin, 2004, pp. 6–8). Besides discrimination that rested on ticket conditions, most airlines also offered two or even three aircraft cabins, each with its own fares and seat densities.

For each origin-and-destination pair, and for each cabin class, an airline then (generally) set a unique *full* fare, and drew no distinction even between peak and off-peak travel. Those fares could be purchased at any time, had few conditions and were intended mainly for business travel. Furthermore, in the case of a seat in the business-class cabin, many airlines gave a total refund if a purchased ticket was not used – even when the passenger did not notify the airline before the flight departed.

To encourage leisure travel, an airline also offered a range of *discount* fares for travel in the economy-class/coach cabin. Each of these had its own (restrictive) conditions. A purchased discount ticket usually lacked *any* flexibility in regard to changes in travel plans. If the traveller did not use (any part of) the ticket, there was no refund. However, some airlines offered 'insurance' on the ticket: for an additional fee, the traveller could be assured of a refund of some or all of the fare paid, in the event of prior cancellation by the passenger. In effect, that arrangement offered another ticket type that had a little more flexibility and a higher price.

Generally, a discounted fare had an *advance-purchase requirement*. For example, the airline might offer a discount of (say) 40 per cent off the full fare *provided* the ticket was purchased at least 30 days before the travel date. For that given travel date, once the 40 per cent discount offer had expired, the airline might then offer a 25 per cent discount on tickets purchased at least 14 days before travel. Once all the discount offers had expired, a late-booking traveller had to pay the full fare. Under those arrangements, the lowest available fare was *increased* as the booking date approached the given travel date.

Another commonly used device was to offer a discount only on simple *round-trip* tickets. This allowed the airline to attach a *trip-duration* condition, commonly one which stipulated that the return portion of such a discounted ticket could not be used until the week *after* the outward flight. In effect, this required the traveller to stay away from home on a Saturday night – which few if any business travellers would be willing to do. In those various ways, the airlines sought to discourage business travellers from taking up a discounted fare.

In summary, (early-booking) leisure travellers were given access to the discounted fares, while (late-booking) business travellers paid the full fare.

For each of the discount offers, the airline determined the maximum number of seats it was willing to sell on each flight. For a flight expected to have few unoccupied seats, the deeper discounts might not be offered at all; and even the smaller discounts might be offered only on a few seats. Once a seat-quota had been sold, the ticket-type was no longer on offer. 'Book early if you want the best fares.'

Of course, the airline's expectation as to how well the particular flight would sell could prove to be inaccurate. If full-fare sales for the flight proved to be greater (fewer) than expected, then under these traditional advance-purchase arrangements, the airline could reduce (increase) quotas for discounted seats, while still honouring the (discounted) tickets already sold.

Quota adjustments apart, the airline had very little flexibility in adapting its offers. In particular, the advance-purchase offers were *defined* by a specified percentage discount and a specified sale cut-off time, for example 30 days before the travel date. The same terms were adopted for all such offers made by the airline; and the advance-purchase period was often common across airlines. (Perhaps, this standardisation was adopted to make it easier for travellers to understand and remember the details of the deals.)

Hence, for a particular advance-purchase offer, the airline could not amend the amount of the fare discount as the booking date approached the travel date. And if the flight was not selling as well as expected, the advance-purchase period could *not* be reduced from (say) 30 days to 25 days. There were similar inflexibilities in the stay-away-over-Saturday-night condition.

9.1.3 The new pricing flexibility: first, some old practices abandoned

The advent of website booking engines made it much easier to introduce greater flexibility in pricing. However, the early low-cost carriers in the US did not immediately take up that challenge. Indeed, it was 1996 before Southwest Airlines started to take bookings on the internet. In Europe, an early mover was the fledgling EasyJet, which followed suit in 1998.

Remarkably, in adopting some new practices for segmenting the market, most of the pioneering low-fare airlines abandoned some of the old devices. *First*, they offered only one cabin class – apparently because they did not expect to be able to attract (many) business travellers. (The simpler cabin arrangements also reduced costs to some degree.)

Second, they chose to sell one-way tickets only. When the traveller specified two flights, for a simple round trip, the airline did *not* treat those flights as being related – apart from noting that both were in the name of the one passenger, and both were to be charged to the same credit/debit card. The airlines thereby sacrificed an opportunity to charge more for a business-related round-trip completed within the one week. Perhaps one reason for that decision was the realisation that the stay-away-over-Saturday-night requirement was difficult to enforce, and enforcement attracted odium (on which see the example at the end of §9.2.1 below).

Third, most new airlines chose *not* to offer lower fares explicitly targeted on particular groups, such as retirees. Even the child discounts were pared back:

in general, a full fare was to be paid whenever the child occupied a separate seat; and only very young children (usually, those under two years of age) were allowed to travel without their own seat. (That change made the fares more closely reflect the costs of supplying the service, rather than parental willingness to pay.)

Fourth, many of the new airlines *initially* offered only one type of ticket, laden with strict conditions regarding cancellation or other change of the booking.

9.1.4 Flexibility in setting the 'main fare'

However, in other important respects, the new approach incorporates *much more* flexibility, notably in the arrangements for differentiating fares across flights at different times of day on the one travel date and across flights on different dates, and for varying the fare offered (for a given flight and travel date) as the booking day gets closer to the travel day.

On the last matter, the airline frequently reviews the prevailing fares, especially those applying for each of the travel dates during (say) the following three weeks. When a fare calls for attention, any change usually increases the fare; thus, as the booking day gets closer to the travel day, the offered fare *generally* increases. (Recall that the same property featured in the earlier arrangements, albeit cast in a less flexible form.)

However, in any instance where the number of passengers booking the flight proves to be less than the number the airline had expected, the new approach does allow the airline to *reduce* the fare offered for further bookings – as the airline *may* wish to do, to help fill seats that it believes would otherwise fly empty.

The flexibility of the new approach deserves emphasis. The fares set for a given booking day do not pre-commit the airline when it comes to choose the fares to offer on any later booking day. For a given travel day and a given booking day, the airline has a wide discretion to set different fares across different flights. Thus, scarce capacity is rationed directly by price, and not by a pre-determined, inflexible quota on the number of discount tickets that may be sold.

On most days, most of the offered fares remain unchanged; others are increased; a few may be reduced. In all cases, changing a fare is administratively entirely straightforward. Furthermore, on each occasion that the airline wants to change a fare (up or down), it has an open choice on *how big* a change to make.

In contrast, the old arrangements left the airline pre-committed on all its fares – except that it *could* close a discount offer early, if it had already sold as many of the discounted tickets as it wished to sell.

The new flexibility also facilitates *implicit* targeting of fares on specific passenger groups. For example, where a route has lower traffic demand on mid-week days, the airline can offer lower fares on that particular route. While the offer goes to all, it is particularly intended to encourage retired persons (for example) to begin and end their holidays on such days, rather than at busier times such as Friday and Sunday evenings.

Finally, in the new arrangements the fare offered for travel from A to B need not be the same as the fare for travel from B to A, even on the same travel date.

Indeed, the profound flexibility of the new pricing approach dispels even the concept of a standard fare.

9.1.5 Ancillary charges for optional services

In the other major innovation, the new airlines chose *not to include in the (main) fare* some of the supplementary services that the legacy carriers did so include. Attracting the most attention initially was the exclusion of inflight food and drinks, where the low-fare airlines instead offered *for sale* items from a modest menu. That helped to keep costs low, *and* resulted in an additional flow of revenue.

More recently, such 'unbundling' (in the jargon long used by economists, and now by airline people) has been taken much further. In particular, new airlines started charging separately for checked baggage.

Though some of the new airlines were the first to adopt the new mechanisms for fare setting, many established airlines soon adopted most of the new practices. Section 9.4 below looks in some detail at how the new ideas are implemented.

9.2 Airlines rely on information revealed by passenger self-selection

9.2.1 Setting the fare and fees payable at the time of booking

Under the contemporary arrangements, the airline discriminates between passenger-groups by making the offered fare depend on quite a number of distinct features. All the usual fare offers are open to all potential customers without restriction (except for the child fare, which has an age maximum). Instead of exclusions based on rules, the airline relies on financial incentives to steer the customers.

As seen in Table 9.1, the total amount paid by the traveller can be described as comprising two parts. The *main fare* is a lump-sum amount determined by the traveller's choice of flight details, together with the choice of ticket type (if the airline offers two or more types). That ticket type sets the conditions that apply if the traveller wishes to change any detail in the original travel plan. Also listed in Table 9.1 are the (unbundled) optional services for which *additional fees* may be payable.

In the beginning, some of the new low-fare airlines (for example, EasyJet and Ryanair) offered just one type of ticket, with a single set of conditions regarding change/cancellation of the flight. Nowadays, however, those travelling in the main (economy/coach) cabin of most new airlines are offered (at the least) a choice between two ticket types: a fare with extensive flexibility that allows a booked passenger to change travel arrangements later without financial penalty; and a lower fare with restrictive conditions that penalise any passenger who later wants to change the date of travel etc. When the airline has more than one ticket type for coach/economy travel, the ticket conditions are more restrictive, the lower is the fare.

Table 9.1 Contemporary practice: factors determining fares and additional fees

Factors	Explanation/comment
MAIN FARE[1]	
Characteristics of booked flight	
Route (city-pair)	origin and destination ports
Direction of travel	fares for the two directions may differ
Date of travel	allows for day-of-week and related effects
Departure time	allows different fares at different times of the day
Cabin class	applicable only when aircraft has two or more cabins
Other passenger choices	
Date of booking	allows airline to discriminate between passengers by reference to their chosen booking date; early bookings *usually* attract lower fares than do later bookings
Ticket type	a bundle of conditions regarding ticketing changes[2] that a passenger *may* seek later
ADDITIONAL FEES[3,4]	
for unbundled supplementary services	
Premium seats having extra leg-room	applicable when the airline makes an extra charge for a bulk-head seat and/or a seat in an exit row
Carry-on bags	subject to usual size and weight limits
Checked bags	together with *additional* fees if bag exceeds standard size/weight limits
Assigned seats[5]	not applicable if airline assigns seats to all passengers (without additional charge)
Preferential boarding[5]	not applicable if airline assigns seats to all passengers (without additional charge)
Meal service	for a meal requiring (advance or contemporary) payment

Notes

1 The 'main fare' is the lump sum payable for the traveller's choices of flight and ticket conditions.

2 The list of possible changes includes: cancellation of the traveller's journey; change of the name on the ticket; change of date and/or time of the flight; change of the route to be flown. Fees charged for any permitted changes requested by a booked traveller are payable at the time the changes are made.

3 Nowadays, almost all airlines charge separately for *some* of these services. Apart from any services for which the airline makes no charge, the traveller can avoid payment only by not using the service – for example, by travelling light and not checking any bags.

4 In general, these fee amounts are the same for all flight circumstances. Exceptions include some of the optional services sold by the American ULCC, Allegiant. On 27 January 2015, *allegiantair.com* reported that checked-bag charges varied by route length; if paid at the time of booking, the amount ranged from US$14.99 to US$35 per standard bag.

5 Many airlines still assign seats (or allow the travellers to choose seats) before boarding, without charging any additional fee. Where such *universal* seat assignment is not practised, the airline may offer seat assignment or preferential boarding, upon payment of an additional fee.

Most *traditional* airlines still have at least two cabin classes (on most if not all their flights), and also offer at least two ticket types for economy/coach travel. Examples include Air Canada, British Airways, Lufthansa, Qantas and the three large US legacy carriers. Furthermore, some of those airlines have continued to offer round-trip fares that are cheaper than the two separate one-way fares.

For example, Delta Airlines (delta.com, accessed on 28 November 2013) then did offer such round-trip tickets; it also maintained a 'Rule 100', which listed 'prohibited ticketing practices' of travellers. These included: *back-to-back ticketing* (using overlapping round-trip tickets to circumvent minimum stay-away require-ments); and *throw-away ticketing* (buying a RT fare for one-way travel). Miscreants who are caught can expect major penalties. At its sole discretion, Delta may cancel the tickets for any remaining portion of the passenger's itinerary, confiscate any unused flight coupons, and refuse to board the passenger. However, no-one goes to prison.

9.2.2 Airline responses when passengers seek changes on booked tickets

If a booked passenger wishes to change some details of the planned flight, the airline's rules for treating such requests usually vary markedly across its ticket types. Those rules may be examined under three headings:

- permitted changes;
- deadlines; and
- charges and penalties.

Permitted changes

For each kind of ticket change that a customer may seek, the basic decision for the airline is whether or not to allow the change. Most airlines do permit a change of flight time and date; but a change of origin and/or destination may not be allowed on a discount ticket. Some airlines allow a change of the passenger name shown on the ticket, while many others do not. For a fully flexible ticket, many airlines grant a refund of the entire fare when the ticket-holder does not wish to travel as booked; in contrast, some low-cost airlines do allow changes, but only under onerous financial conditions.

Deadlines

For discount tickets, the airline typically requires notice of change no later than the day before (or, sometimes, 24 hours before) the booked departure. Changes of refundable fully flexible bookings do not require prior notice; usually a no-show triggers the refund. If the flexible fare is not refundable, the airline requires notice of any change, usually to be given no later than the day of departure.

Charges and penalties

If a passenger holding a discounted ticket decides not to fly *exactly* as booked, the passenger must tell the airline by the deadline; otherwise, the entire fare paid is forfeited. When a passenger notifies the airline before the deadline of a change that the airline *permits*, the penalty fee is usually a fixed money amount, sometimes as much as US$100. That fee can be a considerable proportion of the original ticket price, especially if the booking was made on a sale fare.

Any balance remaining after deducting the penalty becomes a credit available to the passenger, for travel within a specified period – often 12 months after the date on which the *original* booking was made.

When the passenger re-books, the applicable fare is that prevailing at that time. Even when the route is unchanged, the new fare may be higher than the one that applied initially. If the new fare is lower, the airline usually retains the difference.

If, at the time of notifying the airline of the desired ticket change, the passenger has not already made a new travel plan, the airline may require the passenger to telephone the airline's call centre when later using that credit. In that case the passenger also has to pay the extra call-centre charge, even when the original booking was made on the airline's website.

Two or more airlines competing on the same city-pair may have quite different policies regarding passenger-initiated changes to the ticket details. Before purchase, a well-informed passenger will allow for those differences when initially comparing offered fares. In practice, many passengers may not be so knowledgeable, and may be unaware that the airline offering the lower fare has a much less generous policy regarding changes to the ticket.

9.3 Fare repertoires

In its booking engine, an airline nowadays states its fares directly in monetary units – dollars or whatever. There is never any mention of discount percentages. Where the airline has more than one ticket type, the website shows the prevailing fare for each (*currently available*) ticket type, for travel on each of the flights the airline intends to operate on the travel date proposed by the prospective traveller.

The booking engine embodies software which reviews all those displayed fares at very frequent intervals, and changes a fare whenever the recent ticket sales and the amount of the remaining seat inventory are such as to require action according to the rules in the software. (Besides that computerised monitoring, the airline also employs staff members to check the outcomes of the automated decision-making, and intervene whenever they think fit.)

When an airline decides to change (some of) the prevailing fares, the computer needs to be given directions on the new fare levels it should display. To help with such tasks, the airline managers make a standing list of alternative fare levels for each of the ticket types and for each route. That list is stored in the computer before the flights first go on sale. Such a list is here called a 'fare repertoire'. The same list is to be used for each and every flight on any given route. Whenever a fare is changed, the new fare is *always* drawn from the relevant repertoire. An airline generally leaves its fare repertoires undisturbed, except on the infrequent occasions on which it implements an overall revision of its fares.

The airline does not announce publicly the fares in each repertoire. However, a search of the booking engine data for a large number of 'nearby' travel dates allows an investigator to build up the list, with a reasonable degree of certainty that all the fares in the current repertoire have been discovered. (The repertoires shown in Table 9.2 below have been discovered in that way.)

In designing a repertoire, an airline has to include a wide range of fares, in order to make available some high (low) values suitable for peak (off-peak) flights and for late (early) booking dates relative to the date of travel. The repertoire also needs to have relatively small money amounts between adjacent values in the list, to facilitate modest fare changes from one day to the next.

Otherwise, if the computer software sets a fare increase that is 'too large', there may be too large a reduction in new bookings. In turn that might lead to the software making an early reduction in fares, soon followed perhaps by another increase, and then another reduction, and so on. Such 'hunting' in the offered fare can prevent effective working of the market, and so should be avoided.

Table 9.2 Repertoires of one-way fares[1] (in Australian dollars), for travel between the Gold Coast[2] and Sydney, December 2013

Qantas	Jetstar	Virgin Australia	Tigerair[3]
Red e-Deal	Starter[4]	Saver Lite[5]	50, 60, 70, 80, 90,
99, 109, 125,	49, 59, 69, 79, 89, 99,	79	100, 110, 120,140,
145, 169	109, 129, 149, 169,	Saver	160, 190, 220
Flexi Saver	199, 229, 259, 319	99, 112, 122, 139, 155	
169, 199, 226,		Flexi	
249, 319		175, 205, 235, 319, 399	
Fully Flexible		Business Saver[6]	
359, 399		419	
Business		Business	
475, 549, 599		559	

Sources: Booking engines on the airline web sites, accessed on 11 December 2013

Notes
1 For each ticket type, these are the main fares before the addition of any fees for optional services. (The amounts of those fees do not depend on the date and time of the chosen flight.) The repertoires are the same for the two directions of travel. The displayed data exclude any (temporary) sale fares.
2 The Gold Coast has many hotels for holiday-makers, and some expensive hotels for conferences etc.
3 All Tigerair (standard) fares ended with 95 cents, for example $49.95. To simplify this presentation, each fare has been rounded up, thereby adding 5 cents.
4 An extensive website search did not find a $289 fare. However the large $60 gap between the $259 and $319 fares suggests that the Jetstar repertoire *may* have included a fare of $289.
5 The Saver Lite ticket differs from the Saver ticket only by excluding 'free' checked baggage.
6 The Business Saver ticket type was later withdrawn.

For examples of small changes, see the fare repertoires displayed in Table 9.2: on occasions where the prevailing fare is less than A$100, the steps between fare levels may be as little as A$10.

In interpreting that table, recall (from Chapter 7) that Jetstar is a wholly owned subsidiary of Qantas, and that, in December 2013, Virgin Australia had a majority shareholding in the low-cost Tigerair. On the Sydney–Gold Coast route, each of the subsidiaries had only a single ticket type. As the Table shows, each deployed a repertoire which, when beginning from the lowest fare, had fare *increments* of A$10, later rising to A$20 and then to A$30.

Qantas and Virgin Australia each had three ticket types for the economy-class cabin, as well as tickets for their business-class seats. In the case of Qantas, the highest fare for the Red e-Deal ticket matched the lowest fare in the repertoire for the Flexi Saver ticket. A word of caution, however: the Flexi Saver treats the passenger more generously in regard to baggage charges, and so (for a given flight) it may be presumed that the A$169 fare for the Red e-Deal ticket was to be used only after the prevailing fare for the Flexi Saver had reached a higher level.

The set of Qantas repertoires covers its overall price range (from A$99 to A$599!) without leaving major gaps. The large jump from A$399 to A$475 buys significantly better cabin conditions, and at the fare level then reached, the next increment of A$74 does not seem proportionately very large.

The Virgin repertoires have much the same general style, except for the very large jump (in business class) from A$419 to A$559. Though the higher fare buys somewhat better ticket conditions, it seems likely that the Business Saver was used mainly for off-peak fights, and was not offered in peak periods – when Virgin expected to be able to sell at the higher fare of A$559.

In studying the fare differences *between* the airlines, it is notable that while Tigerair and Jetstar start at similar fares, the latter had a repertoire that goes higher. That is probably explained by Jetstar being well established, while Tigerair was still only a little beyond its entry date.

In general, Virgin Australia had lower fare repertoires than Qantas, with the difference probably arising from market-share considerations. (The Qantas + Jetstar share was almost twice that of Virgin + Tiger.) In particular, Virgin was trying to increase its share of business travel.

Perhaps Virgin rarely used its Saver Lite fare, whose role may have been to allow Virgin occasionally to undercut the available Qantas Red e-Deal fare, on booking dates that are close to the date of travel. However, any detailed examination of the inter-airline fare differences needs also to consider differences in the ticket conditions.

9.4 The pricing of unbundled services

While the airlines have (quite reasonably) presented unbundling as giving passengers an opportunity to pay *only* for those extras that they want to have, it is not always obvious (to say the least) that the *amount* of each charge matches the (short-run) incremental cost incurred by the airline in supplying the service.

Pricing for checked bags attracts the most attention. For domestic flights in the US, several airlines have tariffs in which the charge for the second checked bag *exceeds* the charge for the first! For example, the American Airlines website (aa.com, accessed 23 January 2015) showed the following charges (per passenger): first bag US$25, second US$35, third US$150 and fourth US$200.

Clearly, such an increasing scale of charges cannot represent the extra costs incurred in carrying each of the bags. Rather, it seems, the airline believes that most passengers with many bags are affluent, and therefore are willing to pay high charges for extra bags beyond the common passenger habit. (A public-interest evaluation of such practices appears in §15.5.2, which also looks at what if any government intervention may be warranted.)

Though it has a much less affluent clientele, Spirit Airlines too has a scale of increasing per-bag charges (spirit.com, accessed 23 January 2015). Perhaps airlines *also* see profits in charging more for those who are simply addicted to carrying a lot of baggage. (Of course, any such addiction is indulged more readily by those who are affluent.)

On the other hand, some airlines do have bag-charge scales that are more closely acquainted with the incremental costs incurred by the airline. As seen in §1.2.5, Allegiant gives limited recognition to the fact that the cost to the airline of carrying a bag does increase with sector length.

In the US domestic airline market, a few airlines (notably Southwest and JetBlue) initially held back from introducing baggage charges. Given their special reputations in the eyes of many travellers, that hesitation may have been a well-considered decision, intended to avoid reputational damage.

Eventually both companies did introduce *some* bag charges. When accessed on 25 January 2015, the website jetblue.com reported that the first bag was free, and the charges for the second and third bags were US$50 and US$100 respectively. On the same date, southwest.com reported that permitted carryon items were without charge, as were the first two checked bags; for each and every checked bag beyond two, the charge was US$75. (For Southwest, at least, few passengers will pay baggage charges.)

9.5 Fare time-paths and through fares

9.5.1 Initial fare levels and later adjustments thereof

When an airline first offers tickets for a particular flight, typically about 12 months before the date of the flight, it has to determine an *initial* fare level for each of its ticket types; such prices are known as 'lead-in' fares.

In most circumstances, those lead-in fares will be relatively low. As time passes, the airline will eventually raise the fares for the flight, in order to charge high fares to late-booking business travellers.

However other patterns can arise. To simplify the discussion, suppose that all flights on the route are performed by aircraft with but a single cabin, in which all the seats are regarded as being in a single cabin class; in other words, the airline ignores any differences in quality between seats in different cabin locations.

Then, if the route is somewhat thin, and is served only by one airline, suppose that company offers just two flights on a weekday, one in each of the morning and evening peaks. If the airline believes it will fill each flight with business travellers, it will not set lower lead-in fares; rather it will charge its full business-oriented fare from the outset.

In a less extreme case, it may expect to sell *most* (but not all) of the seats to business travellers. It will then set a lower lead-in fare – in order to try to fill the other seats to leisure travellers. It will be for the airline to judge how many seats to offer at the lower fare. Its aim is to sell all the seats, but it will not wish to sell cheaply any seats that it could later sell at the business-oriented are.

Alternatively, now suppose the route is served by two airlines – a long-established incumbent, and a new airline which entered the route recently, and which is actively competing with the incumbent. It is likely that, in total, there will be more seats offered, and that the new airline will offer most if not all its seats at a low lead-in fare. In that case the other airline too is likely to offer a low lead-in fare, though only to fill a small proportion of its seats on each (peak-period) flight. When it raises its fare offer as the booking date approaches the flight date, the new airline may well set a lower fare than that charged by the established incumbent, which often can rely on its reputation to sell at a higher price.

(The plausibility of such a narrative is supported by outcomes on various routes in Australia, especially in the period *before* Qantas and Virgin Australia had launched or acquired in-house low-cost carriers. A specific example is presented below, in §10.2.4.)

9.5.2 Other features of the fare-path

As the booking day approaches the travel day, most of the changes in fare levels that an airline makes serve to *increase* the prevailing fares. This leads to a common exhortation: book as soon as you can. However, other fare-change patterns can arise.

In particular, the airline staff who are responsible for monitoring bookings and adjusting fares may initially have been too optimistic. This problem can arise especially for travel on unusual days, such as on a long weekend for which the Monday is a public holiday. While incumbent airlines will have valuable experience of the corresponding periods in earlier years, there can be contextual circumstances which do not repeat themselves in exactly the same way each year.

Holiday weekends can cause especial difficulty for *new* airlines, with limited staff experience and few years of formal records. Following excessive optimism, the new airline may reduce fares, at one and the same time, for several or all of the flights on such a day, once the problem has been recognised. (Of course, an airline can be too pessimistic in its expectations, in which case there may soon be a general and unusually large *increase* in fares for the particular travel date. But, given the usual upward trend in available fares as booking days go by, such an increase is less prominent than a general reduction in such fares.)

Some booking-engine data for the very dense route between Melbourne and Sydney supports the remark about fare reductions. In its (relatively) early days, Virgin Australia scheduled a group of six Monday-evening flights on the very dense route from Melbourne to Sydney, on 13 June 2005, which was a public holiday. Some 15 days before that travel date, the Virgin booking engine recorded modest reductions in the lowest available fares for each of the flights; and there were further, steep reductions six days before the travel date.

The history of those flights also illustrates a general practice. After those fare reductions, Virgin *increased* the lowest available fares over the last two or three booking days. Many airlines do this – apparently believing that anyone who books so late has very pressing reasons for travel and so is willing to pay a high fare. In the Australian market, the long-established Qantas has usually increased its late fares to a greater extent than Virgin.

Finally, where an airline has two or more ticket types, each with a fare repertoire, it has available a further important mechanism for increasing the lowest available fare as the booking day approaches the travel day. Besides increasing the lowest available fare by moving up the scale in the repertoire, the airline can, without prior notice, withdraw that ticket type from further sale. The potential traveller then finds the lowest available fare buys the next ticket type, going up the price list.

9.5.3 Setting through fares

In operating a hub-and-spoke network, a profit-seeking airline should keep open the possibility of charging a through fare – say, for a journey from port A to hub H to port B – that *is lower* than the sum of the separate fares it currently charges for travel on the sectors A to H and H to B. That might be especially appropriate when the airline seeks to compete with a recent entrant that offers non-stop service between A and B.

For a point-to-point airline that permits passengers to transfer at an intermediate port, the same issue may arise. Again the airline may find it advantageous to offer a through fare that is less than the sum of the separate fares. Such an offer would not oblige the airline to transfer the bags between flights; that responsibility can remain with the traveller.

9.6 Making an internet booking: the customer experience

Because the website booking engine has become the dominant point of sale for many airlines, it is important for the airline that both the presentation of information and the booking procedure be clear and well organised. For the potential clients, and for the government agency charged with protecting the interests of consumers, it is also important that the website presentation be without obscure and misleading procedures that may trap the unwary customer, especially one who is *not* very experienced in the use of computer display screens.

To reach a well-informed decision, the ideal is for the traveller to learn of the airline's flight times on the intended day of travel (and *perhaps* on nearby days as well) and, for each of the flights of interest, the fare levels and ticket conditions for each *available* ticket type. This is especially important for leisure travellers, because their choice of flight time, and even of the date of travel, can be influenced by the differences in fare levels between the various flights.

Where the route is served by more than one airline, the traveller may benefit by having such information for each of those rivals. And the information field may be further broadened if there are flights from and to alternative ports, each serving the area of the traveller's origin or destination.

In large measure, the following discussion is based on a survey (made in January 2014) of the websites of twenty (old and new) airlines.

9.6.1 Presentation of fares

Nowadays, many airlines present a table of fares (usually, for travel on a single day chosen by the prospective traveller) in which each flight is assigned a row in the table. Where the airline has two or more ticket types, and where the airline chooses to show the details, each ticket type is given a column in the table. *Most* such airlines then use each cell to report whether the ticket type is available for the corresponding flight; and when it is, they report the prevailing price.

In that situation, the user of the booking engine can readily see how the price varies by flight and ticket type, and hence can arrive at a well informed decision. To implement a decision the traveller clicks on the relevant cell, and goes on to provide the personal and financial information needed to complete the deal.

However, in that table, some airlines do not report fare levels, and may not identify *all* their ticket types. Some cases are examined below. Also, in case the user wishes to consider travel on alternative dates, some airlines follow a different approach; that too is considered below.

Airline practices differ also in respect of the information the user is *obliged* to provide before the website will disclose information on available ticket types and fare levels. Clearly, the airline *needs* to know the number of passengers to be served by the booking, together with the intended date of travel and the origin and destination ports for each flight in the proposed itinerary. Beyond that, some airlines ask for further information, and then use it to limit the information they provide to the traveller.

Among the twenty airlines in the survey, eight asked only for the minimal prior information, and then presented a table showing the pertinent fare levels for *all* their ticketing options, for the one date set for each flight in the itinerary. Those airlines were: Air Canada, WestJet, Ryanair, WizzAir, Tigerair, Southwest, JetBlue and Virgin America. (Note that Ryanair and WizzAir sold only one ticket type.)

While that approach suits the business traveller, whose travel dates are unlikely to be influenced by fare-level differences between travel dates, some airlines recognise that most of their customers are leisure travellers. Accordingly, they present lowest-available-fares for alternative dates for each flight in the itinerary.

With the exception of Southwest Airlines, each of the airlines listed above showed those fares for a period of between three and eleven days, centred on the proposed date of travel for the flight sector; and they did that on the same screen as the detailed table of flights and ticket types (for the nominated date). A traveller who wanted to explore fares on an alternative date could then click on the relevant date/fare cell to obtain the detailed information about flight times and ticket types for that day. (While Southwest did not present *fares* for alternative dates on its initial screen, it did provide clickable date cells to allow the user to access full tables for alternative dates.)

Those companies provided the alternative date information without first asking the user. Four other airlines (EasyJet, Norwegian, Turkish and Jetstar) asked (in varying words) whether the user was interested in alternative dates, and then presented such fare data when the user so indicated. In those cases, the purpose of the airline inquiry was to allow it to add *more* information on its initial response screen.

The remaining airlines sought prior answers to additional questions. Lufthansa asked whether the potential traveller wanted economy or business-class seating. On its English-language site, Air France asked the traveller to choose between Business, Premium Economy and Economy tickets – though those terms did not always match the choices available on individual routes! British Airways asked questions on two preferences, namely choice between lowest available fare or flexible ticket conditions, and choice between four cabin classes. Qantas required the traveller to choose between economy and business, and also invited a response on flexibility on dates. Virgin Australia issued a similar invitation regarding flexibility of travel dates, and required a choice between economy, premium economy and business seats (with occasionally much the same ensuing difficulty as reported above for Air France).

Finally, and asking the most questions, came the booking engines of the three legacy (network) carriers in the US: American (inspected before implementation of its merger with US Airways), Delta and United. Unlike their large rival (Southwest Airlines), each of these three asked the potential customer to state a preference on most if not all of the following matters: cabin class, travel date flexibility, time-of-day for flight (one permitted answer was 'any time'), fare preference (lowest/restricted, refundable, business etc.), and a choice between being interested in schedule (only) and price-and-schedule.

An airline seeking such extensive pre-commitment typically uses the answers to help it select information focussed directly on the stated preference. For example, when the user has nominated refundable fares, the booking engine typically does not display the lower fares being charged for non-refundable tickets. In that situation, the user can not immediately check *how much* the fare is reduced in exchange for accepting non-refundability, and so is unable to make a well-informed *immediate* judgement on whether to change the initial preference and choose one of the lower fares. Unlike the inquiry about interest in alternative travel dates, the airline here uses the extra information to *reduce* the amount of information that it supplies to the traveller.

In the case of the three US legacy carriers, the reasons for the airline parsimony are not as clear. It may be a benevolent wish to help the user to find quickly the type of fare the user has nominated. On the other hand, some of the booking engines supplement a display of the user-chosen fares with corresponding information on fares in the next *higher* fare category. For example, alongside the requested economy fares, the airline might show the corresponding premium economy fares, with an exhortation such as: *Why not upgrade? Only $90 more!* The survey of the airlines did *not* encounter any case where the user was asked to consider switching to a lower fare.

This suggests a direct airline interest in increased revenue rather than a concern to keep the response simple in order to make the site user-friendly. Whether or not that is so, there remains the fundamental observation that display of full information helps the user to become well informed. Provided the table is well designed, the downside for the user of having to scan and compare a larger number of fare alternatives seems of little consequence.

Despite that concern, the survey of the booking engines of the twenty airlines did *not* yield evidence suggesting the airlines were using information about individual customers to set so-called 'customised' fares (on which, see §15.5.5).

9.6.2 Presentation of ticket conditions

There are two ways of organising the information on ticket conditions relating to post-booking changes or cancellation of the travel. One is to give a link from the table of flights and fares to what is often called a 'fare type guide' (or similar), which presents on the one page the details of the conditions associated with every one of the alternative ticket types.

To aid comparison between tickets, the most effective presentation employs a tabular layout, with ticket types as column headings, and with row headings that identify the types of permitted changes in travel arrangements, together with the corresponding fees levied by the airline. (That orientation of the table is preferred because there are rarely more than five or six ticket types, while the list of changes and other topics is often longer.) Among the 20 airlines sampled in January 2014, Air Canada, Qantas, Jetstar and Southwest provided well executed tabular presentations.

In the second commonly used approach, when the first page has tabulated flights and available fares for each of the ticket types, some airlines offer links to information on the conditions for a user-selected ticket type.

For example, Turkish and Virgin America allow the user to click on the column heading for any one ticket type of interest; the booking engine presents (in a box) a summary of the conditions *for that ticket type only*. In an alternative variant (used by both Air Canada and WestJet, for example), the user places the cursor over the column heading, without actually clicking; the ensuing display of conditions remains on the screen until the cursor is moved.

With such selective link access, the displayed fare conditions are sometimes only a summary. Furthermore, the approach often makes it difficult for the user to compare alternative ticket types – because the screen shows only one box at a time; to make a comparison, the user needs to refer to separate pages. To address that issue, Air Canada and WestJet give conditions for the one ticket type when the user hovers, and gives lists for all types when the user clicks!

Typically, airlines do not give explicit instructions on the existence of these website features. Rather, they seem to rely on users learning 'on the job'. Furthermore, the quality of the wording of the explanation of the ticket conditions varies greatly.

Traditionally, the 'conditions' referred only to those ticket features that could be altered, and what if any fees were charged for such changes. Nowadays, some airlines also include positive information on what supplementary services are available for each ticket type, for example meals and other cabin service, together with prices. The additional information helps to give a better balance to the user's comparisons between the alternative tickets.

9.6.3 Presentation of all-inclusive fares

To help the consumer compare prices, especially across airlines, the airline should show the fares on the first screen that identifies individual flights. Unfortunately, it is rare for *all-inclusive* prices to be stated on that screen. Instead, most airlines state a basic price to which they add (later in the booking process) so-called 'taxes and charges' – which can be considerable in amount. A consumer who does not anticipate such an impost may be encouraged to make a booking that would not have been made in the event of earlier disclosure. And where the potential traveller wishes to compare fares of different airlines, it is even more important to know the fully inclusive prices.

In the US, the seemingly universal practice of delaying disclosure of all-inclusive prices may not be thought a major failing, because the amounts added later are usually modest, and seem not to vary much if at all between airlines. In Europe, however, some airlines add large extra amounts, and this can result in a total price that is as much as *twice* the price initially quoted. Such tactics greatly hamper price comparisons, and hence damage the process of price competition.

The Australian traveller *was* well served in this regard. In May 2002, the general-purpose regulator (the Australian Competition and Consumer Commission) brokered an informal agreement whereby Virgin and Qantas undertook to advertise fares on an all-inclusive basis (for their domestic flights). When this agreement broke down (in 2005), the Australian government announced that it would introduce legislation to require all-inclusive pricing (in all industries), and the airlines immediately reverted to showing all-inclusive fares for domestic flights. (It was late 2008 before the government brought the legislation to parliament!)

However, since that time, the force of such an arrangement for the air traveller has been reduced by the widespread unbundling of the services previously included in the package sold to the customers. The most important of the now separated services is the carriage by the airline of checked baggage. The traveller does not *have* to carry any baggage at all. Thus the charges levied on checked baggage are optional outlays, and so need not be included in the basic fare shown on the website 'first page'. Thus the stated 'all-inclusive' price has become merely the total of all *compulsory* charges that the traveller cannot avoid paying.

Scrutiny of the EasyJet booking engine on 25 June 2015 showed that the airline stated its basic fare on its first screen (after the user has stated route and date of travel). That screen also displayed a list of additional services, all of which were included for the flexi fare; the standard fare included the flight itself and carriage of a cabin bag, and allowed the traveller to check bags and select seats at extra charges.

9.6.4 Unbundling adds to the complexity when using an airline booking engine

The unbundling of service components adds to the steps needed to make a booking. For example, the introduction of separate charges for the carriage of checked bags results in extra questions, inviting or requiring the traveller to decide (at the time of booking a seat) how many checked bags to take on the journey. Such matters may make the booking process a little more stressful for the traveller.

Furthermore, many airlines have sought to increase revenue and profit by including in the booking process offers to supply other products that have no physical link to the carriage of the passenger. Thus, the user may have to respond to offers of hotel rooms, hire cars, and travel insurance, with each demanding up-front payment at the time of booking the aircraft seat. Even worse, one or two of the offers (notably, travel insurance) may appear on the screen with acceptance as the default condition. The hapless traveller who fails to notice and cancel the tick in the box can end up with an expensive and unwanted service.

Caveat emptor.

10 Airline entry and the processes of competition

10.1 Starting a new airline

10.1.1 A complex task that needs capable managers

In almost any industry, the task of launching a new company is challenging. For all but the smallest ventures, the appointment of managers having experience in the industry is – at the least – helpful, and may be well-nigh essential. Of course, those managers must also bring a willingness to change their ways when faced with novel situations.

In the case of passenger airlines, the launch task is particularly difficult. First, the airline CEO has to coordinate the work of diverse production departments, with much of the work performed in widespread geographical locations.

Second, in its day-to-day operations, the airline is at the mercy of factors that it cannot fully control: weather conditions; industrial relations issues, especially regarding workforces that report to other parties; unexpected safety alerts concerning performance of aircraft components; quite big swings in demand levels, some of which are not well predicted, especially by a new company with limited knowledge of conditions in the local market; and the obligation to serve customers whose human idiosyncrasies are heightened by their exposure to the vagaries of travel.

And last but not least, unlike the situation in *most* manufacturing – where firms can build up product stocks to help ensure continuity of supply – the product of a passenger airline perishes immediately; today's empty seat cannot be sold tomorrow. In consequence, the airline has to perform many of its complex tasks in 'real time'. As a result an airline's operational, engineering and administrative adversities/mistakes can have immediate and direct damaging consequences for the customers.

In contrast, the manager of a franchise outlet that cooks and sells hamburgers has a comparatively simple task.

10.1.2 Barriers to airline entry

The would-be airline also faces many 'barriers to entry' – a term that economists use to describe hurdles the newcomer has to overcome in order to gain access to an industry. While some of the barriers have natural, inevitable presence, there may be others that are artificially created or fostered by incumbent airlines that seek to discourage or hinder entry.

In many industries, there are barriers to entry arising from the presence of economies of scale and scope. As already noted (§8.1.5), some of these are important for airlines.

There are also entry barriers arising from the specific circumstances of aviation. The importance of aircraft safety makes the market entry of a new airline a matter of public interest. Accordingly, a start-up airline needs to obtain an *air operator certificate* (AOC) from the government of the country in which the prospective airline is to be domiciled. One pre-requisite for that certificate is the preparation by the airline of operating manuals. Usually a government also examines financial fitness, to check whether the company can fund initial outlays. It thereby hopes to reduce the risk of passengers losing their money when purchasing tickets before the date of travel.

Depending on the precise nature of the institutional arrangements, such governmental scrutiny may result in official publication or unofficial leaking of the plans of a new company, thereby disadvantaging it *vis-à-vis* its incumbent rivals. For an account of one start-up experience, see Beesley (1986). (The late Michael Beesley was a leading academic in the field of transport economics. For a time he became an airline entrepreneur – though, in the end, his intended UK–Hong Kong charter airline did not take to the air.)

In countries where government commitment to deregulation of airlines is not whole-hearted, incumbent airlines may be able to bring political pressure to bear on government, to prevent or hinder/delay the launch of a new airline company. In the US, the experience of Virgin America (§1.2.6) illustrates how, even after entry, the incumbents may campaign on alleged shortcomings of the entrant (in that case, by claiming – unsuccessfully – that the ownership structure of the company did not meet government requirements for control by US citizens).

A special but important case concerns the difficulties often experienced by an airline seeking to enter an international route under bilateral agreements made between the two governments concerned. A striking example (noted above in §6.5) concerns the delays experienced by Fastjet before it won access to the Republic of South Africa for flights from its base in Tanzania.

In contrast, some barriers to entry have become *less* onerous in recent times, mainly because of the development of markets in which a new airline may purchase services or lease assets. Several categories are discussed in the following paragraphs.

Computerised reservation systems

Given the complexity and real-time character of airline operation, it is no surprise that the airlines were early adopters of electronic computers. In the beginning, a major airline would develop its own software for its own use, though common-user reservation systems soon became available.

For the specific requirements of low-cost airline entrants that do not issue paper tickets, Navitaire was one of the earliest computer-based reservations systems, and it was widely adopted. Typically, the fees for such software depend on the amount of use, and this helps a small start-up company to organise its reservation system at modest *initial* cost.

Of course, as an airline grows, those software payments also grow in total amount. That may have encouraged EasyJet (an early user of Navitaire) to switch to a software package written by its own consultants. In 2003, Navitaire began legal action, claiming breach of copyright. In a very detailed statement (England and Wales High Court, 2004), the judge found for EasyJet. However, Navitaire continued to press its case. Eventually the parties reached 'an amicable agreement' in which Navitaire provided 'all the necessary rights, licences and permissions' for EasyJet to use its own software, while EasyJet 'agreed that it will not sell or licence [its own software] to third parties' (EasyJet media release, 10 November 2005).

Aircraft leasing

The (now) well-established market for aircraft leasing (of both new and second-hand aircraft) greatly reduces the amount of capital needed by a new airline. In earlier times, a small start-up airline bought very old aircraft at very low prices, notwithstanding their consequent high operating and maintenance costs – and their reduced safety margins. In contrast, many of the low-cost airlines have started with new aircraft, though at the very beginning some (for example, Virgin Australia) started with older aircraft that were soon replaced once the owner was reassured about company prospects.

Aircraft maintenance

In times past, major airlines did all their own aircraft maintenance. Nowadays, specialist companies offer services to airlines that wish to contract out such work. Some of the companies are independent organisations; others are subsidiaries of major legacy airlines. Some new airlines state publicly that they have contracted out aircraft maintenance, to help convince travellers that the work is in safe hands. For instance, Jazeera Airways (of Kuwait) (§3.3) announced it had engaged Lufthansa Technik to service the engines of its (new) A320s. Following the loss of an aircraft in 2005, Mandala Airlines began building a new fleet of A320s, and announced in June 2008 that it had engaged Singapore Airlines Engineering Company to undertake their maintenance.

Airport access

Finally, a new airline may face a literal barrier to entry, namely difficulty in gaining *access to airport infrastructure*. Incumbent airlines sometimes have control of passenger terminals, and may thwart entry by newcomers. (§7.3 reports on an Australian situation.) At congested ports, runway access may be rationed, with all the rights to land (so-called 'slots') being held by incumbent airlines. Even where slot-trading is allowed, the incumbents may be unwilling to sell or lease to newcomers. If a new airline cannot land at peak times, it may be commercially impracticable for it to serve the airport at all.

10.2 Route entry and incumbent responses

When formulating a business model, a company thinking of launching an airline will proceed only if it believes it can establish a *route network* that will be profitable. As we have seen – notably, in the discussion of Virgin America (§1.2.6) – overall profitability may be a distant prospect. Nevertheless, the initial foray, perhaps the first six or eight routes, must be coherent and balanced, even if not immediately profitable. For example, each of the first few aircraft must be gainfully employed over a long day, and so the initial network must include routes that can be operated early in the morning and/or late in the evening. Perhaps the airline will serve some business routes during peak periods, and fly leisure routes during the remainder of the day. While such network coherence is important, the basic building block is the individual route, which is the main subject of this section.

10.2.1 Entry to a city-pair route

To simplify the analysis and the exposition, suppose that there is only one incumbent. Suppose also that the incumbent offers travel via its hub, but does not offer any direct flights between the city-pair of interest. If the potential entrant expects to have cost levels below the incumbent's prevailing fare levels, then the entrant's offer of direct service at lower fares may readily prove to be successful. Thanks to the lower fares, the total number of travellers will increase, and (at least) some of the extra passengers will fly with the entrant. Further analysis requires consideration of how the incumbent may respond.

For a *first case,* suppose the incumbent starts its own direct service, with fares set at levels that are lower than its previous indirect fares but not as low as those of the entrant. (The case is realistic: the incumbent previously enjoyed a route-monopoly, and set (high) profit-maximising fares; in the new situation, its profit-maximising fares will be lower than before. The next section looks at some real-world examples.)

If some passengers see the incumbent's new direct service as being of higher quality than that of the entrant, they will choose between the competing airlines after considering whether the extra quality is worth the extra price. In general, some will prefer the incumbent and others the entrant. This applies both to passengers already flying between the city-pair and to potential (extra) passengers whose travel is stimulated by the lower fares of both of the airlines *and* by the extra convenience of direct travel. Where the route has a considerable number of potential passengers with non-essential travel purposes and/or low incomes, many of them will choose to fly with the entrant.

A formal analysis for this case is given in Table 10.1. Using the notation introduced there, the *extra* travel on the incumbent is $G2 - N3$ passengers, and this

Table 10.1 Incumbent starts direct city-pair service to compete with an entrant

Scenario	Incumbent initially offers indirect travel only. Entrant starts direct service at lower fares. Incumbent responds by starting direct service at reduced fares, which are still higher than entrant's fares. Entrant's service perceived to be of lower quality (perhaps fewer flights, limited cabin service, no business class, no frequent flyer scheme, no airport lounges).
Journeys made between city-pair before entry	N travellers per period (total for both directions).
Outcome for those N passengers after entry	The total N divides into three groups:
	$N1$ remain on incumbent's indirect service (some may do so, because of schedule convenience).
	$N2$ fly at reduced fares on direct flights of incumbent (travellers who prefer incumbent's higher quality to *further* fare saving attainable by switching to entrant).
	$N3$ on direct flights of entrant (travellers who value fare saving more than extra quality).
Extra journeys after entry	Responding to lower fares, reduced journey time, and convenience of more frequent flights – $G2$ journeys per period on incumbent and $G3$ on entrant.
Net extra journeys (passengers) for each airline	For incumbent, $G2 - N3$; for entrant, $G3 + N3$.

number may be negative or positive – that is, the incumbent may carry fewer or more passengers in the new situation. The number of passengers won by the entrant is $G3 + N3$. However, after entry, the total travel on the incumbent is $N - N3 + G2$ passengers. That may still be the major part of the total travel between the city-pair, especially if the incumbent's flight frequency is much greater than that of the entrant. Even so, the entrant may still earn profits from a relatively infrequent service.

In a *second case*, the incumbent decides not to start a direct service; instead, it reduces its fares for indirect travel. That response is more likely if it thinks that there will be few *extra* passengers responding to the convenience of direct travel. However, the entrant wins *all* the extra passengers who choose direct travel, after taking into account the fares offered by the two airlines. *Dear reader*: try your hand at devising the similar algebraic representation.

10.2.2 Route entries observed in several countries

In the US, because the major incumbent airlines developed a post-deregulation enthusiasm for hub-and-spoke networks, a very large number of city-pairs had jet aircraft service; in many of those cases, though, travel was only via a hub port. Moreover, some of those indirect services required travel over a much greater distance than the direct route. In consequence, Southwest Airlines was able to enter and (eventually) thrive by providing direct service on many (relatively) thin routes.

Another kind of route entry succeeded when the entrant chose a port in a metropolitan area that differed from the port already served by an incumbent. For example, Ryanair's first *Dublin–London* service flew to London Luton, while the two incumbents (Aer Lingus and British Airways) used London Heathrow. Similarly, when EasyJet started operations, its first routes were all from Luton rather than from Heathrow or London Gatwick, the ports used by the incumbents. One factor that helped these Luton services to thrive was the greater convenience of access to that port from some northern parts of the London metropolitan area.

In Australia, Virgin Blue as entrant brought jet service to several thin routes that Qantas served with turboprops. One example concerns Coffs Harbour, a small coastal city with tourist hotels, some 440 km north of Sydney. In mid-2002, Qantas operated small turbo-props on direct services from Sydney, serving business travellers as well as tourists. Virgin started one daily RT using B737-700 or -800 aircraft, and later increased its service to twice daily. (The use of a jet shortened the flight duration only by 15 minutes. Previously, the conventional wisdom had been that jet service on such a route would be unprofitable.)

By introducing lower fares, Virgin was able to attract enough passengers for its jets. Yet Qantas was able to remain on the route, in part because it served some business travel not addressed by Virgin. In particular, it stationed an aircraft in Coffs overnight, and so attracted business travellers keen to spend a long day in Sydney. By 2006, the annual passenger numbers on the route reached 301,000, compared with 146,000 in 2001. In early 2015, the service pattern was much the same in style as before: Virgin had downsized to an E190 jet for each of its two daily flights; Qantas flew five times each weekday, mostly using Q400 turbo-props, one of which overnighted at Coffs. For 2014, the route had 344,000 passengers, down from 368,000 in 2013 (Bureau of Infrastructure, Transport and Regional Economics, Domestic Aviation Activity Annual 2014).

Hamburg–Bristol

Another case of jet entry by a low-cost airline (on a route where an incumbent operated turbo-props) gave a very different outcome. On 1 December 2005, EasyJet started a daily service between Bristol and Hamburg, a route already served twice daily by a small German carrier, OLT, using a Saab 2000 turbo-prop (with 50 seats). However, EasyJet withdrew from the route in October 2006. The Hamburg route was said to be mainly one for business travel, with frequency winning over low fares ('OLT celebrates reaching 50 [years] . . .', anna.aero, 19 September 2008; 'Route launch dates', corporate.easyjet.com/media, accessed 7 July 2009). A few years later, however, OLT ceased flying, and filed for bankruptcy (ch-aviation.ch, 1 February 2013).

10.2.3 Incumbent fare responses to new-airline entry

Where new-airline entry induces incumbents to reduce their fares, three interesting issues arise: the size of the reductions, whether they are made *before* the date of entry, and the motive(s) of the incumbents.

Those issues are examined in Goolsbee and Syverson (2008). For domestic services in the US, the impact of the growing network of Southwest Airlines provided a significant natural experiment, with outcomes that are evident in fares data collected by the US Department of Transportation. In an earlier study of such data, Morrison (2001) constructed an aggregate measure of the savings to passengers in 1998 arising from the low-fare strategy of Southwest Airlines. Of his estimate of total savings of US$12.9 billion, about US$3.3 billion arose on routes where incumbents *feared* that Southwest might be about to enter.

Following that work, Goolsbee and Syverson used the Department of Transportation data collections from 1993 Q1 to 2004 Q4, to study the (many) route entries made by Southwest. They looked particularly at the *timing* of incumbents' fare responses.

In their account, a city-pair route not served by Southwest was 'threatened' if the airline already had a presence at both of the route ports. When Southwest already served just *one* of the ports, it could announce its route-entry at the same time as, or later than, it announced that it was to start service at the second of the route's two defining ports. Goolsbee and Syverson concentrated on the time interval between Southwest announcing it would serve the second port, and actual entry on the route. Their conclusions were:

1 In most cases, incumbents did reduce fares when they thought Southwest was likely soon to enter a route.
2 Fare reductions were confined to routes *directly* threatened – in particular, an incumbent did not reduce fares when, in a metropolitan area, it flew to a port other than that expected to host Southwest's new route (for example, when the incumbent flew to Chicago O'Hare rather than to Southwest's base at Chicago Midway).
3 On average, more than half of the fare-reduction came before Southwest's actual route entry.

The authors found that where Southwest announced route entry at the same time as it announced establishment at the second port, there was little or no fare response from the incumbents until *after* the route entry. The absence of any *prior* response could reflect an incumbent understanding that deterrence would be ineffective in such situations.

To complement those results, it is worth mentioning the timing conduct in the (much simpler) domestic market in Australia. When Virgin Blue was rapidly expanding its route network, its entry fares for fully flexible economy tickets were often about 30 or 40 per cent below the prevailing Qantas fares. The latter airline usually did respond, with fare reductions that took effect on the date of Virgin's route entry.

Generally, a Virgin entry was in direct competition with a Qantas service. There were no other companies serving the main-line network. Qantas had little or no hope of deterring, and little or no benefit from diverting, the various Virgin route entries. Thus, Qantas had little incentive to reduce its fares for travel taking place before the date of Virgin's route entry.

A further issue is how (if at all) incumbent fare responses vary across ticket types. For the US, Gerardi and Shapiro (2009) studied similar US DOT data on fares paid. For routes having significant amounts of both business and leisure travel, they found that upon route entry by another airline, the incumbent reduced the high fares it charged for flexible tickets (used mainly by business travellers) towards the fare levels paid by leisure travellers. In other words, the entry by a competing airline had the effect of reducing the difference between the incumbent's fares for the two ticket types.

Casual inspection of fares offered by Qantas and Virgin suggests a simple pattern of differences between the fares of the two Australian carriers. Upon entry by Virgin, Qantas reduced its full-fare economy prices, while still keeping them higher than the corresponding Virgin fares. However, for discounted tickets with restrictive conditions, Qantas and Virgin set much the same fare levels, especially for tickets bought well before the date of travel.

For another case, see Bilotkach (2005) which reports fares in 2002 for five airlines selling direct round-trip tickets between New York and London.

10.2.4 Selective fare response by an incumbent: an empirical example of fare paths

With fares generally rising as the booking day approaches the date of travel, each of the airlines serving a particular route generally keeps a close eye on the offered fares of the other(s). Even so, the airlines do not necessarily set the same fare levels. Nor do they necessarily choose the same fare increases, day by day.

For an example that illustrates some of the practicalities, consider the very dense Sydney–Melbourne route, which (in 2005) was served only by Qantas and Virgin Blue. At the time the fare data were collected, Virgin was about five years old. It still operated aircraft with economy-class cabins only, and was still a low-fare airline that emphasised its appeal for leisure travellers. Even so, it did carry some passengers travelling on business, especially those on limited expense accounts that did not accommodate business-class fares.

With its dual-cabin aircraft, Qantas had, in effect, a monopoly on the more affluent portion of the business-travel market. Yet, even on routes dominated by business travel, it still carried economy-class passengers – in order to make up the numbers needed to support its frequent service. Thus on many routes, and at booking dates well before the travel date, it too offered low fares for its most basic ticket class, in order to compete with Virgin.

In order to capture and portray the overall patterns of the *competing* fares of the two airlines, the analysis reported here considers only the *lowest available* fares of each airline on a single day of travel. For each flight on that day, the lowest available fares were observed once daily for the 42 booking days immediately preceding the chosen day of travel.

Table 10.2 Time-paths of the lowest fares of Qantas and Virgin, Sydney to Melbourne,
          Wednesday 15 June 2005

Regression statistics
No. of fare observations, $n = 2390$; adjusted R-squared $= 0.78$; (F-value $= 557$)

Fare components
Constant term: A\$105.4 ($t = 35.0$)

Time periods[1]	Qantas (A\$)	t statistic	Virgin (A\$)	t statistic
Periods of the day[2]				
am peak	204.1	45.9	8.7	2.9
pm peak	186.5	43.8	17.2	6.9
off-peak	62.6	15.9		
Days before travel				
7 to 13	−17.1	−5.2	0.2	0.1
14 to 20	−42.0	−12.7	−14.7	−3.8
21 to 27	−71.1	−21.4	−29.6	−7.6
28 to 34	−80.2	−24.1	−28.3	−7.3
35 to 42	−75.1	−23.3	−11.9	−3.2

Source: fares from Qantas and Virgin Blue websites

Notes
1 Each airline is interacted with the time-period of the day; the base case is Virgin in the off-peak
   period. Secondly, each airline is interacted with the *grouped* values for the number of days between
   the booking day and the travel day; the base case is the group of days from 1 to 6 days before travel.
2 Here, the morning peak includes all departures between the hours of 0630 and 0800, while the
   evening peak extends from 1600 to 1900 (both inclusive).

The model puts three features at centre stage: the variation in fares as the
booking day approaches the travel day; the differences in fares across the various
flight times; and the fare differences between the airlines.

To obtain a simple model – without a *very* large number of categories – the day
is regarded as comprising two peak periods (for the morning and evening peak
travel periods, as defined in Table 10.2), and a third period comprising all the
other hours, here regarded as off-peak. Each flight is assigned to one of those three
periods by reference to its departure time. Similarly, booking days are pooled, to
give the five booking periods listed in the table together with a sixth period for
bookings made in the period from one to six days before travel.

Each *observed* lowest available fare is then regarded as being influenced by
three factors: the identity of the airline, which of the six booking periods applies,
and which of the three departure time periods applies.

The purpose of the statistical modelling is to calculate *estimates* of the fares for
each airline for each booking period and each departure-time period. The statistical
layman may immediately object: why prepare estimates when the actual fares
offered on each booking day are already known? A plain-language response is
that, as always, the actual fares display many minor, random variations which
obscure the overall message. The statistical (regression) procedure serves to
smooth out those effects, and thereby reveal the underlying pattern.

Now consider how to interpret the numbers in the table. In the statistical model, the *estimated* fare is regarded as being the sum of three components: an airline-specific component for the time period, an airline-specific component for the booking period, and a constant amount. For the two airlines, the numerical values calculated for those components are shown in (respectively) the first and third data columns in Table 10.2. (Data columns two and four give standard statistical measures that a statistician or econometrician expects to see. Those without such expertise or interest may disregard those measures, and instead focus on the following text.)

To help interpret those data, consider an example. For a booking made in the period 14 to 20 days before the day of travel, on a Qantas flight departing within the pm peak, the Qantas component for the booking period is *minus* A\$42.0, and that for the pm peak is A\$186.5. Upon adding those to the constant term, which is A\$105.4, the estimate for the (rounded) total fare is A\$250. The corresponding estimated fare for Virgin is A\$108.

The overall pattern of the results may be summarised readily. The time-of-day components for Qantas are large and similar for the two peak periods, while the off-peak component is much smaller. For Virgin, the corresponding components are small. (That for the off-peak is zero, because 'Virgin off-peak' is part of the default case). For both airlines, the booking day components mostly diminish in (absolute) amount as the booking is made closer to the day of travel. As these components are negative, this means that the estimated fares generally *rise* as booking is postponed. (Because booking between one and six days before travel is part of the default, those booking day components are zero.)

However, there is an important limitation: the analysis pre-supposes that the peak/off-peak differentials do not change in amount as the booking day approaches the travel day. In reality, these differentials may well change over time. Even so, the simple model does capture a large proportion of the variation in the data. And (almost) all the differences recorded in the table *are* significant – that is, they are big enough to be very unlikely to have arisen by chance.

Thus the results are plausible. Generally, the Qantas fares are much higher than those charged by Virgin. However, the (identified) *off-peak* differences are 'only' about A\$60, rather than the peak-period differences of roughly A\$180.

Probable reasons for these fare differences are that, at the time:

1 Virgin was *relatively* new on the route;
2 it attracted few business travellers, and so it did not experience morning and evening peaks to anything like the same extent as Qantas did; and
3 it was trying to build up market share by matching the Qantas frequency while selling at much lower fares; and, at certain times of the day, the Qantas fares included meals.

For a much larger and more thorough study of the fares set by Qantas and Virgin on domestic routes in Australia, see De Roos, Mills and Whelan (2010).

10.2.5 The value of information on route passenger numbers for the prospective entrant

A potential entrant can usually study published airline timetables or industry sources to estimate, for each flight, the number of *seats* offered by the incumbent(s). While some governments do publish the route-specific *passenger* numbers for each airline, these are usually no more than aggregates for a time period, typically a calendar-month. The prospective entrant does not learn how the passenger numbers vary by time of day and day of the week, though it can gain *some* insight from the seat data revealed by incumbent timetables.

Where airline-specific route *load-factors* are publicly available, an unusually high value will often suggest the route is 'under-served', thereby implying that entry prospects may be better than average. The potential entrant can also monitor daily the fare levels offered on (each) incumbent's website; again, unusually high levels suggest the route may be worth entering.

Where a government publishes route passenger numbers but only after aggregation over the incumbent airlines, the potential entrant does not learn about the distribution between those airlines. When there are only two incumbents (as in Australia, where published government data is not disaggregated by airline) each incumbent can calculate the passenger numbers of the other. Yet, a potential airline is not a member of the club, and remains in the dark.

Almost invariably, published passenger numbers refer to *traffic-on-board by stage*, that is, the total number of passengers flying non-stop from port A to port B. Such data do not identify how many of those passengers have journey origin and/or destination at other ports. However, an incumbent (even one that is largely a point-to-point airline) will know the number of such connecting passengers travelling on its own network. On the other hand, a new airline with little or no network presence will not know that number, and hence will find it difficult to judge how many *indirect* passengers (say, those travelling from A to C via B) it may attract if it were to start a direct service between A and C.

The growth of point-to-point airlines has increased the proportion of passengers travelling non-stop between journey origin and journey destination. Yet information about indirect journeys can still matter. For example, when the six-year old Virgin Blue announced (media release, 19 March 2006) that it was starting *direct* flights between Rockhampton and Sydney, it said its entry decision was encouraged by the number of connecting passengers it already carried between those ports, with change of aircraft at Brisbane.

A prospective entrant also needs to consider the nature of the travel on the route. A low-cost entrant offering basic service at low fares may not do well on a route where a large proportion of journeys are for business purposes.

10.2.6 Competition in the raw

When a new airline is about to enter a city-pair route, it faces several significant risks. For a route not already served, there is uncertainty about the likely number of passengers willing to pay for travel. If the route *is* served, there is uncertainty about how many passengers can be won from the incumbent(s), about how many extra passengers will want to travel as a result of the lower fares the entrant proposes, and about how the incumbent will respond.

In the face of all these risks, the airline offers tickets for sale, and hopes. As the days pass on the way to the launch date, an anxious management monitors its reservations. If there are few takers in the early days, there is little that management can do in order to increase their number: some more advertising, perhaps, and possibly some special ticket offers at even lower fares.

Meanwhile if the (area) incumbent thinks *it* needs to act, it can prepare its responses. Where it already offers direct or indirect service between the city pair, then (at very short notice) it can offer special, reduced fares of its own. The scheduling of extra flights – perhaps at times that match those of the entrant – takes rather longer to organise, though even so, the time-horizon is likely to be weeks rather than months.

The entrant risks financial losses arising when passenger revenues fall short even of the direct operating costs. Because most of those costs are not dependent on passenger numbers, any significant shortfall in passenger numbers can bring considerable deficits.

Even a route launch that is well judged and ultimately 'successful' may incur early losses while the passenger numbers build up over the weeks and months following the start. If there are very few bookings, the possibility of an *eventual* satisfactory passenger response makes more difficult the decision on whether or not to go ahead with the launch.

Even so, poor advance bookings sometimes *do* induce a withdrawal before the launch date. That requires a courageous decision, though the required degree of courage is modest if the new route is but a small venture for an expanding airline that already has a solid foundation.

In another Australian example, Virgin Blue (after many successful route entries) announced (media release, 28 January 2005) that on 7 April it would enter a regional route, Perth to Kalgoorlie (already served by Qantas and by a (then) independent regional airline, Skywest). On 4 April, when Virgin announced 'postponement' of the entry, it cited (among other matters) 'less than acceptable load factors'. Virgin (itself) never did enter that route.

At the other extreme, an entrant can be so successful (initially) that it drives (one or more) incumbents from the route. For example, Sky Europe (which started in Slovakia) established a base at Prague in April 2006, and started flying its new B737-700 aircraft from Prague to London Luton (Sky Europe Airlines, Annual Report 2007, p. 13).

In a later media release ('SkyEurope wins battle for Prague', 5 October 2007), the airline claimed that both Czech Airlines and Thomsonfly (a British company) had withdrawn their Prague–London services. (Even so, Czech Airlines *was* again flying to Heathrow in September 2008.) Sky Europe argued that its success was due to its low fares and punctuality, and to schedules that allowed the Prague-based business traveller to spend a full day in London before going home.

That last point referred tacitly to EasyJet which (at that time) operated two round-trip flights daily from London Gatwick and a further two from London Stansted, but did not overnight an aircraft in Prague. So Sky Europe did indeed offer a better schedule for Prague business travellers.

The penultimate word here comes from Michael Cawley, then deputy CEO of Ryanair, who was quoted ('Ryanair reveals Nike-style approach to new route planning', anna.aero, 9 February 2010):

> The cost for opening a route is low. So we don't bother trying to analyse the living daylights out of it, we have a look at the demographics, and then make a decision to do it – we accept that around 7-10% might not work but we don't see this as a failure – we see it as 90% success. We leave routes if we don't make sustainable profits after six months.

Now for three last words: The claim about the low cost of starting a route must have raised a few eyebrows in the industry. However, such failed entries may indeed be a necessary part of the learning process. Once an airline is so large as to be operating a few hundred routes, the occasional mistaken entry is by no means fatal.

10.2.7 Route profitability varies across an airline's network

It is common for there to be considerable variation in profitability across routes, even when an airline's network is preponderantly mature.

Because of the jointly incurred nature of many costs, an airline may be content to keep flying a poorly performing route, provided that the incremental revenues from the route outweigh the incremental costs. Here, those costs are (principally, if not entirely) aircraft operating and maintenance costs, together with any extra costs of station operation at the two ports connected by the route. As discussed in §8.1.3, the relevant cost concept *excludes* those of the indirect costs – such as the holding cost of the aircraft – that would not be saved if the route were not operated. Thus, for a route flown at a time when an aircraft has no alternative 'profitable' use, a route can be incrementally profitable even when it does not contribute to aircraft capital costs. That argument has particular importance when evaluating the performance of routes served by off-peak flights.

Some of the airline's other routes may earn super-normal profits. However, if there is no government regulation that restricts route entry, any such financial boon *may* be competed away in the longer term. However, competitive processes usually take time to work out. Moreover, aircraft indivisibility precludes very fine adjustment of capacity deployed on a route, and may result in some (modest) level of excess profits persisting even in the long term.

In short, it is common for the network of (even) a well-managed airline to have some routes that are very profitable, many routes that earn about a 'normal' profit rate on capital, and some that (generally) cover the direct costs but make little or no contribution to capital and other indirect costs. (Of course, operation of poorly performing routes may be justified by expectations of good profits in the future.)

One implication is that if an airline's *overall* profit does go into decline (or remains marginal, for whatever reason) the company may need to cut back on some of its worst-performing routes. (Two examples are reported elsewhere: SpiceJet's reduction in the size of its network, made in response to major financial losses (§4.3.2); and Virgin America's reduction in capacity operated, when preparing the airline's financial condition for an IPO (§1.2.6).

10.3 New-airline networks in the early stages of the company

10.3.1 The choice of port for the initial base

When choosing a port for its first base, a new airline needs to consider the implications of that choice for the subsequent development of its network. However, in the initial management thinking, the immediate factors involved in launching the airline will be crucial, and may well dominate.

In looking at the histories of the four US point-to-point carriers that eventually became sizeable, we have already seen that for Southwest Airlines, the initial choice of base and routes reflected its ability to serve *intra-state* routes without Federal regulatory permission.

However, each of the other three sought a base location and initial network where the services of the incumbent airlines were *relatively* weak. Recall that AirTran chose Atlanta when Eastern left a void there, and Frontier started at Denver when Continental greatly reduced the scale of its flights there.

The situation of JetBlue is not so clear-cut. It seems the company chose New York because even by 2000 the north-east region was not served by any other *low-cost, point-to-point* carrier. And it chose JFK to allow it to tap into the major routes that radiated from New York's premier port.

Broadly similar factors have been at work in Europe too, where each national carrier chose the national capital for its (initial) hub, even though that was not always a good location for the development of a hub-and-spoke network.

When the EU legislation came into full effect, there were many regional cities with few, if any, *international* routes. Being more nimble than the national carriers, some of the new companies were able to establish themselves readily at regional ports, or at other ports not (much) used by the national carriers.

When EasyJet began service in 1995, it chose London (Luton) for its base. Despite the capital-city appellations, Luton (and Stansted) were (and, to some extent, still are) 'local' airports for considerable portions of the London metropolitan area, thanks in part to London's very large spatial spread. Thus EasyJet's choice gave it a local market, *and* helped it to avoid head-to-head competition with British Airways and the other national airlines that used Heathrow and/or Gatwick.

As already seen (Chapter 2, Table 2.1), some other new LCCs chose bases well away from capital cities – sometimes preferring to locate in regions not so well served by the national carriers. For example: *Wind Jet* located in Sicily rather than on the Italian mainland; *Germanwings* based at Cologne–Bonn rather than

Frankfurt or Berlin; and in Spain, *Vueling* and *Clickair* both chose Barcelona rather than Madrid.

WizzAir launched when the EU extended to the east. Its initial bases were at Budapest and at Katowice (Poland), and it soon introduced non-stop services to Western Europe from two other regional cities in Poland, namely Gdansk and Poznan, as well as from the capital, Warsaw (where it grasped an opportunity arising from the demise of Air Polonia).

10.3.2 Adding further bases, and deploying the fleet

A new company that makes a *successful* initial entry as a low-cost airline soon faces important questions concerning further growth. It will almost certainly wish to establish further bases, in order to extend its geographical reach. Each aircraft is assigned to a *base*, to which it returns, usually every evening. Accordingly, a base usually has both pilots and cabin crew reporting for duty there. Generally, short-haul aircraft are not flown during the night, and so engineers stationed at the base perform routine maintenance tasks during the night.

In starting a new base, an airline gains several benefits. If it seeks to serve business travellers, there is the particular advantage of readily enabling early-morning departures from, and late-evening returns to, the base city. Establishment of the base generally makes it easier to serve the smaller ports of the surrounding region. Indeed, where an established airline has already exploited much of the potential of its existing bases, opening further bases may be the most profitable way for the airline to grow.

As with other station facilities, there are economies of scale in base operation, notably in aircraft crewing and maintenance. Yet an airline may open a base initially with (say) just two aircraft, especially if it thinks it can soon increase the number of aircraft based there.

In arranging the deployment of aircraft assigned to a base, a common building block is a *rotation*, in which the aircraft flies from port F to port H, and then immediately returns to port F. A sequence of rotations can have the aircraft returning to its base throughout the day, which may be appropriate when the base city is large. Otherwise, the aircraft might, for example, visit two or three other ports during the day, and return to its base only at the end of the day.

10.3.3 Opening (and sometimes closing) further bases: some European examples

In the early stages of an airline's growth, the list of ports already served will be relatively short, and the establishment of a new base may add only a small number of new routes to its network. Later, however, an airline may establish a base at a port that already receives flights from a considerable number of other ports in its network. In such a case, the airline needs to decide which (if any) of those pre-existing routes are to be flown by aircraft quartered at the new base.

Ryanair provides an example. When operating about 180 aircraft, it announced (media release 2 July 2009) that it was to open its 33rd base at Porto, to which it already flew 12 routes. At Porto, it would position two aircraft and start four new routes – to Basel, Eindhoven, St Etienne and Tours.

In 2008 EasyJet flew about 165 aircraft. During that year, it continued to expand its base at Milan Malpensa, where at the end of the year it had 11 aircraft serving 21 ports, including several within Italy (EasyJet, Annual Report 2008, p. 7).

At that time, EasyJet also had some setbacks. Besides quitting 24 routes during the financial year, it announced that while continuing some flights to Dortmund, it would close its base there in October 2008. Of course, closure of a single (small) base does not endanger the continued existence of a large airline.

In contrast, the demise of Sky Europe (§2.3.3) followed early closure of bases at Budapest (Hungary) and Krakow (Poland). No doubt, those woes stemmed in part from the successful growth of its neighbour, WizzAir. Though headquartered in Budapest (Hungary), WizzAir's first base was at Katowice (Poland). By July 2009, its fleet of 26 A320 aircraft was spread over 11 bases, which included three further bases in Poland, namely Gdansk, Poznan and Warsaw, as well as Budapest, Sofia (Bulgaria), Kiev (Ukraine), Bucharest and two other bases in Romania, together with a new base then just opened in Prague (Czech Republic). ('Company Overview', accessed at wizzair.com, 25 July 2009). (The country list demonstrates vividly how the EU legislation supports expansion across national borders.)

10.3.4 The character of multi-base networks

By the time a point-to-point airline has grown large enough to establish several bases, its network map may begin to look a little like that of a hub-and-spoke airline, in that each base port has routes radiating from it – sometime, many such routes. Even so, there are several important differences between the two types of network.

Point-to-point airlines establish their bases at places where there is a large population in the catchment area and/or a tourist attraction or business centre. The principal role of the base is to serve travellers that have the port as (air) origin or destination.

Although a hub-and-spoke airline, such as a US legacy carrier, may have four or five hubs, these are generally at large cities. Even such lesser hubs as Salt Lake City (Delta), Charlotte (American), and Miami (American) have metropolitan-area populations in excess of two million persons. In contrast to the point-to-point case, however, many of the travellers at the hub port are there in order to transfer from one flight to another.

When a large new airline has more than (say) twenty bases, the airline's total traffic divides between many ports, unlike the concentration of traffic found in a hub-and-spoke network. Furthermore, in some large metropolitan areas, a point-to-point airline may fly to more than one of the area's ports. In London, for example, EasyJet has come to serve Luton, Stansted and Gatwick airports. One purpose is to allow passengers to use the airport that is nearest to or most convenient for their journey origin or destination. On the other hand, serving multiple airports does not promote, and may even hinder, connections between flights; in other words, it does not promote hubbing.

Finally, note that some new airlines do *not* shrink from carrying connecting passengers. For example, in its 2006 Annual Report, JetBlue noted that, as the largest *domestic* carrier at New York's JFK port, it benefits from serving some prime routes from JFK. It continues: 'Although an increase in connecting traffic is a by-product of our growing flight concentration at JFK and at our other focus cities [bases], 87% of our passengers and 91% of our passenger revenue in 2006 resulted from point-to-point travel' (pp. 2–3). Nevertheless, it goes on to say (p. 29) that one of its aims is 'in certain markets, [to] utilize our network to maximize connecting opportunities'. Of course, that may reflect an increasing interest in serving business and international travellers.

10.3.5 The growth of EasyJet's network

As is inevitable, EasyJet began as a hub-and-spoke airline! By the end of 1996, it flew to seven ports from its London (Luton) base. After such an initial phase, a fledgling airline can choose whether to develop further as a hub-and-spoke airline or focus on establishing other main network cities. The latter strategy can result in larger average numbers of routes per port and of flights per port per day, and thereby economise on station costs per passenger flown. It also helps the airline to avoid putting very many of its eggs in the one basket.

In 1997, EasyJet added routes from two existing ports (not Luton) to a new port (and base) at Liverpool. When EasyJet started a third base at London Stansted (in May 1998), the initial routes there all went to new ports – perhaps to avoid the risk of Stansted services reducing passenger demand at Luton.

The airline's annual reports soon emphasised the virtue of network density: 'Our business model is based on high network density and high frequency, which management believes is attractive for business travellers. As a measure of this density, the airline averaged 11.5 departures per day per city across its network during September 2001' (EasyJet 2001, Annual Report, p. 2).

And in the 2003 Annual Report (p. 14):

> Our first priority continues to be increasing frequency on existing routes as this brings economies in terms of the operations and increases the attractive-ness of EasyJet's service to consumers – particularly in the business sector. It is also the lowest risk route to growth and in the year to September 2003 this accounted for approximately two thirds of the net growth in capacity. Our second priority is to add flights between existing destinations, known as joining the dots, which benefits from synergies with existing operations and customer relationships at each destination. Our third priority is to add new destinations to the network. These collectively accounted for the other one-third of the net growth in capacity in 2003.

From the year 2000, Table 10.3 shows the upward time-trend in the average number of routes served at each of EasyJet's ports. (Of course, the daily station

Table 10.3 Network features and sold output (RPK), EasyJet, 2000–14

Year (at 30 Sep)	No. of routes flown	No. of ports served	No. of routes per port	RPK in year ending 30 Sep (billions)
2000	28	18	3.1	4.7
2001	35	17	4.1	5.9
2002	83	35	4.7	9.2
2003	105	38	5.5	17.7
2004	153	44	7.0	21.6
2005	212	64	6.6	27.4
2006	262	74	7.1	31.6
2007	289	77	7.5	37.0
2008	380	100	7.6	47.7
2009	422	114	7.4	50.6
2010	509	125	8.1	56.1
2011	547	123	8.9	61.3
2012	605	133	9.1	65.2
2013	633	138	9.1	67.6
2014	675	135	10.0	72.9

Sources: EasyJet Annual Reports for years ending 30 September

Note: The calculation of routes per port supposes that each route serves (only) two ports.

work-load – and the prospects for keeping the station staff busy – depends also on the number of flights on each route.)

Although EasyJet has been able to increase its total sold output (RPK) each year, even in difficult years like 2008 and 2009, the process of network growth is not without risk, even for a well-managed company. In a fair number of cases, EasyJet has soon withdrawn from new routes where traffic levels were lower than anticipated. (Further, it has sometimes abandoned established routes when traffic levels decreased as a result of route developments of other airlines *or* because demand for travel to a hitherto less accessible destination declined once the backlog of unmet demand had been worked out.)

Once EasyJet had become a sizeable airline, it became possible – when starting at a new port – soon to link that port to a large number of ports already in the network. At Berlin Tegel, for example, EasyJet started its first route, which was to London Luton, on 28 April 2004. By the end of that year, it operated 19 routes from Tegel.

10.3.6 Network characteristics for some large new airlines in Europe

In 2006, the three largest of the *new* airlines in Europe were EasyJet, Ryanair and Air Berlin. They had launched with, or switched to, a low-cost business model at approximately the same date. And, as seen in Table 10.4, by 2006 they were much the same size, as measured by aircraft numbers and capacity deployed (available seat kilometres, ASK). (After 2006, Air Berlin became less focussed on the LCC business model.)

Table 10.4 EasyJet, Ryanair and Air Berlin: network comparisons in 2006

	EasyJet	Ryanair	Air Berlin
Date of year end	30 Sep 2006	31 Mar 2006	31 Dec 2006
Number of ports	74	111	97
Number of routes[1]	262	305	n.a.
No. of flights (000s) for the stated year	254	227	171
Average no. of routes per port[2]	7.1	2.7	n.a.
Average no. of flights per port per day[3]	9.4	5.6	4.8
Number of aircraft in fleet	118	103	88
Annual ASK (billions)	39.1	37.1	31.4

Sources: EasyJet, Annual Report 2006 (p. 26); Ryanair, 2006 Form 20F Statement to US Stock Exchange Commission (pp. 6, 26, 28); Air Berlin, Annual Report 2006 (p. 38)

Notes
1 For Ryanair, approximate number of routes operated at 15 September 2006.
2 This calculation supposes that each route serves (only) two ports.
3 The number of flights in the year is divided by the number of ports at the end of the year. To the extent that the number of ports has increased during the year, the average figure is biased downwards.

Despite the similarities in size, there were major differences between the networks of the three carriers, even at that relatively early stage of their development. The most appropriate choices for network characteristics depend on several factors, including the kinds of travel targeted by each airline. By 2006, EasyJet sought to serve business travellers flying to major cities; such travellers favour flight frequency. In contrast, Ryanair emphasised very low fares for holiday makers, and for that situation, the best strategy may be to operate one or two flights per week per route, to minor destination ports.

11 Regional services and route subsidies

11.1 Regional carriers and their relationships with mainline companies

11.1.1 The concept of a regional route

The airline industry commonly makes a distinction between mainline routes and regional routes. Although it is difficult to define a 'regional route', it is useful to have a term for routes that are too 'small' for them to be served economically by a mainline carrier that operates a fleet of sizeable jet aircraft, each having *at least* (say) 100 seats per aircraft.

Regional routes are usually 'thin': that is, they have too few passengers to justify use of such sizeable aircraft; and they *may* be unable to support the presence of more than one airline. Also they are usually short, up to (say) 400 km in sector length. Often they are local routes in the sense that they connect a small city or town with a major city *in the same region.*

Many small-town passengers travel to the local big city in order to do personal or commercial business there, or to transfer at that port to a flight on a major carrier taking them to a distant port – in order to holiday, visit friends or relatives, or undertake business.

When the regional route is both thin and short, it is usually best to provide service using turbo-props, these days generally having between 50 and 80 seats. In contrast, jet aircraft are cost-competitive now only in larger sizes; and their deployment on thin routes may result in inadequate frequency and/or excessive cost. On a short route (say, up to a flight time of one hour) the use of a turbo-prop, rather than a jet, results in only a minimal penalty in increased journey time. And the turbo-prop uses considerably less fuel, which has become more important as fuel-prices have risen during recent decades.

However, in a few parts of the world that have low population densities, there are some very long regional routes. For example, in Western Australia, some such routes have sector lengths exceeding 1000 km. Where a turbo-prop has sufficient range, the flight duration may be too long to be acceptable; the practical outcome can be less-frequent jet service.

On some routes, where the choice between turbo-prop and jet service is not crucial, the advent of low-cost airlines has sometimes resulted in turbo-props giving way to jet aircraft. And for a route with sufficient passengers, there can be competition between two airlines – with one operating a frequent turbo-prop service, and the other using jets to provide a less frequent service. From §7.8, recall the mention of Virgin Australia deploying B737 jets when it entered the Sydney–Coffs Harbour route. In 2015, Qantas still offered a more-frequent turbo-prop service, usually with Q400 aircraft; it also overnighted an aircraft in Coffs, to serve business travellers; Virgin Australia provided twice daily flights, using E190 jets (104 seats).

11.1.2 Mainline and regional services are usually provided by separate operators

Often, a regional route is served by a separate (even if not always independent) company rather than by a major jet airline. If the mainline carrier were itself to serve regional routes, it would find it difficult if not impossible to avoid granting there the same pay and working conditions as it offers to its mainline aircrews.

In contrast, it is usually possible for a separate 'regional airline' to staff regional services in a less costly manner, by offering pay and working conditions that recognise that most regional services are rather marginal in regard to profitability. Furthermore, for pilots, flying for a regional is a common early-career opportunity.

The regional airline can be a subsidiary of the mainline jet operator that serves the major cities in the region. Otherwise the regional may be independently owned, but contracted by the major airline to provide services that connect with the flights of the major. Alternatively, an *independent* regional airline may operate without any such contractual relationship.

One reason for establishing a relationship between a regional airline and a main-line jet operator is to make arrangements for *through fares* for passengers whose journeys require the services of both companies. In the absence of airline competition, however, the through fare may be simply the sum of the two sector fares. Even then, the two airlines will probably want to make arrangements for (1) transfer of checked bags from one airline to the other, and (2) joint ticketing.

11.1.3 Setting through fares when two airlines cooperate in carrying a passenger

As already noted (§9.5.3), where *one* airline carries a passenger over two (or more) sectors, it may be in the financial interest of that airline to charge a through fare that is less than the sum of the two (or more) applicable sector fares. Where the establishment of such a through fare requires the cooperation of *two* airlines, the fare-setting process becomes very much more complicated – because the two parties have to negotiate an agreement for sharing the revenue from the ticket.

Here it is sufficient to sketch some basic ideas. The starting point is the determination of a through fare. Then, when sharing the revenue from the through fare ('prorating'), the dollar amounts going to each airline might be made proportional to the sector lengths. (To assist in such matters, IATA has prepared manuals which codify administrative procedures.)

In a competitive airline sector, there is a strong case for leaving such bargaining matters to individual airlines, while procedural details might be resolved by reference to standards established by industry cooperation. However, in the absence of vigorous competition within the regional or national route network, this approach may not serve the public interest.

For the US market, that point is brought home by comments made in 2015 by David Cush, the CEO of Virgin America ('Virgin America's CEO on his plan to force legacy carriers to let him use their feeder networks', crankyflier.com, 3 September 2015). As a relatively small mainline jet carrier, Virgin America was unable to get the large network carriers in the US to negotiate prorate agreements with Virgin America. Thus passengers travelling part of the way on Virgin America could then complete their journey only by paying a 'full' fare for the other sector, thus making the total fare significantly higher than the through fares offered by the large airlines and other companies having agreements with them.

Specifically, Cush claims:

> American, Delta and United have dozens and dozens of airlines selling into their system and [yet] they exclude low cost carriers in the US . . . we want to make sure that people who live in 90 percent of the airports that aren't hub airports can get low fares . . . when you had 6 or 7 carriers feeding these places, that was fine. There was enough competition. Now with only 3, maybe 4 if you include Southwest, how do we ensure there's competition there?

Cush wanted government intervention to correct a market failure by *requiring* the network airlines to grant uniform access to their flights, and thereby prevent the big three airlines from hindering the growth of the smaller companies such as Virgin America by refusing to deal with them.

Of course, there are some related world precedents, notably legislation that requires (monopoly) owners of essential infrastructure to grant access to rival suppliers. The case is a little harder to argue in the case of the US airline market since, in the main, the *national* industry comprises three (or perhaps four) large carriers, and formally it is not a monopoly. However most routes to smaller ports have service from only one airline (§1.3). Thus the precedents have some legitimacy.

11.1.4 Regional services in the US

Following the 1978 deregulation of inter-state aviation, many of the established trunk (network) airlines arranged with other companies to operate (mainly) short-haul services under brand names that generally included the name of the (respective) main airline. Such names included American Eagle, Continental Express, United Express and Delta Connection.

Although regional airlines in the US still have an important role in flying turbo-props on *local* routes, a major regional activity now is flying smaller jets on thin routes, sometimes over long sectors. Indeed, such 'regional' routes are much like the thinner of the routes operated by the major airlines themselves, except that they are often financially marginal.

Initially, many of the contracted regional operators were small local companies. Nowadays much of the regional service is provided by a few large companies. In 2012, several of them each carried more than 8 million passengers, and the average passenger trip length was 469 miles (Regional Airline Association (RAA), Annual Report 2013, p. 13, accessed at www.raa.org, 15 January 2014).

The same report put the 2012 aggregate regional fleet at about 1700 jet air-craft and 600 turbo-props. The so-called regional jets generally started at about 50 seats, though models introduced recently have from 70 to 115 seats. The proportion of larger jets is now increasing; and some of the shorter routes may be switched to the new, larger turbo-props.

Most of the important regional companies have grown large by contracting with more than one of the major airlines. In turn, most majors have contracted with more than one regional airline. The largest of the regional groups, Skywest (58 million passengers emplaned in 2012) operated services for American, Delta, United and US Airlines (RAA, Annual Report 2013, p. 17). That output measure is not far short of the 65 million passengers emplaned by American Airlines in that year (Bureau of Transportation Statistics, carrier snapshot, www.transtats.bts.gov, accessed 4 February 2015). (Of course, American flies longer routes on average, and so it is much further ahead of Skywest on revenue passenger miles.)

Much of the service provided by the regionals is performed under capacity purchase agreements. Though these give the regional only a modest level of operating risk, conditions in the US market sometimes induce a mainline carrier not to renew its contract, thereby leaving the regional with insufficient flying to employ a major part of its labour force, as well as its (owned) aircraft. Furthermore, the capacity purchase agreements are usually detailed and complex, which can result in costly legal battles, especially if they also contain some performance incentives. In such contexts, the size, wealth, relative security and market power of the majors can place a regional in an insecure situation. In addition, the recent and continuing need to dispose of many of the smaller jets has also disturbed the regional sector.

On the other hand, a regional *can* fly on its own account, provided that the routes it enters are not served by any of the majors with whom it has a current contract. This strategy is tried out from time-to-time, though often without success. A seeming exception was the June 2005 Mesa initiative in starting *Go!* – an inter-island low-fare carrier in Hawaii. While Go! flew for several years, it was closed by its parent in April 2014. The Mesa announcement placed empha-sis on the growth in Mesa's contracted flying for mainline carriers. However, the statement also noted that the long-term increase in the price of fuel had 'caused sustained profitability to be elusive' (Terry Maxon, 'Mesa Air to end its Hawaiian operations, Go!', *Dallas Morning News*, 17 March 2014).

11.1.5 Regional services in Australia

Although the land area of Australia roughly matches that of the 48 contiguous states in the US, most of the Australian hinterland is very sparsely populated.

In the six states and two territories, traditional business ties – formed in the nineteenth century when Australia comprised a collection of separate British colonies – were between each state capital and its in-state hinterland.

To this day, almost all the regional routes that serve small communities connect with the capital city of the state in question, which is generally also the nearest major city. In short, each state capital is a hub for *intrastate* services. To serve business travellers, a regional airline may overnight an aircraft in the small community, to allow local business people to spend a full day in the state capital.

After many airline exits and consolidations in recent years, there remain only four regional airlines of note. In 2015, an independent company, Rex, operated about 50 Saab 340 B-plus turbo-props (34 seats) on routes in New South Wales, South Australia, Victoria and Queensland. In 2014, QantasLink, a (wholly-owned) subsidiary of Qantas, operated 49 turboprops (including 30 Q400s and 16 Q300s), together with 18 B717s (Qantas Data Book, June 2014), mainly on routes in Queensland, New South Wales and Western Australia.

In Western Australia, the independent regional company Skywest was taken over by Virgin, which gave it a new name (Virgin Australia Regional Airlines), added ATR 72s to its fleet, and greatly expanded its regional territory. Air North (an independent company) operated four E170 jets and several smaller turboprops, mainly on regional routes around its Darwin base in the Northern Territory.

The sector has several distinctive features. With few exceptions, each regional route (in the strict sense) is served by only one airline. Neither of the independent companies have US-style formal contracts with the mainline jet operators. For QantasLink, small-sample studies of fares prevailing in July 2015 suggest the quoted through fare is simply the sum of the prevailing fares for the QantasLink sector and the mainline Qantas sector. A similar study for Virgin suggests that the through fare for a journey comprising one sector on Virgin and another sector on Virgin's Regional Airlines can be significantly less than the sum of the component fares.

Since 2002, several routes between state capitals and coastal holiday resorts that were previously operated by turbo-props, have been served by Virgin and Jetstar, flying (respectively) B737 and A320 aircraft. More recently, when Virgin Blue introduced Embraer E170 and E190 jets (respectively, 78 and 104 seats), it deployed them on a few of the major regional routes in New South Wales and Western Australia. Again, it becomes difficult to draw a sharp distinction between regional and mainline services.

In Australia, it is the *state* government that (may) control airline entry to *intrastate* routes. Three states pursue active roles, and all the regional airlines have received assistance of one kind or another. For some detail, see §11.2.6 below.

11.1.6 Regional services in Canada

Canada too has a large land mass with many small, remote communities, especially in Canada's north. Unlike Australia, however, it still has a significant number of small, local carriers – notwithstanding the amalgamation in 2001 of four major regional airlines into a company now called Chorus Aviation. Though the ownership of Chorus is entirely independent of Air Canada, almost all the services operated by Chorus are flown on behalf of Air Canada, under the 'Air Canada Express' tradename. Chorus thereby serves 54 ports in Canada and 25 in the United States (Chorus Aviation Inc., Annual Information Form 2013, p. 4, 28 March 2014).

At 31 December 2013, those services employed a fleet of 127 aircraft, comprising 26 CRJ 200 jets (50 seats) and 16 CRJ705 jets (75 seats), together with 64 ageing Dash 8 turboprops and 21 Q400 turboprops (74 seats) (Annual Information Form 2013, p. 7).

Previously, Chorus had a very detailed Capacity Purchase Agreement (Annual Information Form 2012, pp. 7–13), under which Air Canada paid fees based on variables such as block hours flown, number of take-offs and landings, together with fixed and variable aircraft ownership rates. The Agreement also provided for incentive payments, including some based on Chorus reaching certain performance standards regarding punctuality, reliability (proportion of planned flights actually flown) and incidence of lost bags.

Notwithstanding the amount of detail in the CPA, a dispute between the parties arose in 2010. It was November 2013 before the arbitration process reached a conclusion ('Chorus Aviation Inc. confirms successful outcome of benchmarking arbitration with Air Canada' Halifax: 26 November 2013).

In a media release ('New Capacity Purchase Agreement with Air Canada to 2025', 2 February 2015) Chorus said that the compensation structure was to change from a 'cost plus a 12.5% mark-up' to a 'fixed fee per aircraft regardless of how much an aircraft is flown'. An agreed fleet plan for the period to 31 December 2025 would see the gradual addition of a further 23 Q400s, replacing the 34 Dash 8-100s and the 25 CRJ 200s. Chorus had also reached a new long-term agreement with its pilots. The new overall style seems to reduce the risks to which Chorus is exposed.

Further, Chorus will divide its business into two operating units: Jazz will operate the 'larger, newer aircraft comprised of Q400, CRJ 200 and CRJ705 aircraft'. The second unit 'will address the requirement for improved economics' in operating the older, remaining Dash-8 100/300 fleet. Reading between those lines, it seems that Jazz will fly (mainly?) thin routes that otherwise might be flown by Air Canada itself, while the second unit will (it appears) serve routes that might be classified as regional routes in the strict sense of the term.

Regional routes to small and remote ports

While Chorus does serve a few of the more remote ports (notably, Yellowknife, Wabush and Goose Bay), most of the Canadian routes that count strictly as 'regional services' are operated by smaller carriers.

The following sample of three carriers demonstrates the character of that sector. Pacific Coastal Airlines serves ports in British Columbia, from its base at Vancouver. Air Inuit is based at Quebec City, and serves ports in northern Quebec.

Provincial Airlines is based mainly at St Johns and Halifax, flying to ports in Newfoundland, Labrador and Quebec. All are turboprop operators, principally of Dash 8 aircraft (35/50 seats) and some Saab 340s (around 35 seats). Each also deploys even smaller aircraft such as the Twin Otter and Beechcraft 1900. Relative to the very great land area of Canada, all are indeed local airlines.

11.1.7 Regional services in Europe

Most European countries have dense populations, and so the concept of regional service differs somewhat from that applicable in Canada, Australia and in some parts of the US. In Europe, flight sector lengths are often smaller, and the remote settlements may have larger populations.

United Kingdom

Although British Airways (and its predecessor British European Airways) did operate *some* domestic services connecting London with Edinburgh, Glasgow, Manchester and Belfast, other regional cities had little service. When charter airlines started flying for tour operators, they introduced *international* leisure travel routes which bypassed London. Later, EasyJet and Ryanair started both domestic and international scheduled services from regional ports, in a manner that transformed the nature of scheduled airlines services in the British regions (Civil Aviation Authority, 2005). Of course, there were also some small, early regional airlines, and some of those businesses continue to the present.

Much the largest 'regional' today began life in 1979 as a local airline serving the Channel Islands; it did not fly to London until 1991. In 2002, it changed its business model, to become a low-fare carrier, operating under the name *Flybe*. In 2007, it acquired BA Connect, a loss-making regional carrier owned by British Airways, which paid about £140 million to cover the costs of integrating the two carriers. In return, BA received 15 per cent of Flybe's shares (British Airways, Annual Report and Accounts 2007–08, pp. 29 and 90). Flybe soon ended the operation of the (50-seat) E145 jets that came with BA Connect, and shaped a new fleet, comprising Q400 turboprops and Embraer 195 and 175 jets.

In dealing with the recent adverse economic conditions in the UK and elsewhere in Europe, Flybe also began 'contract flying' (broadly similar to the capacity purchase agreements in the US). In particular, in 2011, it formed a joint venture with Finnair; this established Flybe Nordic, in which Flybe held 60 per cent of the shares, while Finnair had 40 per cent.

Flybe Nordic bought *Finncomm*, an established local carrier, and reshaped its domestic and regional services. Flybe managed the flying, but did not secure profitability. In January 2015, Flybe announced it had sold its shares (for a nominal monetary amount) to two commercial investors in Finland (Alan Dron, 'Flybe draws line under Finnish venture', *Air Transport World*, 12 November 2014; Flybe, 'Q3 2014/15 Trading Update', 26 January 2015).

Meanwhile the company was making some headway in lifting the performance of Flybe UK, the largest division in the group. At end-March 2015, the UK (committed) fleet comprised 43 Q400 turboprops, 11 E175 jets and just three remaining E195s (FY 2015, Results Presentation, 10 June 2015).

In addition, *Loganair* (which became a Flybe franchisee in 2008) continued to serve routes in the north of Scotland, including services to the Shetland Islands.

Eastern Airways launched in 1997. In June 2015, it had a fleet of 18 Jetstream 41 turboprops (29 seats), together with 9 Saab 2000s (50 seats) serving (mainly) small ports in the UK (Wikipedia article, accessed 29 June 2015). It is based at Humberside and has hubs at Aberdeen and Newcastle. It targets business travellers, to whom it sells convenient direct services, inevitably at high fares (CAPA, 'Eastern Airways expansion moves it up the ladder', 7 October 2010).

In 2009, it established a small base at Dijon (France), with services to Bordeaux, Toulouse and Nantes (anna.aero, 29 September 2010). In recent years, it has launched some international routes, notably from Aberdeen and Newcastle to Stavanger and Bergen.

Germany

Despite the entry of new carriers, the established national airline Lufthansa is still a major presence on domestic and other short-haul routes, in part because of its ownership of smaller low-cost airlines, including Eurowings and Germanwings, which hub at ports such as Munich, Frankfurt and Cologne. One of their tasks is to fly thin routes for Lufthansa, serving Germany and nearby European countries. Thus they have little of the character of a regional airline in the strict sense.

Otherwise, Germany seems to have remarkably little in the way of local, regional airlines operating aircraft of modest size. A small aviation company, Air Hamburg, engages in a range of activities, including scheduled service from Hamburg to Sylt and other German islands in the North Sea, flying BN-2 Islander and Cessna 172 aircraft (Wikipedia on Air Hamburg, accessed on 6 February 2015).

Operating under EU rules, a Dutch regional carrier, AIS Airlines, started a second route from Munster/Osnabruck on 13 January 2014, this one to Zurich, using a 19-seat Jetstream 32. Its first route at Munster is a domestic service to Stuttgart (anna.aero, 15 January 2014).

France

As in Germany, *mainland* France has few if any remote regions for which air service might be of particular social importance. Nevertheless, the size/terrain of France lends support to a considerable number of inter-regional routes, even after the development of TGV (rail) services that can offer competitive door-to-door journey times in some cases.

From the 1950s onwards, the presence of such routes encouraged the establishment of a number of significant domestic airlines. Sooner or later, Air France developed links with many of these (including Air Inter, and – later – Brit Air). Ultimately they became wholly-owned subsidiaries of Air France, as did three other companies merged by Air France to form Régional. Two other companies,

Air Liberté and TAT, were taken over by British Airways which did not manage to make them profitable, and ultimately closed them.

Eventually, it was the entry of EasyJet and Ryanair that yielded better service and more passengers on a number of important inter-regional routes (cf. Chapter 2). Air France then began to pay more attention to those routes.

Italy

Unlike Germany and France, Italy has a marked regional economic disparity between north and south, and the latter region includes some islands that are distant from Milan and Rome. Furthermore, the national airline Alitalia has gradually lost its dominant position. In 2015, when Etihad bought 49 per cent of its shares, Alitalia became an Etihad Airways Partner (Alitalia media release, 'Alitalia looks at the future . . .', 4 June 2015).

Of the remaining independent airlines that are domiciled in Italy, two significant companies had their origins in the south. The larger of the two, *Meridiana*, was founded in Sardinia in 1963 by HH Prince Aga Khan, whose aim was to develop the island's north east region (Olbia and the Emerald Coast). The Italian government granted route concessions, which eventually included some routes *between* major mainland ports. The company also started services to Sicily.

In February 2010, Meridiana took over Eurofly, a company providing charter flights to long-haul destinations. Then, in October 2011, it acquired Air Italy, another charter airline which however 'now operates connections on behalf of Meridiana' ('About us', meridiana.it, accessed 21 January 2014). With these acquisitions, Meridiana became the second largest carrier domiciled in Italy!

Meridiana also embarked on restructuring to reduce costs and improve revenues, a campaign that was not rewarded by early profitability. Nevertheless, despite recent adventures, the company still provided important service between mainland ports and the islands of Sardinia (Olbia, Alghero and Cagliari) and Sicily. In that sense, it remained a regional carrier, despite its variegated all-jet fleet of MD 82s, A320s and B737s.

The second company, Wind Jet, had a much shorter history. Founded in 2003, with headquarters at Catania in the island of Sicily, the company quickly developed a sizeable network with hubs at Catania, Palermo and (in northern Italy) at Forli, later shifted to Rimini. The difficult trading conditions following the general financial crisis endangered Wind Jet. In 2012, when Alitalia decided eventually not to make a takeover bid, Wind Jet soon ceased flying. It had enjoyed major market shares at several island ports ('Wind Jet collapse bad news for Catania', anna.aero, 16 August 2012). Nevertheless, there were other airlines (notably Meridiana) which could fill the gaps.

Other European countries

Notable remote communities in Europe include the sparsely populated areas in the north of Scandinavia and Finland, and various islands in north-west Europe and in the Mediterranean.

Several *Greek islands* too have important airline service. In 2009, three airlines shared the role: the declining Olympic Air, the rising Aegean Airlines and a privately owned newcomer Athens Airways, operating Embraer ERJ-145 jets, configured with 49 seats. The newcomer ceased operations in September 2010, after losing governmental route subsidies following complaints of performance shortcomings (Wikipedia entry on Athens Airways, accessed 22 January 2014). In late 2013, Aegean's purchase of Olympic left the island routes being flown by the turboprops formerly operated by Olympic.

While *Norway* is not an EU member state, it has adopted EU aviation rules. The sparsely populated northern part of the country is served by Wideroe, whose fleet comprised 42 turboprops (11 Q400s with 78 seats, and 31 Dash 8s, mostly 39 seats) (wideroe.no, accessed 9 February 2014).

In *Finland*, the entrant Blue 1 started services even to ports in the north, eventually including Ivalo (the most northerly port in Finland with scheduled service), which Blue 1 served three times per week, using MD 90 aircraft with 166 seats (Blue 1 media release, 3 November 2008, blue1.com). However, by 2014, Blue 1 no longer served Ivalo and Rovaniemi. Indeed, since becoming a subsidiary of SAS Group, Blue 1 flies B717s (115 seats), and seems somewhat more directed to providing passenger feed for SAS, with less emphasis on serving as a regional airline.

At the same time, EU policy *has* supported the establishment and growth of truly *local* airlines. In Finland, for example, Air Åland was founded in 2005 by Åland residents and business people, in order to provide services from Mariehamn (on the main island of Åland) west to the (nearby) Swedish capital (Stockholm) and east to mainland Finland, initially to Helsinki, but later to Turku instead. On the routes to Stockholm and Turku, the flight time is 30 minutes. The services *were* flown for it by a Swedish company, NextJet, using Saab 340A aircraft. In 2012, NextJet assumed direct responsibility for the flights (airaland.com, accessed 6 February 2015).

Aer Arann provides another example. Founded in 1970 to serve the Aran Islands off Galway on Ireland's west coast, the company started with Britten-Norman Islanders (9 seats) for a 10-minute hop to each island destination, from Connemara Regional Airport (about 40 km from the city of Galway). In due course, the company entered other routes, with larger aircraft. The expansion gathered pace in the 1990s and 2000s, first within Ireland, then to the UK. Later, it started summer services to ports in northern France.

In January 2010, Aer Arann and Aer Lingus established a franchise arrangement under which Aer Arann flew some routes to the UK under the Aer Lingus Regional brand. In March 2012, the partners extended the franchise, so that *all* flights branded as Aer Lingus Regional were operated by Aer Arann, which took the commercial risk, and paid franchise fees to Aer Lingus. From such services to Scotland and northern England, Aer Lingus also sought passenger feed for its transatlantic services to several ports in the US and Canada.

In late 2010, financial problems had put Aer Arann into 'Examinership' (broadly, the Irish equivalent of Chapter 11 in the US) for a couple of months, while the company sought additional investment funds. The immediate result was that the Stobart Group became a shareholder in Aer Arann. Continuing the company's turboprop tradition, Aer Arann then ordered eight new ATR 72s, with delivery of the last planned for mid-2014.

By March 2014, the Stobart Group had become the largest shareholder. That Group then announced that the airline name was to become Stobart Air, which would acquire a further eight new ATR 72-600 (turboprop) aircraft and extend its franchise agreement with Aer Lingus (media release, 'Aer Arann is to change its corporate name to Stobart Air', 20 March 2014).

Within weeks, Stobart Air announced it had entered into a similar franchise agreement with Flybe. From (London) Southend Airport (also owned by the Stobart Group), Stobart Air was to launch six routes, each having a short sector across the water to a nearby port in France, Belgium, Netherlands or Germany. For these routes, Stobart was to base two ATR 72 aircraft at Southend (media release 'Stobart Air announces partnership with Flybe' 25 March 2014).

Meanwhile the Arann Islands services continue to be flown with Islander aircraft, now operated by a separate company, Aer Arann Islands, with its own Air Operator Certificate.

11.2 'Public service obligations' and regional air services

11.2.1 A public service obligation as a justification for government subsidy

For a thin regional route, the prospective revenue may be insufficient to cover the costs of supply no matter how efficient the airline and how well designed the service. For the provision of many *other* goods and services, that would be the end of the story: markets offer supply only when the revenue is large enough to reward the supplier.

In the case of airline service, however, governments sometimes consider there are public-policy grounds for ensuring some provision. Where airline route-entry is regulated, a government sometimes requires an airline to operate some unprofitable routes, with the deficits funded out of the profits it earns on its other routes.

Upon deregulation, that cross-subsidy mechanism is no longer available. Then the government may decide to provide a direct financial subsidy. For any government committed to market capitalism, this extreme step may be justifiable only to support an over-arching political and social policy, typically one involving economic support for citizens living in 'remote' regions, in which – the government considers – it is in the national interest to maintain human presence and economic activity. (Sometimes, the underlying rationale rests on national security or other geopolitical considerations.)

While the subsidy will benefit the airline as well as those who travel, the government can try to ensure that the supplier receives no more than a 'normal' rate of profit. To obtain some sort of 'value for money', the government can select routes for subsidy by employing a simple rule-of-thumb, for example by setting an upper limit on the subsidy amount per passenger-journey. Such scrutiny may help to determine in a sensible manner which routes get priority, and how much service might be provided on each.

Whenever a 'worthy cause' has been identified, a common terminology is to identify that act of supply as a 'public service obligation' (PSO). For low-cost provision of the service pattern that the government wants, the government may invite bids for individual routes and/or for groups of routes that may be combined to allow cost savings in provision. Then, for each route entity, the government can award an exclusive contract to the airline requiring the smallest subsidy, subject to conditions for minimum service quality.

Sometimes, the lowest bidder may not require *any* subsidy. The grant of *exclusive* access to a route or group of routes assures the winning airline that no other company can 'cherry pick' – that is, operate on the route at times when the service is profitable, while not serving the route at other times for which the government wants service. For example, *exclusive* access to a route to an island which attracts large numbers of tourists in summer might induce an airline to offer year-round service without (any) *government* subsidy. (Of course, that deal is likely to involve a form of cross-subsidy between passenger groups.)

11.2.2 The legislated situation in the EU

As noted in §2.2.2, the European Union has adopted a formal framework to outlaw 'state aid' except in a few circumstances – which include situations in which a Member State wishes to grant financial assistance (under Article 87 of the Treaty) to support remote regions that suffer economic disadvantage.

Under that provision, a Member State may declare that the provision of air services on a route is a 'public service obligation', because such service is needed to support the economic development of the region. The rules for the PSO mechanism were first set down in 1992, in (EEC) Regulation 2408, where Article 4 allows the Member State to specify the service it requires on such a route. (Regulation 2408 was superseded in 2008; on that, see §11.2.4 below.)

Where commercial provision is not forthcoming, Regulation 2408 allowed the State to limit access to the route to only one air carrier (for a period not exceeding three years, following which a review was required), and then announce its willingness to provide a subsidy. The right to supply air services (for a period of up to three years) was then offered for public tender – either for the single route of for a group of related routes (as determined by the Member State). *Any* airline domiciled in the Community had the right to tender. Although international routes were not excluded, in practice almost every PSO route has been between an airport pair within a single state.

11.2.3 Some contentious PSO cases arising in the EU

There have been complaints (especially from low-cost airlines) that in a few cases, the government of a Member State has arranged the procedures in a manner that favours airlines based in that Member State. A considerable controversy arose in Italy. The discussion below deals also with PSO cases in Ireland. The details show that, in awarding PSO routes to individual airlines, commercial and political realities can lead to extraordinary situations.

Routes serving Sardinia

In a media release (7 April 2006), EasyJet said it had announced plans to fly between Milan Malpensa (where it had a new base) and Olbia (in Sardinia). In response, 'the Italian Civil Aviation Authority (ENAC) took the unprecedented step of writing to EasyJet to request that the airline stopped selling seats on the route'. On 21 April, EasyJet reported it had:

> filed a legal challenge in the Italian courts and lodged a complaint with the European Commission. While the court case is pending, the airline [had] planned to continue to operate the route, taking the dramatic step of flying all of the passengers for free. This was a perfectly legal alternative as the European regulation 2408/92 . . . clearly states this [regulation] applies only to 'the transport of passengers for remuneration. . . . However, this morning . . . ENAC representatives at Milan Airport, backed by Italian police, closed down the EasyJet check-in for the Olbia flight.

In consequence the airline had to cancel the flight; and its 149 passengers had to 'travel with the monopoly carrier – who had an aircraft prepared especially for the occasion.'

In the outcome, the administrative court of Lazio found against EasyJet and blocked its flights from Milan to Olbia for the time being. The airline noted (media release, 12 May 2006) that the European Commission was already investigating the matter, and 'we are confident that Commission will soon end this abuse of these subsidised monopolies in Italy'. Meanwhile, some Italian airlines would 'continue to share a nice, rich cake presented to them on a silver plate by ENAC and the Transport Ministry. But it is the people of Sardinia and the Italian taxpayer who have to foot the bill.'

A year *earlier*, Ryanair had 'welcomed the announcement by ENAC, the Italian Civil Aviation Authority, which yesterday cleared the way for Ryanair's low fare flights to commence on the Rome Ciampino–Alghero (Sardinia) route' (media release, 20 April 2005). However, a year later, in a media release of 20th April 2006, Ryanair voiced concerns broadly similar to those of EasyJet, regarding the future of its services on that route from Rome, following a separate ENAC decision. It added: 'Ryanair has already carried 100,000 passengers on the Rome–Alghero route in its first year of operation with fares of less than 40 euro and with no subsidies, which also means that the Italian taxpayer is not being gouged either.' On 12 May, Ryanair said it too would appeal the decision of the regional administrative court of Lazio.

It was April 2007 before the Commission published its decisions. In its report (European Commission, 2007b), it noted (paragraphs 20–2) that the rules on

PSOs must be 'interpreted strictly and in accordance with the principles of non-discrimination and proportionality'.

Concerning the geographical and social context, the Commission accepted (pars. 29 and 31) that Sardinia is a peripheral region with a vital need for the air connections concerned. Accordingly, it judged 'that imposing PSOs concerning frequency, capacity and fares may be necessary' (par. 36).

However it judged also that 'some of the conditions imposed [by the Italian authorities] are unduly restrictive or disproportionate'. These undesirable conditions included:

- the 30-day deadline that had been imposed for airline responses to the tender invitation (par. 38);
- the requirement that an airline should guarantee service for at least 36 months (par. 42);
- the requirement to offer discounted fares to persons born on Sardinia but not resident there (par. 62); and
- the grouping of routes – which put Alghero–Rome and Alghero–Milan into a single package, and likewise for Olbia–Rome and Olbia–Milan – and required that any bidding airline must offer to serve both of the routes in a package (par. 58).

In that last regard, the Commission noted that total passenger numbers in 2005 were about 731,000 for the two Olbia routes, and 503,000 for the two Alghero routes, and concluded 'it is unlikely that these routes . . . are so unattractive that they need to be grouped in order to attract operators' (par. 57).

At the time, EasyJet operated from its Milan (Malpensa) base, but had no services at Rome. And Ryanair operated from its base at Rome Ciampino but did not serve Milan (Malpensa or Linate). Thus neither airline could readily serve *both* Milan and Rome in the manner specified by the Italian authorities. On the other hand, it seemed that local airlines (such as Meridiana and Air One) could base aircraft at the two Sardinian ports, and would thereby find it easy to operate from each to both Milan and Rome.

In the outcome, the Commission decided to allow the PSO arrangements to stand, subject to removal of several offending restrictions. In effect (and as demonstrated by the February 2008 (*winter*) airline timetables) the Commission's decision allowed Ryanair and EasyJet to serve the (thinner!) routes on which they had embarked, while allowing the Italian authorities to select which companies were to serve the other routes.

Some Irish routes

The EC publishes a table listing PSO routes in the European Union, and updates it from time to time. The table dated 21 January 2009 showed that the Irish government had awarded (for three-year terms, starting 22 July 2008) exclusive route subsidies for domestic services from Dublin to Derry, Donegal, Galway, Kerry, Knock and Sligo. The Kerry route was awarded to Ryanair, and the others to Aer Arann. Using data reportedly released by the (Irish) Department of Transport, Ryanair (media release 21 May 2008) claimed that on *its* route the subsidy per passenger-journey would be about €18, while the corresponding figures for the other routes ranged from €46 to €99.

Ryanair interpreted the subsidies as benefiting mainly airlines and airports, and suggested that the total taxpayer funding of €45 million (over three years) could be better spent on health and education services, while the passengers travelled by bus. It seems the Irish government did not (immediately) act on the advice.

11.2.4 PSO routes in the EU considered as a whole

Following such experiences with the initial EC regulation made in 1992, the EC adopted a new text for PSO provisions, set out in Articles 16–18 of Regulation (EC) No 1008/2008 . . . on Common Rules for the Operation of Air Services. The new regulation sought to provide a more careful statement of *all* the legal provisions for EC air services, in the hope of reducing the incidence of controversies; it also included some substantive changes.

Among the latter was a PSO contract length of up to four years (rather than the previous limit of three years), and up to five years for a route to an airport serving 'an outermost region' (as defined) (Article 16, clause 9). The new regulation also introduced some explicit empirical criteria. For example, in considering whether an airline service is needed at all, the Member State proposing a PSO is required to consider the possibility of using some other transport mode, especially when rail services offer 'a travel time of less than three hours' (Article 16, clause 3).

Comparison of the PSO tables published on 21 January 2009 and on 25 February 2013 suggests that there has been a reduction in the number of PSO routes. The PSO payments are still almost always made to a local air carrier, rather than to an airline from another Member State. Even so, the use of the PSO arrangement as a back-door means of paying subsidies to local airlines seems to have diminished. (The cautious wording here reflects the apparently haphazard and incomplete compilation of the table. Even the February 2013 table records that 'This table is a working document . . . [and] may contain errors and omissions'.)

Nevertheless, that table (accessed on 3 February 2014) serves to give a useful broad impression of the programme. Only six EU countries make a substantial appearance, together with Norway (which follows the EU aviation rules). In the case of the UK and Norway, the PSO routes serve very small and remote communities, with the subsidies going mainly to Loganair and Wideroe respectively. Greece, Italy Spain, Portugal and France all include routes serving islands, but there are also some mainland routes that are less obviously deserving. In those countries, the airlines flying PSO routes are generally more substantial operators, and some fly jet aircraft. In Greece, however, the Aegean takeover of Olympic (cf. §2.4.1) may result in a renewed focus on turbo-prop services on the island routes.

The 2013 table also seems to show that some specific PSO arrangements have been ended. That includes the services between Alghero and Bologna and between Alghero and Turin, whose PSO status was repealed on 13 January 2014, with notice given by Italy, and published in the *Official Journal of the European Union* of 31 January 2014. Ryanair then entered the Bologna route, starting daily service on 3 February 2014, with the aircraft flying from and returning to Alghero! (The 'new routes' record on the Ryanair website indicated that the company would also fly 15 other routes from Alghero, beginning on dates in April and May 2014; however, those appear to be summer routes only, with limited frequencies.)

Also noteworthy is the continued presence on the (active) PSO list of routes from Strasbourg to Amsterdam, Copenhagen, Madrid and Prague. Perhaps those services benefit some of the Members of the European Parliament, and European Commission staff members.

11.2.5 The 'Essential Air Service' arrangements in the US

Upon the enactment of the (US) Airline Deregulation Act 1978, Congress established an 'Essential Air Service' (EAS) programme to provide scheduled airline service to small communities which might otherwise lose service following deregulation. In §278 of the Federal Aviation Reauthorization Act 1996, Congress found that the programme 'is necessary for the economic growth and development of rural communities' and put the programme on to a 'permanent' basis. In recent times, Congress voted funds annually; for the financial year 2012, the amount was US$214 million.

Beginning in 2011, Congress has passed a series of reforms. Now, the Department of Transportation is prohibited from making any EAS payment for a community where the annual average per-passenger-journey subsidy exceeds US$1,000. The FAA Modernisation and Reform Act 2012 requires that a subsidised service must carry an average of at least ten passengers per service per day. Subsidy is available only for those communities that received EAS support at any time between 30 September 2010 and 30 September 2011. However, exceptions from those requirements apply for those communities that are more than 175 driving miles from the nearest large or medium air-services hub, and for all communities in the states of Alaska and Hawaii (Department of Transportation, Essential Air Service, updated 29 June 2015, accessed at transportation.gov, 23 September 2015).

The Regional Airline Association reported (at p. 27 of its 2014 Annual Report, accessed at raa.org, 3 June 2015) that 'While the Department had initially used its discretion to waive enforcement of the new criteria, more recently, DOT has begun measuring compliance, a step towards enforcement. Such enforcement could have broad implications for the program, as dozens of communities would need to increase enplanements or risk losing air service.' It also noted: 'Funding for FY2015 is authorized at approximately $258 million.'

Since 2002, however, the Department of Transportation has also run a Small Community Air Service Development Program (DOT media release 'U.S. Transportation Secretary Foxx Announces $5.5 Million in Grants to Small Communities to Help Develop and Improve Local Air Service' 15 September 2015). That annual expenditure was to support eleven communities which themselves were to contribute a total of US$4.6 million, together with some in-kind support.

11.2.6 Government support in some of the Australian states

Among the Australian states, New South Wales, Queensland and Western Australia are spatially large enough to have significant numbers of intra-state routes. Each of those states has legislation allowing its government to regulate intra-state services. Government interventions are of particular interest in the cases of New South Wales and Queensland.

New South Wales

Under the Air Transport Act 1964, the state government has chosen (since 2002) to regulate entry only on routes which connect a small or regional community with Sydney (the state capital) *and* have less than 50,000 (one-way) passenger journeys annually. The more dense routes, from Sydney to several coastal and other cities, attract holidaymakers as well as business and other local travellers; on those routes, airlines are free to compete. (Those routes accommodate about 87 per cent of the intra-state passengers.)

In March 2013, the government issued *exclusive* five-year licences for some 15 routes, each giving non-stop service between Sydney and a single port. As before, while offering route monopolies, it did not offer *any* direct subsidies. The licences went to: Rex (flying Saab 340 turboprops) 9 routes; QantasLink (one route, to Lord Howe Island); and a small independent company, Brindabella (5 routes averaging about 13,000 passenger journeys annually) (transport.nsw. gov.au, accessed 7 February 2014).

From time to time, some of the thinnest routes go unserved, especially when a small licence holder goes out of business. In December 2013, the (Australian) Civil Aviation Safety Authority required Brindabella to perform maintenance reviews on a further six of its aircraft ('Brindabella Airlines maintenance reviews', casa.gov.au, 13 December 2013). This effectively grounded the aircraft, and Brindabella ceased flying.

In the outcome, the route between Mudgee and Sydney remained unserved until June 2015. Then, following a state government decision to *deregulate* the route, *FlyPelican* started twice-daily round-trips upon receiving financial support from the Mid-Western Regional Council.

The route from Narrabri to Sydney was also without airline service for a period in 2014. There is a daily train service, with a journey time exceeding seven hours.

Queensland

In contrast to the NSW practice, the Queensland government allows airlines to bid for individual routes and/or for self-formulated groupings of routes. (The settlements in much of the northern part of the state are small, remote and numerous.) In 2008 the government sought tenders for ten routes, most of which had several intermediate ports.

In the outcome, the successful route groupings were unchanged. Exclusive five-year route-licences were again assigned to QantasLink (*without* route-subsidies) and to MacAir (an independent company). However, after MacAir had obtained some better aircraft in order to honour new quality commitments, it became financially unable to continue even its subsidised services, and went into voluntary administration in January 2009.

After making temporary arrangements for those routes, the government invited new tenders. In December 2009, it issued new five-year licences. This allowed (the NSW-based) Rex to gain a substantial presence in Queensland. Other routes were licensed to Skytrans, then a Dash-8 charter operator based at Cairns, in far north Queensland. The annual subsidies for the re-issued licences amounted to a total of about AU$8.5 million (Queensland Department of Transport and Main Roads 'Contracted air services', and 'Map of Long-distance Passenger Services', both accessed 7 February 2014 at tmr.qld.gov.au). The government extended the QantasLink licences to December 2014, at which date it was to make new arrangements for all the licensed routes.

After undertaking a review of long-distance passenger services on all transport modes, the Queensland government decided to deregulate (from 1 January 2015) three air routes previously operated by QantasLink under exclusive service contracts but without subsidy. Those services included two long routes north from Cairns to Weipa and Cairns to Horn Island (Department of Transport and Main Roads 'Revocation of Service Contract Routes – Air Services' 1 December 2014, accessed at *tmr.qld.gov.au*). (However, the Qantas and Virgin booking engines, when accessed on 30 June 2015, showed that Virgin was not flying the Weipa route, whereas Qantas offered three round-trip flights on weekdays, and fewer flights at the weekend.

For the *other* previously contracted routes, the government invited tenders for five-year exclusive contracts. In the outcome, QantasLink retained its two routes, Rex retained its two routes and also bid successfully for three other routes then being operated by Skytrans (Department of Transport and Main Roads, 'Long distance passenger services', 31 December 2014, accessed at tmr.qld.gov.au). Having thereby lost its government subsidies, Skytrans ceased trading, after 25 years in business ('Skytrans ceases trading', www.skytrans.com.au, accessed 2 January 2015). This resulted in termination of services on three Skytrans *commercial* routes in the Cape York area. For those routes, the state government made a temporary arrangement with another small operator, while other airlines considered their positions ('Long distance passenger services', 31 December 2014).

11.3 Airlines sometimes receive financial support for launch of new routes

Other route-specific subsidies are commonly offered to airlines by airports, tourist authorities and governments, in order to promote the launch of routes not previously served. Among many recorded instances, a notable case arose in 2006 when EasyJet was expanding its Edinburgh base (media release, 'EasyJet announces *massive* expansion from Edinburgh: three NEW direct European routes – Madrid–Milan–Palma', 18 December 2006).

The media release reported:

> The daily Edinburgh – Madrid service that commences on 25 February and the daily Milan service that commences on 21 May are a result of investment from the Scottish Executive, in the form of the route development fund. This is a scheme introduced to support new direct air links, which will bring economic benefits to Scotland. EasyJet will also benefit from funding, in the form of marketing support, from VisitScotland, to help promote Scotland as a destination in Spain and Italy.

11.4 Concluding remarks

11.4.1 The rationales of regional airlines

As the examples have shown, regional airlines vary markedly in their roles. Some operate only turbo-prop aircraft, often of no more than 50 seats, and fly genuinely local routes, often with sector lengths of around 250 to 300 km. In that context, there is rarely more than one company serving the route.

Other (so-called) 'regionals' fly small jets, with capacities of between 50 and 110 seats. The typical number of seats is increasing as rising fuel costs make the use of small jets too expensive. Many of those jet services are distinguished from those of the main airlines only by the number of passengers. When a regional airline flies such routes, it secures lower cost-levels and/or higher flight frequencies than would apply if a main airline were to fly the route with larger jets, crewed at higher rates of pay.

11.4.2 The pros and cons of declaring public service obligations

After allowing the legitimacy of a sovereign government's authority to subsidise airline service to promote government regional policies, there remain two major issues. First, does any particular route make a deserving case – that is, does it meet the criteria laid down for the government's regional policy? And if it does, are the proposed contractual arrangements well designed, in the sense of being proportionate with the policy goals, and providing subsidy to the users rather than excessive funding for the airline (that is, funding over and above the minimum needed to secure supply through a well-designed competitive tender).

The examples considered above suggest that the routes seen as public service obligations, and hence given government financial support, are very varied, in respect of both passenger numbers and the remoteness and other characteristics of the communities served. In the US, the long-overdue reform of the Essential Air Service programme may help to blunt the earlier strong criticisms. In the Australian states, the route-choices seem sensible, but the information publicly available does not always allow judgement on whether the scale of support is appropriate.

In most of the European countries – where it is island or other very remote communities that are served – the same qualified approval seems appropriate.

In the last few years, even the previously questionable matters concerning the Italian routes to Sardinia and Sicily have been resolved in large measure: in particular, more routes have been opened up to allow operation of the standard EU rules on route entry.

In almost all cases in the EU and elsewhere, the arrangements for public service obligations are predicated on the idea that the route will be served by only one airline. In one or two exceptional Australian cases, where the annual passenger number might approach or exceed 100,000, there have been attempts to license two airlines, without subsidy but with assurance that no other company may enter the route. This modest experience suggests that in general, a *stable* two-airline equilibrium may not be achievable.

The likely reality is that any route which is (at best) commercially marginal will be served by one airline only. In such cases, it may well be in the public interest for government to grant an exclusive licence, on condition that the airline meets service standards specified by the government. Of course, the onus is then on government to ensure that it specifies sensible standards.

12   Airlines and airports

12.1 Changes in airline–airport relationships

Because airports and airlines *together* supply services to air passengers, they have an incentive to cooperate in order to secure large (net) revenues from those passengers. Of course, when it comes to sharing out those revenues, port and airline interests often diverge.

The level and style of airport charges are influenced by several underlying factors. Broadly, the greater the airport's market power, the higher will be the charges. In turn, market power is increased by proximity to one or more large population centres, by the amount of airline traffic the port has already attracted (because that traffic gives each airline an opportunity to exchange interlining passengers), and by the absence of *competing* airports nearby. In particular, where a large conurbation has two or more airports owned by the one company or government agency – a common situation – there will rarely be any price or other competition between them.

12.1.1 Relations between airports and regulated airlines

When economic regulation sheltered airlines from competitive pressures, air fares could be high enough to yield rather handsome airline revenues, often exceeding the norm that would apply in a competitive market. While the airline itself would prefer to assign any such surplus to its own interests, airports could sometimes use *their* market power to extract a handsome share.

At large ports, such extra airport revenues often encouraged additional capital expenditures – in particular, lavish expenditure on larger and more luxurious passenger terminals – ostensibly intended to enhance the service to passengers. However, the expenditure sometimes seemed to go beyond the level that the passengers would have preferred, had they been allowed to choose a lower standard offered at a lower level of airport charges.

One motive behind the lavish standards may have been to enlarge the 'empire' of the airport managers, who thereby hoped to increase their personal remuneration. At privately owned ports subject to economic regulation, such 'gold-plating' often serves also to increase the owners' profits. (That is examined in §12.4.3 below.)

In contrast, small airports – including most ports serving small-population areas – generally had little or no market power. In many cases it was local pride and ambition that led local government authorities to build and operate such ports. Even with user charges set at low levels, there were often few flights and few passengers. Financial deficits were common – with revenues sometimes failing to cover operating costs, let alone fund the capital costs.

In the early years after World War II, even a very large city typically had only a single airport, which usually enjoyed a *regional* monopoly. The airline that wished to serve such a major market (and perhaps also attract transfer passengers) had no practicable alternative to paying the charges sought by the airport operator.

As the number of passengers increased, second airports were built at some of the very largest cities. In the beginning, at least, these were but poor relations. Often the established national airlines were unwilling to switch *any* flights, if only because of their interest in serving transfer passengers. At the most, those airlines might operate some minor routes from the second airport.

On the other hand, in some European countries, the new ports attracted charter flights, especially those operated on behalf of package-holiday companies. For such travel, there was no airline advantage in operating from a major port. Rather the charter airlines were glad to use a small port with lower charges and (often) a quick turnaround, thanks to less runway congestion.

For example, in the 1960s, a few European charter services were the only users of the (then) new Malpensa Airport, which is about 45 km from Milan (while the close-in port at Linate is some 7 km from the city centre). Many years passed before Malpensa attracted scheduled airline services. (And only *after* such development did Malpensa gain a passenger rail service.)

London Gatwick provides another example. Built as an alternative to the increasingly congested London Heathrow airport, Gatwick's early users were charter airlines and some foreign scheduled airlines that could not obtain access at Heathrow or preferred not to pay the higher charges levied there.

12.1.2 The airport preferences of low-cost carriers

However, in Europe in particular, the dominance of the major airports diminished as the low-cost airlines entered the industry. In the early days, *all* the new carriers worked very hard to achieve cost levels that were well below those of the so-called legacy airlines – in order to be able to offer lower fares and hence gain a place in the market. And besides pressing for lower airport charges, the new airlines sometimes managed to persuade airports that any increase in terminal capacity should be effected in a low-cost manner.

As in the case of charter airlines, the LCC aimed to carry passengers directly to their final destination. Thus, the LCC had no particular reason for using a major port served by many airlines, rather than a (cheaper) secondary port.

Furthermore, in its early days especially, a LCC might have a wide choice of ports that it could add to its list. If airport A was rather expensive to use, the LCC might instead start flights to airport B or airport X, in another region or even another country.

One further factor that encouraged the low-cost carriers to choose low-cost airports was the willingness of many low-fare passengers to fly to a minor or secondary airport at (say) 50 km distance from the major urban destination, and then complete the journey by bus or train. That was particularly important in Europe, where there were many alternative ports – usually little used and hence ready to offer facilities at low charges. Some of those ports had been built for military purposes, during or after World War II (Barbot, 2006, p. 197). Examples include Charleroi (in Belgium), Frankfurt-Hahn (Germany), Bergamo–Orio al Serio (Italy) and Prestwick (Scotland).

In their different ways, the two European early-mover LCCs – EasyJet and Ryanair – have made considerable use of low-charge airports. The next section considers those and other specific airline cases.

12.2 Initial airport strategies of some new airlines

12.2.1 Southwest Airlines opted for in-town airports

By 1969, all the major airlines had left the close-in Houston airport, Hobby, and had switched to the new Houston Intercontinental Airport, which was about 30 km from down-town Houston. Initially, Southwest Airlines too chose Houston Intercontinental. However, finding few passengers on its flights, Southwest soon switched to Hobby, and its passenger numbers increased significantly. Though Hobby had no other airline presence, passengers liked the Southwest service, because of the more convenient airport location, and because the uncongested conditions there promoted flight punctuality, and a quick passenger transit through the terminal (Freiberg and Freiberg, 1996, p. 23)?

Dallas presented a broadly similar situation. In the early 1970s, construction was underway of a new, very large 'hub' airport, Dallas–Fort Worth (DFW), at a greenfield site located between the cities of Dallas and Fort Worth. The incumbent airlines serving Dallas had signed an agreement to help fund the new airport, and to accept *some* responsibility for operating losses incurred there (Freiberg and Freiberg, 1996, p. 23).

When DFW opened in January 1974, the established airlines serving the downtown port, Love, moved all their Dallas flights to the new airport ('Texas maverick', *Newsweek*, 6 May 1974, pp. 43–4). But Southwest Airlines, which was not a party to the agreement, again thought that its (short-haul) passengers would prefer to use Love rather than travel 30 km from downtown Dallas to DFW.

When it became clear that Southwest would remain at Love, Braniff and Texas International moved some flights back to Love. Fearing a financial disaster at DFW, the airport board and the cities of Dallas and Fort Worth pursued several legal approaches in an attempt to resolve the issue. In particular, Dallas tried but failed to evict *all* the airlines from Love.

Southwest was pleased to be able to remain there, and by 1977 its legal battles seemed to be over. Furthermore, when the 1978 (US) Airline Deregulation Act allowed new airlines to apply for CAB (Civil Aeronautics Board) licences for interstate routes, Southwest obtained authorisation to fly between Dallas and New Orleans.

However, the local opposition was intense. In the US Congress, Jim Wright (Fort Worth member and House majority leader) sought a ban on all interstate services at Love Field. After many months of wrangling, a compromise was reached: the so-called Wright amendment (to the *International* Air Transportation *Competition* Act of 1979 – italics added) banned direct (non-stop or through-plane) service from Love to any city beyond Texas and the four contiguous states (Louisiana, Arkansas, Oklahoma and New Mexico) (Freiberg and Freiberg, 1996, pp. 25–6). In response, Southwest developed its longer interstate routes from other ports, notably Houston.

Regarding the Wright amendment, there was no further legislative change until 2006, when Southwest entered into an agreement with the City of Dallas, the City of Fort Worth, American Airlines and the DFW International Airport Board. These parties then persuaded Congress to pass the Wright Amendment Reform Act of 2006, which repealed several through-service and ticketing restrictions, and provided for removal of all remaining restrictions with effect from 2014 (Southwest Airlines, Form 10-K for 2007, p. B-4).

Southwest's battles regarding Love Field illustrate a further general proposition: incumbent airlines sometimes attempt to use limitations on airport access to prevent or hinder route entry by a new airline company.

12.2.2 EasyJet's early relations with airports

Though EasyJet has chosen to serve many major-city airports, it also sought ports with low charges. After choosing the (minor) London Luton port for its initial base, rather than at one of London's major ports, EasyJet placed its second base at Liverpool – rather than at nearby Manchester, which had services operated by British Airways and some other national carriers. At another early port (Amsterdam's Schiphol) it chose a minor gate with limited gate-lounge space.

After a few years, the (new) owners of Luton airport wished to increase the fees when EasyJet's initial contract expired. Because the airline then had a considerable base there (including the company's headquarters), it was reluctant to move out – but it did say it would direct more of its expansion to other ports.

One port from which EasyJet did withdraw (for a while!) was Zurich. Announcing the closure of its Luton–Zurich service (media release, 18 August 2004), EasyJet complained that some airports 'assume they can charge whatever they want, use cost-plus pricing models, and charge for services that airlines don't want or use . . . [rather than] provide the right infrastructure at the right price'.

12.2.3 Ryanair's airport strategy

Ryanair has chosen minor European ports of two kinds: those serving small cities that have (some) tourist potential in their own right; and secondary ports for major cities, often at some distance from the major city.

In the first category is the port at Carcassonne, an attractive old city in southern France, where (it seems) there was no scheduled air service *at all* until Ryanair started its Dublin route in 1999. In the Ryanair timetable for summer 2014, Carcassonne had service on eleven routes – from Billund, Bournemouth, Brussels Charleroi, Cork, Dublin, East Midlands, Eindhoven, Glasgow Prestwick, Liverpool, London Stansted and Porto – with a total of 36 flights per (summer) week (carcassonne.aeroport.fr, accessed 13 February 2014).

Then, Ryanair was still the only scheduled airline flying to Carcassonne. Though passenger numbers have remained relatively modest, Ryanair has shown that the Carcassonne region can support a viable year-round operation. (The nearest alternative is the well-established port at Toulouse, some 90 km distant.)

In the 'secondary port' category comes 'Frankfurt–Hahn' (the legal name of the port, even though the city of Frankfurt is at a distance of about 120 km). Ryanair launched its first route there in April 1999 (Annual Report 2000, p. II), and soon established a base there (Annual Report 2002, p. IV). Elsewhere in Europe, Ryanair later developed services at a few other secondary European ports, including Beauvais (Paris) and Memmingen (to Ryanair, aka Munich West).

Like EasyJet, Ryanair too has sometimes withdrawn from an airport which increased its charges. For example, it switched its Dublin service from Cardiff to Bristol, when (as Ryanair claimed, media release, 25 April 2006) Cardiff airport sought a 350 per cent increase in charges following the termination of a five-year contract. While Ryanair had some 24 routes from Bristol in 2014, Cardiff did not then appear on the Ryanair route map. (In one or two other cases, however, individual ports have been reinstated.)

Such instances show how a *major* airline can sometimes enjoy considerable market power when dealing with airports outside the top rank.

12.2.4 JetBlue started at New York's J F Kennedy Airport

In contrast, JetBlue chose a markedly different initial strategy. In choosing New York's prestigious JFK Airport as its (initial) base, the company noted (Annual Report 2002, Form 10-K, pp. 5–7):

- Kennedy provides access to about 21 million potential customers in the New York area (of whom, about six million live within 15 miles of the airport).
- Planned improvements in ground transport were to increase JFK's accessibility.
- New York lacked significant low-fare services (compared with the situation in other US city-pair markets), and there were good prospects for stimulating extra travel by introducing low-fare, point-to-point services at JFK.

Of course, JetBlue later started to move up-market. (Perhaps that option was already in mind when the airline's founders chose JFK.) The case shows that while low airport costs have been significant factors in the airport choices of the new airlines, demand considerations can also be *very* important.

12.2.5 The early airport woes of Virgin in Australia

Though the Queensland state government offered a financial inducement to Virgin to locate in Brisbane, this may have been only a minor factor. (Unlike the EU, the state governments in Australia have no qualms about giving 'state aid', even when that aid advantages one firm over its rivals.)

For Virgin, an important advantage at Brisbane Airport was the availability of several unused, high-quality common-user gates. These were better gates than Virgin could then hope to find at any of the other major airports, where the incumbents (Ansett and Qantas) controlled *all* the terminal capacity, and (as noted in §7.3) had only limited obligations to offer gates to an entrant airline.

With hindsight, it seems Brisbane may have been favoured also because it supported early entry to both the under-served Brisbane–Adelaide route, and the not-well-served Brisbane–Melbourne route. Perhaps the Queensland government was spending taxpayers' money needlessly!

To support its choice of Brisbane–Sydney as its first route, Virgin rented terminal space in an old wooden hut at Sydney. When it began service on 31 August 2000, Virgin shared the hut with Impulse Airlines. Virgin's next port was Melbourne (starting on 1 October); following a period of temporary initial arrangements, it moved to a superior prefabricated building, newly constructed by that airport. At Adelaide, Virgin used part of the international terminal, with a temporary structure added alongside, when it opened there on 7 December. It was a year later (9 December 2001) before Virgin arrived at the other major state capital city, Perth, where initially it used part of the international terminal, which is on the opposite side of the runway from the domestic terminals, and is inconveniently located for domestic flights.

After Ansett finally ceased trading (in March 2002), its administrator took some time in negotiating transfers – to the recently privatised airports – of the various long-term terminal leases. Eventually, Virgin gained access to gates previously used by Ansett at all the major ports– even including Brisbane, where it moved gates from its initial location. At Sydney, Qantas leased many of the gates vacated by Ansett, in order to accommodate some of its own expansion – and perhaps to limit Virgin's opportunities for later growth. It was 12 December 2002 before Virgin was able to move in there (Virgin media releases, 6 November and 12 December 2002).

12.3 Airport charges for runway use

12.3.1 Traditional and recent tariff structures

Airlines generally face separate charges for the various airport services they use. The principal aircraft-related charge is that for an aircraft movement on a runway. Other aeronautical charges are for subsidiary services such as parking an aircraft for prolonged periods. (An airline also pays big money for its use of an airport-owned terminal to accommodate its boarding and disembarking passengers. Such charges are considered below, in §12.4.)

For the landing and then the take-off of an aircraft, a port usually levies separate charges. Traditionally, the amount charged is based on the maximum take-off weight (MTOW) of the aircraft, and sometimes also on the length of the flight sector just flown *or* to be flown.

On the whole, heavier aircraft require more runway investment (in runway length and sometimes in pavement strength). Thus the MTOW basis can reflect the long-run incremental cost of runway provision. It is also (loosely) related to the aircraft's wear-and-tear cost for the runway pavement. That measure of short-run cost serves as a floor for the movement charge, because if the charge were less than that cost, the airport would be out of pocket when it hosted the movement. (The public-policy aspects of the charge are discussed later, in §14.2.2.)

If *all* movements were charged at that short-run cost, the airport's *runway* revenue would fall short of the long-run cost of provision and maintenance of its runway(s). Specifically such revenue would not cover the cost of constructing the runway in the first instance, nor would it cover the continuing economic cost of using the site for aviation rather than for some other purpose. (Here, we ignore the congestion costs that arise when the number of movements is so great as to result in aircraft delays. On that matter, see §14.2.3.) Thus, to seek economic and financial viability of runway provision, some at least of the aircraft movements have to pay charges that exceed the short-run maintenance costs.

For the use of capital facilities, a customary commercial aim is to charge higher prices for those uses that will not be deterred by high prices, while otherwise charging a price not less than the short-run maintenance cost. It turns out that the MTOW basis, when appropriately calibrated, does quite a good job in serving that commercial aim – especially if the charge is related to flight-sector length as well as MTOW. (Because the cost of a flight increases with sector length, a high movement charge for a long flight can still be a small proportion of the total cost.)

When almost all airports were owned and operated by government agencies, each port had a published list of movement charges; and the same list applied for all comers. That notion of a published standard tariff generally persisted even when ports were corporatised.

However where a major port has been privatised, it *may* no longer have a standard tariff. Indeed, such a port may vary its tariff by airline – unless there is a legal prohibition of such price discrimination. And some ports do discriminate, in an attempt to gain more revenue (and hence more profit) than would be forthcoming from *any* uniform tariff. One strategy is to levy higher charges on the more profitable airlines, while giving discounts or other financial support to airlines (or, sometimes, to routes) with only marginal profitability.

Of course, the potential for such discrimination is limited by the extent of the port's market power. In particular, if an airport has no competitor in the region, it may be able to use its market power to obtain revenue well in excess of its runway costs. And even that revenue can be increased by discriminating between airlines.

Whether a targeted and aggrieved airline can do anything (about the aircraft movement charges it is required to pay) depends on whether the regulatory structure has an appeal mechanism. An Australian case, involving an airline appeal against the tariff set by a privately operated airport, is reported in the next section.

In the US, because airports have remained in the public sector, the principle of a common tariff (offered to all airlines) remains supreme. This follows because almost all ports receive *some* federal funds (to supplement revenues earned from users), and such funding is conditional on the port being 'available for public use on reasonable conditions and without unjust discrimination' (§511 of the Airport and Airway Improvement Act of 1982, quoted and interpreted at p.51 of Levine, 2009).

In some other countries, however, even some *government-owned* airports have set aside the public-utility concept of a common tariff. As already noted (§2.2.2), the European Commission has taken the position that a government-owned port *can* give special, advantageous terms to an individual airline, but only if a privately-owned airport would offer such terms in the same situation. Section 12.3.4 below reports a famous case, involving a contract between Ryanair and Charleroi Airport in Belgium. (A public-interest analysis of aircraft movement charges is given in Chapter 14.)

12.3.2 Airport privatisation and new runway charges: an Australian case

On 1 January 1988, most Australian capital-city and other major airports were transferred (from direct government ownership) to a newly-established government corporation, the Federal Airports Corporation (FAC), which was required to run them on a more-commercial basis (Mills, 1989, p. 216).

The new Corporation inherited and maintained an MTOW basis for the determination of aircraft movement charges. It published a runway tariff for each of its ports; and those tariffs did not discriminate between airlines.

When the government decided to privatise operation of the major airports, each port was offered on a 50-year lease; some came with an option for a lease for a further 49 years (Airports Act 1996). In the case of Sydney Airport, some special provisions delayed bidding until 2002. Section 18 of the Act gave the lessee of Sydney Airport the right also to lease and operate Sydney West Airport. The latter did not then exist. Rather the term refers to a site the government had selected for a second Sydney airport, and for which it had assembled the necessary land parcels.

Furthermore, §248 of the Airports Act *deemed* that, for the purposes of §50 of the Trade Practices Act 1974, acquisition by a single company of both leases does not by itself substantially lessen competition in any market, nor does it make it likely that competition will be substantially lessened in any market.

This deemed outcome is, of course, an empirical nonsense. Its (un-blushing) purpose is to preclude the application of that §50, and hence rule out any legal challenge based on considerations of market competition. The government's desire for a high price for the lease outweighed any policy stance in favour of market competition.

The government moved also to promote higher aeronautical charges just before the sale. When the ports were assigned to the FAC, the assets had been significantly under-valued (Mills, 1991, pp. 291–2). This had resulted in a modest financial target for the new Corporation, and consequent modest levels for landing and some other charges (Mills, 1995). For Sydney Airport, the government put various arguments to the Australian Competition and Consumer Commission (which had regulatory authority at that time) and the ACCC then allowed increases in charges that were expected to almost double Sydney's aeronautical revenues (ACCC, 'Decision on Sydney airport prices', media release, 11 May 2001).

In the 2002 auction, the successful bid amount (from a consortium led by Macquarie Bank) was so large that the airlines using the port feared the new company would be profitable only if there was a *further* large increase in the movement charges.

Under its new operator (SACL), Sydney Airport introduced new aircraft movement charges to be paid by all those airlines (other than local regional carriers) that were also using the common-user domestic passenger terminal. (As before, those airlines also paid separate charges for their use of that terminal.) The new movement charges depended on the number of passengers travelling in the aircraft, rather than aircraft MTOW; for a detailed illustration of that approach, see (for example) Sydney Airport Conditions of Use (v. 2.5), July 2003.

12.3.3 Virgin Blue's dispute with Sydney Airport

When Sydney Airport introduced its new movement charges, all the Qantas domestic flights used that airline's own domestic passenger terminal. The airport's new published tariff did not refer to the charges to be paid by Qantas. Whatever those details, however, it seems the new tariff(s) effectively increased the total movement charges paid by each of the two airlines. Certainly, Virgin later claimed (media release, 23 May 2007) that the switch to passenger-based charges had 'severely disadvantaged our business, increasing our landing fees by approximately 53 per cent.'

Indeed, the lure of extra profits may have been the main reason for the airport's switch to per-passenger charges. However, for a very different picture of the motivation, see Schuster (2009), which states clearly the author's affiliation with the port's owner.

Of particular interest here is that the new charges policy had different effects on the two airlines. When operating equivalent B737 aircraft, Qantas had fewer seats in its two-class cabin than did Virgin in its one-class layout. And, given its more limited interest in business travel, Virgin may have operated with higher load factors, at least on business-oriented routes. Thus under the new policy, Virgin lost at least part of the per-passenger advantage it had enjoyed when movement charges were based on MTOW. Furthermore, as Fu, Lijesen and Oum (2006) show in some formal modelling, an increase in movement charges (even without any change in the charging basis), does more financial harm to a low-cost carrier than to a competing full-service airline, essentially because the passengers of the LCC are more averse to paying higher fares.

Faced with the airport's unilateral initiative, the only opposing action open to Virgin was to seek a 'declaration' (under Part IIIA of the then Trade Practices Act) that the Sydney airport runways were essential infrastructure for its airline business. Such a declaration would ensure that, if the airport and Virgin did not reach a 'commercial agreement' on the terms of access, the Australian Competition and Consumer Commission (ACCC) would itself determine the access charges.

Accordingly, Virgin (media release, 1 October 2002) asked the National Competition Council (NCC) to recommend declaration of the use of runways and taxiways at Sydney Airport. There followed a protracted and extraordinary sequence of steps.

In June 2003, the NCC issued a draft recommendation *for* declaration; yet in its final recommendation (NCC, January 2004), the NCC recommended *against* declaration, and the Minister accepted that recommendation. Virgin then appealed the decision to the Australian Competition Tribunal, which handed down *its* decision – to declare the services – on 9 December 2005. The airport then sought review of this decision in the Full Court of the Federal Court of Australia, which heard the matter in May 2006, and dismissed the airport's appeal on 18 October 2006. The airport then sought special leave to appeal to the High Court, which refused that application in March 2007.

Meanwhile, on 29 January 2007, Virgin had notified the ACCC of an access dispute regarding airside services at Sydney Airport – in effect, asking the ACCC to arbitrate. Once the High Court had refused to hear an appeal, the airport had to choose, in effect, between an ACCC determination and a negotiated settlement with Virgin.

On 23 May 2007 both Virgin and SACL issued media releases. Virgin said it was 'pleased [that] Sydney Airport has now agreed terms to return to MTOW [charging]'. SACL said it was 'pleased that this agreement has been directly negotiated and resolved on a commercial basis to the satisfaction of both Virgin Blue and ourselves', and welcomed 'a sensible commercial outcome that provides for pricing . . . [based on] MTOW, in place of a price per passenger charge.' It noted also that the two parties had agreed that further details of the agreement were to remain commercial-in-confidence.

Thus, because of the many steps in the legal process, it had taken more than 4 years before Virgin was allowed a decision to set aside the airport imposition of higher charges, based on passenger numbers rather than aircraft MTOW.

Later that year, the airport announced it had reached new agreements on movement charges for international flights and for Qantas domestic flights, with details also to remain commercial-in-confidence.

Some reluctance to disclose persisted. The Sydney Airport Conditions of Use v. 2.28 states aeronautical charges effective from 1 January 2014. For domestic (other than regional) flights using passenger terminal 2 (a common-user terminal), schedule 5 stipulates (in paragraph 2) levels for *per-passenger* runway charges. On the other hand, paragraph 4 – which, it says, applies where paragraph

2 does not apply – specifies levels for runway charges based on aircraft MTOW. Yet the 42-page document seems not to explain how and when paragraph 2 does not apply, and also seems not to state the applicable runway charges for those domestic flights that use (domestic) terminal 3, which belongs to Qantas.

Given that Sydney Airport has a de facto monopoly in the Sydney area, there is an obvious public interest in knowing what runway charges are levied on Qantas, Virgin and their subsidiary airlines. The choice between per-passenger and aircraft MTOW charges raises important efficiency and equity issues; these are considered in §14.3.1.

12.3.4 The EU challenge to the agreement between Charleroi Airport and Ryanair

In 1997, Ryanair started a service from Dublin to Charleroi – a little used airport about 50 km south of Brussels, in the Walloon region of Belgium. In April 2001, after signing a formal agreement with the Walloon government (the airport owner), Ryanair started Charleroi services to London Stansted, Glasgow (Prestwick), Shannon, Carcassonne, Pisa and Venice (Ryanair, Annual Report to the SEC (Form 20-F) for 2002, p. 18). In the agreement, Ryanair undertook to establish a base at Charleroi, initially with 4 aircraft. Over the years, Ryanair has prospered at Charleroi. In the summer of 2014, it was flying more than 60 routes from that port, albeit mostly at low frequencies.

However, the venture also embroiled the company in some lengthy legal proceedings. As Ryanair noted (Form 20-F to the SEC for 2003, pp. 83–4), the European Commission had announced in December 2002 that it was to investigate the Ryanair–Charleroi agreement. The investigation followed a complaint by Brussels International Airport that Ryanair's arrangements with Charleroi constituted illegal state aid. (The Brussels port seems to have regarded Charleroi as an uncomfortably close substitute, despite that airport's distance from Brussels.)

The agreement gave Ryanair concessions with regard to aircraft movement and passenger handling charges; and the airport contributed to the initial marketing costs for new routes. In its 2003 report, Ryanair argued that the arrangements did not constitute illegal state aid. In particular, it claimed that:

- the arrangements complied with the 'Private Investor Principle' which requires that any agreement be entered into on a commercial basis, and be one to which a rational (private) investor would have agreed; and
- the agreement was not exclusive to Ryanair – the same terms were offered, at the same time, to other carriers such as Sabena, EasyJet, and Virgin Express, but none of those airlines accepted.

Even after acknowledging the force of those Ryanair observations, it is worth noting that there remains a legitimate public-interest concern. At Charleroi, Ryanair had got in first. Its presence made it less likely that any other airline would wish to follow, because of the natural limits on passenger demand in the local area. In signing up a first-mover airline, a rational private owner of the airport would recognise that the presence of that airline would discourage other airlines from using the port. The rational owner would then drive a harder bargain, to compensate for sacrificing the opportunity to make profitable deals with other airlines. Furthermore, the structure of the Ryanair deal – essentially that of a quantity discount – favours large, well-established airlines, and so may have significant anti-competitive consequences.

The EC judgement

In announcing its decision in February 2004 (European Commission, 2004b), the Commission noted that while landing charges for other users were determined by aircraft weight, the charges for Ryanair were based on the number of embarking passengers, and the Commission considered that the arrangement gave Ryanair a discount of about 50 per cent (§7). 'In addition, the price fixed for ground handling services for Ryanair is EUR1 per passenger, a mere 10% of the price published by [the airport] for other users' (§10). And the contract put these and other arrangements in place for a period of 15 years (§12).

In its analysis, the Commission noted the primacy of certain economic principles: effective competition between airlines requires a level playing field; in Europe, the development of under-used, (so-called) regional airports will help to moderate levels of congestion at the established hub ports; and competition from the former group will put pressure on the latter to operate more efficiently.

On the other hand, the Commission criticised the way in which the Walloon government had handled the contract negotiations, especially a lack of consideration of several pertinent issues. It believed that 'a private cautious and well-informed investor would not have signed this contract' (§207).

It also judged that although there was some public knowledge of the negotiations with Ryanair, 'the precise terms of the contract . . . were covered by a publicity and confidentiality clause' (§241), and 'the measures granted were not offered to other companies in a transparent way and were in fact offered only to Ryanair' (§242).

The Commission concluded (§250) that the advantages granted to Ryanair *were* State aid within the meaning of Article 87(1) of the Treaty. While recognising that the aid may help the Walloon region, the Commission observed that most of it was operating aid (§§255–6). While Charleroi is eligible for regional aid under Article 87(3) (c) of the Treaty, that article allows only initial investment aid (§257), whereas the contract granted aid over its entire 15-year period.

After prescribing principles by which the Walloon region was to calculate the amounts of aid to be recovered (§§339–44), the Commission formally ruled:

• while a general Wallonia Government Decree allows some reduction in airport landing charges, the additional discounts were not allowable (Article 1);

- the discounts relative to the official airport tariff for ground handling services were not allowable, and the aid to be recovered was to be calculated by comparing the costs of provision with the invoiced amounts (Article 2);
- only part of the marketing contributions and the other one-shot payments were allowable as start-up aid for new routes (Article 4); and
- Belgium was to immediately recover the amounts of aid unlawfully made available to the airline, with interest added (Article 5).

Further legal examination

In two media releases, Ryanair said: it had filed an appeal to the European Court of First Instance (25 May 2004); and it had agreed with the Walloon authorities to repay €4m, to be put into an escrow account until its appeal was heard (28 October 2004).

Then, on 14 December 2005, Ryanair announced it had signed a new 10-year deal with Charleroi Airport, committing Ryanair to further expansion of its base there. Two years later, on 11 December 2007, Ryanair announced it would base a fifth aircraft at Charleroi, and would then operate 26 routes there.

On 12 March 2008, the airline confirmed that the Court had heard its appeal. Finally, in a press release issued on 17 December 2008 (the Court of First Instance, 2008), the Court *annulled* the decision of the European Commission. The Court criticised the Commission for failing to consider the Walloon government and the airport management authority as a single economic entity, taking a decision for which the private investor rule could be applied. Thus, the Court concluded, the Commission decision was vitiated by an error in law.

Section 14.3.3 of this volume gives a further, comprehensive discussion of public-interest principles for the determination of airport access charges; that section includes an account of how EC thinking has developed in recent years.

12.4 Passenger terminals

12.4.1 The basic role of a passenger terminal

For departures, a terminal building provides a sheltered space in which the passengers check in for the flight (if they have not done so by using the internet before coming to the airport), hand to the airline (any) baggage to be checked, and assemble at the nominated departure gate (lounge area). When the flight is ready for boarding, the passenger moves from the gate to the aircraft.

For arriving passengers, the basic sequence is simpler: move from the aircraft to the terminal, collect (any) checked bags, and proceed to ground transport. (Of course, *connecting* passengers use further facilities as well.)

At many ports, aerobridges are attached to the side of the terminal building, at a height that is matched to the height of the aircraft door(s). An aerobridge allows walking passengers to pass between the terminal and the aircraft without exposure to the weather; it also keeps them well clear of baggage handling and other activities near the aircraft. Further, the aerobridge serves wheelchair-bound and other passengers who cannot negotiate the aircraft steps that would be the alternative means of access. Given the size and height of modern jet aircraft, installation of aerobridges requires the terminal to have at least one floor *above* ground level. In turn, this usually leads the terminal designer to include passenger escalators and sometimes lifts too.

Baggage-handling arrangements usually involve moving belts – not only the belts that the passenger sees at check-in and baggage collection, but also behind-the-scenes equipment, used for transfer of bags between the aircraft and the terminal. At major ports, the terminal may be fitted with an *automated* baggage system – which sorts and sends departing bags to the appropriate aircraft, and *may* direct bags from one flight to another, so that connecting passengers need not handle their (checked) bags.

Because the equipment items for baggage handling and for moving passengers are costly, many new airlines prefer to do without – whenever the terminal owner (usually the airport owner) can be persuaded not to install such sophisticated equipment – or (at least) not to charge for it when an airline refrains from use.

When an airline operates a point-to-point network, few passengers transfer at an intermediate port. Usually those few are required to collect their checked bags upon arrival, and present them again when checking in for the next sector. Thus such an airline can readily do without automated or other complex baggage handling.

A point-to-point airline has another reason for not wanting to use automated baggage systems – namely to avoid the risk of bags becoming 'lost', by passing into the hands of other parties, and perhaps being loaded on to a flight of another airline. Instead, a point-to-point airline sometimes prefers to keep the bags under its own control, with its own staff sorting and transferring bags to and from the company's aircraft.

Similarly, some low-cost carriers do not wish to use (and pay for) aerobridges. Instead, their passengers walk across the apron between the terminal and the (mobile) aircraft steps. Well-designed aircraft parking positions can give an outside walking distance of no more than 20 metres. (The few wheelchair passengers and others who cannot negotiate steps can be lifted in and out of the aircraft by using a fork-lift.) Thus a terminal without aerobridges can be a simple, inexpensive single-storey building.

In short, many low-cost airlines seek very low terminal costs, and thereby aim to secure a significant cost advantage over traditional airlines, whose high level of customer convenience results in higher terminal costs.

12.4.2 Charges for terminal use: some airports discriminate between airlines

The terminal operator may wish to set different terminal charges for different airlines, whenever such price discrimination is legally permissible. Sometimes, an airport discriminates by charging the same price for terminals of differing quality – a practice that may go unchallenged even when discriminating differences in nominal prices are prohibited.

An interesting case arose at Paris Charles de Gaulle Airport (CDG). According to EasyJet (media release, 12 January 2006), the per-passenger charge for airline use of the high-quality Terminal 2 (assigned to Air France) was the same as that for use of the lower-quality Terminal 3, (then) used by EasyJet. Much to EasyJet's 'chagrin', the company thereby got less value for the same money. The airport's motive may have been a desire to support the national carrier, as much as a desire to increase its revenues.

However, despite that complaint, and other airline complaints about the Paris airport charges being simply too high (IATA, Annual Report 2007, p. 42), EasyJet went on to expand its operations and establish bases at CDG and at Orly, the other main Paris port (EasyJet media release, 7 February 2008). So a low-cost airline may be willing to pay high terminal charges for access to routes on which passengers are ready to pay relatively high fares.

12.4.3 Gold-plating of passenger terminals

An airport may prefer to build or refurbish terminals to a higher standard than airlines want to fund. For airport management one motive for such 'gold-plating' is to increase the size of the managerial empire. Where the port is privately owned and subject to economic regulation, another motive can be to enlarge the asset base in order to increase the permitted profit for the private owners – an outcome that can ensue under so-called 'rate-of-return regulation', and may arise under some related forms of regulation. Though the adverse incentive has long been recognised, the problem persists in the new world of privately-owned airports.

While the established airlines often protest, it is usually the low-cost airlines who are the most displeased – because their targeting of passengers who seek lower fares makes terminal luxury particularly inappropriate.

Among such protests was a campaign by Ryanair. It wanted the extra terminal (T2) that was to be built at Dublin Airport, to be of a modest standard. In the direct language that it sometimes uses (media release, 'DAA lies exposed in An Bord Pleanala's hearing on €800m gold plated second terminal', 4 May 2007) Ryanair claimed that Dublin Airport Authority plc sought 'to justify a massive increase in the size of T2 and a quadrupling of costs from €170m to over €800 [million]'.

Though Ryanair was the port's largest airline customer, with its passengers accounting for just over 40 per cent of the passenger total (DAA Annual Report, 2007, p. 18), the government backed the DAA's plans.

When the 'smart new €600 million Terminal 2' was opened in 2010, the Irish economy was in some trouble; and the number of passengers served at Dublin had fallen by about 14 per cent compared with the 2007 figures ('Dublin opens Terminal 2 amid economic crisis', anna.aero, 24 November 2010).

The plans for a new terminal at London Stansted Airport (owned by the privately owned company BAA plc) provoked similar criticism. An EasyJet media release (18 May 2005) said:

> EasyJet and Ryanair, which between them account for almost 80% of Stansted's passengers, have always argued that it is necessary to develop

Stansted Airport – providing the infrastructure meets the needs of Stansted's customers. This means constructing a new runway and associated terminals that are fit for low-cost airlines. It doesn't mean building a long-haul airport capable of taking an A380 with marble-lined terminals to match.

Perhaps that protest encouraged the UK Competition Commission to propose separation of ownership for some of the ports owned by BAA plc (Competition Commission, 2008). (The outcome is reported in §14.2.1.)

12.4.4 Terminal diversity to meet airline preferences

Where a major port serves enough passengers to merit construction of more than one terminal, the low-cost airline preference for low-cost terminal services may be met by establishing some diversity of service standards across the port's terminals. Some years ago, a number of ports became willing to develop a low-cost terminal (LCT) alongside their full-service terminal(s).

At Singapore's Changi Airport, the Civil Aviation Authority of Singapore (CAAS) secured a firm user-commitment from Tiger Airways, and built a 'Budget Terminal', which opened in March 2006. The 'operating costs at the Budget Terminal would be kept low to meet the needs and operating models of LCCs . . . the compact layout of the single-storey terminal has no need for travelators, escalators and aerobridges' ('Fact Sheet on Budget Terminal', accessed 29 May 2008, at changiairport.com).

The 25,000 square-metre terminal had a manual baggage handling system. In the absence of aerobridges, passengers walk about 20 metres between aircraft and terminal, and enter/exit the aircraft by mobile steps. However the terminal was somewhat removed from the two main terminals, and (initially) had inferior access to public transport (buses only).

For some years the terminal played a significant role, while the airport's continuing expansion was supported also by the building of a new Terminal 3. However, the life of the Budget Terminal came to an end in September 2012, when its (then) six low-cost airlines and their passengers (about 5 million annually) were transferred to Terminal 2. This allowed construction of Terminal 4 to begin on the site previously occupied by the Budget Terminal (Changi Airport Group news release 'Terminal 2 prepares to handle more passengers', 30 August 2012).

Similarly, the almost new Kuala Lumpur International Airport built a sizeable low-cost terminal, designed to handle 15 million passengers annually, in a building of modest design, located at some distance from the new, main KLIA terminal (see various media releases at malaysiaairports.com.my). Intended, above all else, to serve the rapidly expanding Air Asia, the low-cost terminal opened in 2006.

The success of the terminal and the success of Air Asia soon led to planning for a new, larger low-cost terminal, intended to handle 30 million passengers annually. As the project proceeded, the concept was enlarged, the cost grew greatly, and the opening date was put back several times. Before the terminal opened (in May 2014), the airport's *third* runway was brought into use; this was adjacent to the new terminal.

Well before that opening date, the function of the new terminal had morphed into that of a general-purpose terminal, to be named KLIA2, and to host some full-service carriers as well as the several low-cost carriers already serving the port. This change in its function mirrored the (by then) well established habit of low-cost carriers to become hybrids that seek to serve business as well as leisure travellers (CAPA, 'Kuala Lumpur Airport's new low cost terminal uniquely aims to be a model of connectivity', 9/10 June 2014).

In recent years, low-cost terminals have been established at various major European ports, including Marseille, Bordeaux and Lyon (all in France), Copenhagen (Denmark), Budapest (Hungary), and Sheremetyevo (Moscow, Russia) (CAPA, 'Copenhagen to charge less at "CPH Go" while Kuala Lumpur's new LCCT will cost more to build', 3 September 2010).

Some of the European terminals have been created by recycling old infrastructure. At Copenhagen: a new terminal building makes use of six old aircraft stands ('CPH Go', Special Report, anna.aero, 10 November 2010).

Also of interest is Ryanair's *outright purchase* at Bremen of 'a low cost terminal facility at the airport for €10 million following an EU tender in which Ryanair was the successful bidder' (Ryanair, media release, 19 September 2006.) The airport map (at airport_bremen.de, accessed on 20 May 2008) shows that Ryanair's Terminal E is next to the main terminals, and enjoys good access to public transport (including a city tramway service). No doubt Ryanair's plans to establish a base at Bremen encouraged the port to sell such a well-located site. More commonly, an airport may locate a new-build low-cost terminal at some distance in order to allow for (possible) later expansion of the main terminal.

At Copenhagen, the initial charges for *international* departing passengers were DKK67.18 per passenger at the low-cost terminal and DKK87.18 at the other terminals (airport media release, 31 August 2010, accessed at cpk.dk). Because the charge per *domestic* departing passenger was DKK39.11, there may be grounds for wondering whether the charge levels reflect airport perceptions of what the market will bear as much as cost levels in the various terminals.

Copenhagen seems to have been one of the first (European) ports to differentiate its charges by terminal. The legacy airlines have realised that such differentiation gives LCCs a cost advantage. At Geneva the airport sought to convert, for use by LCCs only, and with lower service levels and lower charges, a secondary terminal that was used previously for charter flights. As reported (CAPA, 'Copenhagen to charge less at CPH Go . . .', 3 September 2010) the scheme was opposed by Air France, KLM and Lufthansa, and the proposal was abandoned.

Clearly, separate terminals with differing service standards present both access and pricing problems that may need the attention of government regulators. Those matters are taken up in §14.3.3.

Besides the terminal issues at major ports, there are (of course) terminals of basic standard at secondary or rural airports that are now operated primarily to serve low-cost airlines. At Frankfurt-Hahn, Ryanair (media release, 30 January 2007) praised the airport for building a terminal to accommodate 15 million passengers per annum for less than €100 million.

12.5 Runway slots

12.5.1 Runway 'slots' introduced to ration runway capacity

At an airport without significant runway congestion, an airline agrees to pay the aeronautical charges levied by the airport, and is then allowed to schedule its flights without specific controls on the timing of its aircraft movements. Of course, on any particular day, there is no guarantee that the runway will be available at the precise moment that the airline's aircraft wants to arrive (or depart). Rather, the air-traffic controllers seek to allow the movement at, or soon after, the desired time.

As the frequency of aircraft movements increases, the degree of congestion also increases, and the air-traffic control task becomes more difficult. Eventually, absent any intervention, the traffic procedure may become unworkable. Then, the almost universal practice is to use a rationing mechanism: an aircraft is allowed to access the runway only if the airline holds a time-specific 'slot' for the aircraft movement, that is, a right to use the airport infrastructure at a specific time on specific dates for the purpose of landing or take-off.

In the past, such slot rights were often acquired informally, through *ad hoc* procedures that were established when an airport first faced a significant degree of congestion. In consequence, an airline that did not serve the port, when all available slots were so allocated, might be unable later to gain access to the port, at busy times of day or at all. The entrenched airlines can then use their hold on slots as a (literal) barrier to entry, which curbs competitive entry – especially entry by LCCs and other new airlines.

Even when a new carrier *can* acquire slots, it may *not* wish to use the congested port. The reasons for this are discussed below in §12.5.2. In cases where a new airline *does* want access, however, the prospects for such entry vary markedly from one port to another. Sections 12.5.3–4 below report on cases in the US and France.

Clearly the disposition of slots at congested ports can have an important influence on the economic efficiency of the industry. The analysis of such matters is taken up in Chapter 14, starting at §14.3.4.

12.5.2 LCC attitudes towards slot-controlled airports

In the main, low-cost carriers prefer *not* to use congested ports. Even with a slot-allocation mechanism in place, runway conditions at such ports often result in delays to aircraft. This makes it difficult, if not impossible, for the airline to achieve the quick 'turn' (the period between arrival at and departure from the passenger terminal) on which such an airline relies in order to secure intensive use of its aircraft, and so keep its costs low.

Furthermore, a busy port may be a hub port for one or more established airlines, and in that case the aeronautical charges may be higher than those at little-used airports. Again, the LCC does not lightly accept such higher charges, especially when (as is usually the case) it has no particular need or even desire to take advantage of inter-airline transfer traffic that may be available at a hub port. If access to the runway requires slot rights that have to be paid for, then that outlay is another deterrent.

Of course, the new carriers vary in their practices. Ryanair has a particular reputation for preferring small and other un-congested ports with low aeronautical charges, to support its low-fares policy. At the other end of the spectrum, JetBlue uses the slot-constrained JFK Airport in New York as its major base, in order to target high-revenue passengers.

Where all feasible slots at an airport are in use, the administrative arrangements for slot allocation may, in effect, simply exclude a new airline that wishes to start using the port. However in other cases, an administered allocation – operated by whatever agency has authority – may assist in enabling access. To illustrate the variety of outcomes, the next two sections report instances of administered allocation in (respectively) the US and France.

12.5.3 Slots for JetBlue at JFK and at Long Beach (Los Angeles)

When JetBlue began service in 2000, the Federal Aviation Administration regulated aircraft movements at JFK during the period 3pm to 7.59pm. Under the FAA's High Density Rule, each such movement required the airline to have either a 'normal' slot or a 'slot exemption'. (By 2007, the peak timing had changed, and the regulation was then altered.)

In the US, it has long been recognised (Levine, 1987, pp. 464–71) that at congested airports, incumbent airlines may be able to rely on slot-rationing to shelter them from competition. In 1994 the (Federal) government embarked on a pro-competitive response at JFK, by introducing legislation for the creation of slot exemptions; these were in addition to the pool of slots long held by the incumbent airlines. As JetBlue has explained (Annual Report 2002, p. 18), the intention was to grant access to other carriers who were able and willing to fill voids in underserved markets and to generate some price competition on specific routes.

Evidently, the FAA saw the entry of JetBlue as a worthy cause. In September 1999, the airline requested and was granted 75 daily slot exemptions, phased in over a three-year period:

> Unlike the FAA-assigned slots held by other airlines at JFK, our slot exemptions, while functioning identically to an FAA-assigned slot, may not be sold, leased, rented or pledged. If we fail to maintain our use of a slot exemption, [it] could be subject to forfeiture.
>
> (JetBlue, Annual Report 2002, p. 18)

Availability of slots was again a key issue when JetBlue chose Long Beach Airport (21 miles south of Los Angeles International Airport, LAX) as its second 'focus city' (JetBlue media release, 23 May 2001). That municipal airport granted JetBlue *all* the 27 daily departure slots then unallocated (JetBlue, Annual Report 2002, p. 18).

Clearly, the municipal government was keen to have JetBlue at Long Beach, to provide convenient access for local residents and visitors, with a prospect of lower fares than could be obtained at LAX. One condition of the grant was that JetBlue should begin using all those slots by May 2003; the airline did (almost) manage to do that (media release, 28 May 2002; see also Annual Report 2007, p. 13 for some later developments).

12.5.4 Runway slots in Paris

Traditionally, Air France dominated France's domestic routes. While Ryanair and EasyJet did begin services from other EU countries to French ports, mainly outside Paris, they found it difficult to obtain slots at the Paris ports of Orly and Charles de Gaulle (CDG).

The interest of EasyJet in serving Paris became manifest in 2002 when the airline announced (media release, 7 February 2002) that it was soon to start three flights daily from Orly to either Geneva or Zurich, and that it had been allocated some slots also at CDG and was currently assessing these. The media release also protested in forceful terms about the failure of Air Lib (then the largest of the small French airlines) to hand back slots at Orly that it did not use:

> Under the terms of the court order, which protected it from bankruptcy, [Air Lib] was obliged to return at least 20,000 slots per year to other airlines; to date it has only returned 12,000. It is a piece of blatant anti-competitive protectionism.

In 2004, EasyJet campaigned to obtain a commercially-viable set of slots at CDG. In media releases dated 12 February, 8 April, 10 May, 19 July and 17 December, EasyJet asserted that:

- Air France (and its subsidiaries) held 53 per cent of the Orly slots and 74 per cent of the slots at Charles de Gaulle.
- Air France had a monopoly on 27 out of 43 domestic routes from Paris, with 'meaningful' competition on only three routes (Marseille, Nice, and Toulouse).
- There were concerns about the independence of the slot allocator (COHOR), and EasyJet was about to take legal action in the Melun Administrative Court.

While EasyJet did soon establish a base at Orly, extra slots at CDG came slowly; it was February 2008 when it established a base there (initially, with three aircraft). It also opened a base at Lyon on 4 April 2008 (with two aircraft); that initiative may have been advanced because of the difficulties in getting slots in Paris.

In 1997 Ryanair began service from the UK to Beauvais, about 80 km from Paris. Its 2003 its acquisition of Buzz (the low-cost subsidiary of KLM) gave it immediate access to 11 further regional airports in France, including Marseille. It was not until 19 March 2008 that Ryanair announced its first French *domestic* route – between Marseille and Paris (Beauvais). Later that year, it started services from Marseille to Lille and Brest, but did not serve Paris CDG or Paris Orly.

On 1 July 2015, the EasyJet website showed flights from CDG to about 40 ports and from Orly to about 20 ports. The Ryanair website still had no presence at either port, perhaps reflecting lack of interest, rather than an inability to obtain slots.

Part III
Conclusions

13 Airline prospects

Lacking access to a crystal ball, this chapter does not attempt to predict the future for individual airlines already in being or yet to come. Rather, it seeks to learn from situations that have arisen in the recent past, and to do so in the light of trends that are already under way and seem likely to persist for a while yet. The focus is on changes in market structure and airline practices, rather than on short term fluctuations in macroeconomic conditions and other magnitudes that drive frequent changes in profitability.

13.1 Further new-airline entry

13.1.1 Diminished prospects for further new-airline entry

Before deregulation led to the launching of LCCs and other new airlines, airline services around the world had become generally somewhat settled. Even when government regulation of the market did not prohibit or prevent competition *between the incumbents*, there was often little display of competitive instincts. Rather, many incumbent airlines had learned to co-exist, and thereby enjoy a quiet life together, with passable if not always large profits.

Upon deregulation, it was those placid conditions that attracted entry by entre-preneurs who hoped that new management practices and enthusiastic staff would lift service standards, reduce operating costs and so yield profits. Furthermore, by offering lower fares, the newcomers could encourage additional travel. That would help to fill *their* planes without necessarily reducing the number of pas-sengers carried by the incumbents. And that *might* encourage the incumbents to refrain from war.

In the face of the invasion, however, some of the incumbents *did* bestir themselves. In order to give the newcomers a hard time, they adopted aggressive strategies, sometimes including predatory conduct on routes entered by new-comers. In some countries, notably the US, the many new airlines found it difficult to attract customers in sufficient number. Only a few of them survived. In other countries, the scale of new entry was more modest, as was the resulting attrition. Those companies who entered just before the general financial crisis (notably those in the Arabian Peninsula) had a particularly difficult time. Even though the permitted numbers of entrants had been modest, some privately owned airlines were soon closed.

Nowadays, in many world regions, the prospects for further entries are diminished. Indeed, where un-regulated domestic airline markets are well served by both long-established legacy airlines *and* vigorous, low-fare newcomers, it has become *very* difficult for a newcomer to succeed. A hopeful entrepreneur needs to find a geographical or other market niche that is not so very well served, and has to learn how to combine low or modest fares with distinctive quality standards.

In recent times, and in some countries, the managerial quality of the few further entrants may have risen. For example, among the very few US airlines that have launched since the year 2000, JetBlue and Virgin America have survived and grown over extended periods, with JetBlue now looking particularly robust.

Even so, there remain some major countries where the airline revolution is not concluded. In some countries per-capita travel has not yet reached a level that matches the (often, rapidly rising) standard of living. In such places, a newcomer can hope to win a share of the forthcoming extra travel. For that reason, it is unsurprising that new-airline entries are continuing in some parts of the world, notably in Asia.

In addition, there are some countries – particularly Russia and China – that have not so far fully opened up entry in their domestic markets. If such governments refrain from *arbitrary* restriction on entry, and yet do engage in financial testing of prospective entrants combined with well-considered judgements regarding likely further market growth, then those countries may well see further successful airline entry.

13.1.2 Conditions supporting further new-airline launches

Table 13.1 identifies the principal conditions that favour *successful* entry. It is also worth recalling some of the examples that have appeared in earlier chapters. Regarding condition 5, airlines such as (the former) Olympic may fill the bill. The long period elapsing before Virgin America secured any profits (§1.2.6) illustrates the importance of condition 7. Because the required launch funding is often so very large, a small start-up may well run out of money, even when well managed otherwise. A large conglomerate may have the funds, but will still need to rely on experienced airline managers brought in from outside. The case of Kingfisher Airlines (§4.3.4) reminds us that conglomerate funding does not guarantee success.

In regard to condition 10, JetBlue (§1.2.2) chose New York City, mainly because there were no other LCCs based in that large market. Furthermore, that north-east region of the US was well away from the areas (then) served by the still-expanding Southwest Airlines. In contrast, the long sequence of financial deficits for Virgin America may reflect the fact that it did *not* start with a poorly-served niche market, other than that it could reasonably claim it supplied main-line routes with better quality cabin service than that offered by the large legacy carriers.

Table 13.1 Conditions that may promote *successful* airline launches in a particular region

Conditions	Comments
1. Regional travel per capita less than level to be expected given present standard of living	An out-of-equilibrium situation, arising when airline-sector expansion has not fully matched *past* growth of potential demand
2. Regional travel growing, thanks to increasing population and/or rising standard of living	
3. Absence of government preference for some or all incumbents	Includes absence of any government-owned airline
4. Legislation prohibiting airline predatory acts	Also requires firm resolve by, and government support for, the regulatory agency
5. Incumbent legacy airlines have become geriatric and/or uncaring	
6. Little or no presence of LCCs	
7. Newcomer owned by private investors with patience and deep pockets	
8. Newcomer has experienced CEO, who can *innovate* as well as manage routine operations, and who values and rewards airline staff	
9. Newcomer is an in-house LCC of an established full-service airline	Parent must accept that its LCC may serve at least some of the routes flown by the parent
10. Newcomer finds poorly served market niche	
11. Newcomer starts on domestic routes only	To avoid complexities of international service

Finally, note the outstanding entry and growth of Azul (§5.6.7), helped by Brazil offering conditions 1 and 2, and by the new company being led by the experienced David Neeleman (condition 8).

13.2 Low-cost airline entry and incumbent responses in the world regions

Because the factors that influence the prospects for a newly launched airline vary markedly between markets, it is helpful to look in turn at individual regions and market areas.

13.2.1 USA

The largest national market in the world has seen the exit of almost all of its many low-cost entrants. And persistent merger and take-over activity by the large legacy carriers has reduced their number to three: Delta, United and American. Alongside those three, Southwest Airlines is the sole independent survivor from among the *early* 'new' airlines. Though it has grown to be much the same size as the other three, and flies many routes at each of a number of large ports, its network is still less hub-oriented than those of the three legacy carriers.

As detailed in Chapter 1, those four companies share the domestic market with only seven other *main-line* carriers: there are two smaller but important recent start-ups, JetBlue and Virgin America; there are two full-service airlines, Alaska Airlines and Hawaiian Airlines, now seeking to expand from regional territory; and there are three small but growing ultra-low-cost carriers (ULCCs): Allegiant, Spirit and Frontier.

On the whole, those seven airlines have done well in recent years. JetBlue marches on. Virgin America has now recorded a second consecutive annual profit. Each of Alaska and Hawaiian has started new routes to more-distant ports. Frontier has changed its business model under new owners, and has entered many new routes. And – after making re-equipment decisions – both Allegiant and Sprit have embarked on growth spurts, perhaps attempting to discourage selective fare predation by the three legacy carriers (Aaron Karp, 'Spirit Airlines 2Q net profit up 18%; faces pricing challenge', *Air Transport World*, 24 July 2015).

Indeed, following the completion of the 'final' mergers of the three network carriers, it seems that *some* aggression may have already begun.

Fares

In 2012, Delta introduced an additional ticket category, 'Basic Economy', initially only on a few routes from Detroit. It then gradually extended the coverage (Kelly Yamanouchi, 'Delta expands bare-bones ticket option', *Star Tribune* (Minneapolis St Paul), 18 November 2014), to other routes that serve leisure destinations and/or have service from smaller carriers. A search on the Delta booking engine (on 23 February 2015) suggests that the Basic Economy fare is commonly only US$10 or US$20 lower than the Economy fare.

Of the 21 routes from Detroit on which Delta then offered the Basic Economy fare, nine were served also by direct flights of Spirit. On the other hand, Delta offered that fare quite widely on other routes that attract travellers who are keen to have the very lowest fare, but were not then served by Spirit. Thus, if the Department of Justice were to become concerned about that situation, it might be difficult for it to secure a win in the courts. (The public-policy aspects of such matters are considered further in §15.3.)

Route entries

Alaska Airlines has long faced little competition on its routes within the state of Alaska. Recently, however, Delta increased its presence at Seattle, and entered some major Alaskan routes. For its part, Alaska Airlines has launched quite a number of new mainland routes. These include new non-stop services from Salt Lake City (a Delta hub) to Boise, Los Angeles, Las Vegas, Portland (Oregon), San Diego, San Francisco and San Jose (press release, 'Alaska Airlines launches service to seven new destinations from Salt Lake City', 9 June 2014). On 6 September 2015, the Alaska Airlines booking engine showed that all seven of those routes were still being served.

JetBlue has also tried its hand. Immediately after Alaska had announced it was to launch service on 29 March 2013 between San Diego and Boston, a route already served by JetBlue, the latter company said it would enter the route between Anchorage (Alaska) and Seattle, starting 16 May 2013 ('JetBlue enters Alaska's bread and butter market', crankyflier.com, 20 November 2012; 'JetBlue enters Anchorage Seattle and challenges Alaska Airlines', anna.aero, 23 May 2013).'

Other network adjustments

The 'final' mergers of the legacy carriers have led to closure of quite a number of their hubs. Though such a closure does not remove the port from the airline's network, it does (taken by itself) materially reduce the number of flights at that port, thereby opening up some route opportunities. Mainly it has been the smaller airlines that have grasped those opportunities.

While each of the big three has recently entered *some* routes already served by one (or both) of the others, a bird's-eye view suggests that a disproportionate number of their network adjustments have brought challenges to the smaller airlines. Is it in the public interest to have the few large airlines seek to increase their collective share in the market? If not, perhaps the individual airlines need to consider whether it is wise to pursue such an aim.

Route frequencies

An interesting example (Delta again) is given by that airline's introduction (scheduled for December 2015) of non-stop service between Tucson (where the city population exceeds 600,000, and where that of Pima county exceeds 1.2 million) and Los Angeles International (Tucson Airport Authority 'Delta to add 3 daily non-stop flights to LAX', flytucson.com, 6 June 2015). Already operating one-stop connections, Delta planned to introduce three round-trip flights daily, each using a CRJ 900 (76 seats), operated by a unit of Skywest (delta.com, accessed 6 September 2015).

On that same date, the pertinent airline websites showed that competing *non-stop* flights were offered by American (two or three flights daily, mostly on CRJ aircraft flown by a unit of Skywest), United (one daily flight of a CRJ 200, operated by a unit of Skywest) and Southwest which offered three flights daily (two on Saturdays) on B737-700/400 aircraft (143 seats). Note that Southwest Airlines first flew the (non-stop) route on 4 October 1994 – using B737s, of course (swamedia.com/channels/By-Category/pages/Openings-Closings, accessed 6 September 2015).

Now, bear in mind that the world's airlines say that they aim to reduce the atmospheric pollution emitted by aircraft, and (in the short term, at any rate) this is to be achieved largely by operating new, less-polluting engines fitted to larger aircraft (§15.6). In that context, Delta's choice of regional aircraft for its new non-stop services seems 'interesting'. Two separate issues merit attention. On such a route, could the benefits from competition flourish with less than four airlines actually flying on the route, especially when potential competitors watch from close by? If so, would it be in the public interest if such routes were served by aircraft with capacity for (say) 140 or more passengers.

Of course, Delta may hope to induce one or more airlines to exit the route, and then itself introduce larger aircraft. And, indeed, the market may so evolve. But in that case, why have the incumbents (other than Southwest) persisted with smaller regional jets, instead of flying B737 or similar aircraft?

Changes in competing network styles

In becoming a very large airline, Southwest relied on developing a point-to-point network, and succeeded in taking market share from the legacy carriers, despite (or, perhaps, because of?) their use of hub-and-spoke networks. In recent years, however, there have been two changes in the aviation environment that may alter the balance of advantage between the two network styles.

First, the recent round of airline mergers may encourage the legacy carriers to fly more direct services. Consider the following hypothetical situation. Before their recent merger, airlines One and Two competed with each other in offering one-stop service between ports O and D, with travel going via different hub ports R and S, respectively. Following the merger, the enlarged airline carries more passengers travelling between O and D than the number previously available to either one of the two (pre-merger) airlines. Thus the per-passenger cost of flying those travellers on non-stop flights is lower than before, and the merged airline may well find that it is now financially advantageous to introduce non-stop flights between O and D, especially if the new service attracts more passengers in total than the sum of the numbers previously flying on the one-stop services of the two pre-merger carriers.

To the extent that such cases arise across the entire domestic network of US airlines, this factor may give significant advantage to the three (merged) legacy carriers, at the expense of point-to-point airlines such as Southwest.

A *second* recent change has a more complicated effect. Notwithstanding the lower fuel prices prevailing in 2015, the trend towards airlines re-equipping with larger aircraft has continued; and given the lags in the production of the aircraft recently ordered, that trend may well continue for some time.

The presence of the larger aircraft in airline fleets may have two consequences: hub carriers may substitute one-stop service on some of the routes they previously served non-stop. And point-to-point carriers may withdraw from some routes they previously served. *By themselves*, both changes would serve to reduce the amount of such travel.

Airline service qualities

While the sector has an outstanding safety record, parameters such as cancellations and on-time performance are not very good by the international standards that prevail in advanced economies. Typically, the smaller US carriers (other than the ULCCs) outperform the big three, among which Delta has recently scored the best. With mergers settled, perhaps the big three will now put more effort into service standards.

13.2.2 Europe

The low-fare airline entrants have won a much larger market share in most European countries than have their counterparts in the US. In part, this is because many business travellers in Europe have been ready to settle for less lavish cabin service on short-haul journeys, while continuing to prefer full-service airlines for long-haul travel. Indeed, the old national carriers have not prospered in the face of the LCC entry, and (unlike the US case) they have been unable to make life difficult for the more competent of the entrants. In consequence, some six or so European LCCs have become large enough to be well-nigh invulnerable to fare predation on particular routes (provided their managements remain competent).

Indeed, it is the legacy carriers that have encountered financial trouble when faced with low-fare competition. In Eastern Europe, Malev has bowed out and CSA appears to be largely controlled by an Asian airline. In Western Europe, financial strength has been sought through merger: KLM and Air France have partnered, as have British Airways and Iberia, who formed a new company IAG, which recently embraced Aer Lingus as well. And the Lufthansa group now includes Austrian, Swiss and Brussels Airlines. In Greece, the legacy carrier Olympic has been taken over by the entrant, Aegean. And in June 2015, the Portuguese government agreed to sell to a joint venture of private owners a majority stake in the national carrier, TAP. In the next several years, some of the remaining smaller European national carriers may well be merged or bought out, or may simply disappear.

In Russia, the government has given financial support for airline services for remote regions, especially in the extreme eastern part of Russia. However, the economic downturn in 2015 has brought new financial woes, especially for several privately-owned companies; in particular, the large airline Transaero (§2.4.7) has ceased operation. The current challenges may give longer-term benefits, as managements learn the importance of nimble feet and well-ordered minds in devising effective policy adaptations, and company boards learn of the importance of employing able managers.

In Europe generally, one factor initially helping the new low-cost airlines has been, of course, their ability to serve short- and medium-haul routes at a somewhat more modest service standard than that which prevailed, and to do so at a *significantly* lower cost. The established national companies have been unable to replicate that performance *within* their mainline carriers, and have restructured accordingly. In particular, Lufthansa has handed over to its own LCC, Germanwings, many of its short-haul routes (other than those from its major hubs at Frankfurt and Munich); it also owns another LCC, Eurowings. To a more limited extent, Air France relies on its subsidiaries to provide domestic services in France. When Iberia became part of IAG, it brought with it the Barcelona-based LCC, Vueling. Conceivably, that successful airline may enter some of the British domestic routes from which British Airways withdrew some years ago.

In short, low-cost carriers seem destined to make further gains in market share, mainly through growth of existing companies. However, the initial success and growth of a recent niche entrant, Volotea, suggests that further entry cannot be ruled out. The surviving national carriers will delegate many domestic services to in-house LCCs, and will focus largely on long-haul routes.

13.2.3 Canada and Australia

In each of these two countries of modest population-size (Canada 36 million people, Australia 24 million), the domestic airline market is dominated by two companies/groups.

In Australia, each camp has three operating divisions. The (mainline) *Qantas* has bedfellows in *Jetstar* (a low-fare jet operator) and *QantasLink* (a regional carrier operating both turboprops and some jets). The newcomer Virgin Australia (mainline) has Tigerair as a low-fare jet operator, and Australian Regional Airlines (flying both turboprops and some jets).

Air Canada also has both a low-cost jet airline, Rouge, and a regional subsidiary Air Canada Express, whose fleet (including many turboprops) is operated mainly by Jazz. Though the recent rival WestJet has established a regional carrier, Encore, which flies Q400 turboprops, it does not (yet?) have a separate low-cost jet operator.

In each country, further (successful) *independent* airline entry seems rather unlikely, even in the medium term. In Australia, Qantas is still much larger than Virgin. However, it is possible that the Virgin camp might grow to match the output of the Qantas group. In that case, both parties might come to accept a rough equality, and that arrangement could become a fairly stable equilibrium. In each of those two camps, the presence of an *in-house* low-cost jet airline will make it difficult for an independent low-cost carrier to break into the market.

13.2.4 Africa

Low-cost carriers have a *very* small share of most African airline markets. The exception is in the Republic of South Africa, where the established LCCs Kulula and Mango (§6.3) have been joined recently by FlySafair, and the market has become very competitive. The only other significant LCCs in sub-Saharan Africa are Fastjet (initially based in Tanzania), Flyafrica.com (initially based in Zimbabwe) – both with pan-African ambitions – and the new Kenya Airways subsidiary, Jambojet.

The prospects for growth of those three LCCs depend significantly on the attitudes of national governments towards the presence of airlines head-quartered in other countries. In September 2015, Fastjet was looking forward to a brighter future, after a long period of travail (§6.5). Following the launch of Fastjet Zimbabwe, the Fastjet group expected that its affiliate Fastjet Zambia would receive its Air Operator Certificate by the end of 2015 'Bases in Kenya, Uganda and South Africa are planned for 2016.' (Fastjet, Interim results for the 6 months to 30 June 2015, 28 September 2015). The holding company was doubling its fleet to six A319 aircraft.

Having experienced less delay than Fastjet, Flyafrica.com was at a roughly similar stage in establishing affiliates. And those two groups may be heading for some lively competition.

The main full-service incumbents are Ethiopian Airlines (which has an outstanding growth record in recent years, and now has a hand in ASKY airlines, in West Africa), Kenya Airways and South African Airways (SAA). After its impressive start, Arik Air (Nigeria) is also worthy of a place on the list.

Of course, it remains to be seen whether SAA will finally make a success of restructuring, and thereby manage to continue serving the regional routes which *have* been profitable for it but now require service at significantly lower fares. On the future of SAA, CAPA takes a positive view. CAPA also wonders whether African governments will (at last) implement the Yamoussoukro Decision, and thereby support the pan-African aspirations of competent entrants (CAPA, 'Liberalisation seeps into African aviation policy – when what is needed is a flood of new services', *Airline Leader* no. 26, February 2015).

Such a change in government attitudes could greatly enhance the role for new entrants offering low fares on routes in East and (perhaps) Central Africa. Regarding full-service airlines, the situation in West Africa looks promising. If the Sénégal government succeeds in restoring the health of *its* airline, is it too fanciful to see Arik Air becoming the partner that the government seeks? Such an outcome would help Arik to strengthen its West African network, and become a *multi-national* airline that competes effectively with ASKY. Such competition between sizeable African airlines might prove to be durable.

Particularly striking have been the good on-time performances of several of the new airlines. In announcing (at flyafrica.com, on 17 July 2014) the departure of its very first flight, Flyafrica used the headline: There Is No Such Thing As Africa Time.

13.2.5 Latin America

As seen in Chapter 5, many of the legacy airlines in Latin America have success-fully rejuvenated. There has also been considerable merger/takeover activity.

In that context, there was at first little by way of LCC entry in the region. In the very large air-travel market in Brazil, GOL launched in 2001. But it was 2008 before David Neeleman's Azul started flying with E190/E195 aircraft (106/118 seats). Just six years later, Azul introduced a small fleet of five A330 wide-bodies, to serve its first international routes – from its Campinas hub to the Florida ports of Fort Lauderdale and Orlando (Ben Mutzabaugh, 'JetBlue founder's Brazil airline now selling US flights', *USA Today*, 21 November 2014). It also planned to lease/buy a total of 63 A320neo aircraft, starting in 2016 (Victoria Moores, 'Brazil's Azul to buy 63 Airbus A320neos', *Air Transport World*, 1 December 2014).

However, Azul then faced two difficulties. A second IPO (Dan Horch, 'Azul, Brazil airline started by JetBlue founder, files for IPO', *New York Times*, 1 December 2014) offered (non-voting) preferred shares; that would allow Neeleman (who owned 67 per cent of the common shares) to retain control. Yet there soon came a report (Rogerio Jelmayer, 'Brazil airline Azul postpones IPO again', *Wall Street Journal*, 16 January 2015) quoting an insider to the effect that adverse market conditions in had again compelled abandonment of the IPO. Of course, if unable to acquire funds through an IPO, Azul may be able to rely solely on aircraft leasing.

The other potential difficulty concerns whether the Brazilian market will have demand levels sufficient to support the continuing high growth rate envisaged by Azul. In the face of little or no underlying demand growth for domestic travel in Brazil, TAM and GOL were said to have begun limiting capacity in 2013, in order to improve or at least maintain yield (CAPA, 'Azul's IPO prospects during 2014 will be challenged by tenuous market conditions', 10 January 2014). In the event of further growth by Azul, will TAM and GOL be willing to suffer further reduction in their market share?

Elsewhere in Latin America, Mexico has seen the entry of three LCCs: Volaris, Interjet and VivaAerobus. While one legacy carrier (Mexicana) went out of business, the presence of three new airlines may discourage further low-cost entry there, for some years.

Although VivaAerobus (which claims to have the lowest costs of any airline in Mexico) launched only in late 2006, the company soon spawned a sister company, VivaColombia, in Colombia. That initiative adopted the practice of establishing associate airlines in other countries, to avoid government bans on majority foreign ownership of subsidiaries. The Mexican company announced (media release, 13 March 2014) it had started flying its first A320, the first of 52 aircraft ordered from Airbus; delivery is to be completed in 2016.

Brazil and Colombia apart, at the beginning of 2015, no South American country had seen the launch of a low-cost airline. Particularly in light of the VivaAerobus order for A320s, it would not be surprising if the owners of Aerobus was soon to launch one or two further affiliate companies. And there could be separate entry by other parties.

13.2.6 The Arabian Peninsula

As seen in Table 3.1, most of the countries in the region have hosted the launch of an airline that operated aircraft with a single-class cabin, though the cost levels of those airlines may have varied somewhat. In each of the Sharjah and Dubai emirates, it was the government that took the initiative, though the Sharjah government subsequently privatised Air Arabia. The general financial crisis and other factors saw off some of the privately owned airlines.

By 2015, only Bahrain had not hosted a low-cost carrier. If some commercial entity in Bahrain wants to risk entry, the government of Bahrain may well agree to the initiative. However, in the Gulf region in general, the prevailing entrants have taken the best market positions. In the near future, further entry seems unlikely.

13.2.7 Asia

This region has been enjoying remarkable growth in air travel, thanks to rising incomes in many countries, and to increased provision of services, mostly of improved quality. Many Asian countries have seen both the launch of new airlines, and the early failure of some of them. While most newcomers have targeted travellers seeking low fares, there has also been entry of full-service carriers.

Even without full deregulation, some Asian governments have readily allowed entry to newcomers. In turn, this has allowed optimistic entrepreneurs to launch flights in abundance, often showing a willingness even to enter routes already served by four or more other airlines. Table 13.2 presents the details for two such cases. Given the lack of experience, and the inevitable uncertainty as to how quickly demand will grow, it is not surprising that markets have sometimes been unstable, and that small, new or poorly managed airlines have met serious financial problems during market downturns.

As aviation experience builds, there may soon come a time when the flow of new-start carriers reduces, and perhaps even dries up. In many Asian countries, however, it is not yet clear that such a time is imminent.

In India, airlines have had to cope with high taxes on aviation fuel, poor governmental decisions regarding passenger airlines, and some instability in the demand for air travel. After the early mergers and amalgamations, the low-cost airlines Kingfisher, Indigo, SpiceJet, Jet Lite and GoAir together grew to take more than sixty per cent of the entire domestic market. Yet, after growing to be the biggest of them all, Kingfisher closed when its conglomerate parent did not provide further funding.

More recently, the relatively successful SpiceJet experienced a run of financial losses (§4.3.2). Its (reinstated, founding) owner lowered unit costs by simplifying the operation, and deploying a smaller fleet on profitable routes only. Soon after that, there were reports of the airline planning to expand its fleet by acquiring new aircraft (Jeremy Torr, 'Reports: SpiceJet looking to buy up to 200 aircraft', *Air Transport World*, 16 October 2015).

The May 2014 election of a new (national) government was regarded as a favourable change for the aviation sector (CAPA, 'India starts to sparkle again – and it could just be for real this time!', *Airline Leader* no. 26, February 2015). In particular, the government adjusted some of the specific regulations to make them a better fit for the economic practicalities of the industry. Yet, after the recent launch of Vistara, the Tata full-service venture, other hopefuls still await the award of air operator certificates. It remains to be seen how many of these will receive them.

Table 13.2 Two Asian routes, each with several incumbents at the time of further entry[1]

Port pairs	Airlines serving the route	Weekly flights[2]	Airline characteristics
Jakarta – Denpasar[3]	Batik Air (May 2013)	14	Full-service subsidiary of Lion Air
	Garuda	103	Indonesian government, national carrier.
	Lion Air	91	Large privately-owned LCC, founded 1999
	Indonesia AirAsia	42	LCC, Indonesian affiliate of AirAsia
	Citilink	21	LCC, subsidiary of Garuda
	Mandala	7	LCC, Indonesian affiliate of Tigerair
	Sriwijaya	7	Founded 2003, privately owned, full service
	Merpati	7	Govt. owned, founded 1962, full service
Shanghai – Osaka[4]	Juneyao (Apr 2014)	7	Privately owned full-service carrier in China
	China Eastern	24	Legacy carrier, formerly part of CAAC
	Air China	14	Legacy carrier, formerly part of CAAC
	Japan Airlines	14	National carrier, Japan
	All Nippon Airways	14	Legacy carrier in Japan
	Shanghai Airlines	7	Wholly owned subsidiary of China Eastern
	Spring Airlines	7	Privately owned LCC in China

Sources: Jakarta – Denpasar: CAPA 'Competition in Southeast Asia's low-cost airline sector heats up as capacity surges' 5 Sept. 2013; anna.aero 'Batik Air starts two domestic routes from Jakarta' 23 May 2013; Shanghai – Osaka: anna.aero 'Juneyao Airlines joins six other carriers on Shanghai to Osaka' 24 April 2014.

Notes
1 For each route, the airline named *in the first row* is the newcomer – which entered in the month shown.
2 Round-trip flights as scheduled by the airlines.
3 On this Indonesian domestic route, each airline is domiciled *within* the country.
4 The airports are Shanghai Pudong and Osaka Kansai. Each airline is domiciled in either China or Japan.

In China, the dramatic development of air travel tends to conceal the problems. As already noted, the airline sector is far from being deregulated. The many share-holding connections between airlines may also hamper competition. The outstanding success in recent years has been the privately owned Spring Airlines. Otherwise, the older airlines are not very spritely, and government regulation of employment contracts makes it difficult to increase labour productivity other than by pursuing growth effected with a less than proportionate increases in employment.

In a situation where the government holds most of the cards, and is not afraid to play its hand, it is particularly difficult to evaluate 'market-place' prospects.

Despite the reduced growth rates of air travel in recent times, there are still quite a number of airlines seeking to launch (CAPA, 'China's 19 new passenger airlines will be mostly full service and along the east coast', 19 November 2014). Given the government's aim to enhance low-cost service, especially for western areas (as part of its regional policy), it is not obvious that many of the nineteen hopefuls will be allowed to enter.

In Japan, low-cost airlines arrived late. Then came the race for entry between Peach, Jetstar Japan and (the first incarnation of) AirAsia Japan. Given the timing, it was almost inevitable that some of the low-cost carriers would struggle to survive. However, in the longer term, it seems that the present number of LCCs is not excessive, given the underlying size and growth rate of the market for air travel. Good managers may ensure survival. And in due course, there may well be further entry.

Safety standards

In several Asian countries, the very rapid growth of air travel seems to have resulted in some airline disregard for the strict operating procedures that are needed to avoid serious accidents. In addition, in at least one country where the government maintains detailed regulation of who may fly where, and when they may fly, minor breaches of the rules have come to public notice. Some of the national governments are now paying more attention to airline conduct.

13.3 Concluding remarks

In most industries, new firms experience financial deficits, especially while they incur the initial establishment costs, and make their products known to potential customers. In addition, if the production processes embody important economies of scale and scope, the unit costs of on-going production will decline eventually, but the initial high cost levels will contribute significantly to the early overall deficits. In part because it is a network industry, airline operation suffers greatly from all those effects.

In some parts of the world, notably Asia, the exuberance of the new-airline entrepreneurs has come face to face with the realities of early financial deficits. For the senior managers, the main task is to judge whether or not current deficits are merely an inevitable early problem, with profitable operation coming soon enough to allow early recovery from indebtedness. The circumstances of airline operation are so complex that such judgements are difficult to make. Thus it is not surprising that some airlines become bankrupt, even (sometimes) in the absence of significant hostile actions from the incumbent airlines.

14 Public policy for airports and air navigation services

14.1 Air navigation services

14.1.1 Air navigation arrangements for domestic airline services

Domestic flights are authorised by the government in question, and are subject to movement controls prescribed by government-empowered (and, often, government-operated) providers of en-route air navigation services, and by local (airport) traffic control services. The provision of such services is a natural monopoly, in the compelling sense that the operation of two separate, *uncoordinated* providers serving the one area would invite the occasional collision between aircraft.

When air navigation services were first established, it was usual for each national government to set up its own agency to operate the service for its own airspace. In recent times, some European governments have established limited companies to provide the service, sometimes on a not-for-profit basis; ownership of such companies *may* remain with the government.

A notable example of a limited form of privatisation is to be found in the UK. Initially NATS (National Air Traffic Services Ltd) was a government-owned subsidiary of the Civil Aviation Authority (the government regulator). When NATS was converted (in 2001) into a public-private partnership (PPP) the UK government retained 49 per cent of the shares, while 5 per cent were held by employees, and 46 per cent were purchased by the Airline Group (of seven airlines, who were clients of NATS). The Airline Group took operational control.

In evaluating the new ownership structure, Steuer (2010) finds that the change brought little or no difference in regard to productivity, flight delays and safety. (No doubt, partial ownership by the Airline Group moderates any financial incentive to cut corners.) In establishing the PPP, the government hoped to tap private (external) funding for capital investment. However, Steuer concludes that the debt-leveraged buyout resulted in new investment capital coming largely from retained financial operating surpluses. In the UK, it seems that privatisation may not have brought significant advantage.

Whatever the precise ownership arrangements, the contract between government and the navigation services provider will generally specify the technical procedures to be deployed, and the hours for which the service is to be provided. The contract may not recognise the possibility of innovation, let alone provide incentives for the adoption of new procedures as these become available.

Recently, the innovation issue has become increasingly important. The traditional radar-based surveillance technique was introduced about seventy years ago. Most countries have complete radar coverage of their own air space, but long-haul oceanic flights may not be served at all stages of the flight. Radar surveillance depends on ground-based stations ('beacons'); pilots are required to fly from one beacon to the next. The consequent zig-zag in the routing often adds significantly to the distance flown. Furthermore, the (rotating) radar receiver 'sees' an aircraft only once every 12 seconds, and thus the precise position of the aircraft at any moment is estimated with a (modest, but important) degree of error.

In recent decades, the introduction of communications satellites and the development of the (United States) Global Positioning System (GPS) have made it possible to bring satellite-based and other digital communication techniques to civil aviation. An important basic piece of new equipment is called ADS-B (Automatic Dependent Surveillance – Broadcast). When fitted in an aircraft, this equipment (operating in 'out' mode) broadcasts signals that allow other parties to recognise the presence of the aircraft, and to know very accurately its location. The signal can be picked up by other (equipped) aircraft in the vicinity, and by similarly equipped ground stations that are within range for a direct signal line. The signal can go also to orbiting satellites whence it can be sent to more-distant ground locations. Once the system has been further developed, the transmitted signals could include information traditionally sent by voice messages between pilots and air traffic controllers.

The introduction of such digital communication permits several improvements. The better knowledge of an aircraft's location allows closer spacing of aircraft along the route. It also allows more precise placing of aircraft during the climb after take-off, and on approach at the destination port; in turn, that can be used to reduce noise disturbance near airports. And there is no need for intermediate beacons: the aircraft can be flown directly between origin and destination ports, thereby reducing the distance travelled. Taken as a whole, these features increase the effective capacity of the system, reduce the amount of aircraft fuel used and lower the levels of atmospheric emissions.

Of course, the new system requires major investment in new equipment. Given the absence of any significant factors that would void the application of the standard 'user pays' philosophy, the conventional argument applies: provided that a cost–benefit analysis demonstrates that the new system will bring positive social returns, then the new techniques *should* be introduced, and the airlines *should* be required to fund all the expenditures.

However, it may be wise for government *initially* to fund the capital costs of the *public-use* assets. Then, over the life of the equipment, the government would recoup those outlays from the airline users, through the charges that are levied on aircraft movements. Individual airlines would still fund the costs of installing equipment on their own aircraft.

In the US, in particular, those basic funding principles have struggled to gain acceptance. Some US airlines have argued that the government should fund all the equipment costs, even including the hardware to be installed in their own aircraft. This attitude stems in part from airline concern about delays and other problems arising in the FAA development programme. (See, for example, Joan Lowy, 'Air traffic control modernization hits turbulence', *Associated Press*, 31 October 2013). The performance of the FAA is discussed in the next section.

14.1.2 Progress in establishing new navigation techniques *in selected countries*

In the *United States*, formal responsibility for such innovation has rested entirely with the US government, represented by the Federal Aviation Administration (an agency of the Department of Transportation). The new approach has been dubbed the Next Generation Air Transportation System (informally, 'NextGen'). (Comprehensive descriptive reports are found at faa.gov/nextgen, accessed 27 May 2014.)

The required new system is very complex, and requires design of and investment in large-scale re-equipment programmes. In the face of continuing criticism of the management of the NextGen program, the FAA began publicising its implementation of particular modules of the program at particular airports. (See, for example, FAA, NextGen Operational Performance Assessment, September 2013.)

Then, in 2015, the DOT announced (US Department of Transportation, 'The backbone of NextGen is now in place', *Fast Lane* blog, 30 April 2015) that installation and deployment of ERAM (En Route Automation Modernization) had been completed at all 20 of the FAA's en route air traffic control centres. (Some further detail is given in FAA, 'Fact sheet – en route automation modernization (ERAM)', 29 April 2015.)

However, as one commentator pointed out (Aaron Karp, 'FAA completes nationwide ERAM deployment', *Air Transport World*, 30 April 2015), the FAA administrator acknowledged that ERAM was originally intended to come into use at the end of 2010, and that the project had overrun its budget by US$370 million.

Nevertheless, the DOT announcement recorded that ERAM was already receiving information from those aircraft that are equipped with ADS-B Out, and that 'ADS-B will replace radar as the primary means of tracking aircraft by 2020'. However, such a mandated equipment deadline was still being challenged by several large American airlines, who argued that they needed a further five years in which to install equipment in about five thousand aircraft (Aaron Karp, 'Airlines, FAA discussing "grace period" for ADS-B Out rule', *Air Transport World*, 14 April 2015).

Much more significant was the continuing dis-satisfaction with the performance of the FAA, together with a recognition that it was singularly inappropriate to attempt such large-scale innovation in a federal-government context in which political battles resulted even in occasional shut-downs when Congress withheld on-going funding. By the end of 2015, there was considerable support for determining some new ownership and administrative structure. That matter is taken up in §15.6.2.

In the *European Union*, the design of the prevailing radar-based system is, in some respects, inferior to that in the US (European Commission, 2008, p. 6). Although the EU aims to treat European airspace as a single entity, the initial air traffic management providers were based on the national boundaries – giving about 60 control centres, compared with about 20 in the US. As a result, many international flights in Europe experience more handovers between controllers than would be needed if the airspace blocks were larger and better designed. Together with the inefficient placing of beacons, that fragmentation results in the average flight being about '49 km longer than strictly necessary'. Even while still using radar-based surveillance and voice communication, improvements in the management of *en route* and airport traffic could reduce both journey time and fuel used by about ten per cent (European Commission, 2008, p. 4).

Under the prevailing reward system for each (national) provider, the flight charge paid by an airline is proportional to the distance flown through *national* airspace, multiplied by a factor for aircraft weight. That mechanism discourages the provider from reorganising in order to reduce flight distances, because that might reduce the provider's revenues (unless the unit charges were sufficiently increased).

The Single European Sky (SES) legislation introduced by the EC in 2004 called for the development of 'functional airspace blocks' (FABs). Initially, that had little effect. In July 2010, however, EC Regulation 691/2010 included decisions establish a single authority to manage the entire European route network, and to introduce a scheme of nine such blocks (FABs), designed without regard for national boundaries.

Of course, a European decision does not always lead to prompt implementation. Though some progress was made during the next few years, the Commission said, in September 2013, 'Despite a binding deadline of December 2012 for Member States to establish FABs, none of the 9 FABs which should have been created under the SES are fully operational' (European Commission, 2013b).

In November 2014, the Association of European Airlines (representing most full-service airlines) wrote to the governments of the EU countries, to complain that, in the ten years since the adoption of the Single European Sky target, there had been almost no progress, and to urge them to end the deadlock (Tim Hepher and Victoria Bryan, 'A decade on, airlines push for delayed European skies reform', *Reuters*, 6 November 2014). One month later, the EC announced an offer of funding for airlines, airport operators and air traffic management stakeholders in order to implement SES projects (EC Press release IP/14/2400, 'Aviation: EU makes €3 billion available to deliver the Single European Sky', 5 December 2014).

In *Australia*, a government-owned corporation, *Airservices Australia*, has focussed on first introducing ADS-B communications *linked to ground stations*.

Because most of the large Australian continent has few if any (human) residents, Australia has never had complete radar coverage. In 2009, however, Airservices Australia commissioned a system that combined some of the extant radar stations with 28 new ADS-B ground stations. For the first time, this gave complete continental surveillance coverage for aircraft flying above 30,000 feet – and almost complete coverage above 20,000 feet (media release, 'Australia completes world-first airspace surveillance system', airservicesaustralia.com, 21 December 2009). (A system with *satellite* surveillance could give complete coverage at all levels; but a ground station cannot 'see' aircraft at low levels except in the vicinity of the station.)

With the required ADS-B equipment installed in about 1100 aircraft approved for operation in Australian airspace, the new system brought *immediate and unequivocal* operational benefit, when dealing with equipped aircraft. Besides supporting less restrictive diversions around bad weather, air traffic controllers became able to reduce aircraft separation from 30 to 5 nautical miles, without reduction in safety levels.

In 2014, Airservices Australia went on to *mandate* installation of ADS-B Out equipment in aircraft flying in Australian airspace, from various effective dates (depending on airspace zone) within the period up to 2 February 2017, ('Carriage of ADS-B avionics in foreign registered aircraft operating in Australian territory' and 'ADS-B mandates 2014–2017', both accessed at airservicesaustralia.com, 3 May 2015).

The modest initial scheme takes advantage of the low installation and maintenance costs of the new ground-based stations (which, on both counts, are much less costly than radar). In planned later developments, *satellite* communication will play a larger role. The target year for introduction of that extension was earlier stated to be 2020 (Department of Infrastructure, Transport, Regional Development and Local Government, 2009, p. 132).

14.1.3 Charging principles for international air navigation services

In oceanic areas without radar coverage, the new satellite systems can track and support aircraft movements to an extent not previously feasible. Of course, this requires harmonised equipment in the various world regions.

Besides addressing that matter, the International Civil Aviation Organisation (an agency of the United Nations) has long taken an interest in the pricing of air navigation services. While implicitly recognising that it does not have authority in respect of services for *domestic* air *routes*, ICAO seeks to shape the charging principles to be applied for *en route* servicing of *international* flights (§III of International Civil Aviation Organization, 2012). The cost to be recovered through such charges is 'the full cost of providing the air navigation services, including appropriate amounts for cost of capital and depreciation of assets' (par. 3 (i)). However, the policy statement limits application of that principle to assets that the users consider necessary. In particular, 'any excessive construction, operation or (*sic*) maintenance expenditures' are to be excluded (par. 3 (ii)).

In allocating costs to individual airline users, ICAO urges that each provider State shall not engage in (price) discrimination between domestic and foreign airlines, nor between any two or more foreign airlines (par. 6 (iv)). And it takes a conventional approach in suggesting that the amount of a route movement charge could reasonably be made proportional to the (great-circle) distance flown (within the area served by the provider), and could increase (but less than proportionately) with aircraft weight (par. 8).

The price-discrimination issue arises also in the context of *airport* services, which are the subject of the next part of this chapter.

14.2 Airport ownership and market power

Many airports – especially those that serve major cities – have features that hinder or exclude the forces of competition. The most notable issues are these: (1) the presence of ownership and administrative arrangements that enhance an airport's market power; (2) the 'lumpy' nature of much airport investment; and (3) important externalities that can affect urban planning – including extra road traffic in a large area around the airport, and aircraft-noise pollution that limits the choice of land uses that may properly be located near an airport. Those matters give problems for all alternative ownership regimes and for economic regulation too. This chapter includes some discussion of the first and second of those issues.

As already noted briefly (§12.1), the market power that an airport enjoys in relation to airlines depends on its geographical location, both in relation to population centres and in relation to other airports that might compete with it.

In the early days of civil aviation, many countries relied on local governments to establish and manage the ports needed to accommodate the new travel mode. In coastal cities, an existing organisation that managed a seaport might be given the responsibility for building and operating the new airport. In the largest cities, where eventually there were two or more airports serving airlines, it was usual for a single authority to be responsible for all the airports in the metropolitan area.

In some of the other countries, the national government took on the responsibility for developing airports, at least in the major cities. Again, the administrative structure resulted in unified control, even when a large metropolitan area came to have two or more major ports. Such common ownership almost always rules out competition *between* the ports.

Even in the absence of common ownership, however, it may be difficult to foster competition between ports, especially where the distances between them are material. Even when the ports are located in a given metropolitan area, each has a natural catchment area, from which the port is more conveniently accessed than is any of the other ports within the metropolis. That difference alone gives each port a (limited) measure of market power.

For distinct but nearby cities each having a single airport, the inter-airport distances are generally much larger and the local market power of individual ports correspondingly greater.

Furthermore, in most urban areas, it is *very* difficult to find a site for a new airport. This often protects existing ports from new competition.

In contrast, a little-used secondary port in a rural location may have very little bargaining power, especially when dealing with a large airline that can choose which of many port(s) to start using as it expands its network. At stake for the port are growth possibilities such as those seen when Ryanair started a base at Charleroi (reported in §12.3.4).

The presence of monopoly characteristics may be thought to favour public-sector ownership of those airports with a significant degree of market power. However, government operation often brings its own problems: cost inefficiency in daily operation, political influences on the setting of charges, uncertain guidance of investment decisions, and a lack of innovation in management thinking. In some countries, those issues eventually helped to promote *corporatisation* of government-owned airports, a movement which began in the UK and some other English-speaking countries several decades ago.

Although transfer of an airport from a government department to a government-owned corporation may seem a small step, in practice it can ensure somewhat greater emphasis on financial discipline. Besides giving the airport corporation financial targets, government may institute formal economic regulation (especially of charges paid by airlines), in an attempt to promote the public interest. Where the airport belongs to a *local* government, either directly or through a port authority, formal regulation by an arms-length regulator does not always materialise. Yet it seems airport corporatisation often has improved economic efficiency.

Nevertheless, some governments have gone on to the next step – the sale of airports to private companies. While the ostensible aim of such *privatisation* has been a more whole-hearted pursuit of economic efficiency, the process of change has sometimes been tainted by governmental pursuit of a conflicting objective, namely the maximisation of revenue from asset sales. This has allowed opportunity for two kinds of shortcoming.

First, where an urban area is served by two or more airports, efficiency considerations suggest sale to separate parties in an attempt to promote competition. But sale of all the area's ports to one company is usually expected to bring in more revenue. It has proved all too easy for governments to prefer extra revenue.

Second, in quite a number of cases, the proposed privatisation of an airport has been accompanied by a push for (so-called) 'light-handed' regulation – which might allow the airport to increase its charges very significantly. Such an expectation has helped to increase the selling price of the airport.

The airports serving *London* provided an early example. While a local government remained the owner of Luton airport (later chosen by EasyJet for its headquarters and first base), the three major ports (Heathrow, Gatwick and Stansted) then owned by the British government were grouped (along with some other UK ports) to form the British Airports Authority, a government-owned corporation. Many years later (in 1987), the UK government privatised the entire group as a single company, called BAA plc.

There followed a long period of airline complaint about BAA's London ports: charges were said to be too high (and the economic regulator too compliant); and on some matters airport management was regarded as paying insufficient attention to service quality. After investigation, the (UK government's) Competition Commission decided (1) to require BAA plc to sell both Gatwick and Stansted, and (2) to recommend that the airport regulator (the Civil Aviation Authority) take certain actions regarding Heathrow 'where BAA will continue to have substantial market power even after the sale of Gatwick and Stansted' (Competition Commission, news release, 19 March 2009).

Although BAA had put Gatwick on the market before the Competition Commission's final decision, it appealed (unsuccessfully) over the ordained early deadline for the sale of Stansted. On 4 December 2009, Global Infrastructure Partners took control of Gatwick ('Gatwick Sale', gatwickairport.com, accessed 16 April 2010). (Global already owned the (short-runway) London City Airport, sited in the former London Docklands, and just a little to the east of the financial district.) And the company that already owned Manchester Airport became the new owner of Stansted.

Thus, some 22 years after the government's foolish decision to privatise the major ports by sale to the one company, competition concerns led to action to reduce the airports' market power. Early experience suggests the new strategy has enjoyed some success. At Stansted, for example, EasyJet and the new airport owner concluded a 'growth framework agreement', intended to encourage the airline to double its traffic there – thereby reversing earlier very sizeable reductions it made there between 2009 and 2013 ('EasyJet's . . . new Stansted agreement will "enable" growth', anna.aero, 19 June 2013). This about-turn by EasyJet strongly suggests an increase in that airline's market power at Stansted. Thus, greater competition between the London airports may well have improved economic efficiency – and airline profits, too.

In the *US*, in contrast, most airports are still in the hands of local governments. However, even at the most important ports, market power can sometimes be shared (constructively) between the port and some of its largest airline customers. In particular, a major legacy carrier may be able to move a hub or other major base from one port to another. That potential can encourage negotiation between the parties – for example, on investment in further passenger terminals, or (more rarely) an extra runway. Even so, in the absence of both vigorous competition and formal economic regulation, the investment and service-level decisions of US ports are often subject to influences grounded in local politics and in the self-interest of *large* airlines (Levine, 2009, pp. 46–9).

With that situation in mind (no doubt), the FAA initiated a *pilot* program for airport privatisation. Under that authorisation, the City of Chicago invited bids for a 99-year lease of its Chicago Midway port. When an issued sale contract did not complete, the City appropriated a non-refundable deposit of US$126 million (cityofchicago.org, 13 May 2009, accessed 19 April 2010). Another privatisation attempt foundered in 2013 when one bidder withdrew at a late stage when the

City was considering just two 'finalists'. The City mayor then abandoned the privatisation attempt ('Emanuel halts Midway privatization bidding', *Chicago Tribune*, 6 September 2013).

Also in the US, a *new* port at Branson was built and is operated by a private company. It is intended to encourage tourists to visit that Missouri city ('the live-music show capital of the world').

Despite its private ownership, Branson Airport *has* received some government support. It is located in Taney County, which 'agreed to accept ownership of the property and provide a long-term lease to Branson Airport LLC' (Branson Airport Factsheet, accessed at flybranson.com, 14 December 2008). One effect of this arrangement was to secure tax-free status for the considerable bond financing raised by the airport company.

In addition, the city of Branson signed a 30-year agreement whereby it pays US$8.40 for every tourist flying in to the port (Christine Negroni, 'In Missouri, investors seek a profit in Branson Airport', *New York Times*, 20 April 2009). Even so, in regard to financial incentives and risk-bearing, that agreement compares very favourably with the customary lump-sum government grants.

However, the airport has had difficulty in attracting and retaining scheduled airline services. Though Frontier maintained its A319 service from Denver for some years, this ceased when Frontier passed to new owners. After AirTran had provided service for several years, its new parent, Southwest Airlines, substituted service by its own larger B737 aircraft from March 2013, only to withdraw entirely in June 2014 (media release, 'Southwest Airlines to cease operations in three cities', 5 December 2013).

On 6 March 2015, the Branson website anticipated summer service by a couple of very small airlines, operating small aircraft. When re-examined on 9 March 2015, the website gave different details. Presumably, the owners of the port had hoped for better when deciding to invest.

In *Australia*, a private venture has had a more favourable outcome. At two hours' drive west of Brisbane is the city of Toowoomba (population exceeding 150,000). Its municipally owned local airport cannot handle the larger turboprops now used for many regional services. On a green-field site outside Toowoomba, a local business family with large-scale interests in other industries built a new port with a runway of length 2870 metres.

When the port opened in November 2014, QantasLink began flights (twice-daily on weekdays) between Toowoomba and *Sydney* (flight duration 95 minutes). The airline operates 76-seat Q400 turboprops, and over-nights an aircraft at Toowoomba every night except Saturday (Jamie Freed, 'QantasLink to fly to $100m privately owned Toowoomba airport', *Sydney Morning Herald*, 3 September 2014; flight details from qantas.com, accessed 9 March 2015 and 29 October 2015). The airport company seeks to host inter-state flights to capitals other than Sydney.

14.3 Pricing and other ways of assigning runway access

14.3.1 Pricing for runway access: public-policy considerations

The analysis begins with the case where there is sufficient runway capacity to serve all flights offering, without significant runway congestion. If the port also enjoys some market power (because there is no alternative port within a reasonable distance), the port may use that monopoly power to set the charges at such a high level that runway use is held to a level *below* that which would best promote economic efficiency. The chosen *structure* of the runway access charges may also damage economic efficiency. In particular, the port may set different prices for different airlines – if that is not prohibited by law. In all those ways, profit-seeking by the port owner may damage the process of airline competition, and result in a pattern of airport use that reduces the level of economic benefit derived from use of the runway.

For an example, consider the case which pitted Virgin Blue against Sydney Airport (reported above in §12.3.3). For Virgin's use of the runways, the airport introduced a charge that was proportional to the number of passengers carried on the individual flight, in place of the traditional movement charge that is based on the maximum take-off weight of the aircraft. Our purpose here is to analyse the public-interest implications of that profit-seeking airport strategy.

The 'ideal' public-interest prescription is that the unit price should match the incremental cost incurred in the production of that unit. If the chosen price exceeds that incremental cost, then some demand is discouraged, even though for those units, the final consumers would be willing to pay more than the incremental cost of production. The suppression of the demand for those units results in a reduction in the total (net) benefit accruing to society as a whole from the production performance.

In the case of aircraft movements, the service to be costed and priced is the provision of a runway for the aircraft to land. (To simplify the exposition, we ignore the fact that every landing is soon followed by a take-off.) That landing cost (the wear-and-tear cost experienced by the port owner) increases with the aircraft weight prevailing at the time the aircraft lands. However, it is not practicable to weigh the aircraft upon each landing. Because the weight of an extra passenger is so small, the maximum take-off weight (MTOW) is an acceptable proxy for the actual weight at the time of the landing.

In contrast, a movement charge that is *proportional* to the number of passengers on board fails to recognise that the weight of the aircraft itself is a large part of the total weight. In effect, it overestimates the weight of an extra passenger. Thus the passenger count is a poor proxy for the cost of the wear-and-tear of the runway. Its use may also discourage an airline from filling as many seats as would otherwise be profitable. In contrast, where an airport has market power, use of a per-passenger charge may be an effective tool for increasing airport revenue from aircraft movements.

In the Sydney Airport case, and in the absence of information on the public record, it is likely that the airport required Qantas to pay movement charges on the same basis as that applied to Virgin. Both airlines were deploying B737-800s. Because Qantas had business-class seating while Virgin had only a single cabin, a Qantas aircraft had fewer seats than a Virgin plane. Furthermore, because Qantas targeted business travellers, it probably had lower load factors than did Virgin (for a given route). Both elements would increase the charges paid by Virgin relative to those paid by Qantas. This would make it harder for low-fare Virgin to increase its market share. In turn, this would sacrifice some of the increased efficiency occasioned by Virgin's market entry.

Potentially, there are several ways in which a government may act to discourage or prevent access arrangements that damage the competitive process. In some countries there is general trade practices (anti-trust) legislation requiring an owner of (so-called) essential infrastructure to grant access to all potential users, on reasonable terms, and to the extent that capacity limits allow. That can help an airline that has been unable to obtain runway access on reasonable terms, or has been denied access altogether.

General trade-practices legislation can also prohibit what is often termed 'abuse of market power'. Despite the difficulties in defining 'abuse', the application of this provision to airports may work passably well in any country that has developed a significant amount of effective case law. Otherwise, an industry-specific regulatory scheme may be preferred. For aviation, the latter can reduce legal imprecision by using terms that relate specifically to the issues that arise in the airport context.

In summary, considerations of equity and economic efficiency motivate two policy rules for an airport that does *not* have significant runway congestion: runway access charges should not depend on the airline name painted on the side of the aircraft; and the tariff should reflect, to the extent practicable, the structure of the movement costs experienced by the airport.

14.3.2 Runway access: pricing principles for dealing with congestion

Even during a peak-period for use of the runway, the hourly rate of aircraft movements is influenced by the charge levels for runway access. This section considers how to set those charges so as to give the greatest economic benefit from use of the runway.

The important additional feature is the presence of queues of aircraft waiting to land. Such queuing results in extra fuel used and extra engine wear incurred, and causes delay for passengers, crew and the aircraft itself. Thus the hourly cost of airborne delays is large. (When the runway is congested, there will be smaller but still significant costs arising from delays to aircraft that are queuing for take-off.)

A pricing principle for a congested runway

Standard runway charging methods, notably pricing according to aircraft weight, have no regard for those aircraft delays. So, what is needed instead is a charging basis that brings home to Alpha Airlines all the extra costs incurred by all the other affected parties if Alpha were to schedule an extra aircraft movement in the peak period. Once such a charging scheme is in place, Alpha has a financial incentive to compare the landing charge it pays with the value to Alpha of the right to make the extra movement.

As will now be argued, that approach serves the public interest well. If Alpha decides to introduce the extra flight, we know that the value to it of the movement is the same as, or (more likely) exceeds the amount of the charge. If that charge accurately measures the extra costs imposed on all other parties, then the value of the movement to Alpha exceeds the extra costs to all other parties. It is then in the public interest to have Alpha introduce the extra aircraft movement – because the value of the extra flight exceeds the total loss experienced by the other parties. And the total social benefit from use of the runway increases.

Similarly if the value to Alpha falls short of the amount of the movement charge, Alpha will not introduce the extra flight. As before, the amount of that charge matches the extra costs experienced by the other parties. Thus the value to Alpha now falls short of the extra costs to other parties. And in that case it is in the public interest that the extra flight should not be introduced – because if it *were* made, the other parties would lose more than Alpha gains. And the total social benefit from use of the runway would be reduced.

Implementation of the new pricing rule

A practicable rule for pricing of runway congestion needs some approximate, simplifying assumptions. During the peak period, the number of aircraft in the queues will vary. It is likely that implementation will be based on average queue lengths during the period. If that approximation seems unsatisfactory, the entire period might be divided into (say) three sub-periods, and distinct averages applied to each.

To a good approximation, each aircraft movement requires exclusive use of the runway for the same time-duration. To a reasonable approximation, the runway-wear-and-tar cost is the same for each aircraft. Then, the new pricing rule has an important feature: each aircraft movement made within a congested period (or sub-period) while the runway has other aircraft waiting (to land or take off) pays the same access charge, regardless of the aircraft type and the other characteristics of the movement.

Where congestion-based pricing is introduced to deal with severe congestion delays, it is likely that the new rule will bring in more revenue than that received under the previous pricing regimes during the congested time-periods. In that case there is no role for a charge related to aircraft MTOW during those periods. In periods without significant runway congestion, the previous MTOW charge can be used. If that combination of charging rules does not bring in enough revenue to cover all the costs of the airport's runways, a MTOW charge may be added during the congested period, at a charging rate that does not exceed that applicable in the periods without congestion.

Adjustments when congestion pricing is first deployed

Where a port previously used MTOW-based pricing (or some other pricing approach that did not distinguish between peak-demand and other periods), the new peak-period charges will be higher than before. In the face of such higher charges, a number of such movements that were previously only marginally profitable then become unprofitable.

In particular, if the airport previously hosted general aviation (small-aircraft) movements, then in practice few if any of those movements will remain in the congested period. Some may be withdrawn; others will shift to periods in which the runway is not congested.

Second, a scheduled airline generally has flights of quite varied profitability. When re-assessing its schedule in the light of the new movement charges, the airline is likely to discontinue at least some of those flight now seen to incur a financial loss – or switch them to a period without congestion.

Such adjustments will reduce the durations of the congestion delays at the airport. The use of a price mechanism helps to ensure that it is the least valuable flights that no longer use up the valuable peak-period runway capacity. The reduction in the number of flights being operated in the peak period will also reduce the aggregate delay cost experienced by the remaining flights. In turn, that should lead to a reduction in the level of the peak-period charges. As in any other market, it may take a little while for the market to settle down to a new equilibrium situation.

Furthermore, a concerned government may formulate and implement a policy in which that market test is not allowed to dispossess certain flights, notably those serving remote areas. Such an approach is based on distributive grounds, which the government thereby deems to be more important than market efficiency considerations.

14.3.3 Congestion pricing: some further considerations

Estimating delay costs

In order to implement the economic principle, the agency responsible for setting runway access charges needs to be able to estimate (for an extra movement) the additional delay costs imposed on all other aircraft movements. Besides collecting recent data on individual aircraft movements and delays, the agency needs to ascertain (or estimate) the numbers of passengers on each delayed flight, and then apply sensible per-minute valuations for both aircraft and passenger delays. While these are major tasks, it should be possible to make good cost estimates. (For an instance, see Prices Surveillance Authority (Australia), 1993, ch. 7.)

A movement may delay other flights of the same airline

At a busy port, a large airline may operate a significant proportion of all the flights at the port. In that case, when the airline operates a flight which delays a number of the ensuing flights, some of those delayed flights belong to the large airline itself. On the congestion-charging basis just prescribed, the large airline finds that a part of the monetary value of those delay costs is imposed twice – once in the form of the actual delays to its own queuing aircraft, and once as a component in the access charge.

However, unless the large airline operates a large proportion of all the flights at the port, the proportion that is double-counted is not so very great, especially because the congestion charge includes the cost of delays to the airline's own passengers, which (it may be argued) will have been disregarded by the airline in assessing the financial reward it gets by operating the flight.

While the rational economic woman or man who serves as the CEO of the large airline will be aware of the self-imposed delay costs, studies in behavioural economics suggest that decision makers do not always fully take into account costs that are not *directly* charged to the pocket or the profit statement.

How should an economic regulator regard airport revenues from congestion charges?

Where a government has appointed a regulator to control the profit level of the airport, and where that airport starts to receive extra revenue from congestion-based access charges, how should the regulator regard the consequent increase in its total revenue?

An airport with congestion charges is a busy airport and its profit before the introduction of such charges is likely to have been up at the limit permitted by the regulator. Then, if the introduction of congestion charging increases the airport's net revenue in the peak period (as is to be expected), the government regulator would require a compensating reduction in other revenue, to get the port back to its permitted maximum profit level.

In pursuing that end, the regulator should *not* seek a reduction in the access charge levied during congested periods, because that charge is – and on grounds of economic efficiency, should remain – set equal to the social cost of the movement, being the delay cost and the runway wear-and-tear cost.

Rather, the revenue reduction can be and should be effected by lowering the access charges in periods when the runway is *not* congested. Those charges serve primarily as revenue raisers. Economic efficiency requires only that each charge should be large enough to recover the runway wear-and-tear cost of the aircraft movement. Generally the charge will be much higher than that, to help recover the indirect costs of operating the airfield. In the new situation, a somewhat greater part of that task is done by the higher revenues resulting from the higher runway access charges levied during the congested periods.

When simple MTOW charging is being used in the periods without runway congestion, the required reduction in total runway revenue raised could be achieved by reducing the charge per tonne of maximum take-off weight. (That approach avoids occasion for *new* arguments about the equity of MTOW charging!)

In short, the two charging regimes, when used *together*, give the airport enough money to pay its bills for the indirect costs; they also ensure that, for each individual aircraft movement the charge is high enough to cover the direct costs (including those falling on other parties).

Does introduction of the equilibrium values for congestion charges guarantee elimination of all delays?

The short answer is 'no, not always – not even after there has been ample opportunity to build more runway capacity'.

For the present purpose, an intuitive explanation should suffice. Building extra capacity costs money. If capacity were increased in successive steps, the benefit of each of the successive increments of extra capacity diminishes. A first increment (if sold to the highest bidders) will eliminate some of the largest of the delays. For a subsequent capacity increment, somewhat smaller delays will be eliminated. And so on. If the delays are very costly, and the construction costs are low, it may be beneficial to add enough capacity to eliminate all the delays. But if extra capacity is very costly, and the *remaining* delays are not very severe, then there may come a stage at which the benefits from adding one more increment of capacity falls short of the cost of that capacity increment. In that situation, the further capacity increment is not worth building, and it is in the public interest that some delays remain.

That account ignores some aspects of the reality of the situation. In particular, runways are indivisible: you can't build half a runway now and the other half later. That reality increases the likelihood that some delays will remain after the best programme of capacity enlargement has been implemented.

Furthermore, Levine (2009, p. 42) points to some ports at each of which a large US carrier 'operates the vast preponderance of [the port's] flights'. His examples include Charlotte, where American Airlines (still) hubs, and Minneapolis (still a Delta hub). At such ports, he notes, the 'amount of delay at peak times is not trivial'. Furthermore, a very large proportion of the delayed aircraft are being flown by the large carrier, which itself suffers the delay. Because the hubbing carrier has great influence at the port, it could persuade the owner to increase runway capacity. However, the long-term persistence of the delay indicates that the hubbing airline prefers to suffer the delay costs rather than pay a correspondingly large proportion of the costs of installing extra runway capacity.

Of course, a hubbing airline may also have a strategic motive, especially when extra capacity comes in large increments. As Levine himself points out (footnote 15), an investment in an additional runway, even if efficient from a public-interest point of view, may not be welcomed by the incumbent large carrier, because the consequent extra 'spare' peak-period runway capacity might attract rival entry at the port; especially feared would be entry by a low-cost airline.

14.3.4 Other methods of assigning runway capacity during peak periods

A 'spot' market?

In a 'spot' market, as is sometimes used for wholesaling of electricity, there are no buy-and-sell contracts with prices agreed in advance. Rather the market price can change from one moment to the next, as a result of on-going changes in the level of demand for electricity, and sometimes in response to changes in the available supply capacity.

Although experience in a specific spot market can help in preparing price forecasts, there is no market agent who plans the price changes. Hence there is no party who can give advance notice of changes. Rather, the price adjusts instantaneously in order to match total quantity demanded with the total amount supplied. (And, unlike the case of aircraft movements, delayed service is not a substitute for immediate service: buyers of electricity are not able to join a queue.)

In the case of access to a congested runway, such a scheme is impracticable. There are no spot markets for access to congested runways.

Prior allocation of capacity

Instead, when there is only a moderate amount of congestion, the usual practice is to institute first-come first-served queuing. Where the congestion is more severe, queuing becomes impractical, and the standard practice is to establish and assign so-called 'slots', as already discussed (§12.5.1). Each pair of slots gives the airline holder the right to operate one landing and one take-off; and each movement has to be conducted within its own predetermined time-period. In using such slot rights, the airline still pays the aircraft movement charges.

The total number of slots is set by an airport planner – or by a government regulator – who decides how many movements can be accommodated on the runway with no more than acceptable aircraft delays. The method for then assigning slots to airlines varies across ports, depending on institutional circumstances.

Besides the time of day at which a slot is available, various other dimensions need to be specified. Should each movement be the subject of a separate contract? If not, what aggregation might be the most useful? Perhaps two slots at the same times every day, to allow an aircraft to arrive and depart? Or perhaps a group of (say) eight slots available every day, at times during the day that allow the airline's staff at the station to work efficiently?

Next, for how long should a contract run? Airlines generally make major timetable adjustments twice a year. Perhaps each contract might provide for daily runway access at specified times of day for several months. Alternatively, a contract might allow the airline to use the slots in perpetuity.

Should an airline be required to give up any slot rights that it fails to use 'regularly' (however that term may be defined)? That question addresses a practice in which an airline holds slots for potential major use later, but wants to deny current runway access to a rival. To thwart a regulator who requires 'regular' use, however, an airline may itself use the slots by operating a small aircraft for minor flights of little or no profitability, until it is ready to use the slots 'properly' for a major purpose.

Incidentally, such strategic hoarding of slots may have occurred at Love Field, Dallas, in the years before the long-heralded termination in 2014 of the Wright restriction on destinations that airlines were allowed to serve by non-stop flights from Love (see also §14.3.6 below).

If and when an airline no longer wants some (identified) slots, there can be arguments about who owns the slots, and about what the using airline can do with them. Those situations are particularly difficult to resolve when the airline acquired the slots informally, sometimes simply by starting regular flights on a daily basis at a port not then significantly congested, and so acquiring what eventually became an entrenched right, arising merely from prolonged use.

One lesson is clear: for any future assignment of new slots, or of old slots that are to be reassigned, the regulator should carefully spell out whether or not the airline is allowed to lease the slots to others, sell the slots outright, and swap slots for some held by another airline. On grounds of economic efficiency, flexible arrangements are to be preferred in many circumstances – but not when there is a risk that an airline may choose not to sell or lease to a potential rival (again, see §14.3.6 below).

An important feature has emerged. The story began with the importance of flexibility in runway access charges. But it has now morphed into a discussion of how to allocate a pre-determined number of slots. Despite the *nominal* difference, these approaches are (broadly) equivalent ways of conveying to users the presence of scarcity. However, the outcome may depend on which allocation method is used.

For a specified busy period, a targeted (given) total number of aircraft movements can be offered by (at least) two alternative methods: *either* by setting an access charge per aircraft movement, *or* by declaring the existence of a number of slots, and allowing those slots to be freely bought and sold. The former is more flexible, in that it readily allows aircraft movements at set times, made by different airlines on different days. In customary practice, on the other hand, the implied or explicit slot contract is for exclusive use over a much longer period.

The alternative approaches can have important differences in financial consequences. Decisions about runway access charges are taken by the airport owner, *who usually retains all the revenue from the charges*. In contrast, airports rarely if ever get (direct) financial benefit from slot prices. In particular, when an airline sells a slot it has been using, it is usual for the *entire* revenue to accrue to the airline.

However, the larger is the airport-charge for an aircraft movement, the smaller is the price the airline receives when it sells a slot, because the sale price reflects the worth to the buying airline after taking into account the movement charges that airline will have to pay (even if it becomes the 'owner' of the slot). It is no surprise that airlines defend their slot rights (including any rights to sell their slots), whereas airports usually prefer that access rationing be done by means of movement charges.

This analysis of congested runway access has been based on standard economic analysis – which pre-supposes the presence of airlines in sufficient number to support competition for runway access. However, analytical modelling of situations with only small numbers of airline players leads Barbot (2005) to conclude that, in practice, introducing congestion pricing may not always be in the public interest. Of course, similar problems arise in a slot market.

14.3.5 Slot management in practice: short-term issues

In practice, the institutional arrangements for the design, assignment and conditions of use of slots are almost always *far* removed from the principled approach set out above. This section looks at a few short-term aspects of efficiency and equity in those common practices. (The long-term implications for the planning of additional runway capacity are addressed in §14.3.7 below.)

At most if not all congested ports, the prevailing assignment of slots owes much to historical circumstance and little to economic efficiency – or, even, to the aggregate profitability of the set of airlines serving the port. In particular, an airline seeking to start (or increase) service at a congested port may be unable to obtain the slots it needs, even when the public benefit of its intended new service is greater than that of some of the existing runway uses.

At a port where the airline users have established a committee (in English-speaking countries, often called a Board of Airline Representatives), the committee members typically attend to the interests of their airlines, and often find it difficult to reach agreement on issues concerning the allocation of further slots. Such failure invites intervention by a government agency, which may apply an arbitrary, default rule perhaps based on grand-fathering or a uniform lottery. A simulation study (Grether, Isaac and Plott, 1981) found that the bargaining within such a committee typically approaches the outcome that the members expect would apply in the event of external intervention. Notions about what allocation would give the greatest overall economic benefit receive little or no weight.

On the other hand, if the institutional setting allows it, later buying and selling of assigned slots – or of short-term leases of those slots – may help to improve the economic outcome. A report prepared for the European Commission (Mott MacDonald and others, 2006) notes that such 'secondary' trading in the 'grey' market for slots at London Heathrow and London Gatwick airports had resulted in increased slot efficiency, as measured there by the (annual) number of available seat kilometres operated per slot.

That increase came as long-haul flights and larger aircraft displaced the operations of some airlines who were the original holders of the slot rights. In particular, some short-haul airlines either went out of business, or moved their operations to other London-area ports. While British Airways had been the largest purchaser of slots, *new* long-haul airlines had also been buyers. Often, direct competitors had been willing to swap slots with each other. However the report has little to say about unilateral sales from an airline *to a rival*.

A sale instance (*not* to a rival) illustrates some of the possibilities. In June 2014, Cyprus Airways announced it was to transfer its London Heathrow service to London Stansted, and to sell its daily Heathrow slot-pair to American Airlines for US$31 million (Paul Riegler, 'American buys London-Heathrow slot for $31 million', *Frequent Business Traveller*, 16 June 2014; Cyprus Airways, Announcement, 17 June 2014). While the airline sold in order to help with a financial problem, it seems likely that the deal served the public-interest as well.

The authors of the 2006 report concluded that, if the EU were to establish well-defined markets for slot sales throughout Europe, there would be *additional* growth in passenger numbers and revenue passenger kilometres. However, the extra growth would not continue indefinitely; such formal markets would simply speed up the adjustments already in train.

The report found that the anticipated effects on competition were mixed: an increase in competition on long-haul routes would be accompanied by a short-haul decrease. Services from a country's regional and peripheral ports to the *principal* capital-city ports would be likely to diminish, unless the Commission chose to give them some measure of priority.

In summary, the report supported an *a priori* expectation: while the common, inflexible arrangements for the allocation of slots do not serve the public interest in economic efficiency, the establishment of a secondary market for slots can give a quite a good outcome – at least for so-called 'static efficiency', that is, for the efficient use of *existing* runways. The only short-term concern is the possibility of adverse effects on airline competition.

14.3.6 Wrestling with the politics of congestion pricing: the US situation

Around the world, the rarity of *implemented* congestion pricing for runway access may reflect political adversity rather than the complexity of the under-lying economic principles. Witness to that proposition comes from the history of runway access in the US.

Government policy on slots

In 1968, the US Federal Aviation Administration introduced limits on the number of aircraft movements at four busy ports, Reagan National (at Washington), and the three major New York ports, LaGuardia, John F Kennedy and Newark. The slot rights thereby implicitly created were assigned without the recipient airlines being required to pay for them (Koran and Ogur, 1983, appendix II). While initially the slots could not be bought and sold, or even exchanged, the FAA reversed its position in 1985, perhaps unwisely!

Absent any regulatory involvement, a prospective seller of a slot generally knows the identity of each potential bidder, and *may* prefer to sell to an airline that will not be an effective competitor, rather than receive a higher price from a strong competitor who then uses the slot to damage the seller's profitability. Similar problems can arise in the exchange of slots. In such cases, the new uses for the slots may not yield the highest possible public benefit (Levine, 2009, p. 58). Levine goes on (p. 82) to urge the use of blind auctions, in which the identities of the bidders are not revealed to the sellers.

In August 2009, Delta and US Airways sought regulatory approval for a swap of daily slot pairs – 125 pairs held by US Airways at LaGuardia (New York) and 42 pairs held by Delta at Reagan National (Washington, DC) ('Delta, US Air to swap slots at Reagan, LaGuardia', *Wall Street Journal*, 12 August 2009). In response, the FAA required the airlines to *divest* a certain number of slots at each port, as a pre-condition for its approval.

In turn, the airlines then offered to sell *smaller* numbers, to buyers of their own choosing, namely AirTran, Spirit, JetBlue and WestJet. This proposal was not acceptable to the FAA. It also upset Southwest Airlines, which wanted slots at both ports (Ted Reed, 'Southwest blasts revised slot deal', theStreet.com, 23 March 2010). In August 2010, Delta and US Airways filed a statement with the US Court of Appeals for the District of Columbia. The case seemed to involve the issue of whether slots are airline property or merely an operating privilege (Andrew Compart, 'Lawsuit raises slot ownership issue', *Aviation Week*, 11 August 2010).

While the wrangling went on, further events changed the situation: in particular, Southwest bought AirTran and so gained control of *some* slots at Reagan. In the eventual outcome (which came only in late 2011!), the Department of Transport approved a revised swap proposed by the two airlines, while requiring a cash-only, blind auction for the divested slots.

In that auction, JetBlue successfully bid US$40 million for eight slot pairs at Reagan. Southwest was the next highest bidder at US$32 million; its CEO was reported as saying that the JetBlue bid was 'absolute madness. A guaranteed money loser.' (Terry Maxon, 'Southwest's Kelly calls JetBlue's bid for Washington National slots "absolute madness"', *Dallas Morning News*, 5 December 2011). (Recall the US$31 million paid to Cyprus Airways for one Heathrow slot pair.)

In an earlier attempt to launch an improved slot policy, the FAA said it proposed to 'retire' (that is, cancel or withdraw) some slots, and to launch auctions for a proportion of the remaining slots at the New York ports. An opportunity for a pilot auction (no pun intended) arose in the spring of 2008 when Eos Airlines ended its daily round-trip service between Newark (New York) and Heathrow (London). The FAA plan, to auction a five-year lease for the vacated pair of Newark slots, drew protests from the major US legacy carriers, on whose behalf the Air Transport Association of America (now, Airlines for America) began court proceedings. In December the US Court of Appeals for the District of Columbia stayed the proposed auctions, and the FAA announced (New York Airports Slot Auctions – Update, 9 December 2008) that it was suspending its intended programme of slot auctions.

In 2013, when American Airlines and US Airways announced that they planned to merge, the US Department of Justice opposed the proposal on the grounds that the merger would significantly reduce competition between the major US airlines (Complaint to the US District Court for the District of Columbia, 13 August 2013). Eventually, the airlines agreed with the DOJ to divest the runway slots and complementary airport assets listed in Table 14.1.

While some of the slot-pair numbers shown in the table are quite large, the divestment is only a modest proportion of the airport totals. At Reagan National, considering American and US Airways together, the divestment reduced their slot use from 69 per cent to 57 per cent of the total number of slots, while for the 'low-cost carriers' (defined as Southwest, JetBlue and Virgin America), the share increased from six to eighteen per cent. For all other airlines (including Delta and United), the share remained at 25 per cent. At La Guardia, the percentage increase in the LCC share was somewhat smaller than at Reagan (US District Court for the District of Columbia, Memorandum Opinion, 25 April 2014, pp. 11–12).

In insisting on the programme of slot divestments, the DOJ aimed to boost competition in domestic airline markets, to offset *in part* the public-interest losses arising from the merger-induced reductions in competition on various routes. Apparently, as part of its settlement with American Airlines and US Airways, the Department of Justice listed airlines that were to be regarded as eligible purchasers. As seen in the Table, all the divested slots were sold to just three airlines: Southwest, JetBlue and Virgin America.

In prescribing financial terms for the required divestments, the Court relied, where feasible, on any existing terms. For example, at Reagan National, American was required to offer the eight slot-pairs already leased by JetBlue 'by making permanent the current agreement between JetBlue and American'. However, where there were no relevant existing terms, the Court said merely that (for example) the divesting airline 'shall divest in Slot Bundles to at least two Acquirers the other 88 DCA slots ... together with any of the JetBlue slots not sold to JetBlue' (paragraphs IV. F.1 and 2, of the Final Judgement, stated in US District Court for the District of Columbia *Proposed Final Judgement* (and related documents) 12 November 2013).

The Final Judgement also required divestment of *gates* and other assets at various ports, to allow the acquirers of slots to operate in the same manner as the previous incumbents, and hence be able to make an immediate start. While new gates may be constructed in due course at most airports, that divestment term in the Final Judgement was of the utmost importance for gates at Dallas Love Field, where an earlier legislative provision *prohibits* construction of *additional* gates! (For those gates at Love, Virgin America was said to be the only airline on the DOJ list of prospective recipients.)

Some general conclusions on slots

Because of the *de facto* ownership by incumbent airlines of runway slots that are to be divested, those airlines are commonly allowed to sell the slots. Hence they

Table 14.1 Slots and gates required to be divested by American Airlines and US Airways, 2014[1,2]

Slots at La Guardia (LGA), New York

Previous disposition			*Divested disposition*	
Held by	*Used by*	*No. of slot pairs*	*Held and used by*	*No. of slot pairs*
American	Southwest	5	Southwest	5
American/ US Airways	American/ US Airways	12	Southwest	6
			Virgin America	6

Slots at Reagan National (DCA), Washington DC

Previous disposition			*Divested disposition*	
Held by	*Used by*	*No. of slot pairs*	*Held and used by*	*No. of slot pairs*[4]
American	JetBlue	8	JetBlue	8
American[3]	American	44	JetBlue	12
			Southwest	27
			Virgin America	4

Gates at Love Field (DAL), Dallas

Previous disposition			*Post-merger disposition*	
Held by	*Used by*	*No. of gates*	*Held and used by*	*No. of gates*
American	United?	2	Virgin America	2

Gates at other ports
Two gates at each of these ports:

Boston Logan, Chicago O'Hare, Los Angeles International and Miami International

Sources: US District Court for the District of Columbia, Proposed Final Judgement (and related documents), 12 November 2013; US District Court for the District of Columbia, Memorandum Opinion, 25 April 2014; US Department of Justice Statement on US District Court Finding that Department's Settlement with US Airways/American Airlines is in the Public Interest, 28 April 2014; airline media releases from JetBlue, 30 January 2014 and 19 June 2014; Southwest, 5 December 2013 and 30 January 2014; and Virgin America, 5 March 2014 and 5 May 2014

Notes
1 The US Department of Justice required divestments as a precondition for withdrawing its opposition to the merger between the two airlines. Eventually, the DOJ and the two airlines agreed on the schedule shown here. The US District Court for the District of Columbia formalised and ratified the arrangements and conditions.
2 In some cases, the named low-cost carriers held/used other slot pairs at Reagan National and/or LaGuardia before acquiring those divested by American Airlines and US Airways.
3 This set of 44 slot pairs includes one pair initially held and used by US Airways (Department of Justice Statement on US District Court Finding, 25 April 2014).
4 At Reagan, one slot-pair remained unsold, apparently because it permitted only weekend flights (Terry Maxon, *Dallas Morning News*, 26 March 2014).

retain at least part of the capital values of the slots, namely the highest money amounts that the *eligible* airlines are willing to bid.

In the American Airlines/US Airways case, the *voluntary* purchase of the nominated slots demonstrates that the acquiring low-cost carriers expected to profit from their slot purchases, even when setting lower fares than those previously charged by the route incumbents. And the merging airlines (and perhaps some other legacy carriers) could expect to *lose* profits on the routes thereby entered by the low-cost carriers. (Note that the new route entries generally do not match the route exits of the merging airlines. To the extent that the slot-purchasing airlines make better use of the divested slots, the improved utilisation of the scarce runway capacity serves the public interest.)

Government policy on aircraft movement charges

In 2007 and 2008, a buoyant economy led to unusually severe congestion at the three main New York City ports. That prompted US Transportation Secretary Mary Peters to announce new rules that would encourage 'overcrowded airports . . . to move away from the decades-old practice of charging aircraft landing fees based simply on the weight of the plane, and instead have the flexibility to vary charges based on the time of day the plane operates' (US Department of Transportation, 'Reducing airline delays and fuel usage', press release, 10 July 2008).

The new policy (US Department of Transportation, 2008) explicitly allows airport operators to levy a two-part movement fee, comprising a 'per-operation charge' (of a particular form) *as well as* the traditional weight-based charge. The per-operation charge may be levied only in periods when the runway is congested. Its amount is determined by including in the cost base certain further costs not previously allowed. In particular, these include 'costs of an airfield project currently under construction' (p. 40,445 in the Federal Register); previously such costs could not be included until the project came into use.

The per-operation charge was intended to influence airline scheduling. Because it is an additional charge and is levied only in congested periods, it gave the airlines an incentive to switch some flights from such periods to less busy times. Further, because it does not depend on aircraft weight, it gave airlines an increased incentive to schedule larger aircraft and so operate fewer flights in the congested periods. (The usual weight-based charge is broadly proportional to the number of seats in the aircraft, and so does not give such an incentive.)

The DOT recognised that the scheme '[does] not represent true congestion pricing because [the scheme does] not authorize airport proprietors to set fees to balance demand with capacity' (p. 40,432). The modesty of the policy change is there attributed to the political need to have charges that are based on the (allowable) costs of the airport. If, instead, the DOT had been prepared to balance revenue with allowable costs *at the aggregate level*, the introduction of peak-period pricing could have been done on a revenue neutral basis. This would have *reduced* the off-peak charges, and enhanced the incentive effects.

While that would have given the Department the moral high ground regarding economic efficiency, the approach might *not* have averted opposition from the major airlines, represented by the Air Transport Association (now called Airlines for America) which petitioned the US Court of Appeals for DC, seeking a review of the policy. And it might have put at risk the support of the major airports, whose association was an intervenor in the Court. Notwithstanding the Court's earlier dislike of DOT policy on airport charges and slots, the Court this time proved sympathetic to the notion of congestion pricing. Despite having a less-than-ideal understanding of some finer points of the economic principles, the Court denied the petition (US Court of Appeals for DC, 2010).

Because the new DOT policy allowed but did not *require* airports to use the limited charging flexibility, it remains to be seen whether the initiative will have much effect.

Concluding remarks on US policy regarding runway congestion

These policy struggles on aircraft movement charges and slots come after almost *fifty* years of government attempts to put in place some sensible arrangements for tackling runway congestion. As the details have shown, the challenge is to devise practicable measures that promote economic efficiency to the greatest degree permitted by the political pressures exerted by the airlines, the airports and the other actors within the aviation sector, and by the governments and citizens in the locality of each port.

A particularly severe problem arises where, as in New York, a single operator controls all the major ports. Levine (2009, p. 77) argues that, in such cases, it is essential to break up the monopoly, in order to reduce the scope for market distortions.

After noting that local pressures favour quiet skies, prestigious terminal buildings and a large number of local jobs, Levine (pp. 75–80) still prefers economic efficiency, and wants:

- the revenue from congestion charges to be used only for (well-conceived) additions to aviation capacity, and *not* for local non-aviation projects;
- the number of slots made available and/or the total price charged for an aircraft movement to be chosen so as to eliminate *inefficient* congestion; and
- an end to exemptions for particular flight categories, such as international routes and small-town services.

In particular, Levine notes, an airport left to its own devices may set and use congestion charges only to supplement its own revenues, and may refrain from investing in more airport capacity, even where that latter is in the public interest (Levine, 2009, p. 80). (Though Levine dos not make the point, such issues suggest that there may be a good case for having the revenues from congestion charges paid in the first instance to a national economic regulator, who then considers whether there is a good case for investment in additional airport capacity.

A further issue concerns the significant periods of *adverse weather* that temporarily reduce runway capacity. There may be a case at some affected ports for designating a proportion of aircraft movements as *interruptible* (Neels, 2002). Such movements could be offered at a lower movement charge, to compensate the holder for the occasions when the flight has to be cancelled, sometimes at quite short notice. On days with bad weather, a pre-planned schedule for a reduced number of aircraft movements could be less troublesome for all than the lengthy delays and flight cancellations that prevail under traditional arrangements. The airlines could use interruptible slots for their less profitable flights, an arrangement that is likely to serve the public interest.

In the overall consideration of the economic management of an airport's runways, the most difficult issues of all concern:

- the likely political need to buy out the holders of any slots that are to be retired, and the consequent reduction in the funds available for the expansion of runway capacity;
- the distribution of the remaining revenues from the sale or lease of slots; and
- discovery of what if any further runway investment best serves the public interest.

The last of those issues is taken up in the next section.

14.3.7 Congestion charges and runway investment decisions

If an airport has congestion-based aircraft movement charges in place for busy periods, and if there remains a significant degree of congestion even when the *equilibrium* values for those charges are in place, there *may* be a public-interest case for further investment to increase runway capacity (supposing that the airport site has space available for such enhancement).

Preparing the analysis to guide such a long-term investment is even more difficult than reaching good decisions about the appropriate levels of the access charges for efficient use of the *prevailing* runway capacity. However, given the general predilection of politicians for taking decisions without much if any analysis, an economic study that is sensible is likely to serve the public interest more effectively, notwithstanding the inevitable use of many simplifications and approximation in the economic analysis.

The public interest criterion requires capacity expansion *if and only if* the (social) value of the economy-wide benefits exceeds the total costs of building and maintaining the extra capacity. In the runway context, the principal benefits comprise the resultant saving in aircraft operating costs (together with the values of the time savings for the passengers) for the prevailing number of flights *plus* the net benefit of any extra flights that are operated as a result of the increase in the runway capacity.

Before embarking on a major project, an airport should ensure that it has exploited all the opportunities for more efficient operation of its existing airfield configuration, including (for example) the establishment of high-speed turn-offs to help arriving aircraft to exit the runway as quickly as possible.

When considering construction of a further runway, the first step in the analysis is to devise one or more feasible options for the location and physical dimensions of the potential runway. As in any investment appraisal, the next matter to consider is the choice of a *time horizon* for the analysis. Here, in estimating the likely pattern of use of the new runway, the analyst has to decide how many years of its operation should be taken into account.

The likely time-trend in use depends on changes in demand factors such as income levels and population growth. On the supply side, the number of aircraft movements may be reduced if there is a continuing shift towards the use of larger aircraft. And so on.

As we look further and further into the future, the forecasts of such magnitudes become more and more uncertain. With time-discounting in the reckoning, the contribution of the present value of future costs and benefits in later years is much reduced. It may be sufficient to work up to a time horizon of only ten or fifteen years, even though the new runway will remain in use for much longer than that.

Perhaps the most important elements in public-interest decision-making are whether the prevailing institutional arrangements contain incentives that will lead to the undertaking of an objective cost-benefit analysis, and whether the politicians will want to implement the results of that analysis. Few countries have politicians who are addicted to commissioning competent cost-benefit analysis and judging on the basis of its analytical insights. Therein lies the major opportunity for failure.

In addition, the prevailing financial incentives often induce parties within the aviation sector to pursue ends that are not compatible with the public interest. In particular, the airport under consideration may prefer, where feasible, to continue collecting the revenue from high levels of congestion charges for aircraft movements, rather than have a new runway which allows more movements, but comes with lower movement charges (as well as all the extra capital costs).

14.4 Regulation of other airport activities

14.4.1 Airline access to passenger terminals

The major economic issues that arise in the provision of passenger terminals have been identified in §12.4. In the absence of *any* legislative requirement or ongoing regulation of terminal services, a terminal operator may deny access to an airline, or may fail to provide the kind of terminal facilities that an airline wants to have. Such conduct can arise in the course of airport profit-seeking, *or* as a result of political pressures that favour a particular airline, such as the legacy national-carrier, *or* when a particular terminal is owned or otherwise controlled by an individual airline.

Of course there can be opposing forces that limit such arbitrary exercise of power. For example, a new low-cost airline may be able quickly to create a terminal of basic quality, either by conversion of an existing structure or by putting up a temporary building – provided, of course, that this is not precluded by space constraints or by a decision of the airport operator.

Furthermore, where a government has instituted essential-infrastructure legis-lation, this *may* be applicable to passenger terminals, though, at a multi-terminal port, and unlike the runway case, a court or other arbitrator may *not* be persuaded that the use of a particular terminal is indeed essential for a particular airline. And the legislation may not apply in a dispute concerning the *type* of terminal service. On the other hand, where an airport is large enough to support more than one terminal, competition between independent terminal operators may give a good outcome (Civil Aviation Authority, 2001).

In some circumstances, a government may be able to embed explicit access requirements in commercial agreements. For example, upon airline deregulation in Australia, the government ensured a very limited availability of gates for entrant airlines (as reported in §7.3). Otherwise, when airlines are faced with market power exercised by a terminal owner or operator, there may be a need for specific legislation. One such instance, which applies to all types of airport infrastructure, is the (European Union) Directive on Airport Charges (examined below in §14.4.3).

14.4.2 Retailing and other airport-located activities

Offers to sell or lease major ports have sometimes stimulated very vigorous bidding. On occasion, this reflects opportunities for developing parts of the site for additional (non-aeronautical) commercial activities. While retention of airports in public ownership need not prevent suitable developments in other land-uses – developments that will not restrict growth in the core aviation activi-ties and are otherwise also in the public interest – managers of government-owned airports can fail to see these opportunities, or fail to act on them. Private bidders may identify previously unconsidered development opportunities, and so have an incentive to bid a higher amount for the purchase or lease of the airport site.

Catering and other retailing in passenger terminals

Private companies that buy or lease airports often seek to increase the retailing activities conducted inside passenger terminals. Unfortunately, the amount of space so assigned can be so great as to hamper the movement of passengers towards the departure gates. Indeed, the plethora of commercial signage may make it difficult for the first-time user of a terminal even to find out where the gates are.

At on-site retailing outlets, prices are often high and the quality can be low. In an attempt to serve airport users fairly, some port operators in the US require so-called 'street pricing'; in response, some outlets choose expensive streets. For example, a turkey sandwich was reportedly priced at US$11 in the airport, and at US$6 at a (same-franchise) outlet near the airport (Roger Yu, 'Travelers chafe at sky-high cost of eating at airports', *USA Today*, 6 August 2009).

When passenger flows are large enough to support several catering outlets, competition might be expected to promote quality and keep prices in check. However, a large firm that seeks to monopolise or dominate inside a terminal may bid higher than a firm that expects to have to compete. Thus competition can be thwarted if the port owner accepts the highest bids for site leases, without regard for the risk of domination by one or a few suppliers.

In 2006, a new (replacement) domestic terminal at Adelaide Airport (South Australia) started with (essentially) just two food-and-beverage companies. One of these had eight outlets each trading under a separate brand-name (Adelaide Airport Limited, Annual Report, 2005–6, p. 12; 'Site profile 01/09 Adelaide Airport', delawarenorth.com.au, accessed 20 January 2010). That particular parent company focuses on catering outlets at airports and other transport terminals, and at sports venues. Such a company may be practised in competing *for* the right to serve a market, as distinct from competing *within* a market.

Retailing of duty-free goods

Many governments exempt from retail taxes the purchase at airports of (packaged) alcohol and consumer durables such as cameras, by passengers travelling on *international* flights. On both efficiency and distributional grounds, there is a strong public-interest case for removing these tax exemptions.

Purchase by a *departing* passenger adds to the aircraft payload. The newly purchased packages can also make it more difficult for other passengers to find locker space for general carry-on baggage. Note, however, that those efficiency losses are not incurred when the goods are purchased by *arriving* passengers, for whom that opportunity often provides a close substitute for purchase before departure (especially because airlines rightly prohibit the in-flight consumption of carry-on alcohol).

An equity concern applies for all purchases, whether made by arriving or departing passengers. Passengers travelling on many international routes have above-average incomes. In that case, the tax exemption is regressive. In other words, the exemption favours the affluent, and a standard public-finance argument supports its removal.

Other types of land-use

If an airport site is large enough, the range of non-aviation commercial activities that a new private owner may establish at the port can be remarkably wide. It may include: supermarkets; retailing of furniture and other large items needing considerable display space; light-engineering premises; hotels; long-term car-parking; business parks; and even (as at Adelaide Airport) low-care facilities (nursing homes) for the aged.

The initiation of such projects may require adjustment of the airport perimeter, in order to place the relevant land parcels outside the area that is made secure for aviation. That can bring the airport company into the land-development business, with consequent involvement with planning-permission (zoning) procedures. In extreme cases, the development profits may exceed the profits received from aviation activities.

When privatising an airport, a government may need to look critically at the issue of how much land is needed for aeronautical purposes. It could then excise from the airport site any land parcels that are not needed.

14.4.3 Economic regulation: the structure of airport charges and related terms of access

Although *general* trade-practices (anti-trust) legislation may be applicable when a major airport abuses its market power, some governments have established aviation-specific legislation, intended to deal more promptly and more certainly with problematic airport conduct. While a major focus of most anti-trust legislation is on general price and profit *levels*, the airport context also presents significant issues in regard to price *structures* and related terms of access. This section considers those latter issues. (Overall price and profit levels are taken up in the next section.)

In the many countries where the *standard* charge for each aircraft movement is based on the maximum take-off weight (MTOW) of the aircraft, there is often little thought given to exactly *how* the resulting charges vary between aircraft types. And in regard to airline access, a common principle is that all airlines should be given the same terms of access, in the case of both runways and passenger terminals. That practice includes setting prices that do not discriminate between airlines. Nevertheless, on occasion, an airport may favour the country's national carrier; see §12.4.2 for discussion of a situation arising in France.

The EU Directive on Airport Charges

An exception to the general lack of formal interest in the structure of airport charges is to be found in the EU Directive on Airport Charges (European Union, 2009), which requires the use of two related *principles*: (1) Airport charges shall not discriminate between airlines (Article 3); and (2) Where airports provide alternative service qualities (for example, in separate passenger terminals), then (a) the various charge levels 'may be differentiated according to the quality and scope of such services and their cost', (b) all airlines are to be allowed access to each of the alternatives, and (c) where capacity constraints are limiting, airline shares of capacity 'shall be determined on the basis of relevant, objective, transparent and non-discriminatory criteria' (Article 10).

The Directive also mandates various *procedures* governing relations between ports and airlines. These include: regular consultation between the parties on the structure and level of airport charges, and on service qualities (Article 6); consultation before finalising plans for new infrastructure (Article 8); and, to secure transparency, the provision of full information regarding airport services, charges and costings, and other financial data (Article 7). Each Member State is to nominate or establish an *independent* supervisory authority (that is, one not associated with any operating agency), to pursue correct application of the provisions of the Directive (Article 11). Also each Member State retains the right (Article 1(5)) to apply additional (compatible) regulatory measures, which may include, for example, price-cap or other regulation intended to limit overall profitability.

The ideas that drive the Directive are based on standard economic analysis. In particular, Article 3 (and, if deemed applicable to runways, the Article 10 provision on allocating scarce capacity) both allow efficient congestion pricing for peak-period runway access, following the principles set out in this chapter (in §14.3.2). If not implemented through a market for slots, such a scheme could have peak-period surcharges for aircraft movements, to be implemented with the help of rules for identifying peak periods and estimating delay costs.

In the Directive, the dangers of excessive regulation are mitigated by the emphasis on *consultation* between an airport and its airline customers. In the US and also in Australia and some other countries, airports have accepted (on occasion) representations from individual airlines about the need not to make terminals too grandiose and expensive; thus, good-sense compromises *can* be reached (sometimes!) even without a formal framework mandated by government.

When the Directive was introduced, the principal *a priori* concern about its efficacy arose from fears that Member States would continue to prefer political expediency over economic principle. While conduct has improved in some respects, an evaluation of the performance of the Directive (Steer Davies Gleave, 2013, commissioned by the EC), records a number of shortcomings, including delays in the transposition of the Directive's terms into national law in some of the Member States. Self-interest continues to motivate airlines: notably, legacy carriers oppose the provision of low-cost terminals, and low-cost carriers criticise the recent spread of passenger-related charges in place of aircraft-related charges. While there have been improvements in transparency and consultation, the Directive has had little impact on the structure and level of airport charges. The consultants urge revision of the Directive, to give greater importance to the principle of relating charges to the costs of provision of the services.

Following submission of the Steer Davies Gleave report, eight months passed before the Commission reported to the Parliament (European Commission, 2014). While the Commission's language is purposive and the direction sensible, the pace of change is likely to be modest. An Expert Group was established. At its first meeting, an exchange of views focussed on transparency of airport charges, the need to avoid discrimination between airlines, and remedial procedures for breaches of the EU policy (EC Summary Record Forum of Airport Charges Regulators, Thessaloniki, 13 June 2014, published Brussels, 3 November 2014).

14.4.4 Economic regulation: the overall profitability of an airport

Government regulation of the profitability of an airport has followed similar regulation in those other industries where sellers have market power. In some countries, the long-established approach of rate-of-return regulation has yielded ground to price-capping, though in practice the latter is often deployed in a way that makes it similar to the former. (For standard text treatments – that require some prior acquaintance with economic analysis – see Viscusi, Harrington and Vernon, 2005; Armstrong, Cowan and Vickers, 1994).

The basic aim in such regulation is to limit total profit to an amount that gives a rate of profit (on the amount of capital employed) no higher than would be achieved in a market that has several or many competing suppliers. The regulator has to try also to avoid giving the supplier an incentive to employ more capital than is needed for efficient production. (If left unchecked, such incentives can lead to 'gold plating', discussed in §12.4.3.)

In the case of an airport, the economic regulator often faces an additional problem, namely how to deal with the presence of any important non-aviation activities, which are not usually regulated when located in a general urban setting. In that case, a regulatory scheme to assess the maximum permitted profit rate has to take a position on two matters. Which of the airport company's activities are to be taken into consideration? And what capital assets are to be included in the calculation of the rate of profit on the capital employed?

Single- and dual-till procedures

One approach is to group together all the activities on the airport site. In this 'single-till' approach, the regulator compares total revenue with total cost, and expresses the profit as a percentage of the capital cost of all the airport assets.

In the alternative 'dual-till' approach, the regulator separates the aeronautical costs from the costs of providing the other services, and relates the revenue from the (regulated) aeronautical charges to the aeronautical costs only. The profits earned on the non-aeronautical activities usually go unregulated – but may be regulated separately (Czerny, 2006, p. 86; Oum, Zhang and Zhang, 2004, pp. 220–1).

A summary of the main characteristics of the two procedures is given in Table 14.2. The dual-till approach gives the airport operator a stronger incentive

Table 14.2 Single-till and dual-till procedures for the economic regulation of airports

Context

Airport is regulated only if it has significant power in its aeronautical markets. In that case, the port generally has strong power in its other markets, with consequent high profits if no economic regulation of those other markets, and may well have periods of runway congestion, which require high aircraft movement charges during peak, and lower movement charges off-peak.

Characteristics of the alternative regulatory procedures:

single-till	*dual-till*
No need to divide airport assets into two classes	Non-aeronautical profits not regulated (unless a further regulatory scheme is added)
High non-aeronautical profits can reduce funding needed from aeronautical charges	Stronger incentive to develop site for non-aeronautical purposes, which may encroach on areas needed later for aeronautical developments
Preferred by airlines, because those non-aeronautical profits can reduce the funding needed from aeronautical charges, and hence the level of those charges	Preferred by airports, because no diversion of non-aeronautical profits to help fund aeronautical costs

to favour the (unregulated) retailing and other non-aeronautical activities, and so increases the risk that airport management may give insufficient attention to, and deploy insufficient resources for, the provision of aeronautical services.

In particular, at in-city ports where the site may be spatially very restricted, pursuit of non-aeronautical profits can result in land allocations that may restrict future aeronautical activity. The *potential* for conflict is illustrated by the 2014 decision of the city-owned Dallas Love Field to close a little-used north–south runway (which intersects the two parallel main runways) in order to allow the creation of more parking space for cars (Daniel Salazar, 'Love Field development plans prepare for take-off', *Dallas Morning News*, 11 July 2014).

Regarding the general choice between single- and dual-till frameworks, Lu and Pagliari (2004) use some formal modelling – which, however, does not have regard for site capacity limitations – to explore how the public interest (as reflected in economic efficiency) varies between the two approaches. They conclude (p. 12) that if runway capacity exceeds the current peak demand level, a single-till approach is preferable, while if the (peak) capacity is fully employed, a dual-till scheme gives a better outcome.

A single-till allows the use of non-aeronautical revenues to fund some of the aeronautical costs when efficient prices for runway use do not give enough revenue to cover all the indirect costs of airport operation. In contrast, the dual-till method allows aeronautical costs to be covered by aeronautical revenues where that is feasible, with the port then free to pursue non-aeronautical profits, supposing – as Lu and Pagliari do – that there is no supplementary regulation of those profits.

In the UK, regulatory policy of airport profit levels has been given particularly close attention – see, in particular, Civil Aviation Authority (2000), Starkie and Yarrow (2000), and Starkie (2008).

For airports that are about to become privately owned, a regulatory scheme has to be chosen *before* privatisation – because, in most legal systems, the regulatory mode cannot be readily changed afterwards. Other things being equal, prior announcement of the employment of a single-till regime may be expected to result in lower bids for the right to operate the airport than would be forthcoming if the government were to announce it will use dual-till regulation – because the latter usually leaves unregulated the profits from the non-aeronautical activities, and hence usually permits higher total profit for the airport company.

A cautionary note

The complexities of airport operation make the regulator's task very difficult, with consequent risk of poor performance. In practice, every regulatory approach has its advantages and disadvantages; regulation of airports is inevitably imperfect, and the aim can be only to limit the imperfections as far as is possible (Starkie, 2005).

With that reality in mind, Fuhr and Beckers (2006, 2009) argue that instead of formal regulation by government, good-faith negotiation between an airport and its airline customers may give better results. While there are numerous instances of successful negotiations, the dispute between Virgin Blue and Sydney Airport regarding runway access charges (§§12.3.2–3) reminds us that, on occasion, an airport's market power may be so great, and the owners enthusiasm for profits so overpowering, as to preclude such an agreement – unless there is some prevailing regulatory scheme which becomes the default power in the event that the parties do not agree.

15 Public policy on airlines

In any country that favours market competition, airline conduct may attract little by way of government *economic* regulation. Yet, around the world, there are still some governments that prescribe in detail who can start an airline, and what each airline can do. A more common problem arises when airlines pursue profits in ways that are not in the public interest – and yet governments *fail to intervene*. Such inaction may reflect a lack of appropriate trade practices/anti-trust legislation and/or an unwillingness to apply the prevailing laws.

This chapter looks mainly at situations in which airline actions do not always serve the public interest. However, there is also a discussion of the public-interest principles to be applied when a government sets aside competitive-market principles in order to favour certain airlines and/or certain airline services.

15.1 Open skies, airline ownership and collaborations between airlines

15.1.1 Regulation of airline entry

In developed capitalist economies, *foreign* companies are usually allowed to own enterprises and assets in the domestic economy – except perhaps in the case of a few industries that are deemed to be of 'strategic importance' (however that term may be defined!).

The list of such industries usually *does* include airline service. Airline deregulation rarely allows access to domestic routes by an airline domiciled in another country. The only significant exception is the EU, where an airline domiciled in *any* EU country is allowed to fly *any* inter-country route within the EU, and also *any* domestic service within *any* EU country. The following remarks on domestic routes apply to countries elsewhere in the world.

Domestic services

Many countries do allow foreign airlines a *limited* participation in domestic services, *provided* the foreign company establishes a subsidiary company that is domiciled in the country whose routes are to be served. Instances of countries accepting that type of arrangement include: Indonesia and Thailand (where the Malaysian company Air Asia has subsidiaries); Ecuador and Peru (each served by a local subsidiary of LAN, which is domiciled in Chile); and some (often, reluctant) countries in Africa, where both Fastjet and Flyafrica have recently sought to establish pan-African holding companies, with subsidiaries in several sovereign countries.

Typically the host country requires that a majority of the shares in the subsidiary be controlled by its own nationals; commonly, 51 per cent of the voting shares is accepted, though some counties require a much higher proportion. The host may also require appointment of some of its nationals to the board of the subsidiary. The underlying purpose of these arrangements is to secure local control of the subsidiary's decision-making. When the local partner is a passive investor without airline experience, however, the judgements of the foreign airline company may readily sway the board. (That was a significant issue in the ostensible reasons for the decision of the Hong Kong government to refuse an air operator certificate for Jetstar Hong Kong (§4.2.5).)

In addition, the host government may require that the local subsidiary operate a separate fleet, with the aircraft owned by the subsidiary. That provision seems to reflect a government wish to have ready access to the fleet in time of war or natural catastrophe. However, the prevalence of aircraft leasing makes it difficult to enforce the requirement. In particular, the parent airline can set up and own a leasing company that leases aircraft to all the airlines in its group.

In regions such as East Asia, where there are many sovereign countries in a proximity that is well within the range of short-haul jet aircraft, economic efficiency favours operation of a homogeneous integrated fleet, from which each individual aircraft can be assigned flexibly to any of the airlines in the group, to help secure high average daily block hours flown per aircraft. In such situations, national autarchy may add to airline costs.

International services

Other than within the EU, an *international* flight between two countries requires a bilateral agreement made by the two governments. Typically each agreement permits designated airlines of both countries to fly designated routes between the countries; usually there are numerical limits on the number of seats that may be flown on each route. Permission to serve a route between two countries is *rarely* granted to an airline that is domiciled in a third country.

The bureaucratic arrangements do not always preclude sensible outcomes. When the British government had occasion to install a designated airline under the bilateral agreement with Russia for the London–Moscow route, it chose EasyJet, to fly between London Gatwick and Moscow Domodedovo, to complement British Airways flights between London Heathrow and Domodedovo. At the time, the Russian nominees were Aeroflot, flying from Moscow Sheremetyevo, and Transaero (from Moscow Vnukovo), both to Heathrow. The addition of EasyJet significantly enlarged the list of options open to travellers, in regard to both service style and airport location ('EasyJet launches London-Moscow route', anna.aero, 18 March 2013).

Further considerations

A state that lacks its own well-developed aviation sector may benefit by allowing a foreign airline to take on important roles. This applies especially when a government seeks to increase the number of visits by foreign tourists. No doubt that aim was in mind when, in 2006, Morocco (in North Africa) signed a Common Aviation Area Agreement with the EU. Tourism soon expanded as European low-cost carriers brought in extra visitors. In addition, Air Arabia Maroc (a locally domiciled subsidiary of Air Arabia) launched *international* routes between ports in Morocco and ports in the EU. In 2012, for example, Air Arabia Maroc was flying four routes from Montpellier (France), to the Moroccan cities of Marrakech, Casablanca, Fez and Nador (anna.aero, 21 November 2012). Thus the parent company, Air Arabia (domiciled in Sharjah, United Arab Emirates), was able to initiate flights between *two other* countries, thanks to the 'open skies' legislation of the European Union.

15.1.2 Planning the transition to airline deregulation

On the other hand, even the *standard* open-entry arrangements of the EU are not beyond public-interest criticism. When a prospective member state completes negotiations for entry to the EU, the date of entry comes not so very long after the signing of the agreement. Even if local entrepreneurs anticipate the signing, and take early steps to establish or strengthen a local airline, it may well be that, by the entry-date, the local venture may not be sufficiently experienced, competent and large to offset the scale and early-mover advantages of airlines such as EasyJet and Ryanair – who, incidentally, have been known to start service from ports in the new member-state on the very first day that EU membership came into effect.

Thus it is not surprising that those two airlines have been able to win substantial local market shares in several of the Eastern European countries that have joined the EU in recent years. Among local start-ups, only the (ULCC) WizzAir has both survived and prospered, to the extent that it has become a sizeable airline – in 2015, a fleet of 55 A320s. Even so, WizzAir remains much smaller than EasyJet (then about 230 A319/A320 aircraft) and Ryanair (some 300 B737-800s).

As a counter-weight to the early-mover advantage, the EU could allow a *prospective* member state to choose whether to have the short-term benefits of immediate entry to its country by experienced Western European airlines, *or* to put in place some restrictions on entry by EU airlines domiciled in another EU country, subject to a sunset clause taking effect after (say) six years. That arrangement would promote the longer-term local benefits that could accrue from successful establishment or up-grading of local airlines.

While the details of any such approach would require very careful consideration, the basic idea is to redistribute the *immediate* aviation-related benefits of EU enlargement, in order to give a larger share to the new member state, and a smaller share to prior members. In addition, such a temporary entry restriction might give a benefit in the longer term, if it resulted in an enlargement of the list of established companies, and if, in turn, that enlargement resulted in a more competitive industry.

In contrast, the present practice in setting the terms of a Common Aviation Area Agreement – that may be signed between the EU and another state that is not (yet) a member – appears to give EU airlines early access (at a fixed date) to *international* routes to/from the new member state, while airlines of that state may have to wait until that that state's aviation sector has adopted various aviation standards of the EU. (For an instance, see European Commission, 'EU and Ukraine for a Common Aviation Area Agreement', Memo 13/1065, 28 November 2013.)

15.1.3 Collaborative arrangements between airlines

While competition between airlines is favoured by those who like competitive markets as a matter of general principle, and perhaps by travellers who seek lower fares, the airlines themselves are not *always* convinced by the public-interest arguments in favour of competition. A newly launched airline has self-interest reasons for welcoming opportunities to compete. But at most times – at least, on serious matters if not on the choice of fillings for the sandwiches – most established airlines prefer to collaborate rather than compete.

This section describes several kinds of collaborative arrangement that airlines favour. All of these arrangements need critical assessment by any government seeking competition to improve economic performance. Accordingly the *next* section gives a public-interest evaluation of the schemes.

These collaborative schemes vary according to the range and scope of the matters that are agreed between the involved airlines. The account starts with agreements of limited scope, and works up from there.

Code-sharing

Two or more airlines can make a code-share agreement for a series of flights – say, a daily non-stop flight between ports A and B, for a six-month period. Each of the participating airlines shows the flight in its timetable and in its website booking engine, using its own flight designator (for example, DL for Delta) and its own (*independent*) choice of flight number.

The agreement has provisions that determine how the seats on each flight are to be shared out between the airlines. The principal alternatives are: (1) each airline takes a pre-determined, fixed number of seats – sometimes called a *hard-block basis*; and (2) each airline keep on selling until all the seats are sold – sometimes called a *freesale basis*. Of course, the agreement also has related terms about how much each airline pays towards the costs of the flight.

The provisions regarding seats become more complicated when the agreement provides for a multiplicity of ticket types and/or cabin classes. The participating airlines then agree on a division of the cabin into sectors. And each sells tickets under its own ticket-type nomenclature, and at prices that it alone choses. Regarding seat allocation, some of the alternative provisions require real-time exchange of information between the computer networks of each of the airlines.

When code-sharing was introduced, many passengers were surprised – and some were displeased – to find that the airline operating the flight was not the airline they thought they had booked. Nowadays, most booking engines say clearly which airline will operate the flight. Those who book through a travel agent have to rely on the agent passing on the information.

Administrative responsibility for the series of flights is taken by one of the participating airlines. That airline must hold all the operating permissions, including any needed airport slots; it organises the provision of passenger handing and other services; and it plans and controls the operation of each flight, which is almost always undertaken by one of its own aircraft. (The Wikipedia article on Code-share agreements, accessed on 15 April 2015, gives additional details.)

Airlines entering into code-share agreements emphasise the (potential) benefits for passengers, including the proposition that on a thin route, there may be no airline willing to offer a daily flight on its own, while a daily flight code-shared between two carriers may be financially attractive. In practice, however, code-shares are established in other contexts, too.

Airline alliances

Many large, full-service airlines that fly on international routes have joined one or other of three (world) airline *alliances* – OneWorld, SkyTeam and Star Alliance. An airline cannot belong to more than one alliance; and (on the whole) each alliance has only a single member from a particular country. Thus, in the USA, American Airlines is a member of OneWorld, Delta is in SkyTeam, and United Airlines is a founder member of Star. On the other hand, SkyTeam has as members no fewer than four large airlines from China (alliance websites, accessed 20 April 2015).

Initially, alliance members were all national carriers or other long-established companies. However, times change. Thus the privately owned, *full-service* Aegean Airlines became a member of Star, *after* becoming the largest Greek airline, but *before* it took over the old national carrier, Olympic Airways (Aegean Airlines, Corporate Presentation, September 2014).

Members of an alliance collaborate on a wide range of matters. When an intending international traveller (or her travel agent) approaches an alliance member, that airline encourages the traveller to fly on the services of members of that alliance throughout the intended international journey. Besides offering ease of ticketing, alliance airlines may use adjacent gates at intermediate ports, thereby making flight transfers easier for the passenger. On a specific port pair, alliance members *may* together offer more frequent flights than would have been flown by any single airline if there were no alliance. Collaboration between airlines may extend to sharing of airport facilities and station staff, thereby reducing the costs of airline members.

Given the importance, within an alliance, of passenger feed from one airline to another, it is unsurprising that the alliances do not (yet) have any low-cost carriers as members.

Joint ventures

Two or more airlines may seek to form a 'joint venture'. Most such initiatives concern a single international route or a group of routes within a specific area of the globe. So they are fairly narrow in scope. They are also of limited duration, often five years.

On the other hand, the relationship is close and deep – and certainly much deeper than those between airline members of a global alliance. While there are no universal standard financial terms, many joint ventures have formal agreements in place to share both costs and revenues between the partner airlines (Carlson Wagonlit Travel, 2012). In effect, the collaboration amounts to almost a complete merger of those activities of the partners that concern the routes within the scope of the venture. (And the sharing of costs and revenues is reminiscent of the old, pre-deregulation agreements commonly made between pairs of European national carriers, who collaborated on the routes between their countries of domicile (§2.1.1).)

For the route(s) included in the joint venture, the airlines establish a joint flight schedule and usually adopt a common list of fare types together with common fare levels for each type. This supports the full cooperation between the airlines, who usually argue that it helps travellers when it comes to making bookings. Especially on a dense route, the joint flight schedule may help the partners to spread out their departure times, rather than have them bunched together in a competition *between* the airlines of the joint venture. The airlines point out that such spreading gives better service to the travellers. Of course, such timetabling also makes it more difficult for another airline to find a flight time for which the joint venture is not operating a close substitute.

The joint-venture conduct amounts to forming a cartel. Such activity is prohibited by legislation in most countries. Accordingly, joint-venture partners usually seek from government an immunity, on the grounds that the venture's public benefits outweigh the public detriments.

The 'Joint Coordination Agreement' (signed on 17 November 2014 by Qantas and China Eastern) affords an instance of the procedure. The case concerned certain air routes between China and Australia, routes that are not identified in the airlines' 'Public Submission' to the Australian Competition and Consumer Commission (ACCC; Application for Authorisation, 18 November 2014, accessed at accc.gov.au, 21 April 2015). (The ACCC generally allows such withholding of material which the applicants claim to be 'commercial-in-confidence'.)

In assessing public detriment arising from the Agreement, the Commission's draft determination (Australian Competition and Consumer Commission, 2015, pp. ii, iii) goes directly to the Sydney–Shanghai route, and notes this route accounts for around 24 per cent of all travel (on direct flights) between Australia and China.

Furthermore, China Eastern and Qantas together were flying 83 per cent of the total number of seats flown on that direct (non-stop) route. After examining alternative routes between the two cities, the Commission concluded that implementation of the Agreement would result in 'significant public detriment' – because the two airlines would then have 'an increased ability and incentive to unilaterally reduce capacity' and to increase airfares on the route.

The Commission acknowledged some public benefits, including greater convenience and (for transit passengers) reduced time at the Shanghai airport, thanks to the handling of Qantas flights at the China Eastern gates.

However the Commission concluded (Australian Competition and Consumer Commission, 2015, p. iv) 'the likely public benefit . . . does not outweigh the likely public detriment. Therefore, the ACCC proposes to deny authorisation' of the Coordination Agreement.

In its final determination, however, the ACCC *granted authorisation* on condition that Qantas and China Eastern 'grow their capacity on routes between Australia and China Eastern's hub in Shanghai by 21% over the five year term of the authorisation' to ensure that coordination between the two airlines does not result in a reduction in flight frequency 'below that which could be expected if the alliance was not in place'('ACCC authorises Qantas/China Eastern coordination agreement', ACCC media release 152/15, 21 August 2015). The ACCC added that it accepts the airlines 'do not want to commit to additional capacity expansion until closer to the time that capacity will be added'. Yet if the airlines did not *increase* capacity in the manner claimed to flow from the agreement, the ACCC might find it difficult to grant any request for re-authorisation at the end of the initial five-year period. (Humph!)

Airlines buy shares in other airlines

In a number of cases, an airline domiciled in one country has bought a minority share-holding in a well-established airline of another country, usually a carrier serving domestic routes, or an EU carrier serving routes within the EU. In an early example, Lufthansa bought shares in the US carrier JetBlue.

More recently, large international airlines domiciled in the Arabian Peninsula have bought shares in airlines domiciled in the EU (and elsewhere). In January 2015, Qatar Airways became the largest shareholder in IAG (the holding company that owns British Airways, Iberia and Vueling) when it bought 9.99 per cent of the IAG shares (Alan Dron, 'IAG hints at future joint Qatar aircraft purchase', *Air Transport World*, 11 March 2015). Furthermore, Etihad purchased 29 per cent of the shares of Air Berlin, Delta acquired 49 per cent of Virgin Atlantic, and Korean Air took a stake of 44 per cent in CSA Czech Airlines.

In April 2014, the range of European purchases prompted the European Commission to consider whether they are entirely in accord with EU legislation on ownership and control of airlines domiciled in the EU (CAPA, 'Airline ownership & control', 28 May 2014). That legislation requires that share ownership by other (non-EU) nationals must not exceed 49.9 per cent of the total equity.

The issue of control is inevitably less clear cut. There have been several suggestions of joint purchasing of supplies (including the purchase of aircraft by Qatar and IAG, noted above). These certainly are at the opposite end of the scale from the passive investor syndrome. However, the evidence *so far* does not appear to raise concerns that the European share acquisitions are having adverse effects on competition in the markets for airline services.

Elsewhere, Etihad, Singapore Airlines and Air New Zealand have bought shares in the Virgin Australia company that operates Australian domestic flights, thereby leaving that company's other shareholders with only a modest minority of the shares. (The company structure avoids allowing foreign airlines control of Virgin Australia's *international* services, which need majority ownership by Australian share-holders in order to qualify for inclusion in the route-access arrangements made under bilateral government agreements.)

International mergers and take-overs

In olden days, when national carriers dominated the world industry, a merger or takeover involving airlines *domiciled in different countries* was unthinkable. In recent years, however, the practice has become rather common, at least in the European Union. KLM (the Netherlands flag carrier) and Air France have joined in a holding company. British Airways and Iberia (Spain) have also joined forces, with their holding company, IAG, taking charge of the low-cost airline Vueling (which previously belonged to Iberia). And Lufthansa (Germany) now includes both Austrian Airlines and Swiss. In South America, the LAN and TAM groups have set up an international holding company.

15.1.4 Public-interest evaluation of airline collaborations

Around the world, most countries have well-developed legal codes for anti-competitive conduct. As in the Qantas/China Eastern case, the usual legal stance proscribes such conduct unless the setting aside of competitive practices brings public benefits of such importance as to outweigh the public losses arising from the absence of competition.

A *network* industry such as airline service brings particular difficulties for both the analyst and the regulator. Unlike other types of industry, a network often serves a very large market in the aggregate, while also having many small sub-markets (for example, city-pair routes) with very strong *supply* interdependence.

Because of their typically small size, *most* city-pair markets have few competing airlines, often no more than two. At the same time, the inherent economies of *airline* scale and scope result in there being only a small number of airline companies, even in spatially extensive market areas. For instance, even after including its small airlines, the US has only ten main-line companies flying on domestic routes, for a population of about 320 million people. On the Australian continent, there are only two companies to serve about 25 million people. (On the other hand, Europe has somewhat more airlines, and presently has much more competition.)

In most *domestic* market areas, the few incumbent airlines experience a high degree of multi-market contact, and the managers of each airline get to know and understand the conduct of the other airlines. In such circumstances, it is hardly surprising that airlines seek to collaborate, in order to avoid the financial adversity that may result from competition. In response, most governments seek to prohibit anti-competitive conduct; and in most developed countries, that government approach can be effective.

But international routes have proved to be a different ball-game. Perhaps because airline deregulation has often promoted competition – sometimes very fierce competition – the political pressure by airlines for governments to allow anti-competitive practices in respect of international routes has grown year by year. The only distinctive economic feature of such routes is that most of them serve a considerable proportion of *foreigners*. Perhaps that helps to explain why airlines have been able to secure government acquiescence when airlines appeal to the 'national interest'.

A brief commentary on the various collaborative categories

The *code-share* version in which the airlines set their fares independently, and then compete with each other to sell seats (without fixed airline seat-quotas) is perhaps the easiest of the collaborations to justify as not damaging the public interest. Even there, government approval is unlikely to be wise unless the route is so thin as to be unable to support the presence of two airlines. One danger is tacit collusion between the participating airlines to maintain high fares, leading to excess profits, and also supporting the impression that the route is not dense enough to support two competing airlines. So the regulatory agencies in the two countries need to be alert.

Alliances have some sound public-interest features: sharing of common-use facilities, such as club lounges in passenger terminals, in order to reduce costs; and good liaison between airlines, which can make it easier for the passenger to arrange and (where desired) amend reservations on multi-airline itineraries, and to transfer between airlines at an intermediate port when the two airlines use adjacent or nearby gates. On the other hand, the inter-airline intimacy that develops in the course of administering the alliance makes it easier for the airlines to engage in public mischief. Beware!

Joint ventures often replicate some of the misdeeds that were heavily criticised before governments finally opted for deregulation. In particular, collusion in setting fares removes *any* price competition between the airline members of the joint venture.

Airline purchase of shares in other airlines may well suppress competition, and may not lead to cost savings.

Mergers and takeovers generally do lead to cost reductions. But they also reduce the intensity of competition on routes previously served by the merging airlines. The financial gains from lower costs then go to the remaining airline, rather than the traveller.

Also important is that each type of collaboration is likely to make it more difficult for another airline to enter any of the routes that are affected by the collaboration, and may make it harder for a new airline to launch at all. Because these collaborations affect international routes, the job facing the regulator is made more difficult whenever there are significant differences in the regulatory codes of the two countries.

However, government agencies have begun to think about such matters. Of particular interest is a jointly produced research report: the European Commission and the United States Department of Transportation's *Transatlantic Airline Alliances: Competitive Issues and Regulatory Approaches* (16 November 2010). Mainly it addresses issues in coordinating the approaches of the two parties to the task of evaluating collaborative airline proposals. While the study is confined to transatlantic routes, application to other regions should not present any *additional* conceptual difficulties. However, the study seems not to have led to much if any progress in policy implementation.

Conclusions

Airlines often like to collaborate with each other. Although such arrangements enhance the market power of the participating airlines, collaboration between airlines domiciled in different countries is often permitted by national governments, even when those governments have strong legislation outlawing *domestic* cartels. Though collaboration between incumbent airlines may improve service quality for travellers, it often enables the airlines to charge higher fares. Furthermore, it often makes it more difficult for low-cost airlines and other new carriers to launch and prosper, resulting in loss of the efficiency gains that come from the entry of new airlines and from the vigorous competition that often ensues.

15.2 Airline presence at route level

15.2.1 Airline conduct at route level

A fashionable catch-cry is 'open skies': for each route, the market should be 'free' to determine which airlines deserve to succeed.

In formal economic analysis, there is indeed an important role for competition *in* a market. However, that analysis pre-supposes 'perfect competition' – or, at least, competition that is not too far from being 'perfect'. For such competition, the main prerequisites are the presence of many actual or potential competitors, together with an absence of significant barriers to entry.

In regard to the number of actual competitors, there are economists who believe that a market with as few as (say) three or four competitors does not *need* a government regulator. In such cases, they argue, it is likely to be in the public interest to leave the market unregulated. So it may be useful to consider how many airlines are to be found flying in city-pair markets around the world.

15.2.2 The numbers of competitors on routes where entry is unregulated

In *Asia*, the rapidly growing traffic on some major routes (and the prospect of further growth) has attracted numerous competitors. Thus some individual routes have as many as seven or even eight competing airlines, as already seen in Table 13.2. In a further case, when Okay Airways (China) started a daily flight on the domestic route between Xi'an and Hangzhou, the route was already served by eight other airlines, namely China Eastern (16 flights weekly), Hainan Airlines (16 flights), Air China (14), China Southern (10), Xiamen Airlines (8), Beijing Capital Airlines (7), Shenzhen Airlines (7) and (the privately owned) Spring Airlines (7). Once Okay had entered, the route had a total of 92 weekly round-trip flights ('New airline routes launched 3 February – 9 February 2015', anna.aero, 11 February 2015 – which remarks that the route 'might be the world's most competitive airport pair').

Even in *Europe* – where, in general, traffic growth-rates are lower than in Asia – there have been recent instances of new-airline entry on city-pair routes that already have several incumbent airlines. Of particular interest is Ryanair's establishment (in late 2015) of a base at Berlin Schönefeld. There, Ryanair planned to start service on *sixteen* new routes, of which over half were already served by EasyJet ('Ryanair makes Berlin [its] base [number] 73 and adds 16 routes for Winter 2015/16', anna.aero, 5 March 2015).

That overlap of Ryanair and EasyJet is the more striking because, in earlier days, the major European LCCs avoided direct competition with each other. Now, the sustained growth of their networks has made such competition well-nigh inevitable, especially because the legacy carriers are shifting *their* emphasis to long-haul routes, and some of them have greatly reduced their intra-European services or have transferred some routes to their own low-cost subsidiary airlines (Justin Bachman, 'Europe's big airlines no longer want to fly in Europe', *Bloomberg*, 11 September 2014).

On the other hand, between European capital cities and other cities that are important for business travel, a small informal survey (conducted on 5 April 2015) suggests that any given *port* pair rarely has service from more than three airlines. The common arrangement includes service by the two national carriers. For example, Amsterdam Schiphol to (in-city) Milan Linate was flown by KLM and Alitalia. (In addition, EasyJet flew to Milan Malpensa.) On London Heathrow to Frankfurt, both BA and Lufthansa provided frequent flights; the same two airlines also flew between Frankfurt and London City. (There were no Frankfurt flights from the other London ports. The nearest LCC service was Ryanair from London Stansted to Frankfurt Hahn, a routing that seems unlikely to attract business travel.)

Between Amsterdam and Oslo (OSL), there were flights by both national carriers, KLM and SAS, together with one daily flight from an LCC, namely Norwegian. On the other hand, there was only *one* carrier, Austrian, flying between Copenhagen and Vienna. And between Oslo (either port) and Rome (either port), *neither* national carrier appeared; rather, there was a single daily flight, offered by Norwegian. Between Madrid and Warsaw (Chopin), the Polish airline LOT flew six times weekly, and Norwegian (using the EU open skies provision) offered a daily service. (Iberia had no direct flights, but offered frequent connections via London Heathrow, with a journey time in excess of 6 hours.)

The other large market-area without any (economic) regulatory restriction on (domestic) route entry is, of course, the USA. There the rates of traffic growth are generally *much* less than those in Asia. The route examples already presented (in Tables 1.3 and 1.4) give Salt Lake City and Oklahoma City snapshots at dates in 2012 and 2014.

In 2014, Oklahoma City had non-stop service to 21 ports, though only four ports had service from more than one airline. And while the larger Salt Lake City port then had direct flights to 82 ports, only 19 routes were contested, and only six of those were served by more than two airlines. Among the *monopoly* routes at SLC were those to Atlanta (eight flights daily) and Minneapolis (six flights) – frequencies that suggest passenger flows were quite large enough to support *at least* two airlines.

In contrast, in the much-less-populous national market in *Australia*, the dominant Qantas and Virgin camps compete on almost all the main-line jet routes. And even on some of the regional routes – usually served by turboprops – Virgin's new turboprop division has started flights that compete with the long-established Qantas services.

Further insight comes from the anna.aero reports on 'New Routes Launched' (worldwide). In a majority of all the cases reported between 11 February and 1 April 2015, the entering airline started on a route not served by any other airline. The other 106 route entries included 53 routes with one incumbent, 30 routes with two, 12 routes with three and 9 routes with four incumbents. In that last category, three routes were in Europe, five in Asia and one in the Republic of South Africa (Johannesburg–Cape Town). The remaining two routes, which had five and eight incumbents respectively, were in Asia.

Some of the routes with larger numbers of incumbents reached the lists because of route entries by new airlines just launching, notably Vistara in India and Skywise in South Africa. In Europe, a large majority of all the route entries came from LCCs.

Of particular interest are the ten routes in the USA that are listed by anna.aero for route entries. Most of those new ventures came from ULCCs; Spirit started three routes from Cleveland (competing with United and Frontier); and Frontier started three from Atlanta, where Delta, Southwest and American were competitors. In starting Seattle to Washington, Alaska was competing with United. Delta started two routes, from San Diego and from Seattle, both challenging Alaska Airlines. The only route-entry involving competition between legacy carriers was American's entry on the dense route Los Angeles (LAX) – Atlanta, where the incumbents were Delta and Southwest.

Some general conclusions

In most regions or countries where route entry is unregulated, the number of competing airlines on any particular (served) route is usually small. Indeed, in many cases, the route has but a single airline. Only dense routes have competing services, and even then the number of competing airlines is often only two, and very rarely more than four. Thus in all but a few cases of *very* dense routes, the typical competitor numbers are far smaller than those required even for an approach towards perfect competition.

In one respect, the common presence of *de facto* monopolies is inevitable. The list of potential routes necessarily includes some thin routes having small traffic flows that can support no more than (say) one daily round-trip. However, where an incumbent has a route monopoly and sets high fares that yield high profits, there may be room for a competitor to enter with lower fares that still give an adequate profit, and are low enough to encourage enough extra travel to support services from the two airlines.

Even so, there will always be some routes that are too thin to support the presence of more than one carrier. The *proportion* of such routes will depend on the size-distribution of the urban populations in the market area. In the USA, for example, there may be an unusually large proportion of smaller communities that are, nevertheless, large enough to attract airline service, given the standard of living and the other factors that influence air-travel demand.

15.2.3 Airline attitudes to competition in the market area

Besides airline numbers, however, there is another very important influencing factor at work. If the number of airlines serving a route is 'small' (say, between two and four *independent* companies), then the chances of a competitive outcome depends crucially on whether the companies *want* to compete. In particular, and as will now be argued, much will depend on whether each airline's owners are content with the company's prevailing *share* of the total RPK output in the national or other market area.

In order to develop the argument, it is helpful to look again at the history of domestic airline services in Australia. Following the very stable equilibrium of the regulation era, almost ten years elapsed before there was any dramatic change. Then, once Virgin had entered, it became obvious that Ansett was in decline (perhaps because of failing management, rather than for any other reason).

Upon Ansett's closure, a still very small Virgin faced an aggressive Qantas which initially greatly expanded its market share. As Virgin grew, the vigorous competition resulted in fare reductions and the launch of many more direct city-pair routes, leading in turn to large increases in total RPK on domestic services. While Qantas still increased its sold output, its market share declined, eventually reaching about 67 per cent. Its attempts to maintain that share led both companies to increase their offered capacity beyond the growth in the market, with adverse financial outcomes for both. In 2015, an apparent truce then slowed the race.

It remains to be seen what, if any, stable outcome will eventuate. Will Virgin be able to move up to a half-share? If so, could that lead to a (fairly) stable outcome, in which both companies tacitly accept equal shares? In that case, because each airline group now has a full hand (a full-service jet operator, a low-cost jet airline, and a regional airline mainly using turbo-props), it would be harder than before for any other company to break into the market. And unlike the previous scheme of government regulation, there would be no mechanism intended to regulate the general level of air-fares in the public interest.

The moral of the Australian story is that in a national market with just a few (independent) airline companies, a competitive outcome is by no means inevitable. Instead, the few may reach a tacit agreement not to compete. While most advanced economies have legislation that makes cartel conduct unlawful, a 'tacit agreement' is not likely to be found to contravene such legislation. Furthermore, such collusion may not be difficult to maintain. In short, the presence of competition depends on company attitudes as well as on the number of competitors.

15.2.4 Airline route competition in the USA

The US Department of Justice has acquiesced in a long-lasting merger process that has reduced (almost) the entire pre-deregulation industry to a list of just *three* very large carriers of substantially similar size and character. The remainder of the industry comprises: Southwest Airlines, about the same size as each of the big three, and launched more than forty years ago, but still having some features that differentiate it from the other three; two long-established jet airlines, Hawaiian and Alaska, each serving their eponymous regions, but now urgently expanding outside its traditional area, apparently in defence against possible attack by any or all of the four big brothers; two new airlines, JetBlue and Virgin America, launched in 2000 and 2007 respectively; and three *ultra*-low-cost carriers, Frontier, Spirit and Allegiant, all still of modest size but *now* seeking to grow rapidly.

The industry outcome is a situation in which the big three may well develop and rely on a tacit understanding about common interests, leading to a lack of vigorous competition between them on essentials (such as route entry) while perhaps still taking solo initiatives on minor matters such as optional service-quality extras – initiatives that would not undermine any group allegiance.

The *recent* performance of the Department of Justice suggests that it too now considers that, from a public-interest point of view, the industry is too highly concentrated. While it did not oppose the merger of US Airways with American Airlines, it did successfully require significant slot and gate divestments by those two carriers, with those resources then made available to JetBlue, Virgin America and Southwest Airlines (as seen in Table 14.1).

However, in the event of predatory low pricing and/or capacity dumping by a major airline that targets one of the smaller companies, the DOJ may need to attempt legal intervention, notwithstanding the previous lack of judicial support for such challenges. The next section presents a brief account of the principles involved in the economic analysis of such predation.

15.3 Predation at route level

15.3.1 Predatory airline response to route entry: the concept and some examples

It is common for established airlines to attempt to prevent a new airline from making successful route entries. The incumbent(s) hope to bankrupt the newcomer or persuade it to withdraw from the route (if not the industry), *before* the newcomer can establish itself. In a less common scenario, a large airline enters a route already served for some time by a smaller newcomer.

In either scenario, the intent of the large airline may not serve the public interest. However, any legislated prohibition needs to be precisely formulated, to ensure that it does not rule out legitimate competitive strategies. This section looks at the definition of *predation* that has been adopted by economists, and gives some examples of the conduct.

The basic idea of *predation* may be stated simply: if an incumbent firm adopts a strategy whose *principal* purpose is to deter a rival from entering (or remaining in) a market, then the firm is said to be engaging in predatory conduct. In the airline sector, a common large-airline strategy is to reduce its fares and (perhaps) increase the capacity it offers, on one or more routes being served by a newcomer or other small airline. That strategy often results in the large airline incurring financial losses on those routes.

In such a situation, the small airline finds it harder to attract passengers and earn enough revenue to cover its costs. If and when it withdraws from the route, the large airline then usually increases its fares and *may* reduce its capacity, perhaps to the same levels as it offered before the route entry. The large airline then earns super-normal profits which soon outweigh its financial losses.

A predator may use other instruments too. For instance, at a particular port, it may occupy more airport gates than it needs, in order to hinder or prevent new-airline entry at that port.

Several instances of *fare predation* in the US are considered in Kahn (1991), a lively account which captures the political and industry practicalities of such conduct. Further US cases are reviewed in Oster and Strong (2001) – see especially Table 2. And the general US experience is covered in US Department of Transportation (2001, pp. 31–6).

Interesting studies of fare predation in other countries include a report (Eckert and West, 2002) on an important case in Canada. In Germany, after a (then) very small airline, Germania, had entered the Berlin–Frankfurt route, the Federal Cartel Office moved to restrain Lufthansa when the latter reduced its fares on that route *only* (Morrison, 2004; Mills, 2003). In Australia in January 2001, Ansett and Qantas responded to route entries by Virgin and Impulse with some *very* narrowly targeted fare cuts (Mills, 2002, pp. 207–8).

In October 2009, the Australian regional carrier Rex secured some recurring charter work in Queensland, its first venture in that state. With Saab 340 aircraft (about 32 seats) thus available, Rex then started three round-trip scheduled services daily between the coastal cities of Townsville and Mackay, offering a best one-way fare of A\$129. The (sole) incumbent QantasLink had been offering twice-daily service, using larger turboprops, each with either 50 or 70 seats; its best fare had been A\$130. In response to the Rex entry, QantasLink started a third daily service, and reduced its best fare to A\$99, which Rex then matched (Clive Dorman, 'Qantas, Rex in coastal stoush', *Sydney Morning Herald* (*Traveller* section), 24 October 2009).

Displeased by the Qantas conduct, Rex lodged a complaint with the (general) economic regulator, the Australian Consumer and Competition Commission. However, Rex later announced (media release, 'Rex exits Mackay to Townsville route' 24 December 2009) that it would exit the route at the end of December, and remarked 'after almost 3 months of determined effort we have been forced to acknowledge that our competitor's predatory practices have been effective'.

In March 2015, QantasLink was still the only airline on the route. It offered four round-trip flights daily on weekdays, three on Saturday and two on Sundays. It was flying the same turboprop aircraft types as before, for a flight lasting between 50 and 60 minutes. The fare repertoires ran from A$130 to A$275 for the restricted fare class, and from A$350 to A$475 for a flexible ticket. No doubt, the route monopoly was a handy earner for Qantas. A further year later, Qantas was still without competition; it then operated a reduced schedule on weekdays – three round-trips instead of four. Even handier? (For an extensive discussion of airline predation, see Forsyth and others, 2005.)

15.3.2 The legal framework for assessing the presence of predation

While the details of anti-trust (trade practices) legislation vary between countries, the underlying proscription is usually of the 'abuse of market power' held by a dominant firm. For the legal details for several countries, see William G Morrison (2004, §2). In applying that stance to instances of alleged predation, many courts and regulatory agencies have adopted a sequence of two or, sometimes, three tests:

1   *Before the alleged predation began, did the accused firm have significant market power?* Here, it is usual to assess market power by noting the firm's market share and by judging the extent to which the firm may choose its own prices, rather than needing to conform to market prices set in a competitive market process.

2   *Are the firm's (allegedly predatory) prices set at levels which are below its unit costs?* The difficulties here lie in choosing an appropriate cost concept, and then in obtaining reasonable empirical estimates; for the airline context, those matters are discussed below.

3   *If the firm has set below-cost prices, can it later recoup the profit it has thereby foregone?* This gives problems in defining an appropriate profit concept; and if the firm's conduct is being reviewed before any recoupment phase has started, it may be difficult to judge whether and to what extent recoupment may be feasible.

In some jurisdictions, the firm is regarded as having engaged in predation only if all three questions are answered in the affirmative. Otherwise, the first two tests are used in reaching a conclusion. In a variant on those procedures, the firm's apparent *purpose* in reducing its previous prices may be taken into account, especially where the new prices are not markedly different from the unit costs.

However, economists and others often note the difficulty in establishing purpose, and argue instead for a test based on effect.

For a brief economics textbook discussion of US antitrust policy in this field, see Viscusi, Harrington and Vernon (2005, pp. 317–22). Also of interest is the treatment found in some manuals written for lawyers; for an example, see Corones (2014, pp. 523–37), which deals mainly with Australian legislation.

15.3.3 Applying the legal framework in the context of airline route entry

In the application of the tests to airlines, it is important to recognise that few air routes have service from more than two or three companies. Thus it is common for a single airline to carry at least (say) forty per cent of the passengers, while many thinner routes are served by only one company. Thus, many well-established airlines do have a considerable degree of market power at the route level. In particular, when such an airline learns that a route-entry is pending, it can fairly quickly switch to that route (any) aircraft capacity not otherwise used. And it can lower its fares within a few days – or even a few hours – of identifying an entry.

For a court or a regulatory agency dealing with alleged or suspected predation by an airline, the difficulties often start with the cost test: what cost concept is to be used in determining a floor for non-predating prices? One candidate is the average unit cost, perhaps per available seat kilometre (ASK). If that measure is calculated for the airline as a whole, however, there can be at least two major objections.

For an individual flight, that unit cost decreases as aircraft size increases and as sector length increases. Thus an estimate based on the airline's entire operation may be significantly inaccurate when applied to a single route. To deal with that issue, the calculation may be based on the costs of operation on the route in question – though that is likely to increase the difficulties encountered in allocating joint costs.

Second, some elements of total cost are not varied in the short-term. An obvious refinement is to classify each of the airline's costs as either variable or fixed, and then calculate the average *variable* cost per seat kilometre (for the route in question). A further refinement might be to estimate costs for the particular route, and seek to include only those costs that would be *avoided* if the airline did *not* increase its capacity on the route; that approach is suggested in Baumol (1996). (For further details on the airline context, see also Morrison, 2004, §3.)

To an economist, the avoidable-cost principle is patently sensible, especially because its effect is to measure the (net) opportunity cost of flying the extra or changed flights. The measure includes not only the direct variable costs (for example, extra fuel used and engine maintenance incurred, being costs incurred while operating the route) but also any indirect costs such as any (*net*) revenue foregone elsewhere if the airline removes an aircraft from another route in order to use it on the route in question.

Unfortunately, a cost analysis that makes sense to the economist is not always accepted by a court. One of the few US airline cases to be heard in recent times was that brought by the Department of Justice regarding some conduct of American Airlines. In finding for the airline, the US District Court of Kansas (2001) relied crucially on what it perceived as a lack of evidence of below-cost pricing.

15.3.4 Other approaches that do not rely on costs tests

The inevitable complexity of cost tests and the difficulties that the courts may have in addressing the predation issue by reference to general anti-trust (trade practices) legislation have encouraged the development of alternative approaches that do not rely on costs tests.

A notable approach (intended for any industry) is the *output restriction rule* (Williamson, 1977). This requires that when an incumbent with considerable market power is faced with entry, then (for a prescribed period of time) that firm's post-entry output offered in that market must be no higher than its pre-entry level.

The rule is relatively easy to apply, and this is particularly important in the airline context, where the customary plethora of different fare types hinders implementation of a comparison between average fare and any measure of unit cost. However, if 'output' were interpreted (weakly) as capacity (seats) *offered*, rather than seats sold, then an incumbent airline could (to some degree) undermine application of the rule. Specifically, it could operate the same flights as before, while lowering its fares to attract more passengers, which it could accommodate by flying with higher load factors.

Even so, in precluding a capacity increase, the rule could become an effective constraint that prevents the more egregious predatory actions. Recall that in the Rex case (§15.3.1 above), Qantas reduced its best fare *and* increased its offered capacity by 50 per cent.

It might be objected that when the incumbent is already flying with a high load factor, the output restriction rule allows little opportunity to respond to entry. Yet the high load factor itself constitutes strong *a priori* evidence that its service is barely adequate, and that the incumbent has chosen to run the risk of attracting entry to the route.

When the US Congress placed a requirement on the Department of Transportation for the latter to block 'unfair' methods of competition in the airline industry, the Department was given an opportunity to plan a method of intervention that did not rely on the standard antitrust laws (US Department of Transportation, 2001, p. 2).

The outcome was a proposal (US Department of Transportation, 1998) for comparing the revenue results of the incumbent's adopted policy (following entry) with the best revenue outcome that could have been obtained if the incumbent had adopted some alternative policy. In general such an alternative would be likely to include smaller fare reductions, and in turn that might support an accommodation in which the incumbent and the entrant shared the route. If the best alternative policy would have given larger net revenue for the incumbent than the adopted policy did (during the period of the contest), the incumbent's actions would be deemed to be predatory. Kahn (1999), Blair and Harrison (1999) and Eckert and West (2002) give detailed commentaries.

A major strength of the DOT proposal is its adherence to economic principle, though even in that regard there were criticisms, especially from airlines. The major difficulty lay in conducting the empirical analysis. The Department soon announced that it would not publish revised guidelines; instead, in exercising its authority, it would proceed by using a case-by-case approach (US Department of Transportation, 2001, p. 4).

Two further approaches for dealing with alleged predation without deploying cost tests may be noted briefly. First, a submission (Starkie, 1999) to the US Department of Transportation suggested that if an incumbent responds to entry by increasing capacity, and the entrant then withdraws, the incumbent could be required to continue to serve the route for a specified period (Starkie suggest three or six months) *without* reducing its capacity and flight-frequency from their *post-entry* levels.

Second, for a case where an incumbent airline has a monopoly before the entry, and the entrant later withdraws, the reinstatement of monopoly could be regarded as showing that the route is not dense enough to support two airlines. Accordingly, the government could then invite bids for an *exclusive* right to serve the route. This would introduce competition *for* the market in place of the (failed) competition *in* the market, with a reasonable prospect of an outcome that would be more favourable for the passengers than if the monopoly was enforced by the incumbent on terms of its own choosing.

15.4 Government subsidies for airlines, especially national flag carriers

In many countries, the early tradition of government provision of subsidies for airlines persisted long after aviation lost its infant-industry status. Indeed, even though deregulation and privatisation has become common, some governments still provide financial aid, especially to their national flag carriers. While *direct* subsidies are no longer paid in many countries (notably USA, Canada, Australia, New Zealand, and UK together with *some* of the other EU countries), there are recent instances of other governments being very reluctant to allow a foundering local airline to go bankrupt.

Notwithstanding the European Union policy to permit state aid only in situations where airline services promote development in remote/low-income regions (cf. §11.2), several EU governments have given general financial aid to flag carriers, often to pay for a restructuring that did not cure the malaise.

The European Low Fares Airline Association (whose membership in 2015 included EasyJet, Norwegian, Ryanair, Vueling and WizzAir) has long campaigned against state subsidies. In particular, it 'called on the European Commission to carry out full and swift investigations into offending state aid cases concerning SAS, Malév, Spanair, and CSA' (press release, 17 March 2010).

Since then, however, the closure of Malév, the effective demise of Olympic and a less tolerant attitude towards financial deficits at CSA and LOT suggest that unjustified state aid in Europe is on the wane.

Elsewhere in the world, some governments have persisted with financial support for airlines in financial trouble. For the privately-owned JAL (Japan Airlines), a detailed account of the problems and the promised reforms is given in Notice of Decision to Provide Support to Japan Airlines, issued by the Enterprise Turnaround Initiative Corporation of Japan, 19 January 2010 (accessed at etic-j.co.jp, 22 March 2010). As already noted, two other state-owned companies, Air India and South African Airways, have enjoyed on-going subsidies.

When governments do support failing airline companies, their primary motives seem to be to maintain employment and to ensure passengers are still served. Experience has shown, however, that after a company failure, *competitive* airline industries soon restore services. Indeed, after the dramatic closure of Ansett Airlines in 2001, Australian route capacity levels soon outgrew those provided by the previous Qantas–Ansett duopoly. In Mexico, after Mexicana closed at the end of August 2010, the market total passengers in December had recovered sufficiently to almost match the December figure of the previous year (§5.1 and Table 5.1).

In general, the *resilience* of competitive aviation suggests that on grounds of both efficiency and income distribution, governments may well do better to put taxpayers' money into the provision of social services such as health and education rather than into the operation of inefficient airlines.

15.5 Protection for airline passengers

To protect the interests of consumers, many governments intervene in markets where the sellers enjoy considerable market power in their dealings with individual personal customers. This section looks at four distinct areas of airline practice. First, however, it is helpful to look at some traditional regulatory practices that have long been used by governments.

15.5.1 Traditional practices in the regulation of public utilities

Governments developed these practices as they began to regulate *public utilities* – that is, the industries which supply, to individual citizens, services such as electricity, gas, water and transport. In those network industries, the suppliers are large, the individual buyer usually had little or no choice of supplier, and market power rested with the supplier.

To protect its citizens, a government traditionally intervened in two ways. First, it placed an upper limit on the overall rate of profit that was allowed to a supplier, as a way of controlling the general level of the supplier's prices. Secondly, it usually required that each and every price offered by the supplier to citizens in a particular area should, as a matter of equity, be made available to all the citizens in the area.

There is also a third principle that was often deployed: each individual price should reflect the cost of supply (somehow defined). That principle sought, at the least, to limit the extent to which consumers of one product were required to subsidise the consumers of another product of the same supplier.

Furthermore, adoption of the third principle implies that, in deploying the second principle, a public utility needs to divide its customers into groups in such a way that the cost of supply is essentially the same for all members of the group, and *then* needs to charge the same price for each member of such a group.

Turning now to present-day *airline services*, deregulation of route entry has reduced the incidence of monopoly supply. And competition between airlines is now presumed to limit overall profitability. However, the equitable treatment of individual consumers is not secured automatically when airline services are provided by private companies, especially when competition is muted – as is the common situation in airline markets for which there are only a few rival suppliers.

Thus (it may be argued), there is still a role for government in consumer protection, especially in ensuring that every price offer goes to all potential buyers (in the group). That consideration can be regarded as banning *price discrimination* – which, in the present context, occurs when the airline *simultaneously* offers sales of a ticket (having certain standard conditions) at prices that differ between buyers.

That word 'simultaneously' is important. A 'no price discrimination' condition does not rule out different prices offered on different days, for example. In particular, an early offer of cheap tickets targeted on leisure travellers, and a later offer of full-fare tickets targeted on business travellers, does not involve price discrimination – provided both offers are made available to all travellers, irrespective of journey purpose.

(In a more general setting in which a firm offers for sale two *different* products, price discrimination is present when the difference in price between the two products does not match the difference in unit production costs of the two products. Economics textbooks explore that extension and much more. That analysis is not pursued here.)

15.5.2 Ancillary charges, especially baggage charges

While the unbundling of optional services allows an airline to sell a cheaper basic ticket, it also gives the airline greater opportunity for engaging in price discrimination, especially because the entire contract between airline and traveller involves the setting of more prices.

In the case of charges for checked bags, the discussion in §9.4 noted that some large airlines set charges on an *increasing* scale, such as US$40 for the first bag, US$60 for the second, and US$100 for the third and each additional bag beyond the third.

Now the unit cost (that is, the variable cost per bag) that the airline incurs in carrying a bag comprises a fixed component (for handling and for some of the extra fuel) and a further fuel cost that is proportional to bag weight and to the distance that the bag travels.

While one (small) US airline does levy charges that vary with sector length, most airlines do not charge according to distance flown. While an airline does set an upper limit on the weight of each bag, it does not charge by weight. Instead, a count of the number of bags serves as a proxy for the total weight of the baggage checked by the traveller. Given that the airline also sets a maximum on the weight of each bag, the proxy might serve reasonably well if the airline then set a uniform charge for each of the bags checked by the traveller. In contrast, the many airlines that charge on an increasing scale impose a total charge that lacks acquaintance with the variable costs incurred by the airline.

On the other hand, an increasing scale will boost the airline's net revenue. The airline thinking may be based on the idea that a large number of checked bags signals that the passenger is affluent, and is willing to pay large sums for *extra* bags. Thus the airline can profit by price-discriminating against such passengers, while still offering to other passengers lower charges for the first (checked) bag or two.

An increasing scale of bag charges does *not* breach the principle that all passengers should receive the same offer. But it does conflict with the proposition that in a public-utility context, the supplier should set prices that reflect unit costs. On that analysis, the public-policy question is whether the size of the divergence from the unit costs is large enough to warrant government intervention.

There is also a public-interest case for favouring simple tariffs. In the case of bag fees, for example, if few travel without any checked bags at all, a passenger's first checked bag might travel without any specific charge; that implies that the cost of the first bag is recouped through the main fare for the ticket. Then, each passengers who wishes to check more than one bag could be asked to pay a *uniform* charge for each *extra* bag.

Perverse financial incentives

In setting its ancillary (and other) charges, it is in the public interest that an airline should not encourage individual passengers to behave in a manner that is not in the public interest. In the case of baggage charges, airlines introduced charges only on *checked* bags. This gave passengers an incentive to increase the amount of baggage they took into the cabin. In turn, that consequence often increased the workload for the cabin attendants, increased the risk of injury to people in the cabin, and sometimes delayed flights, especially when the crew had to transfer large or surplus bags to the hold.

To secure more sensible incentives, it might be better to charge for *cabin* baggage (with exemption for minor items, somehow defined), and refrain from charging for the first checked bag. Yet, when the US niche airline, Spirit, started charging for cabin bags in 2010, there was much outcry.

Governments too sometimes create perverse incentives. The US government levies a 7.5 per cent charge on the price of each airline ticket; the revenue goes into the Aviation Trust Fund. However, airline revenues from ancillary charges on 'non-essential' services are *not* subject to this levy. Thus airlines have a (modest) incentive to increase revenue by raising bag and other ancillary charges, instead of increasing the price of the basic ticket, on which the levy is paid.

If the aviation levy is accepted as a proper way of raising revenue to support government aviation outlays, then it may be wise to avoid slippery concepts such as 'essentiality', and simply apply the tax to all types of airline revenue received from passengers, except possibly fees paid for travel insurance – since that can be purchased by travellers directly from third parties, and so requires a level playing field for competition reasons.

15.5.3 Protecting and compensating passengers when flights are delayed or cancelled

For most airlines, flight delays are commonplace. The consequent damage to an airline's reputation gives the airline *some* incentive to avoid delays – or, at the least, to moderate their extent. However, the observed incidence of both delays and consequent complaints has convinced some governments to act to reduce the incidence of delays, and sometimes to introduce mandatory schemes of compensation for delayed passengers.

Government setting of safety requirements is well-nigh universal. In addition, some countries set further quality requirements, with fines payable for breaches. For example, in 2010, the US Department of Transportation implemented several new rules (media release, 'Airline consumer protection rules take effect tomorrow', 28 April 2010). The rule that attracted the most airline protest was one requiring (with minor exceptions) that a US airline which has boarded passengers on a domestic flights *must allow passengers to deplane* after a tarmac delay of *three hours*. And the maximum fines for breaches are so large as to ensure compliance. Mainly, the rule targets the major departure delays that occur at a few US airports under adverse weather conditions.

The DOT rules also prohibit the largest US airlines from scheduling flights that have a record of 'chronic' delay. Miscreants are threatened with DOT enforcement action for unfair and deceptive practices. Again, the underlying purpose is to give airlines an increased incentive to avoid scheduling (and other) practices that make significant delays somewhat likely.

In contrast to those specific, narrow American initiatives, the EU introduced a comprehensive *passenger-compensation* scheme, EC Regulation 261/2004. Before looking at the details, it helps to identify and consider five main entities that need to be considered when developing any such scheme:

1   *Events that cause delays* fall into two categories: (i) events *arising from the airline's conduct*, such as failure of aircraft systems (perhaps because of poor maintenance), crew illness or other crew shortages, industrial action by the airline's employees, and simple lackadaisical turn-round of aircraft; and (ii) events *not under the airline's (direct) control*, such as adverse weather conditions that reduce runway capacity, the (rare) presence of

airborne volcanic ash that results in airspace closure, unavailability of an airport gate because of delays to flights of other airlines, and industrial action by employees of other parties.

2   *Airline attempts to keep the delay to a minimum.* When a passenger still wishes to continue a (delayed) journey, the opportunities for prompt re-arrangement of travel will depend on the airline's flight frequency on the route, seat availability on its other flights, whether the airline gives delayed passengers priority over accepting *new* bookings, and whether the airline is willing to transfer the passenger to another airline, at its own expense.

3   *In-kind assistance provided by the airline.* This can include meal vouchers valid at local restaurants/cafes, overnight accommodation at hotels, and transport between airport and hotel. It may be reasonable to relate the extent of (any) such assistance to the amount of the delay and (perhaps) to the distance that was to have been travelled on the delayed/cancelled flight.

4   *Circumstances that qualify the passenger for financial compensation.* A ticketed traveller may seek financial compensation when the flight is cancelled with little or no notice, or is significantly delayed. However, it seems reasonable to require the airline to pay only when certain conditions are met, notably relating to what caused the delay/cancellation, how much delay is experienced, and whether or not the passenger accepts an offer the airline makes for travel on another flight (perhaps by another route).

5   *Arrangements for funding the costs of compensation.* A compensation package is akin to the benefits offered by an insurer in exchange for a premium paid by the traveller. There are two main funding options. One is to have the traveller choose whether to buy such a policy from an insurance company, while leaving the passenger without recourse to claims on the airline. In the second, the airline includes a standard compensation package in the price of the ticket.

A proposal to amend EC Regulation 261/2004

This 2004 legislation placed substantial obligations on every EU-domiciled airline to provide, at its own expense, 'assistance' to any confirmed passenger who checks in at an EU port for a flight that is delayed, or is cancelled without sufficient notice.

For delays beyond a minimum duration (which varies with the distance to be travelled by the flight) and for cancellation without 'sufficient' notice (as defined), the regulation specified (a) 'care' payments for meals and perhaps hotel accommodation (depending on the extent of the delay), and (b) for delays beyond a longer duration, reimbursement of the ticket price *or* (at the passenger's choice) re-routing by the airline, without further charge.

In the case of cancellation without sufficient notice, the airline is required *also* to pay financial compensation (of an amount that depends on the distance of the flight). The amount to be paid is reduced by 50 per cent if the passenger accepts re-routing. No compensation is payable if the event causing the cancellation is 'unavoidable'.

The introduction of the Regulation drew immediate protest from low-fares airlines, especially because – except for reimbursement of the fare paid, where applicable – the monetary cost to an airline of the prescribed assistance had no regard for the fare paid by the passenger (ELFAA media release 'European Low Fares Airlines ... challenge flawed new EU passenger compensation legislation', Brussels, 20 February 2004). Also of concern to airlines was an obligation to pay for passenger meals and accommodation *even when the airline had no control over the events that occasioned delay or cancellation.*

Later, in 2010, when a volcanic eruption led to closure of some European airspace for several days, Ryanair announced it would limit reimbursement of additional expenses 'to a maximum of the original air fare paid' (media release, 20 April). After public pressure, Ryanair said (media release, 22 April) that 'it will comply with EU261 regulations under which EU airlines are required to reimburse the reasonable receipted expenses ... of disrupted passengers'.

Later, a passenger from Ireland who had been stranded for seven days in Faro (southern Portugal) – because of the airspace closure – brought a case in a Dublin court seeking reimbursement from Ryanair of her additional expenses. That court sought a ruling from the Court of Justice of the EU on some points of law.

The EU court ruled (CJ of the EU, Press Release No 8/13, 31 January 2013) that, under the terms of the Regulation, (1) volcanic activity was an 'extraordinary circumstance', which (however) did not release an airline from its obligation to provide *care* – that is reimbursement of additional expenses incurred by passengers, (2) there was no limitation, either temporal or monetary, on that obligation to provide care, and (3) an airline was under no obligation to provide *compensation* if it could prove that the flight cancellation was caused by an extraordinary circumstance.

Earlier concerns about the Regulation had led the EC to commission a study (Steer Davies Gleave, 2010) which concluded that some clarification and revision of the rules was desirable, and also put emphasis on the widespread failure in many EC countries to enforce the rules, leaving passengers unable to obtain redress. In March 2013, the EC presented to the European Parliament a proposal (European Commission, 2013a) for a regulation to amend Regulation 261/2004.

Apart from moves for more effective enforcement, the proposed regulation made significant changes to the financial terms. In order to better recognise the financial capacities of the air carriers, the right to compensation becomes available only after a delay of five hours (previously three hours) for flights within the EU, and for flights to/from ports outside the EU, after delays of five, nine or 12 hours depending on the sector distance to be flown. A passenger's right to accommodation funding was limited to three nights, with a maximum of €100 per night.

On the other hand, given the prevailing airline reluctance to transfer passengers to the flights of other airlines, the new text said that if an airline cannot reroute a passenger within 12 hours, it must seek to put the passenger on a flight of another company. It also outlawed a common (legacy) airline 'no-show' policy, whereby the airline denies boarding for a return journey where the passenger has not flown as booked on the outward journey.

Economic principles for determining an airline's liability

Turning from institutional matters to the underlying economic principles, the first question is whether the airline's financial liability should depend on the nature of the event(s) causing the flight delay or cancellation. Where the event is clearly the responsibility of the airline – for example, when the delay arises from an aircraft maintenance problem – a rule that makes the airline pay has the effect of giving it an additional incentive to set good maintenance and other service standards. The rule is also equitable.

On the other hand, no airline can hope to control a wayward volcano. In that case, there is no efficiency argument for requiring the airline to make payments to a delayed passenger (provided that the compensation rules were made clear before the ticket was sold).

Thus the in-principle argument is clear: the airline should pay only when the delays arise from events for which it is responsible. In practice, however, the issue is not always clear-cut. Consider, for example, a rain-storm which reduces runway capacity and causes aircraft delays at the affected port. The immediate argument is that the airline can't control the weather, and so should not be held liable for the passengers' delay costs. *But*, without such liability, the airline has a greater incentive to knowingly schedule more flights than the port can handle on bad-weather days. In contrast, when the airline is held responsible for those passenger costs, it is encouraged to have regard for *all* the costs that arise when bad weather causes delays, and thereby act in a manner that is closer to the public interest.

Of course, all parties must know in advance where the delay costs will fall. To that end, a practical approach is to identify and categorise each of the possible types of event, and then require the airline to bear the passenger delay costs in all the circumstances (such as bad weather) where the airline has some *significant* role in choosing to operate in a way that increases the risk of passengers experiencing delays.

On 19 April 2013, the EC published a Draft List of Extraordinary Circumstances for the Application of the Current Regulation (EC) 261/2004, the Regulation that was still in force at that date. This categorised as 'extraordinary' a considerable number of events, including 'Weather conditions resulting in capacity restrictions at either the airport of arrival or the airport of departure'. This follows the economic principle just stated regarding extra passenger costs. (But again note that the airline has no obligation to pay compensation in the event of an extraordinary circumstance.)

On the other hand, the list also included airspace closure necessitated by volcanic activity, which seems inappropriate when judged by the argument set out above. (For such an 'act of God', a passenger may be unable to buy cover from an insurance company either. Travellers who are so venturesome as to wish to travel by air have to recognise that they may experience an un-insurable adverse outcome!)

The principled economic analysis can be extended in order to deal with the objection that the EU scheme offers the same level of payments, regardless of the fare paid. A traveller who seeks out a low fare is likely also to prefer a smaller amount of cover for delay costs. The EU scheme could be adapted to offer (say) two alternative levels of such cover. An individual airline could choose between those levels, with the cover again bundled within the fare, and the potential traveller clearly informed.

15.5.4 Airline-website booking engines

An early regulatory concern arose from biases in the major computer reservation systems used by travel agents when serving their customers. In particular, the software was sometimes designed to favour certain airlines when reporting competing airline services. To help travel agents and others become well-informed, governments introduced regulation of such software practices; see, for example, European Commission (1989).

With many travellers now using airline websites to make bookings for themselves, the current focus is on the way the booking engine presents information to the prospective traveller. The earlier exposition in §9.6 reports on airlines practices, and notes how unbundling has made the booking process more complex. The question now is whether those practices serve the public interest.

Many airlines have made considerable efforts to design their electronic forms to make the booking task as simple as possible. However, studies reported in Torres, Barry and Hogan (2009) suggest that some low-cost airlines (in particular) engage in web practices that seem to be designed to deceive. A useful list of issues and practices concerning passenger needs and rights is given in Abeyratne (2001).

There seems to be a solid case for regulation to proscribe misleading airline conduct – whether based on omission of important information or on other marketing practices. In particular, an airline may disclose a basic fare initially, and then as the customer pursues the booking process, the booking engine adds further components (including so-called 'taxes and charges'), giving an eventual total that is much higher than the fare first stated. The effect is to encourage travel that might not be contemplated if the full amount of the fare were made obvious at the outset. The *delayed* display of charges for optional services also makes it harder for the traveller to compare prices across airlines.

Furthermore, some airlines include in the fare calculation charges payable for some supplementary services, notably travel insurance. To avoid paying for such services, the traveller has to cancel each offer, usually by removing a pre-placed 'tick' from a box. That 'opt-out' approach amounts to a form of *inertia selling*, which has been prohibited in some countries.

For air travel, a common regulatory response has been to require the *total* fare to be displayed on the first web page appearing after the customer has specified a route, date and flight time. However, as already noted, that rule can refer only to charges that every traveller is *obliged* to pay.

15.5.5 *Price discrimination between individual passengers*

For a given route, and on a particular day, the 'traditional' on-line booking engine presents a standard set of fares, which vary by the day of the flight; and, on a busy route with two or more flights each day, the fares may vary by the time of day at which the flight departs. When *offering* its 'fares of the day', the airline does not know anything about the individual who seeks the fare information. (Of course, someone who wants to accept one of the airline offers is obliged to disclose name, contact details, and details of the financial account from which the airline will obtain payment; but that disclosure comes *after* the airline has offered its fares.)

Even so, a passenger who chooses a full economy fare or a business fare (rather than a discounted economy fare) is (in effect) saying to the airline: 'I am travelling on business, *or* I am quite well off; and I don't want to accept the restrictive conditions that come with the discounted ticket.' That shows how the airline has successfully targeted a group of such travellers, and induced one of them to buy one of the more expensive tickets. Self-selection has worked in the airline's interest because of the skilful way in which it has conditioned its alternative ticket offers.

In contrast, in the non-electronic world, street hawkers (who generally refrain from posting prices) can learn much more about their customers before making an offer. In particular, a hawker sees the prospective buyer's clothes and body language, and can take into account the manner of speech, and what the buyer says in any haggling that takes place – before the hawker makes a 'final' offer.

In recent years, airlines have become interested in using analogous procedures when deploying an electronic booking engine ('In the future, fare search engines will know who you are', *Air Transport World*, 26 May 2010). Such an approach may allow the airline to price-discriminate between individuals – and not merely between groups of individuals.

For an individual who has already travelled on the airline, storage of prior information could reveal, for example, the residential postcode and/or the identity of the company for which the business traveller works. That raises the prospect of an airline charging a higher fare to someone living in a wealthy post-code area than the fare it offers to someone from a poorer area. By definition, the introduction of such personalised pricing would mean that an airline's fare offers are no longer available to all.

For a traveller who is a member of the airline's frequent flyer scheme, or is addicted to membership of electronic social media, the airline may be able to collect further information about the individual, in order to build up a detailed portrait – which it then uses as a basis for making a personalised fare offer.

In 2015, when that approach was discussed at an airline-industry conference, it did not receive universal approval (Jamie Freed, 'The price you pay for an airline ticket is becoming personal', *Sydney Morning Herald*, 10 July 2015).

When a company does offer various different prices, *and* makes all its offers available to all potential buyers, the discrimination is generally seen as reasonable and 'fair'. However, whether that discrimination helps to improve economic efficiency depends on the detailed circumstances (Viscusi and others, 2005, p. 290).

When price offers are restricted to some individuals or particular groups, it seems less likely that the practice will improve economic efficiency.

The last word goes to the European Commission. Upon receiving a complaint that an EU airline rejected bookings placed by residents of country A on a website targeted on residents of country B (a website that offered some lower fares), the EC Commissioner responsible for Mobility and Transport responded thus: 'Although individualised pricing is not necessarily considered unfair per se, the Commission is currently assessing under which circumstances such practices may become illegitimate' under The Unfair Commercial Practices Directive 2005/29/EC (*DG Mobility and Transport Newsletter,* 13 July 2015).

15.6 Policies for sustainable aviation

15.6.1 Introduction

Today's concerns regarding sustainability of the world's physical environment raise questions about the eventual viability of aviation. Indeed, doomsayers suggest that within a few years, we shall see most of the world's airliners parked in the Arizona desert. In contrast others see little if any need for lifestyle changes that sacrifice present enjoyment of the fruits of technical progress. In such a crucial context, excessive reaction and gross neglect both risk sorry outcomes.

Accordingly, the following sections offer some thinking for a world in which the nations have been persuaded to moderate and then reduce the level of environmental degradation, and perhaps even *halt* some of the degrading processes. The discussion here supposes that in regard to aircraft propulsion, limitation of environmental damage is best sought through the introduction of market-based financial incentives, in preference to reliance on the direct physical controls of governmental central planning.

Unless there emerges a new technology that allows aircraft-propulsion without atmospheric pollution or other adverse environmental effects, government policies will make air travel more expensive, and the *aggregate* amount of air travel may well be significantly reduced. Fewer people will be able to afford air travel for holidays. And for the conduct of business, there will be greater reliance on imperfect substitutes based on digital communication.

In the case of aviation (as in many other sectors), there will certainly be pressures to modify the manner of production, so as to secure 'more bang for the (environmental) buck'. Section 15.6.2 below examines how fairly simple changes in operating procedures can improve the level of economic efficiency in the sector, and also offer a bonus of some modest but significant reductions in the prevailing levels of aircraft-induced atmospheric pollution.

To go beyond such improvements will require action to discourage demand for air travel. The fundamental analysis needed to steer such a policy was developed more than a century ago. The (then, few) professional economists realised the policy importance of what are now called 'negative externalities'. Section 15.6.3 below gives a brief account of that basic thinking, which takes a market-based approach to remedying what is otherwise a market failure. Sections 15.6.4–5 develop ideas about how that approach works out in detail in the airline context. Finally, §15.6.6 looks at the modification required *now* in the procedures for the evaluation of additional long-lived aviation assets, such as new runways and new airports.

15.6.2 Eliminate inefficient aviation practices, and thereby reduce emissions

Given the presence of both imperfectly executed government policy-making, and the financial interests of airlines, it is not surprising that the outcomes sometimes include efficiency losses that are avoidable. This section looks at three policy areas.

(a) Air traffic control (ATC)

As already seen (§14.1), two major issues arise. In some world regions there is need to divorce the boundaries of the air traffic control areas from national borders, in order to give more direct flight routings, fewer air traffic control areas, and hence fewer (flight) handovers from one controller to another. Secondly, in several countries – notably the US – ownership and administrative structures could be changed to facilitate the phasing out of radar aircraft-tracking, and the introduction of digital electronic transmission of flight-related information, including the current location of each and every airborne (commercial) aircraft.

In Europe, the self-interest of the separate national governments and their ATC service providers has hindered the current EU campaign, which seeks only to improve the traditional radar-based system. The planned new scheme has fewer and larger control areas, and will reduce both airline costs and atmospheric pollution (§14.1.2). The EU has now started to offer financial assistance to service providers, to help fund the costs of change.

For the US, there have been proposals over recent years for administrative reform, but these did not lead to legislative action. Then, in 2015, the Eno Center for Transportation established a working group to study possible alternative ATC administrations to replace the prevailing management by the FAA.

In its report (Eno Center, NEXT GEN Working Group – Final Report, Washington, DC, July 2015, accessed at enotrans.org), the Group reviews experience in several other countries that have transferred the ATC role to some form of independent or quasi-independent organisation. It particularly admires the performance of the independent provider in Canada.

It gives support to two options: a government corporation placed outside the Federal government system; and an independent non-profit organisation. Neither would be constrained by Federal government procurement rules and other inflexible arrangements that the Group considers to be inappropriate for a large and complex system such as Next Gen. Both options would (or could?) allow stakeholders (airlines) to play a role in governance, and thereby promote decisions that best serve the stakeholder interests. And both options would also separate the ATC service provider from the safety regulator, thanks to the latter role remaining with the FAA.

In both options, funding comes from user fees. This could encourage the supply of services well suited to prevailing airline operations, and should promote economic efficiency in the production of those services. Despite that stance, there are occasional references to (tax-payer-funded) 'grants' (pp. 61–2 of the Report), perhaps coming via the budget of the (new) FAA. Because there is no public-interest reason why commercial aviation should be subsidised by taxpayers, it would surely be important to specify an explicit prohibition on such subsidy for the new corporation. The temptation to breach that principle may be particularly great when a cyclical downturn in travel reduces the revenue coming from user fees.

In late 2015, the ideas explored in the ENO report began to attract attention in Congress and elsewhere. In January 2016, the US House Transportation and Infrastructure Committee chairman Bill Shuster (R-Pa.) expressed support for having ATC services provided by an organisation separate from the FAA (Kerry Lynch, 'Shuster highlights independent ATC in campaign kickoff', *AIN Online*, 13 January 2016).

Yet some in Congress were concerned about the proposal (Keith Laing 'Private air traffic control plan hits turbulence in Senate' *The Hill* 29 January 2016). And there was also opposition from general aviation, and from Delta Airlines (Paul Bedard, 'Delta CEO: GOP's FAA bill will slash flights, boost delays, user fees', *Washington Examiner*, 10 February 2016).

In Congress, a bill for the Aviation Innovation, Reform, and Reauthorization Act of 2016 was published on 3 February 2016. Its 273 pages are devoted to several other matters besides the establishment of the 'ATC Corporation'. The Act sees the Corporation as a federally chartered, not-for-profit corporation, and not a federal entity (§90301). The bill is long on administrative detail and legal considerations.

On charging *principles*, however, §90311 says only that 'Charges and fees shall be consistent with the International Civil Aviation Organization's *Policies on Charges for Air Navigation Services (italics added)* Ninth Edition, 2012.' While that ICAO stance gives sensible guidance, there are likely to be matters on which the Corporation will not be bound by the ICAO policy. The influence of the large US airlines with membership of the board of the Corporation might result in pricing and runway-access policies that favour the interests of those large companies, at the expense of other industry parties.

After a long hearing, which considered many amendments and adopted about half of them, the House Transportation Committee divided mainly on party lines; a majority approved the bill (Keith Laing, 'Panel approves plan to spin off air traffic control', *The Hill*, 11 February 2016). In an editorial ('Air traffic change gains altitude: Our view', *USA Today*, 2 March 2016), that newspaper argued that the independent corporation promises to bring benefits 'but gives big carriers too much clout'.

At the time of writing, it is expected that Congress will determine the fate of the bill in late 2016.

(b) Access rules for congested runways

When runway congestion results in airborne delays of incoming aircraft, extra fuel is burned, and extra atmospheric pollution is created. To help keep such delays to an operationally reasonable minimum, it may be helpful to review runway use at any busy port that is presently without slot assignments, to see whether the introduction of a peak-period slot system would reduce the total amount of aircraft delays.

Of course, for any new slots, legal ownership must be clearly established before they are assigned. In many countries, it may be wise to vest ownership with the *national* aviation regulator, which then leases slots to airlines at prices that are determined in airline bidding competitions. Each lease fee should be levied daily, whether or not the holder uses the slot every day. The regulator *could* pass on the revenue to the individual port, provided the port meets specified public-interest conditions regarding airport runway charges and investment in runway capacity.

(c) Air passenger duties

Some national governments impose a charge on every air passenger departing on an *international* flight. The list includes the UK and other EU countries, and also Australia and New Zealand. Initially, such imposts were intended merely to raise revenue, though later some have been represented as levies related to environmental pollution.

In Australia, a uniform 'passenger movement charge' was introduced in 1978, initially at a rate of A$10 per person. After several increases, the rate reached A$55 in 2012 (Passenger Movement Charge Act 1978, as amended in 2012).

When the UK government introduced an 'Airport Passenger Duty' (APD) in 1994, the charges were higher for longer flights. Some European LCCs complained that the rates had no other relation to the fare paid; later, the British government did alter the structure.

Because the pollution source is the aircraft, not the passenger, the LCCs also argued that, on economic-efficiency grounds, any pollution charge should be levied per *aircraft* departure, with rates that reflected the polluting characteristics of the individual aircraft types, as well as the length of the sector to be flown. (The LCCs often operate newer (less-polluting) aircraft, and – for a given type – generally have more seats per aircraft, with a higher proportion of those seats occupied. Thus such a modification would – quite properly – benefit the LCCs relative to the legacy carriers.)

Subsequently, the UK government planned to replace the APD with a duty payable per aircraft. However, in the face of industry opposition, successive governments left the APD unchanged, *ostensibly* because – as *some* parties claimed! – a per-plane charge could be interpreted as a tax on fuel, which is prohibited by Article 24 of the 1944 Chicago Convention ('International law forces UK U-turn on tax per plane', *Wall Street Journal*, 23 March 2011).

That history illustrates a general proposition: it is all too easy for governments to take decisions which are in conflict with sound environmental policy. Those decisions can damage other aspects of economic efficiency, too. In particular, a per-passenger charge does not give an airline any additional incentive to reduce runway congestion, whereas a (sensible) charge per plane encourages the airline to fly larger aircraft with more seats, and to secure higher load factors.

15.6.3 A levy on activities that adversely affect other parties: the basic concepts

For more than a century, economists have argued for financial levies upon human activities that damage the wellbeing of 'third parties' (that is, all parties other than those directly involved in a particular economic transaction). In the early days, a classic example of such a 'negative externality' was smoke from a factory that soiled domestic washing hanging outside nearby houses.

A levy scheme requires the polluter to pay for each unit of emitted pollution. In the early thinking, the 'price' for the right to pollute was to be determined directly by the government, which could then adjust that price in the light of experience in using the scheme. The revenue from such a scheme flowed to the government. While businesses are commonly averse to making such payments, that revenue also has an important indirect *beneficial* consequence – namely it reduces the need for government to tax business earnings that come from 'good' activities, namely supplying other goods and services whose production does not impose negative consequences on other parties.

In contemporary thinking about the physical environment, however, most discussion centres not on levies, but on the use of an 'emissions trading scheme' (ETS). Though very different in its institutional form, an ETS is fundamentally somewhat similar to a direct government levy, in the sense that in both schemes, the polluter can reduce its *total* financial outlays arising from the pollution it emits by reducing the amount of those harmful emissions.

To do that, a polluting firm can reduce the scale of its production activity and/ or change its production technique. Such adjustments often increase its other costs and/or reduce its revenue from sales. However, upon the introduction of either a direct levy *or* an ETS, a polluting firm may find it more profitable to make the adjustments, and thereby reduce the pollution charges it pays.

In the airline context, an airline can benefit by reducing the number of flights (perhaps, in part, by using larger aircraft), and/or by using aircraft with modern engines which have been designed to secure lower amounts of noxious emissions.

The remaining question concerns the manner of implementation. Where the government introduces a direct levy, the policy instrument is the monetary value per unit of the emitted noxious pollution, a 'price' that is set by a government authority.

In the case of an ETS, the policy instrument is a *quantity* 'cap'. With a certain total pollution limit in mind, the government assigns to each incumbent polluter an individual cap (or permit), which limits the pollution amount that the firm can emit. Sometimes, the trading scheme is established by *initially* setting each individual cap equal to the prevailing level of emissions created by the firm. (Of course, there are pros and cons in that approach.)

The government agency also establishes a market in which emission permits can be traded. A firm that can reduce it emissions easily (that is, with only a small increase in its other costs) can then profit by selling, on that market, a part of its allowed cap. Such a sale allows other firms, especially (but not only) those that are expanding their production and therefore increasing the pollution amount they want to emit, to buy additional emission rights. (For a more detailed account, see the lengthy but very thorough Wikipedia article on 'Emissions trading', here accessed on 24 July 2015.)

Such an initial step allows the government to prevent the total amount of the specific type of pollution from increasing. Once the scheme has been introduced, and the market in the specific pollution rights has been established and has settled down, the government agency may reduce the total cap by a small percentage, and reduce each individual cap by the same percentage. Repetition of that arrangement allows an orderly sequence of reductions of the total pollution, while the market in permits allows each individual polluter to adjust its production, and its emission of the pollutant. Such adjustments are made in a manner that is more flexible (and so at lower social cost) than would prevail if there were no such market in permits, and instead the government itself determined each new individual emission level, which could not be altered by the polluting firm.

So, in summary, when introducing an emissions trading scheme, a government establishes an *initial* individual quota (a quantity) for each polluter, and then from time to time it may reduce those individual quotas. Those decisions in effect limit and may reduce the aggregate pollution amount. The market in pollution rights then converts that regulated aggregate quantity into price signals, which influence the individual polluter who decides how, if at all, to trade on the permits market.

Those firms that can reduce their pollution with little difficulty (and hence little cost) may find it profitable to sell some of their pollution rights on the market. And those that find it difficult (costly) to reduce their pollution may instead find it profitable to buy some pollution rights from other firms.

The overall outcome is *somewhat* similar to that achieved when the government directly sets (and later adjusts) the price (or levy) per pollution unit. However the differences between the two approaches are important. First, the market in pollution rights allows more flexibility in the adjustments made by individual polluters. Secondly, the ETS does not give the government a revenue source that could be used to reduce conventional taxation on the profit earned from other (non-polluting) production activities. And thirdly, the ETS reduces the financial total of the pollution charges paid by polluting firms. (The ETS achieves that by focussing on the marginal changes in pollution levels, whereas a government levy scheme imposes a charge on *all* the units of the pollutant.) No doubt, it is that third difference that accounts for the preference of businesses for an ETS rather than a direct pollution levy.

Finally, note that in the case of pollution of the environment in general, it is extremely difficult to conceptualise, let alone measure, the *socially optimal* amount of total pollution. Accordingly, an ETS does not necessarily result in the (socially) best price per unit of emitted pollutant. Rather, each government deci-sion – to reduce the total permitted amount of the specific pollution – remains somewhat arbitrary, and therefore at the mercy of political forces that are based mainly on sectional interests. Rather, what an ETS does do – and do well – is to provide an economically efficient process for implementing any *given* target level of total pollution.

15.6.4 An ETS for pollution arising from aircraft engines: principles

In designing such an ETS, the first task is to identify and define the pollutant(s) whose production is to be discouraged by the financial incentive mechanism. In the airline case, the pollution comes from the gases emitted by the operation of aircraft engines.

In order to obtain a basis for determining the pollution charge, each engine-type needs to be rated according to the pollution amount per unit distance flown in level flight. (The implicit assumption is that there is a single pollutant, or an acceptable index number in the case of two or more pollutants.)

Then, to a good approximation, the total amount of damaging emissions for a given flight and given aircraft type may be taken as being proportional to the multiplicative product of sector length, the number of engines, and the emission propensity of the engine type.

As already noted, the most difficult task in the implementation of an ETS lies in choosing the reduced aggregate pollution level to be set by government at each subsequent revision of the scheme. Accordingly, in choosing each of a set of consecutive pollution levels, the aim can only be to *improve* the prevailing situation, rather than find the very best level.

Given the widespread industrial and political opposition to paying charges intended to reduce pollution levels, it seems reasonable to say that initially (and for quite some time thereafter) any reduced pollution levels nominated by governments will be higher than those that would be found to be socially optimal, if calculations for the latter were feasible!

15.6.5 An ETS for pollution arising from aircraft engines: some practicalities

Who administers such schemes?

In the absence of a world-wide inter-governmental agreement on aviation pollution charging, the design of any airline ETS needs to recognise the presence of several regional authorities. Potential regional areas include the EU, North America and perhaps multinational areas such as Latin America and a major part of Asia. Most *inter-regional* flights would also pass through (oceanic) areas not having a regional authority. Such circumstances would be likely to result in jurisdictional issues.

Non-discriminatory treatment of airlines

For reasons of both equity and economic efficiency, every flight having some travel within the area of a regional authority should be included in that regional scheme, regardless of whether or not the airline in question is domiciled in the regional area. Furthermore, the pollution measure (and hence the consequences for pollution charges) should be the same for all airlines flying a given route, save for the standard differences arising from differences in engine type.

Industrial coverage of an ETS

There is an economic-efficiency argument for having a single broadly based ETS which is applied to all industries operating in the region for which the ETS is applied. Firms that want to buy (or sell) pollution permits can then deal with firms in any industry operating in the region. And the market price paid/received by a firm that wants to buy/sell additional pollution rights is the same across all the industries. In turn, that allows the greatest possibility flexibility in sharing out the target pollution level among the various industries, and hence keeps to a minimum the social cost of meeting the targeted *aggregate* pollution level.

Frequency of scheme revision

In the early stages, at least, the ETS might be reviewed, and perhaps amended, at frequent intervals – say, every three years. Of course, that matter too needs international cooperation.

15.6.6 The position of the IATA airlines on aircraft emissions

Apparently, the world's airlines see only a limited role for emission charges, according to statements posted on the website (*iata.org*) of the International Air Transport Association (IATA) – whose membership includes almost all the world's airlines of any significant size.

When accessed on 2 August 2015, that site displayed a two-page document, Fact Sheet: Climate Change (dated June 2015), which states (on p. 1):

> The aviation industry is confident that technology, operations and infrastructure measures will provide long-term solutions for aviation's sustainable growth. However, the industry accepts that some form of market-based measure (MBM) may be needed to fill any remaining emissions gap.

Specifically, the Fact Sheet (p. 1 again) sees a need to '[adopt] a set of ambitious targets to mitigate CO_2 emissions from air transport'. Those targets comprise: 'an average improvement in fuel efficiency of 1.5 per cent per year from 2009 to 2020'; then, for some years (detail not specified), deployment of a market-based 'cap on net aviation CO_2 emissions from 2020 (carbon neutral growth)'; and finally 'a reduction in net [annual] CO_2 emissions of 50 per cent by 2050, relative to 2005 levels', thanks to *anticipated* improvements in the technology used by the industry.

That position has some striking features:

1   before 2020, IATA sees no role in aviation for emissions charges to be paid by polluters;
2   the aggregate aviation pollution level reached by the airlines in 2020 (in the absence of any charging disincentive) becomes a baseline; and
3   after 2020, any market-based mechanism (details not specified) is intended only to keep the aggregate aviation pollution amount to that base-line level.

In that view of the world, there is no place *in aviation* for any governmental decisions about ETS or other market-based mechanisms that seek *reductions* in aggregate (all-industry) atmospheric pollution levels below the 2020 level. Furthermore, the IATA stance presupposes *successful* introduction of 'biofuels and additional new-generation technologies'.

Further insights on airline attitudes come from a second document on the IATA website, 'Fact sheet: "green" taxes' (December 2014; despite its title, the document is largely polemical). It asserts that pollution charges (1) 'do not incentivize investment in new technology but, on the contrary, weaken the ability of the sector to dedicate resources to the acquisition of newer, cleaner equipment', (2) 'will not create any additional incentive to reduce its emissions' (that is, beyond the incentive arising from the cost of fuel), and (3) will 'discourage families and businesses from traveling'. The last point implies that the whole or a part of the cost (to the airline) of its payment of pollution charges would be passed on to the travellers in the form of higher fares; in turn, that reduces the weakening effect to which the first point refers. That third point seems also to imply that *any* reduction in air travel is not in the public interest.

Overall, those two documents appear to signify opposition to any form of aviation pollution charging, other than the very limited role noted above. Meanwhile other industries do have to pay up, in the EU at least. Does IATA really intend to claim a distinct, privileged position?

15.6.7 The International Civil Aviation Organization

The International Civil Aviation Organization (ICAO) is a UN specialized agency. It was established in 1944 upon the signing of the Convention on International Civil Aviation (the Chicago Convention). The ICAO Assembly is the organisation's ultimate decision-making body, has members drawn from 191 Member

States and has (regular) meetings once every three years. At those meetings, it elects a Council whose 36 members come mainly from Member States with large roles in air transport.

In 2015, the then President had tertiary education in aeronautical engineering. The Secretary-General, appointed for a term of three years from August 2015, was trained as a lawyer (www.icao.int, accessed on 5 August 2015).

On that date, the ICAO website listed the organisation's Strategic Objectives 2014–16. The last of the five objectives on the list is 'environmental protection':

> Minimize the adverse environmental effects of civil aviation activities. This Strategic Objective fosters *ICAO's leadership in all aviation-related environmental activities* and is consistent with the ICAO and UN system environmental protection policies and practices. [Emphasis added]

The website also notes that ICAO *has* engaged in studies of market-based mechanisms designed to reduce atmospheric pollution arising from aircraft operation.

Its recent activities in environmental protection are detailed in the next section. The suitability of ICAO for *any* role in environmental protection is considered in §15.6.9.

15.6.8 Battles over jurisdiction

In 2003, the European Union resolved to start an ETS that covered land-based industrial activities in the EU (Directive 2003/87/EC). The scheme launched on 1 January 2005. The EU then waited for ICAO to propose an *international* market-based mechanism to help reduce aircraft emissions. In the absence of any such initiative, the EU extended its own ETS scheme to include, from 1 January 2012, all flights arriving at and departing from airfields within the 27 member states of the EU, together with Norway and Iceland. Its initial position – to charge according to the entire distance of each flight (including any travel in airspace outside the EU area) – embodied an unreasonable asymmetry. Perhaps the EU sought to prompt some long-awaited proposal from ICAO.

In the event, the immediate response was very different: various countries and airlines (1) objected to the imposition of charges on non-European airlines *and* to charges on the travel of flights outside the EU area, and (2) refused to comply with the ETS provisions, even after the EU had offered a compromise. Besides diplomatic pressures, one or two countries are said to have taken retaliatory actions in trade relations (EurActiv.com, 'EU aviation carbon charge compromise draws industry fire', *Reuters*, 17 October 2013). In response, the EU Commissioner for Climate Action pointed out that the EU had a sovereign right to regulate aviation within its own airspace.

However, there were also some ICAO Council discussions that did seem to favour some movement towards a world-wide market-based mechanism. The EU Climate Commissioner grasped her opportunity, and said 'Now it seems that because of some countries' dislike of our scheme many countries are prepared to move in ICAO, and even to move towards a Market Based Mechanism (MBM) at global level' ('Stopping the clock of ETS and aviation emissions following last week's ICAO council', EC memo, 12 November 2012). Accordingly, upon the recommendation of the EU Commissioner, the EU member states had agreed to 'stop the clock' regarding enforcement of the ETS provisions in respect of 'flights to and from non-European countries, until after the ICAO General Assembly next autumn'.

In the event, at that 2013 Assembly:

> following a long and difficult debate between Member States who held a wide range of divergent views, it was agreed by consensus to develop a global MBM scheme for international aviation. This decision reflects . . . [a preference] for a global solution in the international aviation sector, as opposed to a possible patchwork of different measures. The Assembly agreed that the Council . . . would make a recommendation on a global MBM scheme . . . and [on] the mechanisms for implementing the scheme from 2020, for decision by the 39th Session of the Assembly in 2016.
>
> (Annual Report of the ICAO Council: 2013 – Strategic Objectives: Environmental Protection – Market-based Measures, accessed at icao.int on 4 August 2015).

So, despite the 12-month limitation on the EU willingness to 'stop the clock', ICAO was not to be rushed. Its studies of MBMs had begun in 2001 (ICAO, Report of the Assessment of Market-based Measures, Doc 10018, 2013, p. vii). Even if ICAO *were* to agree, at the next meeting of the Assembly, on the design of a market-based mechanism, implementation would not come until almost two decades after those studies began.

15.6.9 The sustainability of civil aviation: immediate actions, and some concluding remarks

While the underlying issues of environmental sustainability are immensely complex, some of the scientific studies suggest there is a risk that Earth *may* reach a tipping point, beyond which recovery to familiar conditions would simply not be possible. For consideration by those who think such a potential outcome can be disregarded, there remains the argument that the negative externalities of environmental degradation *already* provide grounds for the use of a market-based mechanism to reduce the extent of further atmospheric pollution, and so curb the less spectacular degrading processes that are already under way.

In particular, a safety-first argument for civil aviation is that it might be prudent now to slow the growth of the industry's output, and also start to reduce the annual growth rate for total atmospheric pollution. Part of such a programme could rest on using larger aircraft with cleaner engines, to operate less frequent services. A market-based mechanism that (in effect) puts a price on atmospheric pollution would encourage airlines to respond promptly and in large measure. Beyond that, the accretion of further scientific evidence may eventually (or quite soon!) persuade government decision-makers that the time has come to *reduce* the output of the airline industry.

Institutional arrangements for curbing growth in airport capacity

Aviation is long past the state of being an infant industry. While direct subsidies for airlines are becoming less common, there remain major issues regarding government support for increases in *airport capacity*. Besides giving direct financial subsidies, governments often assist by using powers of compulsory purchase of land parcels.

Around the world, many parties still make 'business cases' for a new airport or an extra runway (think Heathrow for a recent example). Those cases often rest on projections of glorious traffic growth over the next thirty years or longer. Surely it is more realistic to factor in the idea that within (say) ten or fifteen years after the date that the new capacity comes on stream, government policy may (or will) *require* a reduction in air travel, perhaps resulting in the extra capacity then being unwanted. To allow for such outcomes, the cost-benefit analyses could include options in which the (*net*) benefit stream simply ceases after ten or fifteen years. To help bring home the financial risks attached to further airport investment, governments could insist on private-investor funding. (In that case, however, it might be prudent to attach a condition that taxes private capital gains on land that has been made available by compulsory purchase procedures, in the event of later switching of that land to non-aviation uses.)

Institutional arrangements for limiting atmospheric pollution
from aircraft operation

Regardless of whether that is done by using a market-based mechanism or in some other way, it will now be argued that ICAO is not suited for the purpose.

After World War II, some national governments promoted civil aviation by establishing airlines within government departments. (In China, the formation of CAAC illustrates the point.) In more recent times, many developed countries have transferred airline ownership to the private sector. They have also separated the government department that 'looks after' civil aviation from the department that engages in economic regulation of all industries. In the USA, for instance, the distinct and separate roles of the Department of Transportation and the Department of Justice illustrate the point.

While the analogy between general economic regulation and environmental protection is not exact, there is a strong argument for bringing together *environmental policy-making for all industries* under the one departmental roof, as the EU has done.

In contrast, ICAO comes from that earlier post-war era. It still serves as a *pro-aviation* body. It has earned a good reputation for unifying procedures within the technical operation in the industry, to help secure safe and not too costly performance. But atmospheric pollution *is* an externality, and not part of the central functioning of the industry. So government policies regarding environmental pollution should be determined elsewhere, in a setting where the public interest is the dominant influence. (That approach also helps to secure the efficiency gain that flows from having all firms able to trade in one and the same market for pollution permits.) In short, environmental policy should not be entrusted to an industry body such as ICAO.

Social equity in arrangements for curbing atmospheric pollution

The airline industry likes to make the point that aircraft-generated pollution is but a small part of total atmospheric pollution; a figure of two or three per cent is often put forward. In contrast, the European Commission emphasises that 'Someone flying from London to New York and back generates roughly the same level of emissions as the average person in the EU does by heating their home for a whole year' ('Reducing emissions from aviation', http://ec.europa.eu/clima/policies/transport/aviation/index_en.htm, accessed 21 July 2015).

In effect, the EU is making a point about an *equitable distribution* of benefits and costs among different groups in the world population. Much aircraft pollution comes from medium- to long-distance flights, carrying an elite minority. In the absence of an effective market-based measure for limiting aviation-generated pollution, the unequal shares in permitted pollution will add to the increasing (financial) inequality now found in many developed countries. In turn this may add to the risk of a break-down in social cohesion.

As already emphasised, economists have long grappled with the difficulties stemming from negative externalities. The fundamental practical difficulty is that self-interested behaviour of the individual often over-rides the protection of the 'commonwealth'. In the case of environmental pollution leading to global warming, such conduct could even undermine entire societies.

References

Abeyratne, Ruwantissa (2001) Ethical and moral considerations of airline management *Journal of Air Transport Management* **7** 339–48

Armstrong, Mark, Simon Cowan and John Vickers (1994) *Regulatory Reform: Economic Analysis and British Experience* Cambridge, MA: MIT Press

Australian Competition and Consumer Commission (2015) *Draft Determination: Applications for Authorisation Lodged by Qantas Airways Limited and China Eastern Airlines Corporation Limited in Respect of a Joint Coordination Agreement* Canberra: ACCC

Australian Transport Safety Bureau (2002) *Investigation into Ansett Australia maintenance safety deficiencies and the control of continuing airworthiness of Class A aircraft* (Aviation Safety Investigation BS/20010005) Canberra: Department of Transport and Regional Services

Barbot, Cristina (2005) Airport pricing systems and airport deregulation effects on welfare *Journal of Air Transportation* **10** (2) 109–26

Barbot, Cristina (2006) Low-cost airlines, secondary airports, and state aid: an economic assessment of the Ryanair–Charleroi Airport agreement *Journal of Air Transport Management* **12** 197–203

Baumol, W J (1996) Predation and the logic of the average variable cost test *Journal of Law and Economics* **39** 49–72

Beesley, Michael E (1986) Commitment, sunk costs, and entry to the airline industry: reflections on experience *Journal of Transport Economics and Policy* **20** (2) 173–90

Bettini, H F A J and A V M Oliveira (2008) Airline capacity setting after re-regulation: the Brazilian case in the early 2000s *Journal of Air Transport Management* **14** 289–92

Bilotkach, V (2005) Understanding price dispersion in the airline industry: capacity constraints and consumer heterogeneity, in Darin Lee (editor) *Advances in Airline Economics, Vol. 1* Amsterdam: Elsevier

Blair, Roger and Jeffrey Harrison (1999) Airline price wars: competition or predation *Antitrust Bulletin* **44** 489–518

Borenstein, Severin (1989) Hubs and high fares: dominance and market power in the US airline industry *RAND Journal of Economics* **20** 344–65

Borenstein, Severin (1992) The evolution of U.S. airline competition *Journal of Economic Perspectives* **6** (2) 45–73

Bureau of Transport and Communications Economics (1991a) *Deregulation of Domestic Aviation – the First Year* (Report 73) Canberra: AGPS

Bureau of Transport and Communications Economics (1991b) *A New Era in Australian Aviation* (Conference Papers) Canberra: AGPS

Bureau of Transport and Communications Economics (1993) *The Progress of Aviation Reform* (Report 81) Canberra: AGPS

Bureau of Transport and Regional Economics (2006) *Domestic Air Fare Indexes Methodology*

Cantle, Katie (2008) China's most successful LCC, Spring Airlines, models itself after Southwest Airlines *Air Transport World* August

Carlson Wagonlit Travel (2012) *Airline Joint Ventures, Alliances Becoming More Commonplace* CWT Viewpoint, April

Caves, Douglas W, Laurits R Christensen and Michael W Tretheway (1984) Economies of density versus economies of scale: why trunk and local service airline costs differ *Rand Journal of Economics* **15** 471–89

Civil Aviation Authority (2000) *The 'Single Till' and the 'Dual Till' Approach to the Price Regulation of Airports* (Consultation Paper) London: Civil Aviation Authority

Civil Aviation Authority (2001): *Competitive Provision of Infrastructure and Services within Airports* (Consultation Paper) London: Civil Aviation Authority

Civil Aviation Authority (2005) *UK Regional Air Services* (CAP 754) London: Civil Aviation Authority

Civil Aviation Authority (2006) *No-Frills Carriers: Revolution or Evolution?* (CAP 770) London: Civil Aviation Authority

Civil Aviation Authority (2007) *Air Services at UK Regional Airports: An Update on Developments* (CAP 775) London: Civil Aviation Authority

Civil Aviation Authority (2009a) *UK Business Air Travel: Traffic Trends and Characteristics* London: Civil Aviation Authority

Civil Aviation Authority (2009b) *International Relations: The Growth in Air Travel to Visit Friends or Relatives* (CAP 787) London: Civil Aviation Authority

Clarke, Peter (1997) *Hope and Glory: Britain 1900–1990* London: Penguin Books

Competition Commission (2008) *BAA Airports Market Investigation: Provisional Findings Report* London: Competition Commission

Corones, S G (2014) *Competition Law in Australia* (sixth edition) Sydney: Thomson Reuters Australia

Czerny, Achim I (2006) Price-cap regulation of airports: single-till versus dual-till *Journal of Regulatory Economics* **30** 85–97

De Roos, Nicholas, Gordon Mills and Stephen Whelan (2010) Pricing dynamics in the Australian airline market *Economic Record* **86** 545–62

Department of Infrastructure, Transport, Regional Development and Local Government (2009) *National Aviation Policy White Paper: Flight Path to the Future* Canberra: Department of Infrastructure, Transport, Regional Development and Local Government

Eckert, Andrew and Douglas West (2002) Predation in the airline industry: the Canadian antitrust approach *The Antitrust Bulletin* **47** 217–42

Economic Commission for Africa (1999) *Decision Relating to the Implementation of the Yamoussoukro Declaration Concerning the Liberalisation of Access to Air Transport Markets in Africa* ECA/RCID/CM.CIVAC/99/RPT/Annex1, Addis Ababa: Economic Commission for Africa

England and Wales High Court (Chancery Division) (2004) *Decision by Mr Justice Pumfrey in the Case between Navitaire Inc (Claimant) and EasyJet Airline Company & Bulletproof Technologies Inc (Defendants)* [2004] EWHC 1725 (Ch)

European Commission (1989) Council Regulation (EEC) No 2299/89 of 24 July 1989 on a code of conduct for computerized reservation systems *Official Journal of the European Union* L 220, 29 July

European Commission (2004a) *Regulation No 2408/92 of 23 July 1992 (as amended) on Access for Community Air Carriers to Intra-Community Air Routes* Brussels, 1 May

European Commission (2004b) Commission decision of 12 February 2004 concerning advantages granted . . . [at] Charleroi Airport to the airline Ryanair . . . *Official Journal of the European Union* L 137. 30 April

European Commission (2007a) *Guide to European Community Legislation in the Field of Civil Aviation* Brussels: EC Directorate General for Energy and Transport, June

European Commission (2007b): *Commission decision of 23/IV/2007 on Public Service Obligations on Certain Routes to and from Sardinia* Brussels

European Commission (2007c) *Vademecum Community Rules on State Aid* Brussels, 15 February

European Commission (2008) *Single European Sky II: Towards More Sustainable and Better Performing Aviation* Brussels: COM (2008) 389/2

European Commission (2009) *EU and Africa Join Forces to Develop Aviation Cooperation* IP/09/541 Brussels, 4 April

European Commission (2013a) *Proposal for a Regulation of the European Parliament and of the Council amending Regulation (EC) No 261/2004* [on air carrier liabilities to passengers] COM(2013) 130, Brussels 13 March 2013

European Commission (2013b) *Commission urges Italy, Cyprus and Greece to implement EU rules to unblock congestion in Europe's airspace* (press release) Brussels, 26 September 2013

European Commission (2014) *Report from the Commission to the European Parliament on the Application of the Airport Charges Directive* COM (2014) 278, Brussels, 19 May

European Union (2009) Directive on Airport Charges 2009/12/EC of 11 March *Official Journal of the European Union* L70/11–16, 14 March

Forsyth, Peter and others (editors) (2005) *Competition versus Predation in Aviation Markets* Aldershot: Ashgate

Freiberg, Kevin and Jackie Freiberg (1996) *NUTS: Southwest Airlines' Crazy Recipe for Business and Personal Success* Austin, TX: Bard Press

Fu, Xiao Wen, Mark Lijesen and Tae H Oum (2006) An analysis of airport pricing and regulation in the presence of competition between full service airlines and low cost carriers *Journal of Transport Economics and Policy* **40** (3) 425–47

Fuhr, Johannes and Thorsten Beckers (2006) vertical governance between airlines and airports – a transaction cost analysis *Review of Network Economics* **5** 386–412

Fuhr, Johannes and Thorsten Beckers (2009) Contract design, financing arrangements and public ownership—an assessment of the US Airport governance model *Transport Reviews* **2** 459–78

Gerardi, Kristopher S and Adam H Shapiro (2009) Does competition reduce price dispersion? New evidence from the airline industry *Journal of Political Economy* **117** 1–37

Gillen, David and William G Morrison (2005) Regulation, competition and network evolution in aviation *Journal of Air Transport Management* **11** 161–74

Gillen, David W, Tae Hoon Oum and Michael W Tretheway (1990) Airline cost structure and policy implications: a multi-product approach for Canadian airlines *Journal of Transport Economics and Policy* **24** 9–34

Goolsbee, A and C Syverson (2008) How do incumbents respond to the threat of entry? Evidence from the major airlines *Quarterly Journal of Economics* **123** 1611–33

Grether, D M, R M Isaac and C R Plott (1981) The allocation of landing rights by unanimity among competitors *American Economic Review* **71** 166–71

Hendricks, Ken, Michele Piccione and Guofu Tan (1997) Entry and exit in hub-spoke networks *RAND Journal of Economics* **28** (3) 291–303

Hergott, Matthew J (1997) Airport concentration and market power: an events study approach *Review of Industrial Organization* **12** 793–800

ICAO/ATAG/WB Development Forum (2006) Implementation of the Yamoussoukro Decision: progressing or stalled? Paper presented by Ethiopia, Montreal, May

Independent Review of Economic Regulation of Domestic Aviation (1986) *Report* (2 volumes) Canberra: Australian Government Publishing Service

International Civil Aviation Organization (2012) *ICAO's Policies on Charges for Airports and Air Navigation Services* (ninth edition) Doc 9082, Montreal: ICAO

Kahn, A E (1991) Thinking about predation – a personal diary *Review of Industrial Organization* **6** 137–46

Kahn, Alfred (1999) Comments on exclusionary airline pricing *Journal of Air Transport Management* **5** 1–12

Kaplan, Daniel P (1986) The changing airline industry, in Weiss and Klass (1986), pp. 40–77

Kilpi, J (2007) Fleet composition of commercial jet aircraft 1952–2005: developments in uniformity and scale *Journal of Air Transport Management* **13** 81–9

Koran, D and J D Ogur (1983) *Airport Access Problems: Lessons Learned from Slot Regulation* Washington, DC: Federal Trade Commission

Levine, Michael E (1987) Airline competition in deregulated markets: theory, firm strategy and public policy *Yale Journal of Regulation* **4** 393–494

Levine, Michael E (2004) *Understanding Airline Strategic Choices: How Much Do Legacy Carriers Have to Change to Survive?* Mimeo

Levine, Michael E (2009) Airport congestion: when theory meets reality *Yale Journal on Regulation* **26** 37–88

Lijesen, Mark G and others (2001) Hub premiums in European civil aviation *Transport Policy* **8** 193–9

Lu, Ching-Chyuan and Romano I. Pagliari (2004) Evaluating the potential impact of alternative airport pricing approaches on social welfare *Transportation Research Part E* **40** 1–17

McGowan, Gerry (2000) Interview with Gerry McGowan, Impulse Airlines *Australian Aviation* September

Mills, Gordon (1989) The reform of Australian aviation *Journal of Transport Economics and Policy* **23** 209–18

Mills, Gordon (1991) Commercial funding of transport infrastructure *Journal of Transport Economics and Policy* **25** 279–98

Mills, Gordon (1995) Airports: users don't pay enough – and now here's privatisation *Economic Papers* **14** (1) 73–84

Mills, Gordon (2002) *Retail Pricing Strategies and Market Power* Melbourne: Melbourne University Press

Mills, Gordon (2003) Customer-class pricing – efficiency and ethics *Economic Papers* (2003) **22**(2) 74–83

Minister for Transport and Communications (1987) *Federal Airports Corporation on Track* Media Statement 53/87, issued 22 December

Morrison, Steven A (2001) Actual, adjacent, and potential competition: estimating the full effect of Southwest Airlines *Journal of Transport Economics and Policy* **32** 239–56

Morrison, William G (2004) Dimensions of predatory pricing in air travel markets *Journal of Air Transport Management* **10** 87–95

Mott MacDonald and others (2006) *Study on the Impact of the Introduction of Secondary Trading at Community Airports* (two volumes), prepared for the European Commission, Croydon: Mott MacDonald

Neels, Kevin (2002) Pricing-based solutions to the problem of weather-related airport and airway system delay *Air Traffic Control Quarterly* **10** (3) 261–84

O'Connell, J F and G Williams (2006) Transformation of India's domestic airlines: a case study of Indian Airlines, Jet Airways, Air Sahara and Air Deccan *Journal of Air Transport Management* **12** 358–74

Oster, Clinton V and John S Strong (2001) *Predatory Practices in the US Airline Industry* Washington, DC: US Department of Transportation

Oum, Tae, Anming Zhang and Yimin Zhang (1995) Airline network rivalry *Canadian Journal of Economics* **28** 836–57

Oum, Tae, Anming Zhang and Yimin Zhang (2004) Alternative forms of economic regulation and their efficiency implications for airports *Journal of Transport Economics and Policy* **38** 217–46

Pandit, Shruti (2007) Praying for time: Air Deccan began India's low fare revolution but has had trouble meeting expectations *Air Transport World* May

Pandit, Shruti (2008) More than a branding exercise: Kingfisher Airlines is not just about selling beer *Air Transport World* February

Prices Surveillance Authority (Australia) (1993) *Inquiry into the Aeronautical and Non-aeronautical charges of the Federal Airports Corporation* Canberra: Prices Surveillance Authority

Schuster, Dominic (2009) Australia's approach to airport charges: the Sydney Airport experience *Journal of Air Transport Management* **15** 121–6

Ssamula, Bridget and Christoffel Venter (2013) Application of hub-and-spoke networks in sparse markets: the case of Africa *Journal of Transport Economics and Policy* **47** 279–97

Starkie, David (1999) The US Department of Transportation's statement on predatory conduct in the airline industry: an alternative proposal *European Competition Law Review* **20** 281–6

Starkie, David (2005) Making airport regulation less imperfect *Journal of Air Transport Management* **11** 3–8

Starkie, David (2008) *The Airport Industry in a Competitive Environment: A United Kingdom Perspective* Discussion Paper No 2008-15, Paris: International Transport Forum

Starkie, David and George Yarrow (2000) *The Single-Till Approach to the Price Regulation of Airports* consulting report prepared for the Economic Regulation Group of the Civil Aviation Authority (UK)

Steer Davies Gleave (2010) *Evaluation of Regulation 261/2004* final report, prepared for the European Commission, February

Steer Davies Gleave (2013) *Evaluation of Directive 2009/12/EC on Airport Charges* final report, prepared for the European Commission, 2013

Steuer, Max (2010) The partially private UK system for air traffic control *Journal of Air Transport Management* **16** 26–35

Sull, D (1999) easyJet's $500 million gamble *European Management Journal* **17** 20–38

Talluri, K T and G J van Ryzin (2004) *The Theory and Practice of Revenue Management* Boston, MA: Kluwer

Torres, Ann M, Chris Barry and Mairéad Hogan (2009) Opaque web practices among low-cost carriers *Journal of Air Transport Management* **15** 299–307

Trade Practices Commission (1992) *The Failure of Compass Airlines* (main report, summary and conclusions) Canberra: Trade Practices Commission

US Court of Appeals for DC (2010) *Air Transport Association v. US Department of Transportation and Federal Aviation Administration: Opinion 08-1293* 13 July 2010 (cadc.uscourts.gov)

US Department of Transportation (1998) *Statement of Enforcement Policy Regarding Unfair Exclusionary Conduct in the Air Transportation Industry* Docket OST-98-3713, Washington DC: Department of Transportation

US Department of Transportation (2001) *Enforcement Policy Regarding Unfair Exclusionary Conduct in the Air Transportation Industry: Findings and Conclusions* Docket OST-98-3713, Washington DC: Department of Transportation

US Department of Transportation (2008) [Amendment to] Policy Regarding Airport Rates and Charges *Federal Register* **73**(135) 40,430–40,445, 14 July

US District Court of Kansas (2001) *United States of America versus AMR Corporation and others – Memorandum and Order* by Judge Marten, 27 April (downloaded from www.usdoj.gov/atr)

Viscusi, W Kip, Joseph E Harrington and John M Vernon (2005) *Economics of Regulation and Antitrust* (Fourth Edition) Cambridge, MA: MIT Press

Weiss, Leonard W and Michael W Klass (editors) (1986) *Regulatory Reform: What Actually Happened* Boston, MA: Little, Brown & Company

Williamson, Oliver E (1977) Predatory pricing: a strategic and welfare analysis *Yale Law Journal* **87** 284–340

Index